*Adventures of a
Home Economist*

Adventures of a Home Economist

Ava Milam Clark & J. Kenneth Munford

Introduction by Betty E. Hawthorne

Corvallis:
OREGON STATE UNIVERSITY PRESS

Introduction

BETTY E. HAWTHORNE
Dean of the School of Home Economics,
Oregon State University

THE MEN AND WOMEN who participated in the ten annual Lake
Placid Conferences at the turn of the century and those who
founded the American Home Economics Association and established
the *Journal of Home Economics* held many beliefs in common. They
believed that the intelligent use of household resources and the application of basic scientific knowledge to the management of homes
would have a beneficial effect on society. They believed that crime
and vice could be prevented more effectively through the development of wholesome values in family life than through the punishment of wrongdoers. They believed that education should do more
than provide money-making skills to advance the industrial revolution, that it should help perpetuate high ethical standards to be
practiced first of all in the homes of the nation. They believed that
skilled home management could improve the physical, mental, and
spiritual well-being of a family and help it form one of the building
blocks of a strong civilization. In short, they saw that applying man's
knowledge to man's basic needs—food, shelter, clothing, and social
relationships—could have a profound effect on a family's health,
vigor, enjoyment of life, and ability to function effectively in society.

Educational programs that grew out of this mode of thinking
have had a variety of titles at different times and places—sanitary
science, household sanitation, household science, household arts,
household economy, domestic science, domestic arts, domestic economy, euthenics, *arts ménagers,* and so forth—but a consensus developed that they should all fall under one all-encompassing term:

HOME ECONOMICS. As the individuals engaged in this field of thought and action banded together for mutual assistance and encouragement, the endeavor they launched became known as the HOME ECONOMICS MOVEMENT.

The author of this book, Ava Milam Clark, has participated in the home economics movement in a unique and distinctive manner. She has watched it grow from its infancy, has known personally many of its leaders, and has made significant contributions to it not only in this country but in other parts of the world as well. In her youth she first encountered a professional home economist at the World's Fair in St. Louis in 1904, when she saw Sara Tyson Rorer giving a demonstration. Later, as a student at the University of Chicago, she met Ellen H. Richards, the founder and "consulting engineer" of the home economics movement, and received an inspiration that has endured throughout her life. Miss Milam's professors at the University of Chicago reinforced this inspiration and helped her in developing vision, resourcefulness, and humanitarian attitudes. Early in her professional career she met and worked with other colleagues who stimulated her interest and helped her realize how much one person can accomplish.

When Ava Milam came to Oregon Agricultural College in the fall of 1911 as an assistant professor of domestic science, she found the School of Domestic Science and Art in a period of temporary crisis because the staff members from the previous year had suddenly resigned shortly before the opening of the new school year. Although she had graduated from the University of Chicago only recently and had taught at the college level only briefly, she was appointed department head at once and appointed dean of the school six years later. In those early years at Oregon Agricultural College, she pioneered in broadening the base of education in home economics. By 1924 courses devoted to housekeeping techniques were reduced while liberal arts courses were strengthened. Science and social science were emphasized in the curriculum. Her philosophy of the importance of the home environment and the breadth of education of the mother in the whole educational process of the young influenced home economics education not only in Oregon but throughout the country. Professional education for the improvement of family life, coupled with education for specific career opportunities in home economics, as introduced at Oregon State, became a pattern followed in other colleges and universities—particularly in land-grant institutions.

Dean Milam's service to the people of the state of Oregon has been far broader than her formal service as an instructor, professor, and dean at Oregon State College. She pioneered in home economics extension and continuing education services long before they were formal units. Through innumerable talks, demonstrations, conferences, and short courses, she took home economics education to the people in many areas of the state, traveling by buggy, car, bus, train, and on one occasion, by railroad handcar. She was quick to respond to particular needs of the state in education and service.

Dean Milam also helped home economics education develop in the Orient. In the early 1920's she visited homes, schools, missions, and colleges in China, Japan, Korea, and the Philippines preparatory to establishing the first collegiate course in home economics in China at Yenching University in Peking in 1923. A decade later she returned to the Far East as a consultant on education for women and the advancement of programs of home economics at Yenching University and at Lingnan University in Canton, Ewha College in Seoul, Korea, and Kwassui College in Nagasaki, Japan. In 1937 she and another member of the School of Home Economics staff conducted a summer tour for home economists to Japan, China, and Korea. Following World War II, she spent nearly six months in the Far East as a consultant on reconstruction of education in China and in conducting a survey of Christian colleges and schools in the Philippines. She also visited Japan and Thailand, encouraging officials to send students to the United States for advanced education in home economics. After her retirement in 1950, Dean Milam was selected as the first technical assistance home economist to be sent out by the Food and Agricultural Organization of the United Nations. She served a year in Syria, six months in Iraq, and briefly in Lebanon and Egypt. Her surveys of homes and schools and her pioneering efforts in emphasizing to government officials the importance of formal and informal home economics education helped lay a foundation in these countries for the development of school and extension programs in home economics which have been advanced by those who followed her.

After her return from overseas, Ava Milam married Jesse Claude Clark, a graduate of Oregon Agricultural College who had recently

retired after a long career as a YMCA secretary and conference center manager. She had first met him and his wife and their three children in China in 1924, and they had all been good friends since that
time. The wife, Julia Fuller Clark, an alumna of our school, had died
in 1951 while Miss Milam was in the Near East. After their marriage,
Ava and J. C. Clark spent four enjoyable years traveling and visiting
with his children, grandchildren, and their many friends—as well as
entertaining members of their families and former colleagues—before a heart attack cut short his life in 1956.

As she nears her eighty-fourth birthday, Ava Milam Clark still
has an office in the Home Economics Building where faculty, alumni,
and students frequently seek her out for advice and encouragement.
Since I have become dean of the school she did so much to develop,
I find it helpful to be able to call on her inexhaustible fund of wisdom,
wit, and optimism. New students who come in contact with her
through her annual talk to the class in Introduction to Home Economics, or in other ways, seem to draw from her something of the
same sort of inspiration she received from Ellen H. Richards six decades ago at the University of Chicago.

Many honors have accrued to Mrs. Clark. She is a member of
Phi Kappa Phi and Omicron Nu honor societies. She has served as an
officer in numerous regional and national organizations. The Business
and Professional Women of Oregon selected her as one of their recipients of a Golden Torch Award and Oregon State University presented her with a Distinguished Service Award in 1966. The College
of Home Economics in Yonsei University, Seoul, Korea, in 1968
honored her with a Distinguished Service Award "in recognition of
outstanding contributions to Home Economics Education in Korea
and meritorious service to mankind." The Citation she received from
Oregon State University reads in part:

> AVA MILAM CLARK . . . distinguished teacher and ad-
> ministrator . . . an inspiration and confidante to her faculty
> and students through 34 years as dean of home economics at
> Oregon State University . . . innovator of professional
> home economics education at Oregon State . . . devoted
> lifetime champion of the highest standards for home and
> family life . . . pioneer of home economics in the Orient,

*Syria, and Iraq . . . active in civilian food conservation and
nutrition programs through two world wars . . . undaunted
by obstacles in pursuit of goals . . . a gentlewoman in the
truest sense—whose friendly twinkle of the eye or warm
smile has solved many a problem over the years . . . and
whose forceful personality has been felt by even casual acquaintances . . . generous contributor for more than half
a century to the welfare of homes and families of the world.*

This book is primarily an autobiography of a great home economist, educator, and humanitarian—but it is also more. It is an
authentic history of the School of Home Economics at Oregon State
University. It reveals interesting and significant facets of the home
economics movement at home and abroad as seen through the eyes
of one who helped influence its course through the years. It provides
illustrations of women who pioneered in seeking educational advantages at a time when they were none too welcome in the universities
and of the problems encountered in developing a distinctive type of
higher education for women. It gives glimpses into the lives, philoso-
phies, and achievements of homemakers, teachers, missionaries, career women, administrators, and others who sought to improve homes
and homelife in many segments of society.

The text is based on personal reminiscences, diary letters, correspondence, official reports, published articles, biographies, files of the
School of Home Economics, and other documents and source material. In selecting material to be included, in organizing it, and in
putting together and editing the manuscript, Mrs. Clark had the
assistance of a co-author, James Kenneth Munford, director of publications at Oregon State University. Since Dr. Munford is an OSU
alumnus and a long-time OSU staff member, he has personal knowledge of many of the people and of the times and events described.
Mrs. Clark has said many times that this book could not have been
completed without his assistance.

Corvallis, Oregon
June 1, 1968

Contents

Adventures of a
Home Economist

Home is not merely the place
where a man hangs his hat at night—
nor merely where he eats and sleeps.
Home is the scene of the greatest events
in life—birth, death, joy, and sorrow.
It is the cradle of the child,
the resting place of old age,
the retreat in which the worker
is to be refreshed
physically and spiritually
for the day to come.
And if governed with firmness
and love and intelligence,
it becomes the nursery of all virtues.
A palace does not increase its value
nor can a hovel take away
the beauty of mother love.

Attributed to ELLEN H. RICHARDS

1. The First Day

AN HOUR BEFORE NOON on October 4, 1911, the wood-burning locomotive that brought the morning train from Portland drew up
beside the railway station in Corvallis. A young woman in her mid-
twenties dressed in a tailored woolen suit stepped down onto the
platform beside the tracks, her long skirt nearly sweeping the planks.
She was tall and slender with masses of dark brown hair wound in
a coronet braid around her head. She looked about to see if anyone
had come to meet her, but seeing no one, she assumed that her telegram to the President of Oregon Agricultural College had not arrived
in time for anyone to come to the station. The driver of a horse-drawn
vehicle that served as a taxi helped her assemble her luggage and
they started for the campus. A gentle rain was falling and the horse
splashed through little puddles as they moved west along unpaved
Jefferson Street. Although the events of that young woman's first day
in Oregon occurred a long time ago, they live vividly in my memory
because they happened to me.

I have traveled the streets entering the campus a thousand
times, but I shall never forget the first glimpse of what was to become
"my college." The vast green expanse of the Lower Campus, with
its curving pathway and clumps of shrubs and trees, provided a
pleasing introduction for the newcomer. Through the Oregon mist
I could see a piece of statuary in a circular pool at one end of the
tree-lined path that wound up toward the campus buildings. I came
to know this pathway well as I walked along it daily in the weeks to
come when I lived in a hotel downtown. I grew to love that beautiful,
shaded lane and often paused at one of the benches or beside the
statue of the Lady of the Fountain for rest and meditation.

The Lower Campus was well named. In fact, it must have been
much lower then than it is now—or at least not so well drained. When
heavier rains came in the winter, the ditch that crossed it flooded and
became deep enough for the college boys to row boats on. The area

1

impressed me so favorably as a magnificent campus entrance and a splendid recreational area—for activities other than boating—that I have hated to see it encroached upon in recent years by streets cutting across it, parking lots gouging into it, and new buildings intruding upon its fringes.

At the far end of the curving pathway, on the crest of a knoll, stood an imposing three-story building with tall windows. This Administration Building (Benton Hall) looked much the same then as it does today, except that it had a two-story balcony on the east side and clock faces painted on four sides of the tall belfry. The trees that surround and shield it from view today were much smaller then. To the north of it stood the smoke stack of the power plant and the two-story Mechanical (Apperson) Hall. To the south were the castle-like Science (Education) Hall and the Gymnasium (Mitchell Playhouse), outwardly appearing much the same then as now. Across the street to the south was the new Armory, a stark, squat, sturdy-looking building.

Two dozen buildings spread out over the green campus with much room for future expansion between them. Each building in its own way had something in its favor from an architectural standpoint, but I must confess that I had a feeling of disappointment. The rutted dirt roads, the raw blank spaces in need of landscaping, the newness and the dampness of it all undoubtedly influenced my impression. The campus seemed undeveloped to me. The campuses I had known best—the University of Chicago, the University of Missouri, and Iowa State Agricultural College—seemed magnificent by comparison.

I am not sure what I expected, nor what I had a right to expect. I had read in its *Catalogue* a good deal about Oregon Agricultural College. It and its predecessor, Corvallis College, had been in operation half a century; it had been offering college-level studies much longer than the University of Chicago, and even slightly longer than Iowa State College. I knew it had an expanding School of Agriculture and at least the beginnings of home economics. I knew it had a vigorous, well-liked president who had introduced a number of changes in his first four years, but on that first day I gained the impression that much more needed to be done.

The driver let me out in front of Waldo Hall, along the new circular driveway that became so familiar to many generations of college girls and their beaux. I was probably too excited that morning to take a good look at the building, which the *Catalogue* described as having "striking proportions." If I had looked above the entrance archway framed by two gray granite pillars, I would have noted the construction date—1907—just four years before. This "home away from home" for all women who lived on campus I later found had "cool mountain water" in every room, pleasant parlors, graceful dining rooms, and "modern appointments." It had 115 rooms for students on the second, third, and fourth floors and on the first floor a large kitchen and dining room, and the classrooms, laboratories, and offices for the Department of Domestic Science.

Dr. Anna Zou Crayne, the physician who looked after the health of the women students and also served as dean of women and preceptress of Waldo Hall, greeted me cordially. A stately, pleasant person with pince-nez glasses, she was dressed in a starched white uniform with a long, sweeping skirt. I soon learned why she and the other college officials eagerly awaited my arrival, even though the school year had started.

The Dean of the School of Domestic Science and Art had married the previous spring and resigned. Shortly before the school year opened, the four other full-time staff members had also resigned, leaving the school unstaffed in the face of a sharp increase in enrollment. The only continuity with the previous staff was an instructor who had just graduated in June. A new dean for the school had been selected, but she could not leave her position at Purdue University until the end of the 1911-12 school year. New instructors in domestic science and art were being appointed, but here I was, not yet a year out of college, the ranking member of the Department of Domestic Science. I was not sure I was ready for such responsibility.

That spring I had received a Master of Arts degree from the University of Chicago. In the summer I had taught home economics courses—to students mostly older than myself—at Northern Illinois State Normal School at DeKalb. The University of Chicago placement secretary had sent me notices of three home economics openings for the coming year, two at teachers colleges paying salaries of $1,350 per year, and one, an instructorship at Iowa State Agricultural College at Ames, paying $1,000 per year. On the advice of one of my University of Chicago professors, Elizabeth Sprague, I accepted the lower-salaried offer at Iowa State despite my university debt. Miss

Sprague believed the greatest future for home economics lay in land-grant colleges.

After my summer job in DeKalb I had reported in August to my new assignment at Ames. A few weeks later the University of Chicago placement office sent a telegram asking if I would accept a more important position at Oregon Agricultural College. I had no desire to leave Iowa and did not answer the wire. Soon a telegram came from President W. J. Kerr asking if I would consider the opening in Oregon. If so, when could I arrive and what salary would I accept? In reply I suggested that he find someone else and told him that I would not leave Iowa if the people at Ames felt I was being unfair, nor would I be willing to leave until a successor had arrived. I indicated the minimum salary I could accept would be $1,800, the salary I was to receive in Iowa beginning in January 1912. Asking for such a high salary, I thought, would settle matters and I would stay in Ames. President Kerr's surprising response came back almost immediately: "YOU ARE APPOINTED. WIRE ACCEPTANCE AND DATE OF ARRIVAL."

I telephoned my parents at Macon, Missouri, to seek their counsel. My father was at his office, but my mother assured me that he would give the same advice that she did—that they would have confidence in whatever decision I made, but that *I* would have to make it.

On Sunday afternoon, a sunny autumn day in Ames, I carried in my hand the telegram from President Kerr as I walked toward the home of Catherine J. MacKay, head of home economics. I was truly puzzled about what I should do. As I crossed campus, the chimes began to play, "I'll go where You want me to go," and at once I decided: "It's Oregon for me!"

When I reached Miss MacKay's home, instead of asking her advice, I told her of my decision. She said she was sorry that I was leaving, but she extended best wishes and told me she did not blame me for taking the new position. She had been in Oregon and she had met President Kerr; she thought highly of both. I helped find my successor, waited until she could arrive so that no class was missed, and then started off on the long trail to Oregon.

Now that I had arrived in the Far West, I began to wonder whether or not I had made the right choice. The new job presented more responsibility than I had anticipated, and I was not fully convinced I was capable of handling it. At the faculty luncheon table that first day in Waldo Hall, however, I met other staff members who began to give me a sense of reassurance. Joining the Dean of Women and me were the Librarian, the Assistant Librarian, the President's secretary, and several other staff members. Their friendly attitude gave me encouragement.

After lunch I met the two other instructors in the Domestic Science Department—Mrs. Lida M. Layton, who had just recently arrived, and Ruth McNary Smith, who had been an assistant as a senior the previous year. Ruth remembers that meeting, too: "When I first saw Ava Milam on that October day, the situation was rather confused, with many of her responsibilities as yet undefined; her manner, while cordial and friendly, was a little uncertain."

I do not doubt that I did appear uncertain, because that is the way I felt. I met two classes that had not met before, one at two o'clock and another at three o'clock, and at four I crossed the campus to the President's office to report officially. In his outer office, I met his executive secretary, Mr. W. A. Jensen. He introduced me to a professor who commented, "Oh, yes, we saw your picture in the paper, and we all decided that you were too young for your job." Although the professor had a twinkle in his eyes and he smiled as he said it, his comment did not boost my morale at that moment.

President Kerr proved to be a tall, dignified, poised, considerate man, whom I came to admire through the years for his many fine qualities. We talked only briefly that day. Then he arose, as he always did when he considered a conference to be of sufficient length, and taking my hand looked straight into my eyes. "Miss Milam," he said, "I realize that you have a difficult job, but we have great faith in you. Make your decisions as you think best, and never doubt that you have the hearty support of this office."

I walked out of that office with a greater feeling of security than when I entered. Never, in the quarter of a century I had the privilege of working with the leadership of William Jasper Kerr, did I have cause to doubt his hearty support for the field of study I represented nor for me as a staff member. He taught me much about administration by precept, example, and wise counsel. I sought no opening elsewhere and declined offers of positions that came to me unsolicited.

Musing about the turmoil I had plunged into, I walked back to Waldo Hall. Many of the women staff members lived there, but all suitable accommodations were filled. I therefore picked up my luggage, arranged for transportation downtown, and moved into the Julian Hotel, on the corner of the two paved streets, Second and Monroe.

This unusual day left me much to think about. The new position looked difficult, yet it appeared challenging. The classes seemed in chaos, but I felt they could be brought into orderly arrangement. I had personal resources I knew I could rely on. I had taught in elementary schools and had some knowledge of how to organize new classes. I had received the benefit of an excellent education in one of America's newer and most imaginative universities, and I had received a personal inspiration from one of the greatest leaders in education for women that this country has known. I sensed, too, that this College, although new to me, had deep roots and that the School of Domestic Science and Art had a tradition of success and service that would help carry it through this period of temporary disorganization.

Before going on with the events of that first year in Oregon, let us first take a glimpse into my personal resources and the background of the College whose faculty I had just joined.

Waldo Hall

2. Early Life in Missouri

Child, your time is coming.

—ELLEN STEWART McGINNIS

M^Y TWIN SISTER, Ada Elizabeth Milam, and I, Ava Bertha Milam, were born on Thanksgiving Day, November 27, 1884, on a farm in Macon County, Missouri. Our mother was the daughter of Scotch-Irish parents, Ellen Stewart and William McGinnis, and her name had been Mary Louisa McGinnis before she married our father, Ancil Milam. Father's parents, Hannah Richardson and Buise Milam, were of English and Dutch ancestry. The Milam name came from the Dutch side of the family and by other Dutch-Americans is sometimes spelled Milham. Both of our parents' families had come to Missouri from Virginia, the McGinnises settling in Montgomery County and the Milams in Macon County. Milam Chapel, a community twelve miles northwest of the city of Macon, still carries the Milam name, although none of the family lives there now.

Since Missouri was a border state between the North and the South, the practice of holding slaves before the Civil War varied from family to family. My mother's family, the McGinnises, apparently did not hold slaves, but my grandfather Milam and his wife's family did. As a boy my father played with a slightly older Negro boy who prided himself on being Father's bodyguard. At the time of my father's funeral, sixty years after the slaves had been freed, this boyhood playmate came 175 miles to attend the services. When my grandmother, Hannah Richardson, was young she had a little Negro maid named Christine, a few years older than herself. When Grandmother married Buise Milam, Christine became part of the dowry and went along with the bride to live in the new home. After Chris-

7

tine was freed, she moved to Iowa, married, and raised a family of her own. The two had a lasting affection for one another. When "Miss Hannah," as many called my grandmother, lived in our home in later years, she told us so many stories about Christine that we felt we knew her. One hot summer afternoon shortly after Grandmother Milam's death, Mother called us to the porch to meet a guest. There was Christine, who had come from Iowa, she said, because she thought Miss Hannah needed her. We knew she was older than Grandmother, but she looked younger and gave an appearance of quiet capability in her freshly laundered black and white calico dress and bonnet and apron to match. Christine was as delighted to see us grandchildren as we were to see her, but she was sad that she had not come in time to see Miss Hannah once more.

The different environments in which our two grandmothers grew up undoubtedly had a marked influence on their attitudes in later years. Grandmother Milam grew up in a family where she had little work to do, and when she came to spend her final years in our home she did no work except occasional knitting. She wore dark dresses with a little three-cornered shawl around her stooped shoulders, sat most of the time in a small rocker, and called each of us "Honey." Her mind was largely on events of the past.

With Grandmother Ellen Stewart McGinnis, it was a much different story. A remarkable, self-reliant woman, she had raised three sons, Evermont, William Erasmus (our beloved "Uncle Roz"), and Leonidas, and twin daughters, Mary Louisa (my mother) and Elizabeth Jane. Although she had lost her husband when her fifth child was a baby, she had managed to send each of the five to college. After they were grown, she came to live with us except in the winter months when she lived with Uncle Roz and his family in Kansas City. Tall, erect, and well groomed, she kept up to date not only in clothes but also in the happenings of the day. She sewed for the family and brought from Kansas City beautiful sashes and ribbons and other clothing—and oh, yes, *perfume*. She was the best looking grandmother around and we were proud of her. She ever kept the future before us. "Child, your time is coming," she said to each of us and kept insisting, "These children must go to college." She eyed carefully any boys who came to our house and never hesitated to pass judgment on them. When vexed, her strongest expression was, "Oh scissors!"

We learned a great deal from our grandmothers. Children lose something when they have no grandparents near as they are growing up. Many students have told me of their affection for their grandparents; how they were attracted by cookie jars at first, but how in later years they came to realize their grandparents had taught them much about life. With Grandmother McGinnis, it was not just "cupboard love." She thought Ada and I should take calisthenics and even paid us a few pennies each night to come into her bedroom to exercise under her supervision. We both grew tall early, and she was afraid we would be stooped. We responded to her encouragement and tried to learn good posture. We did not want to become bent over like Grandmother Milam in our old age.

My parents were leaders in the community of Milam Chapel. Father had studied at the normal school at Kirksville, forty miles north of Macon, and had taught school for a while. Mother had attended Hardin College at Mexico, Missouri, and Howard-Payne College at Fayette, Missouri, and also had taught for a year before her marriage. Father served many years as a school board member. Both were active in church as well as school affairs, and the neighbors called on them for help and counsel. They sometimes made up the church deficit out of their own funds.

My mother was easy to live with—so joyous. As we hurried home from school and called, she was always there, usually with a slice of fresh bread and perhaps a lump of brown sugar. When there was illness in the community, Mother often sat up all night with a sick child or neighbor. Early next morning she would ride her horse home, and if the illness was communicable, she would change her clothes in the smokehouse and wash her hands and face carefully before coming in to greet her family and preparing breakfast.

She seemed to have a reservoir of strength. Daily she read and studied her Bible, and each morning about ten o'clock she was not available for about twenty minutes or half an hour. She was in her bedroom on her knees praying or meditating. We all learned early to respect that quiet time of Mother's. It was, I always believed, a part of the secret of her radiance and joyousness and readiness to meet whatever the day brought.

When Ada and I first left home, Mother filled our little trunk with what she considered necessities, including two small New Testaments. On the flyleaves she had written, "Trust in the Lord with all thy heart and lean not unto thine own understanding," and Father had finished the quotation from Proverbs in his own handwriting, "In all thy ways acknowledge Him and He shall direct thy paths." I have often recalled these passages, especially when faced with important decisions in school, in professional life, or on overseas assignments. Each time before any of her daughters left home for boarding school, for college, or for new teaching positions, Mother always took us into one of our bedrooms and knelt down with us— between us if there were more than one—and put her arms about us, offering a brief prayer asking God to protect and direct us. The faith that my parents helped establish in me as a child, through their examples and their admonitions, has been a significant force in my life for more than eight decades.

My parents had five daughters: Eleanor, whom we called Nell or Nellie, who was three years older than Ada and I; and another set of twins, Lottie and Lora, who were three and a half years younger than Ada and I. When one of my father's men friends would ask, "Ancil, didn't you ever wish to have a boy?" he would quickly reply (at least when within hearing distance of one of his daughters), "Oh, I couldn't get along with less than *five* girls." We knew then that we were wanted. I have had students tell me with concern, "My father wanted a boy when I came." Children are more sensitive than parents sometimes realize about remarks thoughtlessly made.

Twins, especially identical twins, have certain problems; they also have an opportunity to get unusual enjoyment out of life. Ada and I, unlike Lottie and Lora, are identical twins, and as we were growing up we attracted so much attention that it made us self-conscious. People would say, "Look at those two little girls, like peas in a pod." Father often mentioned our likeness and always wished us to be dressed alike. Mother tried to please him and to keep from showing favoritism between us. The younger twins often had to wear Ada's and my dresses when we had grown out of them, whereas Ada and I had only one older sister and felt fortunate to escape wearing outgrown dresses. Sometimes Eleanor would feel lonely and would claim mother as her twin. Ada and I wished to have separate identities, but schoolmates and teachers often confused one of us with the other. When people mistook us we avoided admitting that we were not the one they took us to be. Sometimes we got into "jams" and had to admit deception.

In college we decided that the time had come to break away from the custom of dressing alike. We intentionally chose different majors. Even so, we still experienced many cases of mistaken identity. One day at the University of Chicago, my French teacher asked me if anyone on the campus looked like me. I told him of my twin. "Well," he said, "that explains it. At times when I meet you, you are very cordial; other times you just don't speak to me." A boy said to Ada one day, "Please explain something to me. Why do you know me in geology class but not in chemistry?" Sometimes when we went to parties or plays with two boys and we both preferred one over the other, we would agree to let one of us go with the favored boy and the other return with him. At times we were accused of doing so when we were not guilty. Students in our Latin class, in which the professor could not tell us apart, accused us of taking turns in preparing the assignments and no matter on which one of us the instructor called, the one prepared would reply.

The similarity in appearance continued as we grew older. Just before Ada was married, the whole family went to Los Angeles for the wedding. Our sisters suggested that I meet Ada's fiance, Edgar A. (Ted) Cockefair, at the train and see if he would realize that I was not Ada. I had never met Ted but had a photograph by which I could recognize him. To be good sports, we carried the idea along for a while, but when the day came to meet the train neither Ada nor I thought the idea a good one. Ada met Ted at the station, and I was relieved of the proposed prank.

Once when Ada came to Oregon to visit, some of the staff members confused our identity. In Madison, Wisconsin, where Ada made her home in later life, people have called me "Mrs. Cockefair." The most startling instance of uncertainty came when Ada's little daughter approached me one day with a puzzled look and asked, "Are you Mother or are you Auntie?"

I AM GLAD my parents lived on a farm and that they considered it important for each of us to learn how to work and to know the satisfaction of a job well done. I believe most children wish to contribute to the family's welfare and work, especially when deserved commendation is given. We walked three miles daily to and from a one-room country school. We helped with the chores—carrying in wood for the cookstove and the big base-burner in the living room, feeding the horses and the cows, taking turns whirling the churn one hundred times each, helping with the milking and with the cooking and dishwashing.

The butchering of hogs was an unusual event because the neighbors came and helped. We girls were too small to assist and I hated to hear the guns go off. Through the frightening process, I preferred to stay in the house. I would lie on the feather bed and bury my head in the pillows. Later, of course, we all enjoyed the delicious hams, bacon, tenderloin, scrapple, headcheese, and sausage.

In addition to the five girls and two grandmothers, a hired man usually lived in our home. Cousins from Kansas City frequently visited in the summer. The spare bedroom was often occupied by our pastor, a circuit rider, who usually stayed with us over the weekends he spent in our community and also when he came for "protracted meetings." We also had other guests frequently for meals and to stay overnight. Father bought and sold cattle, and cattlemen often stayed all night in our home and had dinner and breakfast with us. Whether friends or strangers they always received our best with no remuneration accepted.

We attended weekly Sunday School and the monthly church services when the circuit rider came. When the younger twins were babies, all five of us girls were baptized by the bishop. Ada and I were about four then, and I recall (or at least recall hearing the family talk about it) being concerned when the bishop, in baptizing Ada, let a few drops of water fall on her new red dress. I reached over and wiped it off, much to the amusement of the congregation. Following the service, the bishop came to our house for dinner. Afterwards, Ada and I, still dressed in our finery, decided that we did not like the odor of our freshly polished shoes. We went into the pantry and washed off the shoes. When Mother discovered us with wet feet, she gave us quinine and put us to bed. That taught us a lesson we never forgot.

Younger sister Lora caused the whole family a great deal of anxiety when she had the croup and diphtheria and had to fight for every breath. Our family physician, Dr. A. B. Miller, told my parents he would have to perform an operation and put a tube in Lora's windpipe so that she could get air into her lungs. Father and Mother

held the lamps, boiled the water, and administered the anesthetic for
Dr. Miller as he performed the tracheotomy. Grandmother McGinnis
took us other girls into another room, but we could still hear something of what was going on. The struggle for breath ceased when the
doctor cut into the windpipe, but the quiet that followed caused us
to fear the outcome. Lying beside us on a four-poster bed, Grandmother soothed and calmed us with her prayers as she held us close
to her. Prayer became very meaningful to me at that moment. The
operation proved successful and in six weeks Lora was back in good
health.

Despite all of her duties and responsibilities, Mother took time
to be with her children. She read to us, played with us, taught us to
keep house, and showed us how to ride willows, to make little mills
at the brook, and to find wild flowers in the spring. She found time
to answer innumerable questions and to quote lovely and exciting
poems she had memorized. She sang songs with us and helped us
with the catechism.

When the family was alone at meals, the table became an educational center. Father would not say Grace until each of us was in her
place. "If your mother can get up early to cook your breakfast," he
would say, "you can come down when it is ready and eat it." Once
Grace had been asked, the table became an open forum. We children
had much to talk about, and Father served as a referee. We each had
our say, but none was permitted to have more than her share. I
remember breakfasts so well—ham and eggs, heaping plates of delicious light buttermilk biscuits, jam, and coffee (permitted for us
children only on Sundays)—and all of it spiced with what we considered brilliant conversation.

We all read a good deal. We girls read the Louisa May Alcott
books eagerly. Whittier and Dickens' *Pickwick Papers* come to mind
quickly when I think of that period. For periodicals the *Youth's
Companion*, the *Ladies Home Journal*, and the *Christian Herald*
were the standbys. Lora kept track of the time when each issue was
due and usually managed to get it first and devour it before any of
the rest of us saw it. She remained an avid reader, and her early
interest in reading led in later years to the collection of a fine home
library.

We did not have to rely entirely on books and periodicals for
contact with the outside world. Ours was one of the first homes in

the neighborhood to have a telephone. The circuit-riding minister, the cattle buyers, the relatives and friends who came to visit, all brought something in the way of news and information. We eagerly awaited one relative in particular. About once a year Grandmother Milam's brother, Howard Haven Richardson, came to see us. Uncle Hāve had traveled to California in the early fifties to find gold. He claimed he had fought in five wars. With one twin on each knee he would regale us with stories of the Far West and Texas and his adventures with Kit Carson and how he had come through New Orleans on his way home and had heard Jenny Lind sing. We would always ask Uncle Hāve to sing. He would throw back his head—he had a shaved upper lip and a rather long beard—and sing for us folk songs of the cattle trails and mining camps. One of our favorites, Lottie recalls, was "The Dying Californian." It is not hard to imagine the effect this romantic person had on the curiosities of bright-eyed little girls.

Grandmothers and parents all encouraged us in music. The old reed organ would not do, they thought, so a grand piano was purchased and Ada and I took lessons for several years. We became so interested in music that we even proposed to our parents that we major in music. They did not encourage the proposal, feeling that we should learn something more practical.

My mother showed great patience in letting Ada and me learn to cook. While she was making cake, pie, or bread, we stood on little boxes one on either side of her. She divided the ingredients to let us make small amounts of the same recipe she was making. Ada and I have always enjoyed cooking and we attribute this interest to Mother's patience in teaching us. She captured our interest when it was strong and did not impatiently suggest that we go away and come back at a later time.

We also had playhouses of our own and in the summer cooked on little improvised brick stoves. The foods we cooked consisted mostly of dried apricots or dried peaches and raisins, and they had a distinctly smoky flavor. They were never completely cooked, but *we* had cooked them so of course *we* ate them. Sometimes on summer afternoons Mother allowed us to use her kitchen. Ada and I could each have one egg, but before we began we had to choose a recipe from Mother's recipe book and calculate how much of each ingredient we needed to go with one egg. We usually chose a cake recipe that called for five eggs. Hence we had to take one-fifth of the other ingredients and in that way learned fractions ahead of most of the rest of our class in school.

THERE WAS NO HIGH SCHOOL in our community. When Nell finished elementary school she went to live with Uncle Roz and attended high school in Kansas City. When Ada and I were ready for high school my parents had to choose between sending us to a boarding academy or employing a young woman to live in our home and tutor us for the school year. Our parents weighed carefully the advantages and disadvantages of these two plans. They finally chose the academy, even though to send us away from home at thirteen years of age seemed difficult at the time.

The first school we attended away from home was the Macon District Academy at Clarence, Missouri, only about twenty miles from home. It was directed by our father's cousin, Sol Milam, who was experienced as a preacher but not as an educator. A number of his students were relatives who helped boost the school's enrollment but whose parents soon became discontented with the policies and the quality of teaching.

For our second year we transferred to Centenary Academy at Palmyra, which is about sixty miles east of Macon not far from Samuel Clemen's hometown, Hannibal, on the Mississippi River. The head of the Academy, Professor James Lanius, had taught at Washington University in St. Louis and, earlier, had been director of the academy in Bloomington that my father had attended. We studied English, mathematics, Latin and Greek, history, and music. Professor Lanius saw to it that his students learned how to concentrate and not waste time. He also insisted that we be in bed with our lights out by ten o'clock. We thought, however, if we were to make good marks in Latin and Greek, which Professor Lanius himself taught, we just had to study late at night. We asked for a kerosene lamp for our room—under the guise of needing it to heat our curling iron. Mother had never approved the use of a curling iron because our hair was naturally curly, but we did not tell the authorities that. Thus, we had a light after lights were supposed to be out.

Professor Lanius became suspicious. One morning about three o'clock, we heard his peg leg coming down the hall. He rapped on our door. "Lights out, young ladies!" he said sternly. Our lamp went out quickly, and the Latin and Greek books slid onto the floor. We had no sleep the rest of that night wondering what our punishment would be.

Later, the professor stood at the entrance of the dining room and as we entered he said, "Young ladies, I would like to see you in the parlor after breakfast." That was not an enjoyable meal for us. The students at our table who had heard the professor in the night felt sorry for us. After breakfast our seemingly gruff old professor said to us, "You girls don't need to study after ten o'clock. I know that you will make good in your studies, and I wish to send you home in the spring with good health as well as good grades. Your father was a student of mine, and I think of you as grandchildren." Ada and I were expecting reproof, but when kind talk, affection, and understanding came instead, we both cried. We went to our room determined not to let our parents and our old professor down.

While Ada and I were still in boarding school, the other twins, Lora and Lottie, finished grade school. In order to be near a high school for them, my parents sold the farm and moved into Macon. Father went into the insurance business and also became a director and a stockholder in the local bank. The latter venture proved disastrous because an employee of the bank absconded with a large sum of money and the bank failed. Helping to make up the loss to depositors put Father in a difficult financial situation. We would have lost our home if Uncle Roz had not bought it and deeded it over to my mother. After the bank failure, Father became postmaster for Macon—a position he held until his retirement.

After four years in boarding schools, Ada and I were graduated from Centenary Academy in June 1903. At once we began to study for the Macon County teachers' examination and were ready to take it in July. After receiving our teaching certificates—we were 18 at the time—Ada obtained a job teaching in the small town of Bevier, while I found one in Atlanta, another small town nearby. I taught the fourth, fifth, and sixth grades. In addition, I gave piano lessons for my room rent. I boarded with a quaint little Irish woman, who was a good cook and an efficient housekeeper.

When Ada and I came back to Macon on weekends we met two young medical students, proteges of Dr. Miller, our family physician who lived a block from our house. We played tennis with the young

The Milam sisters of Macon County, Missouri, about 1894.
Left to right: Ava, Lottie, Eleanor, Ada, and Lora.

The Milam twins, Ada Elizabeth and Ava Bertha, at sixteen years of age, students at Centenary Academy in Palmyra, Missouri. *Above:* Their father Ancil Milam, and mother Mary Louisa McGinnis Milam.

Cadets and teacher at Blees Military Academy, Macon, Missouri, 1907.
Standing: Eddie Busch, Coy Worden, Pope Dodge, Harry Cantrell, Sidney Busch.
Seated: Roy Solari, Miss Ava B. Milam, Frederic Liebing. *In front:* Maurice Duncan.

The campus of Oregon Agricultural College, 1912, Jefferson Street on left, Monroe Street on right. The pathway through the Lower Campus winds from The Lady of the Fountain at the head of Madison Street to the Administration Building (Benton Hall). Other buildings from left to right include the Armory with athletic fields beyond, Waldo Hall, old Gymnasium (Mitchell Playhouse), Science Hall (Education), Cauthorn-Kidder-Fairbanks Hall surrounded by trees, greenhouses and new Agriculture Hall, Agricultural Engineering and other agriculture buildings, Dairy Building (Social Science Hall), Alpha Hall-Pharmacy building, Shepard Hall, Mines, Industrial Arts (Production Technology), and Apperson Hall, *Lower right.*

men and enjoyed their company. The next summer they invited us to
come to St. Louis where they were in school and offered to show us
the World's Fair. We explained to our parents that Fairs were considered educational, and they gave us permission to go. Ada and I
stayed at the YWCA in St. Louis, and the four of us had great fun
seeing the Louisiana Purchase Exposition together. In one of the
exhibits of household science, Mrs. Sara Tyson Rorer, head of the
Philadelphia Cooking School, demonstrated how to bone a chicken
in preparation for making a fancy dish. As she carved, she emphasized
that for skillful boning one needs to know the anatomy of the chicken.
Just about that time in her demonstration, her knife failed to hit the
joint. Without batting an eye she looked up at her audience and
explained her failure: "Malformation of the joint!" I never did meet
Mrs. Rorer after that but came to know her by reputation as editor
of the food and domestic science section of the *Ladies' Home Journal*,
as author of more than a dozen books, and as an active pioneer in the
home economics movement.

IN THE SUMMER after my second year at Atlanta I was invited to
tutor the daughter of a banker in Macon to prepare her for entrance
to a "prep" school in Illinois. Through this banker, General William
F. Blees heard of my work and invited me to call at his residence.
Timid but excited, I rang the bell on the big front door of his "castle."
A uniformed butler ushered me into a deeply carpeted room filled
with beautiful paintings.

General Blees, an imposing Prussian-type officer, soon appeared
and greeted me pleasantly. He explained that he would like me to
give up my teaching position in Atlanta and devote myself to tutoring
his two daughters. He said that he would pay me $10 a month more
than the $45 I was then receiving and that I could live at home with
my parents. Although our home was within walking distance of the
Blees residence, a driver would call for me each morning, take me
home at 11:30 for lunch, and call again at 1:30 p.m. In mid-morning
the butler would bring sandwiches and milk. I would be free at
3 o'clock, or if I would care to go with his daughters for a ride, a
driver and carriage would be at our disposal. Since the General had
beautiful prize horses and high carriages, the prospect of riding
behind those prancing horses was quite an inducement to me. General Blees explained that the schoolroom in the tower of his castle-

like residence had a good children's library and, in addition, the many other books in the house would be available to me.

Awed but excited, I went home to discuss the offer with my parents. They told me I should make my own decision but that they would be very happy to have me home again. I accepted the General's offer and began the daily routine as he had outlined it for me.

General Blees, a dignified, well-educated gentleman, had a deep interest in music and good literature and always chose excellent books as gifts from his daughters to me. He had been commandant of a struggling military academy in Macon when copper ore had been discovered on his family's estate in Germany. He came into so much wealth that he built a very fine military academy a mile from Macon on grounds of 1,000 acres with two artificial lakes. He also paid for paving several miles of street in the town. He owned a carriage factory in Macon and several business establishments in St. Louis. His academy was popular, especially among German families in many parts of the country.

The Blees daughters, Marie and Elise, were ten and nine years of age. General Blees invited me to move out to the academy, where the Blees family had moved for the remainder of the school year, and told me I would have a suite consisting of a living room, bedroom, and bath on the first floor of the academy and would eat my meals at the Blees table there. On weekends I could be with my family. This arrangement seemed so practical that I accepted.

I found life at the academy stimulating and delightful. The exceptional staff of teachers gave the rich young boys excellent training and discipline. I loved little Marie and Elise, and my work was intriguing. The Blees family once expressed a desire for me to accompany them on a European trip, but my parents discouraged my acceptance, thinking I was too young. Consequently, I did not go with the family on any of their travels, even though they had a private railroad car when traveling in the United States.

My situation was so pleasant that it became very difficult for me to consider continuing my education, but I knew that I should. Therefore, during the summer between my first and second years of teaching for General Blees, Ada and I decided to follow our sister Nell to the University of Missouri to begin college study. When I told the General our plans, he expressed the hope that we would attend the University of Chicago instead. He said that he believed the new university William Rainey Harper had organized was one of the most promising in the country. I expressed some doubt as to whether or not we could gain admission to an out-of-state university since a fire at Centenary Academy had destroyed our records. He said, "I know a member of the University of Chicago's Board of Admissions, Professor Frank J. Miller. I will write him about you." This he did, and the University of Chicago admitted Ada and me for the summer quarter of 1906.

At the beginning of my second year at the military academy, General Blees invited me to take ten young boys, ten to fourteen years of age, into my classroom. He knew it would be good for his daughters to have added competition in their studies and in this way he could also comply with the demand of parents who wished to send younger boys to the academy. He offered me a raise in salary and I accepted.

I became deeply interested in this group of cadets, rich and yet in many respects poor because their parents spent so much time traveling that they had little time for the youngsters. The boys had been accustomed to having a great deal of spending money, but as privates in the academy they were allowed only 25¢ a week. Since buglers had a higher rank and were allowed $1.00 a week, several of the boys decided to become buglers. They often came to visit in my living room and to share with me their improvement in buglery. At mealtimes, I sat with my boys at a separate table. If one of them came in late to the dining room, he had to go first to the commandant's table and salute him. Then he came to our table, saluted me, and said, "I wish to report my presence." One morning I slept through reveille and was late in "reporting my presence." I apologized for not hearing the reveille bugle. Sidney Busch, son of the St. Louis brewer, was by then quite a bugler. He piped up and said, "I'll fix that!" The next morning—and thereafter at reveille—Sidney turned his bugle so that the sound would strike the metal door of my living room. I did not come late for breakfast again.

Before one vacation period, Sidney wrote a note that contained only thirteen words in a boyish scrawl that took a whole sheet of paper: "Good bye dear teacher. Hope you will have a good time this Easter. S. W. Busch." Another cadet wrote after he reached home: "Dear Miss Milam. I was lying down and happened to think of you and how good you were to me and thought I would drop you a line

immediately to let you know that I did not forget you. . . . I went
to school with my sister and all of the teachers were glad to see me
the principal said that they were not 10 boys in that school that
could stand as strait as I could. With Love, Roy Solari. P.S. Don't
forget my love to your sister."

The parents of my cadets were appreciative and generous, often
bringing gifts to me from their travels and showing gratitude for my
interest in their children. One Easter I was invited to the home of the
mayor of St. Louis, the father of one of the boys. It was a delightful,
memorable vacation with operas and other fascinating experiences
included in the two-week period. Opportunities such as this enabled
me to observe some of the problems as well as the pleasures associated with great wealth. I learned that money alone cannot guarantee
happiness to a family, and that it brings its own problems.

After teaching at the academy for three years, I regretfully left
my position at the end of the school year to complete my college
education.

3. University of Chicago

ON A JUNE EVENING in 1906, Father took Ada and me to the Burlington station in Macon and put us on the train. After a night in the chair car, we arrived in Chicago in early morning and transferred our luggage to an elevated train that took us to the south part of the city. After we left the elevated we walked across the Midway Plaisance, site of the World's Columbian Exposition of thirteen years before, and reported at Cobb Hall to enroll for the summer quarter at the University of Chicago.

We had not decided what courses to take but thought that this would be a good time to start going our individual ways in classwork. A summer student from Texas suggested that we would have more freedom in choice of courses if we registered as Unclassified Students rather than as regular freshmen. We took her advice and did not enroll in a prescribed curriculum. In the academy we had liked the classics, languages, and literature. At Chicago we both registered for the fifth course in Latin, Selections from Livy, even though we should have had the fourth course, Cicero, as a prerequisite. We persuaded the instructor we could handle the advanced course because of our preparation in the academy. I enrolled in an elementary course in French; Ada, in German. In science Ada chose a class in geology; I signed up for Principles of Geography, which I found was a "senior college" course; that is, an upper division course for which I was supposed to have had two junior college courses as preparation.

We enjoyed our courses but had to do quite a bit of stretching because, as freshmen, we found ourselves among upperclassmen who were more mature students. Our preparation for advanced work was a bit weak, but we studied hard and made a creditable showing. We had much reading to do and, fortunately, found a place to room near the library.

The instructor in Principles of Geography was Assistant Professor John Paul Goode, one of the country's foremost young geographers, who later became noted as the author of several atlases. He was a dynamic teacher and often took students on field trips. A tour through Swift's slaughterhouse took away from me all desire to eat meat for some time. I shuddered to see the conditions under which the men had to work. Standing in what seemed inches of blood, they slashed the throats of squealing hogs dangling by one hind leg from a moving trolley line. Other men stunned beeves with heavy hammer blows and then cut them so that they would bleed to death. Although seeing the slaughter, hearing the animals' screams of fear and pain, and smelling the stench was a traumatic experience for us, I could see why Dr. Goode had brought us. He wanted us to see firsthand what the revolution in the preparation of foods was costing in terms of its effect on the men engaged in it. Having dreaded butchering day on the farm, I could understand how mass slaughtering was a more efficient method than each family doing its own. But I could also see that an industrial operation such as this could have a brutalizing effect on the men engaged in it and, probably, an undesirable effect on their homes and families. I could understand why Upton Sinclair had called the book he had recently written on this subject *The Jungle*.

My association with Professor Goode was a long and interesting one. For one of his classes, I wrote a paper on the U. S. and British postal services. Father came for a visit while I was working on the paper and, as a postmaster himself, he added to my information and experience by taking me downtown to see the inner workings of the mammoth Chicago postal system. My paper was thus based on firsthand observations as well as extensive reading. In addition to the university library, I discovered the resources of the Crerar Library in Chicago, where my cousin, Carl Milam (later executive secretary of the American Library Association) was employed. I learned much from writing this paper, and as we shall see later, it served a dual purpose.

Dr. Goode took a great deal of interest in his students. He knew us not only on an academic basis but also on a friendly, personal, social basis. He often invited students—sometimes parents, too—to his home. When my parents came for graduation, for example, the Goodes included them in the invitation to a dinner in their home.

Dr Goode and I kept in touch with each other for many years. On several occasions before I selected a major he encouraged me to specialize in geography and, shortly before he died some years later, he sent me a copy of the latest edition of his *School Atlas*. Geography would have interested me as a field of specialization, except for the fact that I was becoming acquainted with a new and to me more fascinating field of study.

At the end of the first summer, Ada and I returned to our teaching positions in Macon, I at the Blees Academy and Ada in the Macon public schools. We went back to Chicago in the summer of 1907 and in the fall Ada stayed to work toward a degree. By continuing her university study then, attending through full years including summer quarters under the Chicago plan, she graduated a year ahead of me, because I did not start full-time study until a year later.

In the summer quarter in 1908, I enrolled for Intermediate German and English Literature 1744-1798. For a third course, I looked through the schedule of classes and found one in household administration called The Application of Heat to Food Materials. It sounded as if it had something to do with cooking and therefore appealed to me.

According to the transcript of my Chicago record, which the Registrar sent me in recent years, I did not do very good work that summer. In German, I received a C grade, and in English Literature and the Application of Heat classes I received D's. I could alibi that I really did not have adequate preparation for these advanced courses, but I suspect that lack of a long-range goal also played a part. In summer study up to that point my grades were mostly C's and D's with only an occasional B. I mention this fact only because of the dramatic change that took place the next fall. Something happened to me that I have seen happen to dozens of other girls through the years. I found a clear-cut purpose for being in college and the whole picture changed. In autumn quarter I brought my average up to B and in succeeding quarters to between B and A. In two terms of my senior year I made a straight A.

In the fall quarter of 1908, the record shows that my course of study took a new direction. I enrolled for introductory courses in physics and in economics (political economy it was then called), for an Old Testament course in the Social Teachings of the Priests, for required work in public speaking and physical culture, and for a second course in household administration: The Organization of the Retail Market. I objected at first to the public speaking course, because at that point I had no intention of ever making speeches, but was persuaded to include it since it was required for graduation.

In order to explain what happened to me that fall of 1908, I need to tell a bit about the University of Chicago and some of the things that were going on in the country at that time. President William Rainey Harper had planned a university in which outstanding scholars, scientists, and administrators would be assembled, in which the wisdom of the ages would be freely studied and criticized, and in which new fields of thought would find a congenial home. The university gained the reputation of being unorthodox in education and religion. I recall my parents being asked, "Are you sending your daughters to the University of Chicago where the Scriptures are criticized?" My parents seemed to have confidence in the university and continued to sacrifice to make university study possible for us. Dr. Harper, who by some had been called a heretic, had also seemed unruffled by criticism. When his benefactor, John D. Rockefeller, or other members of his Baptist-dominated Board of Trustees protested that some professor was too strong in his unorthodox opinions, Dr. Harper's characteristic response was not to throttle the professor but to seek someone equally strong in the opposing view to present the other side of a controversial question.

President Harper had died six months before I arrived in Chicago, but his lengthened shadow was present everywhere. The whole university continued in the form and spirit in which he had molded it. In many fields of knowledge he had brought to the campus eminent scholars. He had shown foresight by appointing outstanding women who became leaders in the home economics movement. These leaders and their colleagues elsewhere were taking a new approach toward the improvement of society. For generations, professors of moral philosophy had been discussing ethics and family relations. Anthropologists and sociologists were expanding their scholarly studies of the family as a basic social unit, but, except in isolated instances, very little attention had been given to the setting in which the family functions: the home. The leaders at Chicago and their associates in other parts of the country had caught a vision that the home is the heart of society and that the fundamental way in which to improve society is through improvement of the home.

A few pioneers in the previous half century had made dramatic attempts to awaken the nation, especially its women, to the fact that the arts and sciences of homelife and the household were badly neglected. Following the inspiration of such women as Emma Hart Willard and Mary Lyon, Catharine Beecher and her sister Harriet Beecher Stowe had campaigned vigorously "to relieve the disabilities and sufferings of their sex." We "are confident," they wrote in 1869, "that the chief cause of these evils is the fact that the honor and duties of the family state are not duly appreciated, that women are not trained for these duties as men are trained for their trades and professions, and that, as a consequence, family labor is poorly done, poorly paid, and regarded as menial and disgraceful."

Others had called attention to the benefits of improving home conditions. Miss Juliet Corson had opened the New York Cooking School in 1874. Miss Maria Parloa had lectured in 1879 at the Boston Cooking School and worked vigorously in other parts of New England. Some study of household arts, especially those related to sewing, had appeared in public schools. The World's Fair in Chicago had stimulated interest in household economy in several ways. The National Household Economics Association had been organized there in May 1893, and this organization, working largely through women's clubs, had continued for ten years before being merged into a department of the General Federation of Women's Clubs. The Massachusetts state exhibit at the Chicago Fair had included a demonstration kitchen as an outgrowth of the New England Kitchen in Boston; it was called the Rumford Kitchen, in honor of an American physicist known in Europe as Count Rumford, who pointed the way toward the scientific study of foods and nutrition and the heating and lighting of houses.

A few colleges for women had opened, and women had been admitted to men's colleges, but for the most part women had been offered only liberal arts courses in which to prove that they had the mental and physical stamina to compete with men in higher education. A few of the new technical institutes, of which Pratt Institute is a good example, had introduced study of household arts and sciences. More than half of the land-grant colleges had added degree courses in the domestic arts and sciences. Some extensive scientific investigations of domestic problems had been undertaken by physicists and chemists. But "the home economics movement" did not get under way in an organized, integrated, national manner until about the time I was at the University of Chicago. As I look back now, I can see that I had an unusual opportunity to grow up with the movement and the good fortune to know many of its leaders.

The words "Lake Placid" have a special meaning for home economists—not as a ski resort in the Adirondacks—but as the symbol of a vision. If one place and one moment in history can be pointed to as the beginning point of the home economics movement, it was late September 1899 in a lakeside club in northern New York State when eleven people found that they had *a cause*. There they discovered they shared a deep concern for the home and its future and became convinced that scientific education for homemaking was a necessity in American society. Melvil Dewey usually gets the credit for having brought this group together, though I suspect his wife, Annie, had an important hand in the project.

Mr. Dewey, a person of ability and imagination, had many interests. By profession a librarian, he helped found the *Library Journal* and the American Library Association; he developed a scheme for classifying books known today as the Dewey Decimal System. As the Secretary of the New York State Board of Regents he had reason to be interested in the emerging field of household arts and sciences, especially as it would affect education at all levels. As an outgrowth of a number of summer meetings of educators and interested citizens who discussed educational problems in general, he assembled a special group in September 1899 to discuss education for homemaking. Although he and his wife were host and hostess for the meeting, the natural leader of the group was Ellen Henrietta Swallow Richards, a friend and fellow Vassar alumna of Mrs. Dewey, who had visited them in previous summers and had discussed her ideas of how homelife could be improved for the benefit of all.

Others at the first Lake Placid Conference in 1899 were: Mrs. Alice P. Norton, Miss Maria Daniell, Miss Emily Huntington, Miss Maria Parloa, Miss Anna Barrows, Mrs. W. V. Kellen, Miss Louisa Nicholass, and Mrs. W. G. Shailer. Of this group I knew Mrs. Norton best since she was my professor at Chicago. I read Miss Parloa's book in my early study of home economics although I never met her. Miss Barrows came to Corvallis at my invitation some years later to speak at one of our farm and home conferences. This group of 11 expanded to 30 the next year and by the tenth year the membership had grown to 201, with 74 attending the conference—which was still called the Lake Placid Conference, although it met in 1908 at Chautauqua, New York.

Five of my University of Chicago professors were active in the Lake Placid conferences—Mrs. Alice P. Norton, Miss Marion Talbot, Miss Sophonisba Preston Breckinridge, Miss Jenny Helen Snow, and Miss Elizabeth Sprague.

Mrs. Norton, a graduate of Smith College, had also studied at the Massachusetts Institute of Technology and the Boston Normal School of Household Arts. She had taught in high school, the Boston Cooking School, and the YWCA School of Domestic Science in Massachusetts before coming to Chicago. For several years after she came, she continued to direct the Chautauqua School of Domestic Science. She specialized in the chemistry of foods and brought with her a wide, practical point of view, having had the experience of marriage, motherhood, and widowhood as well as teaching in public schools. In later years she became the third editor of the *Journal of Home Economics*.

Miss Talbot had given a report at the second Lake Placid Conference in 1900 describing a survey she had made of home economics courses in colleges and universities. A graduate of Boston University and MIT, she had taught domestic science at Wellesley College before coming to Chicago in 1892 as Assistant Professor of Sanitary Science on the University's first faculty. When I first knew her she was Dean of Women and Professor and Head of Household Administration. She taught House Sanitation, Food Supplies and Dietaries, Administration of the House, and Modern Problems in Household Administration. I took all of these and for two years served as reader for her courses—receiving the really munificent wage of 75¢ an hour. Her book, *The Education of Women*, was published while I was working for her. She became my major professor in graduate school, and after I came to Oregon she wrote me many times. The last note I have from her was written on New Year's Eve in 1944.

Dr. Breckinridge, a cousin of the John C. Breckinridge who ran against Lincoln in the election of 1860, had graduated from Wellesley College and had taught mathematics before coming to Chicago to study and teach political science. She received her Ph.D. *summa cum laude* in 1901 and the first Doctor of Jurisprudence degree granted to a woman at the University of Chicago (1904). She joined the

faculty of the Department of Household Administration to teach
courses dealing with the legal and economic position of women and
the family. Miss Breckinridge worked closely with Jane Addams at
Hull House in Chicago in addition to her teaching and advisory
duties on the campus. I kept in touch with her also after I left Chicago and have a telegram from her and Miss Talbot dated February
29, 1940, a congratulatory message on the occasion of the 50th anniversary of the School of Home Economics at Oregon State College.
Miss Breckinridge once made a remark I have thought of many
times. "Ava," she said, "one thing which troubles me about your
teaching in Oregon is that I don't see how in that favored section of
the United States, you can teach students how the other half lives."

Miss Snow — I remember her for her snow-white hair — had
taught in public schools before coming to study at the University of
Chicago. As she continued graduate study, she also served as an
assistant in home economics in the School of Education and in the
University High School. Her long experience as a teacher gave her
a great advantage in training students for the teaching of home
economics in the public schools. She was well trained in chemistry
and was scientific as well as practical in her approach to home economics courses.

Elizabeth Sprague, the member of the Chicago group whom I
knew best and who was probably the one nearest my age, had studied
at the Boston Normal School of Household Arts and MIT and had
taught several places. She had also done research work in foods and
cookery at the University of Illinois before coming to Chicago about
the time I entered the University. A pioneer in the use of oven ther-
mometers, she and a man who was an agricultural chemist at Illinois
had studied a precise method of cooking beef. They developed a
method of inserting a thermometer into the center of a roast—as we
all do today—to determine the degree of doneness. After she left
Chicago, she became head of home economics at the University of
Kansas, a position she held until retirement. I kept in touch with her
through the years. She was a fine teacher, as well as a friend, and
held her students to their best. She would often say, "That's good,
Ava, but not your best." I would go back and struggle arduously to
measure up to what she expected.

The only time I met Ellen H. Richards, the founding mother of
the home economics movement, was when she came to the Univer-

sity of Chicago in the fall of 1908 to speak to the Household Administration Club. The club president could not be present that day; I was asked to introduce Mrs. Richards. To me as an undergraduate, she seemed very old—and indeed she was well along in years, being in her 67th year at that time. She did not appear much concerned with stylish dress or such, but she held us enthralled with her sparkling grey eyes and her great enthusiasm for home economics and the future she saw for it in service to mankind.

Mrs. Richards told us of her plans for founding the *Journal of Home Economics* for which she was to serve as the first editor in January of the next year, 1909. She described the new national organization which was to be devoted to the advancement of home economics. I do not remember her exact words that day, but I remember well the spirit and the inspiration her talk conveyed.

This remarkable little woman, I learned later, was just coming to the climax of an almost lifelong struggle. I was fascinated when I heard her story. From earliest girlhood in New England, Ellen Swallow had been striving for something greater than was expected of her. She had attended an academy in Massachusetts, taught Latin a few years, and then entered the newly established Vassar Female Institute, where she developed a desire for further scientific study, especially in chemistry. Because no school of science was open to her, she tried unsuccessfully to apprentice herself to a commercial chemist in Boston. In 1870 she applied for admission to the five-year-old Massachusetts Institute of Technology. After due consideration the faculty admitted her but made it clear that the admission of a woman was in the nature of an experiment. In January 1871, Ellen Swallow became the first woman ever to enter any such strictly scientific school in the United States. In 1873 she received a B.S. degree in chemistry from MIT and the same year a master's degree from Vassar. She became a water analyst and developed a large private practice in sanitary chemistry, analyzing water, air, and food. She also analyzed wallpapers and fabrics for traces of arsenic. In 1876 she joined the MIT faculty, first as an instructor in the woman's laboratory and from 1884 to 1911 as a professor of sanitary chemistry.

Miss Swallow married Professor Robert H. Richards, head of mining engineering at MIT, and broke still another tradition by continuing on the staff after marriage. Filled with the scientific spirit, she made her home an experimental laboratory. She investigated house furnishings in relation to time and energy expended in housekeeping; she studied food as it affects the body; she assembled data on costs of using various types of equipment. Instead of hiring housekeepers, as was the custom of the time, she made her house into a home for girls eager to get an education and allowed them to work for their room and board.

She carried on many activities in addition to teaching and consulting. She directed correspondence courses for women who could not go to college. She urged the introduction of science and domestic arts into the public schools in Boston. In demonstration kitchens she experimented in improvement of the food habits of families. She developed the first school-lunch program in Boston and in later life turned her attention to the preparation of home economics teachers.

With the help of Mrs. Mary H. Abel, she set up the Rumford Kitchen at the Chicago World's Fair, and after the Fair closed she arranged for the equipment used in the Kitchen to be moved over to the women's residence halls at the University of Chicago. "It occurred to Mrs. Richards," Marion Talbot wrote in an article for the *Journal of Home Economics* "that the new university, already conspicuous for its freedom from academic traditions and for its readiness to follow new paths, might consider the housing and feeding of its women students as a matter worthy of scientific investigation and experiment. . . .Her anticipation was in large measure realized."

In late December after Mrs. Richards visited our club at Chicago, she joined a group assembled in Washington, D.C., to found the American Home Economics Association. They convened at 2:45 on New Year's Eve in 1908 in the McKinley Manual Training high school in Washington. Miss Josephine Berry from the normal school at DeKalb, Illinois (where I later taught my first classes in home economics), made the motion on which Mrs. Ellen H. Richards was declared the unanimous choice of the Association for President.

Miss Isabel Bevier of the University of Illinois became First Vice President; Dr. C. F. Langworthy of Washington, D.C., Second Vice President; Miss Mary Urie of Macdonald Institute, Guelph, Ontario, Third Vice President; Benjamin R. Andrews of Teachers College, Columbia University, Secretary. I later met all of these first officers of the AHEA except Miss Urie from Canada. Dr. Andrews came to Oregon State College twice to teach summer sessions and helped me to write a book. Miss Bevier visited Chicago while I was there and came to Corvallis twice in the 1920's.

In her inaugural address on January 2, 1909, Mrs. Richards revealed a great deal of her accumulated wisdom, conviction, and philosophy. The shocking thing about reading her remarks today is that so much of her vision is yet to be realized. She protested the influence of commercialism, but it is still a dominating factor in decision making. Her proposal that "a sense of what is worth while in living" be cultivated in the schools, especially for those who do not have the right kind of home, is just as basic today as it was then. The problems that discourage the beginner have not become any less complex today than they were in her time.

Let me quote a few excerpts from Mrs. Richards' speech as recorded that day. It is quite possible—most likely, in fact—that these were somewhat the same ideas she had passed on to us that day in the Household Administration Club at the University of Chicago. This was at a time when Darwin's theory of natural selection in biology was much discussed and was applied to many fields. She began with a reference to it:

> The papers on the Darwin celebration in Baltimore yesterday, gave many illustrations tending to be a hopeful outlook for further progress in the living conditions of the human being. One illustration was that of a fertile field when it by some need had been flooded with water and for years had presented a dreary waste so far as vegetation was concerned, which drained of the water immediately showed signs of life in the dormant seeds which sprang into full life, and the once disused swamp became again a flowering garden, showing the persistence of inherited and individual characteristics.

> At present we feel that our homes are covered with a flood of commerical ideas. When these are drained off we have full hope that the best kind of home will emerge. Again, the eyeless fishes found in caves have degenerated because they have stayed under these conditions of darkness. Their neighbors who made their way out in time have developed normally. The lesson is that we should get out of the degrading conditions before we are trapped by the changes, mechanical and social, which are coming upon us. . . .

We cannot have a free country without homes of nurture for citizens, we cannot have homes without ideals and very few of us can maintain ideals on bread and water with bare boards and worn out clothes. Physical comforts may smother ideals, if excessive, but the law of progress demands at least enough physical well being to allow of freedom from galling tyranny of daily want. In this country we have wealth and opportunity, but our ideals seem to be sadly mixed, or wanting altogether. . . .

Home Economics demands a study of ways and means to maintain a training school for good citizens at a cost within the reach of all. It is not so much money as ideas and ideals we need. Can a young man marry on $1,000 a year with a reasonable hope of success in his venture? It depends on the ideals they both have and what a home means to them and on their sense of values. This sense of what is worth while in living is to be insensibly cultivated in school for the great majority who have not the right kind of homes and it is in these lines of what is worth striving for that we need just such an authoritative association as we are forming. We are stemming a tide. I hope we are not sweeping back the ocean with a broom—an ocean of fashion, of commercial exploitation, of mercantile temptation. . . ."

As I look back on it now, I can see that the day when Ellen H. Richards spoke to our Household Administration Club at Chicago was a turning point in my life. Her gripping presentation of this young, new field into which she had poured all her energies convinced me that I no longer needed to hesitate as to where I should pour my own. From that day on, the dead languages held little interest for me. Mrs. Richards spoke to us in a fresh new language—a language based on science but filled with hope, promise, and vision. I set my sights on the vision also. I vowed to subscribe to the journal she was about to establish—and I did. Even though I had to borrow money to carry on my university studies and I soon went to work as a reader for Dean Talbot's courses, I set aside a few dollars to become a charter subscriber. And how pleased I am today that I made that decision. On a shelf above my desk are all of the handsomely bound volumes of the *Journal of Home Economics*, from

February 1, 1909 to the present time—an almost endless source of information and inspiration for anyone interested in the profession of home economics.

Promptly, I set out to prepare myself for my life's work through university study. I concentrated on chemistry, physics, mathematics, physiology, and bacteriology. I took as many courses in household administration and the teaching of home economics as I could work into my schedule. My program also included courses in philosophy, religion, and literature as part of a broad liberal arts program leading to a Bachelor of Philosophy degree.

Just as the University of Chicago's founder, William Rainey Harper, was known as "the young man in a hurry," I became a young woman in a hurry. I continued as an unclassified student as long as I could, selecting—with my dean's approval—the courses I wanted for my program. For living quarters, I chose a single room in Foster Hall; a tiny room with a single bed, a corner closet, a little study table, and a straight chair. From the window I had a view of the tree-lined Midway, where the sunken gardens in winter were flooded with water. On cold evenings after the library closed at ten o'clock, I would come into Foster, head for the pantry for a glass of milk and a few crackers, and then out to the Midway to skate for half an hour before retiring. Living alone, I could retire and get up when I wanted to without disturbing anyone. Each day I went to classes with great anticipation and high hopes. I too had *a cause*.

Lest I give the impression of being a recluse, let me say that I made a practice of taking Sundays off for recreation and personal reflection and let me mention too the built-in social program that was part of the Chicago plan of education—another tribute to the vision of President Harper. Each of the five residence halls for women had a Head appointed by the President. These were women of high standing on the campus, usually deans or professors. Dean Talbot was Head of Green Hall. At Foster Hall we had Dr. Myra Reynolds, Associate Professor of English Literature, who was a Vassar graduate and an authority on Tennyson. She was my well-remembered instructor in the course in English Literature in the summer of 1908. The Heads had no housekeeping responsibilities but lived with us and, by their example, taught us a great deal about good manners and gracious living. About once a week, Miss Reynolds invited other professors as dinner guests, and those of us whose turn it was for sitting at Miss Reynolds' table joined her and the guests for coffee in her rooms afterward. There we heard lively conversation, since Miss Reynolds was a great story teller and some of her guests were masters of the art. Dr. Charles Judd, the psychologist, once asked her, "How do you account for your ability to tell stories so well?" Miss Reynolds replied that her father, a circuit-riding minister, always asked his children to relate something that had occurred during his absences from home. Then he would point out ways in which the stories they had told could be made more interesting.

The University of Chicago did not permit sororities, but after a girl had resided in a hall for two quarters the other girls voted on whether or not she should become a permanent member of the group. A single negative vote would make it necessary for the one under consideration to seek lodging elsewhere. A thoughtless new student soon learned not to evade explaining her lateness to Miss Reynolds by climbing up the fire escape instead of ringing the doorbell and being admitted by the maid. Any girl not making good scholastically soon learned to mend her ways. We developed pride in our associates and felt it an honor to be a Foster woman. Foster Hall was much a part of my University of Chicago education.

One great lesson I learned in the University came not from a professor but from an Irish woman named Hannah, head maid at Foster Hall. She had a commanding presence and took pride in her job; we respected and admired her. When she received an offer of a better job in Iowa, Miss Reynolds tried to keep her by asking for higher wages for her. At first Miss Reynolds had no success with the increase in wages and Hannah left for Iowa, but after a few sad days without her we saw her one morning at breakfast in her accustomed place behind Miss Reynolds' chair. As Miss Reynolds looked up to indicate to the maid that she was ready to be served she saw Hannah standing there. She was so pleased that she reached up and kissed her. "How did you happen to return to Foster?" Miss Reynolds asked. In her musical Irish brogue, Hannah quickly replied, "Oh, Miss Reynolds, I couldn't work where my heart isn't." This apt retort has run through my mind countless times since then. How dreadful it must be for those people who work in quiet desperation.

When I view college residences as I have seen them in recent years, I question whether the best educational use of campus living facilities is being made. Residence halls today seem to be planned largely as places to eat quickly, to sleep, and perhaps to study; they seem to provide little or no leisurely contact with professors. I appreciate the fact that hiring Irish maids or other comparable help does not seem feasible now, but I believe that dormitory life need not seem so factory-like. Assembly lines of tray-carrying students do little for student culture. It seems to me that a reasonable amount of leisure and good conversation at meals, at least in the evening, would be more inviting to students and would perhaps contribute more enjoyment at the family table later.

The school years 1908-09 and 1909-10 passed swiftly for Ada and me. Financial help from home was quite restricted after the bank failure and by that time there were three of our family in college. Nell had joined Ada and me at Chicago. Because I was in a hurry to graduate and get on with my life's work, I took a heavier load than was normally permitted. By examination I completed language requirements in German and French in the fall of 1908. I completed the second public speaking requirement by examination early the next quarter, but English I and III requirements, both theme courses, were yet to be satisfied. Taking these courses would consume two-thirds of a quarter's time, so I "screwed up my courage to the sticking point" and went to see James Weber Linn, Dean of the Junior College of Literature and University examiner in English, and asked for credit for English I and III. Dean Linn asked what basis I had for such a request and I told him I had taken a number of senior college courses and had written term papers on which I had received good marks. He asked to see two of them. On my way to trigonometry class, I left my papers on "The Postal Service of the United States and Great Britain" and "The World's Sugar," which I had written for one of Dr. Goode's courses. On my way out of the class I stopped again at the Faculty Exchange and found a note from Dean Linn saying: "Knowing the quantity and quality of work done by this student, I grant her full credit for English I and III." Years later after reading his biography of his aunt, Jane Addams, I wrote him: "Dr. Linn, I never had a course with you at Chicago, but I have had a warm spot in my heart for you because you granted me credit for English I and III. That may have been a disservice to me, but I certainly felt it a great service at the time." He replied that he remembered me very well and that he remembered my handwriting and could scarcely believe that I had not had a course with him.

The experience in obtaining credit for the English courses spurred me on to try to reduce my four years' work for a bachelor's degree by studying psychology and taking an examination in that subject. After weeks of devoting Saturday mornings to reading William James, Charles Judd, and Angell's psychology, I passed the examination. Receiving credit for psychology and English reduced my time in the university by one full quarter. I was permitted later to carry four major courses rather than the usual three, and by attending half of the summer quarter in 1909, I was able to complete requirements for a Bachelor of Philosophy degree and to graduate in June 1910. Because my record the last two years was good, I graduated with honors and was granted an honors scholarship which made it possible for me to stay on for a year of graduate work.

In graduate study in the summer of 1910 through the year of 1910-11, I concentrated on advanced courses in household economy, household administration, chemistry, physiology, bacteriology, and textiles and by the end of May was ready for my oral examination. I had reviewed thoroughly all of my courses, both undergraduate and graduate, and fortified by the glass of grape juice my sister Nell had poured for me, I walked over to the examining room. A master's examination at Chicago at that time was quite a formal affair. There were eight or ten professors present, garbed in cap and gown as I was. Miss Talbot, Miss Breckinridge, and Miss Sprague were all there, and I felt that to some extent I was among friends. For two hours they questioned me, especially in home economics and chemistry, and I thoroughly enjoyed the stimulation of it all. They excused me while they reached their verdict. Miss Sprague told me later that members of the committee commented that I had done well and that the examination was almost worthy of a doctorate. It was quite a thrill to be ushered back into the room and find this distinguished group of professors standing ready to congratulate me.

Sister Nell, worried about her little sister, was waiting in the hall. "Ava," she said, "you look as though you have enjoyed it all."

"I have," I replied. I felt as though a great weight had been lifted from my shoulders and I was ready for some new challenge.

4. Oregon Pioneers

It was a pretty sight in those days to see,
when her class time was up, a great group
of girls clustering round her
on the green campus,
and choosing study places under the big trees.
Her influence rose beyond her teaching,
for it was personal.

—WALLIS NASH

THE FIRST PROFESSOR OF HOUSEHOLD ECONOMY in the Far West,
Margaret Comstock Snell, M.D., had retired three years before
I came to Oregon Agricultural College. As I was leaving Iowa,
several people suggested that I would have an opportunity to become
a pioneer in Oregon, but I soon learned that the fundamental pioneering had come twenty years before my time. Dr. Snell had remained in Corvallis after retirement and gave me a good deal of
help with my early problems. I could look into her lovely, calm face
with its twinkling eyes, beautiful skin, and rosy cheeks framed with
snow-white hair and know that I could go to her easily and receive
the best of sympathetic assistance. In order to appreciate what a
remarkable pioneer this sturdy, purposeful woman was, we need to
understand something of the situation as she found it and the conditions under which she worked.

Oregon State University began as Corvallis Academy, a community school incorporated in 1858 and purchased by the Methodist
Episcopal Church, South, in 1860. At first, Corvallis College stressed
the work of its primary and preparatory departments. By 1865, when
Reverend William A. Finley became the first president, it had added
a four-year liberal arts curriculum leading to a bachelor of arts degree. In 1868, the state Legislature designated Corvallis College to
receive the benefits of the federal Morrill Act of 1862 (the Land-

Grant Act) and required that courses related to agriculture and mechanical arts be added. In the early years the liberal arts dominated the curriculum, but gradually the applied sciences were added. In 1870 the College held its first Commencement and granted three bachelor's degrees—the first degrees granted by any state-assisted college or university in the Pacific Northwest.

Benjamin Lee Arnold became the second president of Corvallis College in 1872. He found, as he later wrote, "The institution was in debt in every department. . . .   There was no money and scarcely any resources . . . all was paralyzed." In the transition from a wholly private college to a state-supported institution, a good deal of bickering and even a lawsuit occurred; but the state finally took control from the board representing the Methodist Episcopal Church, South, and the Legislature began to make regular appropriations to ease the financial situation.

Early in President Arnold's administration, a wing was added to the college building, which at that time stood on the block bounded by Fifth and Sixth and Madison and Monroe streets in downtown Corvallis. On the college farm a mile west of town, gifts from the citizens of Benton County made possible a fine new three-story brick structure, now called Benton Hall. The College moved into this first permanent building on the present campus in 1888.

In 1888-89, the year before Margaret Snell joined the faculty, Mr. Arnold was in his 17th year as president. He had the support of a vigorous Board of Regents, which included William S. Ladd, president; Wallis Nash, secretary; Thomas E. Cauthorn, treasurer; Governor Sylvester Pennoyer, ex-officio; and Captain J. T. Apperson, James K. Weatherford, and seven others. In fact, the Regents outnumbered the faculty thirteen to eight!

In order to teach the basic subjects in the arts and sciences and at the same time add the new applied sciences, some of the eight faculty members had to handle more than one field of subject matter. John D. Letcher, a civil engineer, taught mathematics and military science and tactics as well as engineering. Frederick Berchtold, who later in my time was head of the English Department, was teaching modern languages and history. President Arnold handled work in English language and literature. W. N. Hull taught physiology and drawing. Edgar Grimm was the professor of agriculture, and E. R. Lake taught botany and horticulture. P. Herbert Irish, the only

Ph.D. on the faculty, taught chemistry and physics, and the versatile principal of the preparatory department, W. W. Bristow, taught the curious combination of bookkeeping and bee culture.

Women had always been part of the student body of Corvallis College and the State Agricultural College. In fact, one-third of the first graduating class in 1870 was a woman, Alice E. Biddle. The alumni directory for 1889, the year Margaret Snell came to the campus, lists more than 25 women who had received A.B. or B.S. degrees and gives their occupations. A few were teachers, one a farmer, one a "Type-Writer," but most of them are simply listed as "Married," as if that were a career in itself.

The Board of Regents saw the need for providing education for young women in the management and improvement of homes. They decided to add to the faculty a Professor of Household Economy and Hygiene. Wallis Nash,* Secretary of the Board, actively pursued the search for the right person to fill the new position. Through a Mr. F. B. Linn, whom he does not further identify, he learned of a doctor of medicine teaching in a girls' seminary in Oakland, California, and began corresponding with her.

The Oregon State University Archives has copies of Mr. Nash's letters to Dr. Margaret Snell but does not have her replies. He wrote first in August 1888; in September he explained, "The influence of a cultivated and high-minded Christian lady is what we are chiefly seeking—whose teaching in sanitary matters for household & person, for sickness & health, may have the most far reaching power of good in this young State." Later letters from Mr. Nash show that he strongly backed her for the position although there was opposition from other Regents: "Various colleagues of mine on the Board are somewhat tender on the Lady Doctor idea: you know how much reasonless prejudice exists." At the December meeting of the Board, objection was raised that she did not have a certificate from a "school of cookery" but, "On this occasion," Mr. Nash wrote, "the physician's qualifications were treated as one of your strongest attractions & no one said us nay."

The discussion of whether or not Dr. Snell should be appointed went on through the early months of 1889. Then, on May 7, Mr. Nash wrote her that his wife, who was staying with an invalid son

---

* See note on Mr. and Mrs. Nash in the Appendix.

at a sanitarium at St. Helena in the Napa Valley in California, would
come to Oakland to see her. On June 7, Mrs. Nash, then back in
Corvallis, wrote this report of that visit for Mr. Cauthorn, treasurer
of the Board of Regents.

*Finding I had some hours to spare in San Francisco on
May 19th, Mr. Nash asked me to call & see Miss Margaret
Snell, & I thought you might like to know my impressions of
her.*

*She is at present helping in her sister's Seminary, a large
& well appointed house, where about 50 young ladies are living, & 150 receiving their education. She is a tall finely developed woman of about 35 years, but looking older from the
fact of her hair being prematurely grey.*

*Her manner is particularly pleasing & genial, & young
people would, I should think, take very readily to her. I noticed
at the table, that she served to take the lead in housekeeping
matters, going to the kitchen to give certain directions. She
seemed to me to be a woman of strong character not caring to
walk in the common groove of either thought or fashion; & has
evidently a warm, large heart anxious to help those under her
influence to a better knowledge of the practical things of life
as far as her working sphere permits her.*

*It was for this reason that from teaching physiology in
her sister's school, she went East to pursue her own studies more
thoroughly. And now that she has her diploma of M.D. she says
she has no intention whatever of practising medicine, but one
of her aims is to teach the young how they may keep well &
to avoid the illnesses that require the doctor's services.*

*She says she is a firm believer in the "manual training"
doctrine, & that girls should be brought up in the Study of the
domestic arts—& then they would not be so apt to despise them,
not show such lamentable ignorance in them. She has been
herself working particularly on this line of Household Economy
since her return from the East, that as a teacher she should be as
well qualified in one department as the other, believing that
both Cooking, Dressmaking & Hygiene Physiology hang together. "What I teach my sister's girls," she said "will I hope
have the effect of making them better wives & mothers than
they would otherwise have been."*

> *That Miss Snell is a truly Christian woman I should be sure from this one remark:*
>
> *"If I remain here, it will be because God has a work for me here, & it is all right; if I should find myself at Corvallis, I shall know that He has my work for me there, & so I am content any way!"*
>
> *That she was well appreciated in her sister's school was plain from the fact of two of the teachers saying to me "I hope Dr. Margaret will not be enticed away from us, for I don't know what we should all do without her."*

In this remarkably perceptive description of Margaret Snell, Mrs. Nash errs on one point. Miss Snell was closer to 45 than 35 years of age. She had been born near Livingston, New York, on November 11, 1843. Her father, Richard Snell, son of an immigrant from England, had helped survey the Erie Canal. Her mother, Margaret Comstock, a native of Adrian, Michigan, died comparatively young after bearing eight children.

Margaret Comstock Snell received her early education in New York and after the family moved to Iowa she entered Center Grove Academy and later attended Grinnell College. From 1872 to 1875 she taught school in Iowa City and then joined two of her sisters and a brother in Benicia, California, where they had opened a school for girls. She taught in the Snell Seminary there and also after the sisters had moved it to Oakland. Becoming interested in the study of medicine, she learned what she could by reading and then in 1883 gained admission to Boston University, whose school of medicine accepted women—it had been founded as the New England Female Medical College. Margaret Snell received the degree of Doctor of Medicine in 1886, her special field of interest being in homeopathy.

Dr. Snell returned to Oakland to practice medicine, but according to a sketch of her life published in 1903, she became "imbued with the idea that the higher and broader function of medical lore was to teach people how to keep well, rather than to cure disease." She returned to teaching in the Snell Seminary. Partly because of a suggestion from Wallis Nash, she returned East in January 1889 to enroll in a cooking class for a few months at the newly established Pratt Institute in Brooklyn, New York. After this further study, she was in a receptive state of mind when the Board of Regents of the

State Agricultural College of Oregon provided her with the opportunity to create the first college department in Household Economy and Hygiene in the Far West.*

Mr. Nash wired Miss Snell on June 26, 1889: "YOU ARE ELECTED PROFESSOR HOUSEHOLD ECONOMY AND HYGIENE. SALARY ONE THOUSAND. DUTIES COMMENCE SEPTEMBER FIRST." The salary, Mr. Nash had explained earlier, included board and room. On August 30, 1889, the Albany *Democrat* reported that Dr. Snell had arrived in the nearby town of Albany that morning "on her way to her new field of labors, and spent the forenoon in the city, making friends with Albany people, which is an easy thing to do, as Miss Snell is a woman of many apparent charms of character. She will fill a new department in the college, one which should become popular."

During Dr. Snell's first year at OAC, there were 24 girls enrolled in the Domestic Economy Course—as compared with an enrollment of 43 in Agriculture, 12 in the Mechanical Course, 6 postgraduates, and 67 in the Preparatory Department. A photograph in the 1889-1890 *Catalogue* shows a group of girls in long dark dresses, white caps, and wide aprons, preparing foods in a laboratory. I cannot believe that anyone other than Dr. Snell wrote the following clear-cut description of the new department:

> The purpose of this department is to teach girls how to cook, to sew, and how to take care of their own health and that of a family. Few things contribute so much to the welfare of the family, and hence of the State, as attention given to secure the good health of the household. The proper preparation of food is useful in two respects: first, it leads to health, and secondly to economy. The best methods of preparing food for the table, as well as the best methods of serving it, are taught in this department. And let no one suppose this matter a small one; there are good methods and bad ones. This department endeavors to infuse refinement into the culinary department of home life. Special attention is given to the subject of hygiene by lectures

---

* Only Iowa State Agricultural College, Kansas State Agricultural College, Illinois State Industrial University, which later became the University of Illinois, and Dakota Agricultural College at Brookings preceded Oregon in offering college-level home economics. The first three introduced subjects related to home economics in the mid-1870's and the Dakota Territory college in 1884. At Illinois, home economics was discontinued in 1880 and not reinstated until 1900; Oregon State is the fourth oldest land-grant institution continuously offering work in home economics.

*and daily precepts, the ultimate of this teaching being to inspire
all with the necessity of hygienic living as the only guarantee
to happiness and success in life.*

Dr. Snell taught her classes in household economy and hygiene
in the high-ceilinged rooms on the third floor of the main college
building (Benton Hall). She also had charge of Alpha Hall, the
girls' dormitory, and for a time lived with her students. Thus she
could focus her attention on education for homemaking both in
classes and in a campus living situation. For laboratory equipment
in her classroom, she had a small wood-burning stove, a few saucepans, and a sewing machine or two. Concerned over the consumption
of too many greasy foods, she often told students and housewives,
"Throw away your frying pans." She often related her early experiences at quiet luncheons in her home with just the two of us present.
The menu she served consisted of a fruit salad and a glass of milk.

Margaret Snell knew that preparation for homemaking consists
of much more than learning to cook and sew. She passed on to her
girls an appreciation of good art and literature and the importance
of human relations. Her graduates have told me that after they had
placed their little saucepans on the stove for cooking they would
pick up their hand sewing and while they stitched away, Miss Snell
would read to them. She read from the Bible, Shakespeare, Emerson,
Tennyson, and Byron and discussed problems raised by the authors.
These readings and the poetry she encouraged them to memorize
had a lasting influence on her students. One of them, V. Esther
Simmons, a graduate of 1896, described Miss Snell for me in terms of
Shakespeare. When I went to interview her in 1966—seventy years
after she had graduated—Miss Simmons quoted without a moment's
hesitation Mark Anthony's final tribute to Brutus. "Just change the
words, she said, "and you have a description of Margaret Snell:

> *Her life was gentle, and the elements*
> *So mix'd in her that Nature might stand up*
> *And say to all the world "A splendid human being!"*

Another graduate of the same period, Carrie A. Lyford, once
pointed out that not all classes indulged in such dual instruction.
"Advanced sewing allowed little time for such esthetic practices as
we gathered our full skirts and leg-o-mutton sleeves, bound gores
and seams, feather-stitched the many stays in our fitted waists,

basted crinoline against the lining of our long skirts which were finished at the bottom with yards of dust braid so necessary where they all but swept the ground."

Miss Snell organized instruction in household economy and hygiene, or as she later called it "household science," into eight courses, beginning with General Hygiene, since "good health is acknowledged as one of the prime factors of success in life." Next came courses in Sewing, Dressmaking, and Cookery. Course V dealt with Etiquette—social forms and usages, the art of entertaining, and the art of conversation. Courses VI and VII were called *Aesthetics*, and emphasized the "kinds and laws of beauty" in the fine arts, literature, music, and architecture. The eighth course, Domestic Lectures, she reserved for the third term of the senior year. It included lectures on "Special hygiene, including parentage, care of children, heredity, etc., sanitation in the home; home furnishing; emergency lectures; fireside practice, etc." Through this instruction Miss Snell inspired her girls to sense the significance of the home and the influence of the wife and mother on the quality, character, and success of the entire family.

A person of dignity and charm, Dr. Snell had a many-sided personality. She took a great interest in civic affairs, working especially to make Corvallis a beautiful and healthful place in which to live. The Corvallis *Gazette* on November 16, 1894, spoke of one such enterprise:

> A very commendable act has been the effort of Miss Margaret Snell to raise the necessary funds to purchase shade trees about the public school buildings. The citizens have been solicited to contribute and it is the intention to purchase white elm trees* to be planted this fall around the school house block on the outside of the walk, and also to plant evergreen vines as a screen to the outbuildings.

The tall trees around the "school house block," now Central Park in downtown Corvallis, and those around the Art Center on Seventh Street and around her apartments and houses on Jackson and on Monroe streets are living reminders of her desire to create lasting beauty.

---

* The trees planted were white birch rather than white elm.

Dr. Snell was a hygienic person. Fairly tall, striking-looking, and robust, she wore loose clothing (in the day of wasp waists and corsets) and shoes with low heels and often walked for miles for the joy of it. She loved the out-of-doors and fresh air indoors. She called one of the houses she designed "Tento." Her plan was to have a canvas roof that could be rolled back in fair weather to provide an abundance of fresh air. She built Tento, but decided that a tent for a roof would hardly be practical year-round in Willamette Valley weather and gave it a shingled roof.

Apparently as a hobby and as a means of having a retirement income in a time when there were no pensions for faculty, she designed and had built several houses. She purchased a half block near the campus and built apartments and houses that are an expression of her personality. Some people called her eccentric because she did not feel bound to follow the crowd. Instead of opening her front door to noise and the dust of the unpaved street, she designed her apartments for privacy. She turned their backs to the street and had the doors open into a shaded courtyard. The wide eaves, the windows protected from the weather, and the heavy beam construction still make this group of buildings distinctive and livable.

After she reached sixty years of age, Miss Snell indicated that she would like to retire. Nothing was done toward appointing a successor until President Kerr came in 1907. Dr Kerr's first year was Miss Snell's last active year on the faculty. That same year her department was moved to better quarters in the newly opened Waldo Hall. After retirement Miss Snell continued in her many hobbies and activities as long as her health permitted. She was nearly 80 when she died in 1923.

In considering the pioneers in home economics, it is interesting to compare the lives and contributions of Margaret Snell and Ellen H. Richards. They were about the same age; Mrs. Richards was born in 1842 and Miss Snell in 1843. Both had an early urge to acquire an education. Both became teachers early in life. Both undertook scientific studies at a time when such endeavors were almost entirely the province of men. Both were among those who had a clear vision that the way to improve society is to improve the home. Both believed that the improvement of homelife could come about most effectively through educating future homemakers. Both carried on experiments —Mrs. Richards in house design, domestic sanitation, and food preparation; Miss Snell in house design. Both were inspiring, well-loved teachers. But there the similarity ends.

In carrying out her ambitions, Ellen H. Richards found herself in a rapidly expanding industrial area of New England. A dynamic leader, she drew to herself followers of a like mind, convinced that homes must be improved through improving the homemaker. She traveled widely, speaking, organizing, writing, teaching, and developing new ideas. She thought in terms of massive group action on a national scale through a national organization and a national journal.

In her way just as devoted to the goal, just as sincere, just as energetic, Margaret Snell found herself in the sparsely settled areas of the West—in small communities in Iowa, California, and Oregon. After coming to Oregon she traveled a little, but mostly to and from her sisters' home in California. She lectured off campus to a limited extent but declined distant speaking engagements. She wrote little for publication.

Ellen Richards received national acclaim in her lifetime and continues to be revered for her contribution to society. Margaret Snell has received little of this sort of recognition, but she was appreciated locally. The students in 1908 dedicated their yearbook, *The Orange*, to her and said of her, "*A woman of fine culture, high ideals, and a winning personality, she has left a lasting impression on the minds of hundreds of young women who have sat at her feet. Who can estimate her influence?*"

In recent years, Margaret Wiley Marshall, the daughter of one of her students, came to this conclusion in an article published in the *Journal of Higher Education*:

> Most of the tributes to Margaret Snell and her teachings are buried, as she would have wanted them to be, in the fertile fields of home life, first in Oregon and then across the continent —to the third and fourth generation.

Under Margaret Snell's guidance the Department of Household Economy and Hygiene granted its first ten degrees in 1892.* From then until she retired, her graduates averaged twelve a year. Beginning in 1895 she had the assistance of other instructors. Mrs. Mary Avery, the new matron of the girls' hall, served as an assistant in

---

* These Bachelor of Household Economy (B.H.E.) degrees were the first such degrees granted, according to Curtis A. Bartholomew in *Epithetology* (Red Bank, N. J.: The Commercial Press, 1948), p. 27.

sewing from 1895 to 1905, when Mary Elizabeth Sutherland, a graduate of 1904, replaced her. For two years, 1896-98, Miss Snell had another assistant, Carrie Alberta Lyford, who received a Bachelor of Household Economy degree in 1896 and Bachelor of Letters degree in 1897. Miss Lyford went on to an outstanding career in home economics—taking further study at Oread Institute in Massachusetts, Drexel Institute in Philadelphia, and Columbia University. She taught in Chicago schools and at Michigan State College, Illinois State Normal University, and University of New Hampshire. She was a charter member of the American Home Economics Association. In 1915, when the U. S. Bureau of Education added its first two specialists in home economics to its Washington, D.C. staff, they chose Henrietta Calvin, then Dean of the School of Home Economics at OAC, and OAC-graduate Carrie Lyford to fill the new positions. In the early 1920's, Miss Lyford became Dean of Women and Director of Home Economics at Hampton Normal Institute. In 1929 she returned to government service as supervisor of Indian education in the Bureau of Indian Affairs, a position she held for sixteen years. She wrote several books on Indian art and returned to the campus in 1950 to speak at our 60th Anniversary celebration.

Miss Snell also received assistance at various times from Mrs. Clara H. Waldo, a member of the OAC Board of Regents from 1906 to 1919. In the 1907 *Catalogue* Mrs. Waldo is listed as a Special Lecturer for the Short Course in Household Science.

When W. J. Kerr became president in 1907 he recommended to the Regents that they establish a School of Agriculture, with Zoology Professor Arthur B. Cordley to serve as dean, and a School of Engineering and Mechanic Arts, with Professor Grant A. Covell as dean. He recommended converting the department of Literary Commerce into a School of Commerce and brought in John A. Bexell as dean. For a School of Domestic Science and Art, Dr. Kerr recommended the appointment of a dean and four assistants and made provision for room space and equipment "coordinate with agriculture and engineering." In one way he gave Domestic Science and Art a little better than equal treatment. He established a salary for the new dean a little higher ($2,000 vs. $1,800) than for either Agriculture or Engineering. From the beginning President Kerr was a good friend of home economics, a relationship for which I had many occasions to be thankful.

In 1908 he appointed Juliet Greer, who for ten years had been a member of the faculty of Pratt Institute in New York, as dean of the new School of Domestic Science and Domestic Art. Miss Greer chose four instructors to assist here: Marion S. Van Liew, Myrtie C. Van Deusen, Helen H. Tobin, and Ariel Ewing. All four were graduates of Pratt Institute, Miss Tobin having received her diploma in 1907 and the other three in 1908. Miss Van Liew and Miss Van Deusen taught cookery, serving, dietetics, marketing, and laundry work. Miss Tobin taught plain hand and machine sewing, dressmaking, and tailoring. Miss Ewing taught house planning, household decoration, hand work, basketry, weaving, and millinery. In addition to other duties, Dean Greer also had responsibility for the management of Waldo Hall.

This period in the development of home economics was one in which some schools gave much attention to "skill in manipulation and time saving methods." It was a time when millinery, basketweaving, and making party decorations were popular in some areas. Certainly, manual skills are a fine thing for a young woman to develop, but the whole field of home economics at the college level has been criticized for permitting too much stress on peripheral activities at the expense of more fundamental, scientific instruction.

Dean Greer and her staff apparently were well liked by their students, but they had all left the campus before I arrived. Miss Greer had resigned at the end of her third year, in 1911, to be married to John C. Bridwell, an instructor in zoology and entomology. I did not meet Mrs. Bridwell until many years later at a convention. She impressed me as a dignified, well-groomed lady whose presence commanded respect and attention. One of her graduates, Helen Gilkey, remembered her as "a sweet, dainty, trim little woman with pretty curly hair—and a long chain of jangling keys hanging from her belt."

The four instructors who had come from Pratt Institute with Dean Greer waited until late in the summer to resign. I never did know for certain why they left, but I suspect that they were waiting to see if one of them would be made dean. When President Kerr appointed Henrietta Calvin, a professor at Purdue University, as dean, they all resigned, leaving the administration little time to search for replacements before college opened in September.

Margaret Comstock Snell, M.D., and three of her students who received Bachelor of Household Economy degrees in 1892: Ora Spangler (Porter), Erma Laurence (Jones), and Anna Samuel (Sansom). *Right:* The same three alumnae at a class reunion in 1940.

Juliet Greer

Henrietta Willard Calvin

Some Early Builders of the School of Home Economics

Helen Lee Davis

A. Grace Johnson

Sara Watt Prentiss

Florence Blazier

Maud Wilson

Gertrude Strickland

Jessamine Williams

Melissa Hunter

Vera Haskell Brandon

Alma Fritchoff

Claribel Nye

Above: A class in Camp Cookery at Oregon Agricultural College, 1913.
Below: Mrs. Sara W. Prentiss, graduate assistants, and a nursery school class, 1926.

5. The First Year

Oregon has long seemed to me
the land of conspicuous promise.

—EDWIN T. REED, 1912

MY FIRST YEAR IN OREGON, 1911-12, proved strenuous but gratifying. As head of the Department of Domestic Science, I found that I had to go at a rapid pace to do the things I could see needed to be done, to do the things others asked me to do, and to carry on at the same time a reasonable amount of social life in the new community.

The girls who had come in September to study in the School of Domestic Science and Art—a record-breaking 213 as compared with 147 the previous year—had been upset with what they had found. Some disappointed girls had not yet registered by the time I arrived in October because the dean and four instructors whom they liked had not returned and the students looked with suspicion upon the incoming replacements.

In the confusion, I made various impressions on my new students. Years later some of them told me how I looked to them then. Winnifred Turner (Loos) described me as having "a reserved manner, a precise way of doing things" and said I "attached great importance to everything in home economics. Many of us undergraduates were scared stiff of you and those stiff examinations. Even as a senior I wondered if I would ever pass." Edith Allworth (Metcalf), a freshman that first year, said, "We had been studying cooking under a middle-aged lady who took things in a leisurely manner. When you took over it sort of jerked us up by the boot straps. You were very little older than many of us. Your uniform was just as it should be. Your petticoats were starched so they rustled and you walked as if you were going places. You seemed most efficient."

49

On one occasion a perky little freshman "stood up to me." Kathleen Armstrong (Plympton) still likes to tell the story: The Governor of Oregon and other dignitaries were to visit the campus one day, and as was customary—I soon learned—President Kerr called on the domestic science classes to prepare a luncheon. We had a small kitchen at the north end of the second floor of Waldo Hall, while the foods laboratory was on the south end of the ground floor. According to Kathleen, I was dashing back and forth urging the girls to do their work promptly. When I asked her group if we would have the meal ready on time, she flipped a lump of butter into a pan with her finger and declared with a touch of Irish temper, "Yes, ma'am, if you will get out of here and let us get on with our work in our own way!"

I knew the girls were sizing me up, and finally one day Hortense Eppley (Smith) called at my office. An intense young woman with dark, snapping eyes, Hortense said that the other seniors had sent her as their spokesman. They had decided before I came, she said, that they would not like any replacement for the instructors they had become fond of. They had come to realize, however, that I was not trying to be a replacement. I had won their esteem by being myself, and they found me acceptable.

Friendly acts now and then bore out what Hortense had to say. Another senior, Nell Sykes (Pearmine), and student body president Ernie Rice invited me to go canoeing on the Marys River. Having rowed boats in Jackson Park in Chicago, I felt I knew enough about boating to accept the invitation. A canoe, I soon learned, is not a rowboat. Nell had to warn me sharply several times that my clumsy movement could tip us over. The skill of my hosts saved us from getting wet, and despite my shortcomings as a canoeist Nell and I became good friends.

One incident shows what a serious young woman I was in those days. In the Julian Hotel where I lived at first, the fire alarm sounded one night. Jumping out of bed, I dressed rapidly, but before rushing out to save myself, I packed a suitcase with papers and articles I thought I would need to carry on my work if the hotel burned down and I lost everything else. It proved to be a false alarm, but it caused me to seek new lodgings. The manager of Waldo Hall cleared out a small windowless storeroom and put in a bed and some other furniture, and there I slept for the rest of the year. I had liked the daily walks to the campus in good weather, but on rainy days I enjoyed being close to my office, classroom, and laboratory. I enjoyed also living with a jolly group of wonderful girls.

Students sometimes invited faculty to take part in their recreation. We took hikes on Saturday or Sunday afternoons—out the railroad tracks to Mount Baldy or out over Cemetery Hill to a hill called The Dimples. Sometimes we took part in the activities of the literary societies and other clubs. I became associated with the Waldo Hall Club which Mrs. Waldo, the only woman on the Board of Regents, encouraged and supported and sometimes visited, and with the special interest group in home economics, the Margaret Snell Club. In retirement, Dr. Snell lived in one of her apartments close to the campus and came occasionally to talk with the girls.

Among the faculty that first year, I came into closest contact with Ruth McNary Smith, the young instructor I had met right after lunch my first day on the campus. She had graduated the previous spring but had served as an assistant in the department during her senior year. We were near the same age and the same level of inexperience. In the previous summer, as dean pro tempore, she had been the only domestic science instructor available to answer letters from housewives who wanted to know how to make dill pickles. We helped each other with our heavy teaching loads and in preparing teaching materials. Later when she returned after a year's advanced study in New York, we roomed together on North Twenty-Sixth Street. The reader will find our lives entwining at several points as this story progresses, especially since in later years we married brothers, Roy and J. C. Clark.

The School of Domestic Science and Art had two departments. Professor Helen Bryce Brooks, new to the staff that first fall, was head of the Domestic Art Department. She and her assistants, Esther Bertha Seleen, Esther Vestal Leech, and Elta Raber (who came later in the year), had their classrooms and laboratories in the north wing of Agriculture Hall. The subject matter of this department included sewing, dressmaking, tailoring, house construction and decoration, basketry, handwork and weaving, costume design, millinery, and teaching methods in sewing.

The Domestic Science Department had all of its classrooms and laboratories in Waldo Hall. Its course work included cookery, laundering, home nursing, marketing, home sanitation, dietetics, household economics and management, and teaching methods in cookery and domestic economy. The staff that first year included Ruth McNary Smith; Mrs. Lida M. Layton, and myself, appointed in October; Lois Failyer, appointed in December; and Margaret Mc-Call, appointed in March as a part-time assistant. Since the others were instructors and I was an assistant professor, the responsibilities of department head fell to me.

Faculty women outside the School of Domestic Science and Art whom I met my first day on campus included the Dean of Women, Anna Zou Crayne, M.D., who resigned in 1914; Librarian Ida A. Kidder, whose remarkable achievements will be discussed in a later chapter; Mrs. Kidder's assistant, Lucy M. Lewis, who later became Librarian and still later the first Director of Libraries for the State System of Higher Education; Mary Bowman (Hull), who had come from Portland the previous year to be President Kerr's private stenographer and held that position for the rest of Dr. Kerr's term as president and after he became the first Chancellor of the State System of Higher Education; and Clytie May Workinger, a stenographer who in later years as teacher placement secretary in the School of Education did a remarkably fine job of finding positions for home economics graduates.

In the coming weeks I met the other faculty women, and as I became acquainted with them found them to be dedicated teachers and sympathetic counselors of students. They worked conscientiously in their departments, in research work, and in other activities and laid the foundations for greater things to come.

My closest friends outside of the School of Domestic Science and Art were Grace Rosaaen (Siefert), an instructor in dramatic art, and Norma Waddle (Cardinell), an assistant in the seed testing laboratory. Ruth Smith and I took our meals in the same boarding house with Grace and Norma for a while and we all enjoyed each other's company. Mabel Withycombe, a graduate student and daughter of the Director of the Agricultural Experiment Station, was also a friend but not as close as the other three.

Most of the younger single men I knew best on the faculty—W. A. Jensen, the president's executive secretary, Ralph D. Hetzel and Sigurd H. Peterson in public speaking, Godfrey V. Copson in bacteriology, B. T. Simms in veterinary medicine, and E. J. Kraus in horticulture—one by one lost their eligibility to be so classified by getting married. All except E. J. Kraus. He remained a bachelor all his life and I am happy to have been counted among his friends through all those years. One of our earliest meetings was at Mabel Withycombe's house, when she suggested we prepare a dinner for him and another bachelor. We roasted wild duck, and although we exerted our best culinary skill, we still had a tough piece of meat. E.J. never let me forget that meal. In later years, when I had lunch or dinner with him in Chicago or met him on other occasions, he seldom failed to make some sly remark about the wild duck. He was a witty man of wide interests, and we had many delightful conversations on a variety of subjects.

His given names were Ezra Jacob, but he liked neither of them and preferred to be called by his initials. He had graduated from Michigan State Agricultural College in 1907 and came to OAC as a research horticulturist and graduate student. He took leave of absence to do graduate work at the University of Chicago and received his Ph.D. degree in 1917. He returned to OAC and in 1918 was named the first Dean of the Service Departments, a grouping of departments that later became the School of Basic Arts and Sciences. In 1919 he accepted a position as professor of applied botany at the University of Wisconsin and held it until 1927, when Chicago called him back. The University of Chicago made him head of its Botany Department in 1934 and named him distinguished professor in 1943. In 1938 he also became Principal Plant Physiologist for the U S. Department of Agriculture at Beltsville, Maryland. Active in many national organizations, he was president of the American Society of Plant Physiologists in 1928, vice president of the American Association for the Advancement of Science in 1930, vice president of the American Society of Naturalists in 1931, and president of the Botanical Society of America in 1933. Oregon State College granted him an honorary Doctor of Science degree in 1938. Much of his research work centered in reproduction and metabolism and the effect of growth-regulating substances and nutrition on plants of economic importance. When he retired early because of ill health in the late 1940's, he returned to Corvallis. He brought his breeding stock of chrysanthemums and day lilies from Chicago and spent his last years growing gorgeous flowers and serving as a much-appreciated consultant for the staff and graduate students in the departments of Horticulture and Botany.

In my first year at OAC I came to know many others in the community. The city of Corvallis (population 4,552 in the Census of 1910) at one time had a reputation as a wide-open saloon town, but by the time I arrived the saloons had gone, and the community had a moral tone "equal to that of any city within the boundaries of the state." According to the OAC catalog at that time, "It is a city of homes and its people are justly proud of the great institution within their midst and jealously guard its good name." It had an uncomplicated social life. Touring companies of actors occasionally presented plays in the Opera House downtown, and W. A. Jensen, who enjoyed this type of entertainment, took me several times to see them. Students annually held a Junior Prom and a few other large dances, but public dances were rare. For the most part, social life consisted largely of visits in homes and in small groups. Normally, a congenial rapport existed between the members of the community and the college faculty.

Faculty wives played an important part in the social structure of the campus and community. Graciously, they invited me to their homes to meet the members of their families, to relax, and to be entertained. Mrs. Grant A. Covell, wife of the Dean of the School of Engineering, was the first to invite me into her home. She and her husband asked me to come one Sunday morning for breakfast. We had ham and eggs and big delicious biscuits that reminded me of the ones my mother baked three times a day. Around the table were three sons and a daughter, Margaret. One of the sons, Walter, had the unusual hobby—for a boy—of baking angel food cakes for home consumption and for sale. One never approached Walter for a cake, I was told; Margaret took the orders and delivered the cakes.

The Covells told fascinating stories of their adventures in coming to Oregon, their courtship and honeymoon, and their lives as part of the developing college and community. Mrs. Covell (Mary Ann Spencer) had been born in England and had been brought to Ohio by her parents as a child. After she had finished her schooling at Grand River Institute near Lake Erie she decided to come west in 1892 with her sister and brother-in-law, Elton Blanchard, who had been appointed superintendent of the Corvallis Public Schools. As they were coming through the Columbia River gorge near The Dalles, a committee of loggers boarded the train looking for a teacher for their children. Because of heavy snows in the mountains, they could hold school only in the summer. Miss Spencer accepted their challenge and left the train in this strange, rough community. She sometimes had to wear loggers' boots on the muddy roads and trails as she collected the children in groups for safety from possible attack by cougars. She found not only children but adults as well in need of education and delighted the community by leading a Sunday School class and holding spelling bees for men and women. She left at the end of the summer feeling that her efforts had been appreciated. In Corvallis she taught school for a short time, met the young engineering professor, and married him in July 1893.

Her husband, Grant Covell, had grown up on a farm in New York State and his father wanted him to remain in that vicinity, but Grant persisted in his desire to get an education. With a suitcase filled with enough food to last him a week he walked miles on Sundays to Troy to attend high school, returning home each weekend to renew his supplies. Later he worked his way through Cornell University and taught there for a year before accepting the OAC appointment. The Covells often laughed about the start of their honeymoon. After their marriage ceremony at Margaret Snell's home on Ninth Street, they boarded a train that had stopped for them beside the house. Before leaving the state to visit relatives and friends in the East, they went to the penitentiary and insane asylum in Salem, where Grant was serving as a consultant on heating plants. In later years their children thought this was a hilarious way to start a honeymoon.

For daughter Margaret and me, that Sunday morning meeting was the beginning of a long friendship. As a student in home economics when she came to college; as a nutrition social worker in New York, where she went after graduation; as she married a Cornell man, Birge Kinne, who became a successful business executive; as they raised their family and sent a son and daughter to Oregon State College; and as they made their homes in Westchester County, New York City, and rural New Jersey—all through the years Margaret and I have kept in touch with each other and have visited in each other's homes many times.

Another early visit to a home in Corvallis came when the frail yet energetic wife of the college president invited me to spend a weekend with them and their delightful family of five children. As I came to know her better, I found that Leonora Hamilton Kerr had

assumed a role of leadership soon after they had arrived from Utah.
Since her husband had been a professor at the University of Utah,
president of Brigham Young College in Logan for six years, and
president of Utah Agricultural College for seven years, she understood what a president's wife could and could not accomplish. A
stately, attractive, rather reserved person, Mrs. Kerr quickly revealed
a warmth and friendliness in working with those who joined in
furthering the projects she initiated.

One of the first of these projects was organizing the College
Folk Club. This group included all women in any way connected
with the college, from the youngest secretary to relatives living in
faculty homes. Committees often met in the Kerr home. On one
occasion, Mrs. Kerr invited a group of mothers with young children
to come and discuss the formation of the special interest group which
became known as the Mothers' Club. Most of the committee members brought their young ones with them. When she saw that they
were not accomplishing much with so many children about, Mrs.
Kerr called in her four daughters ranging in age from eight to fourteen and instructed them to take the children into the garden and
entertain them. As would any other girls of that age, they registered
their objections, but Mrs. Kerr quietly opened the door and indicated
the sunny back yard. The process of organizing the Mother's Club
continued uninterrupted. One part of their plan was to assemble
books on child psychology, child training, foods and nutrition, and
related subjects. They asked Ida Kidder, the Librarian, to assist in
selecting and buying books, and provided her with a list they thought
would be suitable. A few days later, Mrs. Kidder called with elaborate apologies for having mislaid the list. The committee chairman,
Mrs. W. E. Lawrence assured her that there was a duplicate list.
"Who ever heard of a woman with a duplicate list!" Mrs. Kidder exclaimed. Thoroughness in organizational and administrative matters
was as typical of Mrs. Kerr as it was of her husband.

Through their studies, the young mothers became convinced of
the value of preschool training to prepare a child for the abrupt
change from home to school. The Montessori method, which was
receiving its first publicity in this country, seemed worth trying.
Since Mrs. Lawrence was the only one of their group with teaching
experience, they prevailed upon her to take a class of a dozen four-
and-five-year-olds into her home for a three-hour session daily. They

set the fee for enrollment at $5 a month per child and in that way initiated the first kindergarten in the city and probably one of the earliest in the state.

The Folk Club became a thriving organization with a number of other interest groups in addition to the Mothers' Club. They sponsored social activities and entertainments. They paid particular attention to welcoming new women who joined the campus community and formed what later became the Newcomers' Club. The Folk Club became the envy of town women, who were not eligible to join. So much pressure was brought to include the wives of ministers, and then the wives of public school officials, that it threatened to get out of hand. Mrs. Kerr's ingenuity came to the fore again. She suggested to some of those clamoring for admission that they form a city Women's Club. This separate-but-equal idea did not appeal to them at first, and they came back with the suggestion that the Folk Club disband and join in forming an all-city club. This looked like defeating an original purpose of the College Folk Club, which was to foster an esprit de corps on campus. Feeling ran high and Mrs. Kerr's position became uncomfortable. It was not helped by the fact that the leader of the town women was Mrs. Rose Wilson, a forceful, commanding person accustomed to seeing things go her way and whose son, E. E. Wilson, was a member of the Board of Regents of the college. The college women stood their ground, assuring Mrs. Kerr of their loyalty to her and their firm belief in her original idea for separate campus and city clubs. Eventually, the Women's Club was formed, and many of the older women connected with the college, who had lived in the town long enough to feel a part of it, became active members. Both clubs have continued through the years, each playing its dynamic part in the life of the community.

In 1931 the Folk Club began an annual full-tuition grant for an Oregon girl. They later named it the Leonora Kerr Scholarship, eventually raising enough endowment to make it self-sustaining. The income from a Thrift Shop managed by the Folk Club provides for another scholarship, and Folk Club dues and other income support two more. Between 1931 and 1967 forty-two young women benefited from assistance provided by the club Mrs. Kerr founded.

In my busy first year in Oregon I became acquainted with many of the campus wives and through them developed new concepts of home life. They treated me so courteously that I began to feel almost a part of their families. Hence, instead of feeling cut off from my own family, I began to feel a part of a wider group of friends and families.

IN THE FALL OF 1911, we had a great deal of ground work to do in the Department of Domestic Science. The departing faculty from the previous year had left no records. To find out what had been taught we asked juniors and seniors if we might see their notebooks and conferred with them so that we would not repeat instruction they had already received.

In the first biennial report she submitted, Dean Calvin (who had been appointed in 1911 but who did not come until the following summer) called the year 1911-12 a period of "serious difficulties and extremely trying conditions." Although she had only secondhand reports to go on, she wrote that we had carried on the work thoroughly, "reorganizing many of the courses and strengthening the scientific quality of instruction in all lines of work." Our main difficulty was that we had few staff members to accomplish the reorganizing and strengthening, and we were all short on experience.

In addition to the 213 young women enrolled in the regular four-year degree course in Domestic Science and Art in 1911-12, we had 103 in the four-week Short Course and about 150 in special classes. Among the six degree-granting schools and departments on campus we were second in enrollment to Agriculture, slightly ahead of Engineering, and much larger than Commerce, Forestry, and Pharmacy. By the end of the year we had graduated 33 women in Domestic Science and Art—as compared with only 14 the previous year.

One type of instruction that took considerable time then—but which diminished rapidly as the years went on—was preparatory work. In the days before high schools were generally available, most colleges had preparatory departments. From its beginning Corvallis College and the State Agricultural College had maintained a preparatory department—and in the earliest years, even a primary department. Teaching students with such a broad range of preparation created problems in organizing courses and instruction.

Low admission requirements in the early 1900's permitted students to enter the Secondary Courses direct from the eighth grade. Although the number of such students entering the college was

decreasing (100 in 1909, 67 in 1910), there were still 55 who entered
with so little preparation in 1911. To enter the regular four-year
degree courses as a freshman, all a student needed was two years of
secondary school preparation. The trend, however, was toward
better preparation. In 1909, 67 had come into the college after completing four years of high school. In 1910 this number increased to
72, and in 1911 it was 139. Eventually, as we turned out more and
more graduates capable of teaching home economics and as high
schools became more numerous, the secondary schools could
strengthen their programs and we did not have to take so much
time in getting the students ready for college-level study.

For the year 1911-12, the Department of Domestic Science
offered eight Secondary Courses—in cooking, simple dietetics, serving, and laundering. It offered twenty-two Degree Courses: seven
in science of cookery and in advanced, special, and fancy cookery;
an advanced course in laundering; courses in home nursing, marketing, home problems, and house sanitation; two courses in advanced
dietetics; two in household economics and management; three in
normal methods for the preparation of teachers; a one-night-a-week
course in home cookery for men; and Plain Cookery I and II for
Foresters.

By conferring with students and examining their notebooks, I
saw that the science subjects—chemistry, physics, bacteriology, and
physiology—were not linked closely enough with cooking and
household sanitation. Fortunately, my background in science at the
University of Chicago had been strong enough that I could draw on
my knowledge of the natural sciences to make lectures and discussions meaningful for classes in cookery, sanitation, and dietetics.

Out of that first year's experience grew my basic philosophy in
regard to the study of domestic science. I began to see clearly that
sciences applied in the home should not be taught as areas separate
and discrete in themselves. We should select principles from all
areas of science, as taught in other subject-matter fields, and apply
them to the fields of home economics. For example, in the studying
of canning and preserving of fruits, it did not seem appropriate to
me to take our time in covering principles of bacteriology, physics,
and chemistry. Rather, we should take for granted that our students
were gaining the basic knowledge they needed in other courses and
that we should spend our efforts in making clear to them how to

apply these principles. This type of teaching is not as easy as it sounds. It takes skillful, well-prepared, and broadly educated instructors to apply such principles confidently and effectively.

BEFORE I had been on the campus long that first year, I began to receive invitations to make talks at various meetings. I had tried to avoid taking a course in public speaking at Chicago because I had no intention of becoming a speech maker, yet all of a sudden here I was lecturing on the basic principles of home economics to a variety of audiences—most of them men. My first out-of-town speech hit the headlines of a Portland newspaper:

THRESHERMEN TOLD
HOW TO TREAT WIVES

(Salem Bureau of the Journal.)

Salem, Or., Dec. 8—Two hundred Oregon threshermen were urged to give their wives vacations at least twice a year, to give them some spending money without their having to ask for every penny, and to put labor saving devices into the houses as well as into the barns and fields. The speaker was Miss Ava B. Milam of the Oregon Agricultural college. . . .

The convention this session has to a greater extent than ever before departed from the routine order of discussion of business exclusively and introduced some broader features along the line of improvement of country life.

Both Salem papers also mentioned the talk. The *Daily Capital Journal* reported:

Miss Milam got a round of applause for her defense of the rights of housewives to have kind consideration, labor-saving machinery, and an annual vacation.

The *Daily Oregon Statesman* called the talk "interesting" and concluded by saying:

> Miss Milam was greeted with applause for her defensive talk of the women.

At a bankers' convention in the Statehouse in Salem, I followed a speaker whose subject was "How hogs can increase the bank account of the farmer." A Salem newspaper reported that "Miss Milam spoke up for the housewife and was heartily applauded" by the all-male audience. In a time when most farm homes in Oregon had neither running water nor electric lights, it must have been something of a revelation to hear hope for improving the lot of the homemaker.

Surprises continued throughout that first year. I learned in the fall that "Winter Short Courses" would begin on January 3. Established originally to help farmers, gardeners, stockmen, and orchardists to keep pace with the rapid developments in the science and practice of agriculture, these 4-week courses in mid-winter had become popular. Since many of the men attending brought their wives and since it was also becoming recognized that women could profit from learning about developments in the science, art, and practice of homemaking, short courses for women had been added. Not only wives who had come to town with their husbands but a number of Corvallis women also enrolled.

In my class that first year I had Mrs. George Peavy, wife of the forestry professor; Mrs. Bexell, wife of the dean of the School of Commerce; Mrs. Wm. E. Lawrence, the first kindergarten teacher and later for many years my next door neighbor; Miss Edna Groves, an OAC graduate who later became supervisor of home economics for the Portland public schools—and dozens of others. In all, we had 103 women in the short courses in domestic science and domestic art.

One professor's wife, Mrs. Hector Macpherson—who had majored in botany at the University of Chicago—took great pride in her accomplishments in a baking class. She turned out a loaf of bread we all agreed looked perfect. Mrs. Peavy wanted to cut and taste it, but Mrs. MacPherson would not permit its destruction. She insisted that she intended to take it home, put it under a bell jar and preserve it so that her young son, then a tiny tot, could see it when he was grown. Edna Groves and Mrs. John Allen always wore hats during the cookery class. This seemed a strange custom to me, but because they were my seniors I did not suggest they change it. We on the staff enjoyed the eager, friendly group and came to know many homemakers from all over the state through these short courses.

Another surprise came before the end of the first semester when George Peavy, the forestry professor, called on me to make plans for teaching Camp Cookery the second semester. I explained to him that I knew nothing about camping, having been raised in the Midwest, and that no one else on the staff had adequate preparation to teach such a class. Besides, we all had full teaching programs. Mr. Peavy, however, proved persuasive. He pointed out that many of his students spent the summer in the forests to gain practical experience and to help earn college expenses. Their health was closely related to the food they took to camp, and the palatability of the food they cooked depended on their knowledge of cooking. "You know the principles of nutrition and cookery," he said, "and I know camping. Harold Newins of our staff and I will help by taking you out to a model camp site on the college farm and demonstrating the use of equipment we use."

Reluctantly at first, I accepted Mr. Peavy's offer but soon recognized the importance of this type of teaching. The class turned out to be quite large, drawing students not only from forestry but also from agriculture and other fields. They proved adept and enthusiastic. Ruth Smith and I both had sections of the night classes the first year and we learned a few things ourselves. We baked quick bread and sour dough bread in frying pans. We coated unplucked fowl with mud and wrapped potatoes and corn in wet paper—then covered them with hot coals for cooking. We baked apples and baking-powder biscuits in reflector ovens.

We found we needed a textbook—a manual of instruction that would serve not only in class but also in forest camps later. The U. S. Forest Service had some material and S. E. White's *Camp and Trail* helped somewhat, but what we needed was a pocket-sized handbook, with information adapted to local conditions. Ruth and I decided to write our own. The College Press printed the first edition in June 1912. A little 32-page paperbacked booklet, it gave suggestions for ration lists and menus, buying supplies, assembling equipment, and dozens of recipes. It proved so popular that we needed a new edition the next year. We increased it to 48 pages and added an index.

Through Ralph Hetzel, Director of the Extension Division, the second edition became an Extension publication and in that way became available at no cost to a wide audience.

Camp Cookery has had an interesting history. As an Extension Bulletin it went through many revisions, the later ones adapted to use by 4-H Clubs. In 1918, A. Grace Johnson became a co-author with Ruth Smith and me in preparing a new edition especially for Boy Scouts and other campers. We added drawings of equipment and suggestions for constructing or purchasing it. The J. K. Gill Company in Portland published and distributed the new edition. Eventually we sold our rights to it to the Youth Library for $150.

Through this publication venture I made acquaintances I valued highly. I also learned a little verse that has helped cheer me up when I get crotchety. I met the Gill brothers, John and J.K., who had founded the J. K. Gill Company, and J. K.'s daughter Frances, a teacher, author, and poetess. Frances once jotted down a verse on a scrap of paper and sent it to me. I have tried her recipe for curing crossness and many times have found it successful:

> *When I am very, very cross,*
> *As mean as I can be,*
> *I go into the garden plot*
> *And stand beneath a tree.*
> *I love its wide green arms so well*
> *It cures the cross of me.*

Benton Hall

6. Home Economics Extension

> As home economics learns to use well the tools at its
> disposal, it has within its grasp the opportunity
> to play a part of far-reaching importance
> in reshaping human relationships,
> in reorienting home and family life,
> in giving to science and art a meaning in terms
> of daily living, in renewing respect for the
> manual labor that is conducted with care, thought,
> and intelligence—in short, in making human health,
> human conduct, and human welfare the outstanding
> goals of human enterprise.
>
> —FLORA ROSE

THE OREGON EXTENSION SERVICE came into being the same fall
I arrived in Corvallis. Although I had many other matters de-
manding my attention, I gradually became aware of what was
happening and found myself involved in a vital new phase of home
economics teaching. The people of the state had been asking for
advice and assistance, mostly in agriculture, but also in engineering, forestry, commerce, and domestic science and art. The college
had tried to meet these requests as best it could with funds and time
available, but responsibility was scattered among several deans and
department heads. On July 24, 1911, the Board of Regents, acting on
President Kerr's recommendation that off-campus educational programs be administerd by one agency, established the Oregon Extension Service as a division of the School of Agriculture. On November
4, 1911—just a month after I arrived—Professor Ralph D. Hetzel was
named its Director.

President Kerr had skill in picking people of ability and foresight
for positions requiring imaginative educational statesmanship. Versatile Ralph Hetzel had come to the faculty in 1907 as an instructor in

public speaking; later he taught business law and political science. He held a law degree from the University of Wisconsin and had been admitted to the bar in both Wisconsin and Oregon. As the officer in charge of information services, he had served as correspondent for three Portland newspapers, started a weekly news service for other papers, and coordinated some of the off-campus speaking engagements of staff members. He therefore had unusually fine qualifications to serve as the Director of Extension at this particular time of lawmaking and policy setting.

The Association of Land-Grant Colleges, the Grange, and other farm organizations had urged Congress to provide federal aid to land-grant colleges for off-campus instruction. Research by the U. S. Department of Agriculture and the state experiment stations had resulted in the accumulation of a store of essential information that would add tremendously to incomes from farming and bring improvements in homelife if put to use generally. Much of the new knowledge was confined to scientific bulletins and other publications not easily available to the farmer and homemaker. A means needed to be found to put it into practice.

In his history of the first fifty years of extension work in Oregon, Frank L. Ballard tells of the part Ralph Hetzel played in getting Oregon ready to participate in federally assisted extension work:

In late 1912, toward the close of the first year of the Oregon Extension Service, it seemed that passage of favorable legislation . . . was quite likely at the national level. It was already evident that if action were taken by Congress, the states would be required to match some of the funds appropriated. Therefore, Director Hetzel began in the late months of 1912 to prepare a bill for the 1913 Oregon legislature, which would provide state funds for Extension . . . to meet the requirements of the Federal Act which had been introduced and was being debated in Congress. . . . The Hetzel bill, in addition to providing the necessary match money, authorized the various counties of the state to make appropriations for Cooperative Extension work under the supervision of the State Agricultural College. . . . This law establishing the state's financial basis of Cooperative Extension work proved, as the years went by, one of the best written in any of the states, and it has been only slightly amended.

In 1914 Congress passed the Smith-Lever Act, which became the basis of the Federal Cooperative Extension Service in agriculture and home economics as we know it today. President Wilson signed the act into law on May 8, 1914. Largely as a result of the preparations made by Mr. Hetzel, Oregon was ready and began at once to expand off-campus instruction through institutes, lectures, demonstrations, correspondence courses, lecture and reading courses, boys' and girls' clubs, railway excursions and exhibits, news bulletins, leaflets, periodicals, monographs, traveling libraries, and individual consultation.

Meanwhile, before the Smith-Lever funds became available, Mr. Hetzel had been busy with many projects. Early in the summer of 1913, he telegraphed me in Los Angeles, where I had gone to attend Ada's wedding and to spend the rest of the summer relaxing with the family. He invited me to join a group of agricultural specialists going throughout Oregon in August and September to visit Granges. He wanted me to give talks and demonstrations for the wives while the men in the party were giving talks and demonstrations for the husbands.

Although I had no specific experience along such lines, I accepted the invitation. It sounded like an important experiment. We traveled by train and, like a touring company of actors, usually spent no more than a day in one location. Often we gave two "performances" a day, usually afternoon and evening, sometimes morning and afternoon, and occasionally morning, afternoon, and evening. We left Albany by train on Sunday afternoon, August 10, and arrived that evening at Yoncalla; on Wednesday, Oakland; on Thursday, Myrtle Creek; on Friday we split the company in two and went to Canyonville and Days Creek, and on Saturday finished the week with three sessions in Riddle. The next week we spent three days at Klamath Falls and then returned to Grants Pass. Stops the third week included Glendale, Creswell, Springfield, Brownsville, and Monroe. After spending Sunday in Corvallis we started the fourth week at McCoy and then went through Portland and out to Tillamook for Wednesday and Thursday meetings, and after returning to Portland finished the week at Estacada. The fifth week took us to the northeast corner of the state to Imbler, Wallowa, Enterprise, and Haines. The sixth week included Vale, Brogan, two days at the county fair at Ontario, and Saturday at the county fair in Baker.

While our touring party stopped in small communities, a second team with Edna Groves as the home economist, met with groups of farmers and homemakers in larger towns throughout the state. These two parties, I understood, were the largest groups of extension people to travel statewide up to that time. No funds were available to supplement our salaries, but our traveling expenses were paid.

Mrs. Austin Buxton, who was in charge of the women's program of the State Grange and whose husband had been a member of the OAC Board of Regents from 1905 to 1910, served as a companion on the early part of the trip. We had adventures that we laughed about in later years. One night in southern Oregon, our hotel room had old-fashioned beds so high that Mrs. Buxton, who was rather short, had to climb up on a chair to get to her bed. Being taller, I had less difficulty. One of the two chairs in the room was a discarded dental chair; sitting in it, I could almost feel the pain of tooth extraction.

Mrs. Buxton helped with my part of the program by talking with the wives about Grange work for women. She soon found, however, that she could not carry on for the full tour. I continued the tour with the men who included Walter Brown from Horticulture, leader of the group; Roy Graves, the new head of the Dairy Department; George Hyslop, Professor of Agronomy; Alfred Lunn from Poultry; and sometimes one or two others. The one I enjoyed most was Al Lunn. An OAC graduate of 1912, he had married a classmate, Bella Ackerman, daughter of the president of Oregon Normal School. Al had been a cheerleader in college and had a broad smile and a keen sense of humor. The story was still being told of a toast he proposed at a poultrymen's banquet: "Here's to the health of the American hen. May her son never set!"

The men were good to me and helped me overcome my inexperience. They also gave me new insight into the various aspects of agriculture and homelife in the different parts of the state. My work on tour was to stimulate interest in improving the diet of rural families by the use of uncooked fruits and vegetables in salads and through cookery that conserved the nutrients of foods. Since mayonnaise and French dressing could not be purchased at that time, I demonstrated how to make salad dressings. The audience had an opportunity to taste the products and ask questions. I also discussed the contribution domestic science could make to homes and answered questions. Because the demonstrations required a trunkful of equipment and supplies, we had much packing and unpacking to do. The men would join me after the meetings, finish eating what was left of the salads, and help me wash dishes and pack up to leave for the next community.

Transportation was not easy at times. Once we traveled between towns on a railroad handcar. Hotel accommodations sometimes were poor. At one stop in eastern Oregon, the men refused to stay in the hotel that had been engaged for us because of the filthy washbowls, dirty rugs, and unkempt condition of the place. They decided to go out to a resort in the country for the weekend. It was the end of the season for the resort and there were no other guests, but the cook had been kept on.

Sunday morning Al Lunn went exploring and climbed a barbed wire fence to get into a pen where chickens were feeding. In doing so he tore an L-shaped rip over the knee of the only pair of trousers he had with him. When he asked me what he should do, I suggested that he borrow a pair of pants from the cook and send his torn pair to my room. I did the best I could to mend the torn place. That afternoon Director James Withycombe of the Agricultural Experiment Station came aboard our train as we were enroute to Vale for our Monday assignment. As we were comfortably seated in the club car talking to him, I noticed that Al kept one hand over that mend of mine. His wife Bella told me afterwards that Al took pride in that pair of pants darned by her former domestic science teacher.

Future Governor Withycombe gave us all such a flowery introduction at our meetings in Vale on Monday and at Brogan the next day that we could hardly recognize ourselves. His oratory did give us a fine buildup and we got off to a good start with our sessions despite the fact that these communities still had the reputation of being "shoot-'em-up" wild west towns.

The six weeks of travel through the state proved stimulating and educational. I enjoyed getting acquainted with a beautiful, diversified section of the country and learning something of its homes and homemakers. The hospitality and graciousness of farm families and other friends we made along the way could not have been exceeded. Not long after that trip, Mr. Hetzel asked me to become the first state leader of home economics extension. I would have enjoyed the work, but I declined the offer because I felt I should continue on-campus instruction.

In addition to programs for adults, Director Hetzel also introduced the forerunner of the 4-H Clubs, "Industrial Contests" for boys and girls begun in cooperation with the State Department of Education. The contests at first consisted of judging and awarding prizes at the state fair for exhibits of vegetables, flowers, bread, preserved foods, sewing, carpentry, poultry, and livestock. The first prize for bread baking, for example, was $12.50 in cash, second prize six cans of Wadco baking powder, third prize $2.00, and fourth prize $1.00. The railroads provided free freight for the exhibits to and from the fair. A "camp" on the OAC campus in 1913 was the forerunner of 4-H Summer Schools. It provided a two-week course in practical agriculture for boys 12 to 16 years of age. Response was good. In 1916 courses for girls were added because, "It is now recognized that woman's work in the home must be as carefully and intelligently planned as that required in any occupation or profession outside of the home."

F. L. Griffin was the state agent in charge of the Industrial Clubs for Boys and Girls for a few years. Then the team of Harry C. Seymour, state leader, and Helen J. Cowgill and Leonard J. Allen, assistant state leaders, took charge of the boys' and girls' club work, which soon became affiliated with the national 4-H Club program. Stressing the importance of creative enterprise in home and community, this program has encouraged hundreds of thousands of young people to make this avowal:

> *I pledge my HEAD to clearer thinking, my HEART to greater loyalty, my HANDS to larger service, and my HEALTH to better living.*

By the time Mr. Seymour and Miss Cowgill retired in 1947 and Mr. Allen became state leader, they had developed one of the finest programs of its kind in the country. Three stone benches on the Lower Campus near the 4-H Tree provide a lasting memorial to this remarkable team.

An OAC graduate of 1913 and 1916, Helen Cowgill guided the club work program for girls. With the cooperation of Dean Calvin, she prepared bulletins, score cards, and record sheets for sewing, canning and preserving, and baking clubs, and later, in many other fields of homemaking. She helped organize youth clubs all over the state, carried on a voluminous correspondence, and supervised the summer school for girls. A witty, good-natured speaker, she traveled widely and was much in demand as a judge in contests and as an adviser, as well as a speaker. She devoted thirty-three years of her life to the 4-H Clubs and won the admiration and appreciation of thousands of girls.

In 1917, Mr. Hetzel accepted a new position as president of New Hampshire College, which at that time was a struggling institution of two or three hundred students. He offered me a position there as Dean of Women and head of home economics, but the West had gripped me, and I had no desire to leave. I never came to the point where I felt my work for Oregon was finished or that I was willing to leave. In the East, Ralph Hetzel continued to show his ability as an organizer and educator, and he once told me that his administration had been greatly influenced by Dr. Kerr's pattern. He rebuilt the New Hampshire college into a state university with an enrollment of 1,500 students supported by a state millage tax. He moved on from there to become president of Pennsylvania State College, where he remained until his death in 1947. The last time I saw Ralph was at the Land-Grant Colleges Association meeting in Washington, when he was president of the organization.

The first state leader for home economics extension work in Oregon was appointed on December 8, 1914. She was Anna M. Turley, a graduate of Purdue University and former member of the faculty of Montana State College. She responded to requests from homemakers for lectures on domestic science. She participated with specialists in agriculture in rounding out the programs of the "movable schools," three to six-day programs of lectures and demonstrations appropriate to farms and homes in various sections of the state. She built her demonstrations around food problems and nutrition, shelter problems including kitchen arrangement, and clothing problems involving both textile selection and clothing construction. In her first year (1915), Miss Turley took part in movable schools in fourteen communities and gave 150 lectures and demonstrations. Partly as a result of her stimulation, six high schools introduced home economics instruction and eight others began hot lunch service.

Miss Turley arrived early at certain basic conclusions that have constituted a strong part of the foundation upon which this phase of extension work has been developed. She pointed out that technical information is important, but the ability of extension teachers to make it an active force is even more important. She concluded that farm productivity depends to a greater extent upon farm home efficiency than is generally recognized. A prime objective of home economics extension teaching, she believed, was recognizing that efficiency in the home must be the homemaker's goal.

Miss Turley served as state leader from 1914 to 1918, when she resigned to be married. She was followed first by Minnie Kalbus for about a year, and then by Mrs. Jessie McComb for about ten years.

In 1929, as I prepared to leave Corvallis for the July meeting of the American Home Economics Association in Massachusetts, Paul V. Maris, Director of the Oregon Extension Service, asked me to look for a new state leader in home economics extension while I was in the East. In complying with this request, I had an opportunity to visit one of the great pioneers in home economics extension work and learn how home economics education had developed in one influential state. On the way to Boston, I stopped at Ithaca, New York, to talk with the co-directors of the Cornell University College of Home Economics, Martha Van Rensselaer and Flora Rose. Since New York was the home state of Melvil Dewey and the Lake Placid conferences, interest in introducing home economics in its land-grant college arose earlier in New York than in other states on the East Coast. It is curious to see the sequence in which various parts of the complete home economics program came into being. In most land-grant colleges, home economics began as part of resident instruction. In some cases research work in home economics began early to supplement the teaching program. Out of resident instruction, or a combination of resident instruction and research, grew extension.

At Cornell University, it was the other way around; home economics extension started first. At the suggestion of Liberty Hyde Bailey, soon to become dean of the New York State College of Agriculture at Cornell University, Martha Van Rensselaer was added to the agricultural extension staff in 1900 to work with wives of farmers. At Martha's request, Mr. Bailey sent out 5,000 letters to farmers (assuming they all had wives), asking whether the wives would like to have assistance in making their housework and homemaking duties lighter. Back came more than 2,000 replies with valuable suggestions and useful requests. Miss Van Rensselaer sent out the first bulletin in her reading series for farmers' wives in January 1901. The course proved very popular and eventually enrolled 50,000 to 70,000 persons.

At the same time that winter short courses for farmers, orchardists, and dairymen were developing at Oregon Agricultural College, Cornell University also had them. As in Oregon, the need for parallel work for farm wives in New York became evident. There was quite a contrast in the way in which the programs for women were conducted in the two states. In Oregon, the regular home economics staff taught the short courses for women. In New York, since there was no regular home economics resident staff—only Miss Van Rensselaer for extension—the classes were taught by guest lecturers. The roster of speakers who came to Cornell in 1906 for from three to ten days each during the first "Winter-Course in Home Economics" reads like a Who's Who in Home Economics: Ellen H. Richards from Massachusetts Institute of Technology, Mary Hinman Abel from Baltimore, Anna Barrows from Boston, Isabel Bevier from University of Illinois, Helen Kinne and Mary Schenck Woolman from Teachers College, Columbia University, Abby Marlatt from the Rhode Island Normal Training School, Alice P. Norton and Marion Talbot from University of Chicago, and fifteen others. As Flora Rose writes in her history of home economics at Cornell, this first winter course in home economics "caused far more than a ripple of interest."

Because of budget limitations, the second winter short course was less extensive but it did bring Flora Rose to Cornell. She had been a staff member at Kansas State Agricultural College and then a graduate student at Columbia University. Director Bailey discussed with her the possibility of introducing undergraduate instruction in home economics on campus and then offered her the opportunity of organizing the new program, which was at first under the College of Agriculture but later became a college in itself. Miss Van Rensselaer and Miss Rose were named co-directors of all the work in home economics at Cornell. They had been carrying on as a team remarkably well for nearly twenty-five successful years when I went to see them in 1929.

When I told Miss Van Rensselaer that we were looking for a new state leader in home economics extension for Oregon and asked whom she could recommend, she replied, "Well, there's Claribel Nye. She could do a fine job for you, but of course you can't have her. We need her here." Nothing Martha could have said would have challenged me more. Oregon, too, needed such a person as she described Miss Nye to be. The position in Oregon would be an advancement for Miss Nye because she was not the state leader in New York. I met and talked with Claribel there in Ithaca and later at the Association meeting in Massachusetts. One afternoon at the convention when we were both free she took me to see interesting places near Boston. At Marblehead, when we visited a small pottery factory where lovely crackleware vases and dishes were made, Claribel bought a small vase and presented it to me as a keepsake from the trip.

When I returned to Oregon with a glowing report on Claribel Nye, Mr. Maris offered her the position—and in the end she accepted it. Several months elapsed before she was free to leave Cornell, but we corresponded in the meantime. Once she asked whether I had reached home safely with my Marblehead piece of pottery. I dictated my reply, and when the draft copy came back from the stenographer it read: "Yes, I reached home safely with it and I like my marble head-piece very much."

Claribel Nye arrived at Oregon State College to become state leader of home economics on February 1, 1930. In the Depression years, development of organized county programs was retarded because the services of Miss Nye and the specialists were needed in the state-wide relief program. Governor Julius Meier appointed her a member of the foods committee of the State Relief Committee and she gave a large amount of time to arranging conferences on relief activities for county relief committees, to editing material prepared chiefly for use of families on relief or on very low incomes, and to providing leadership for the State Relief Committee in food preservation programs.

Frank Ballard, Emeritus Director of the Federal Cooperative Extension Service for Oregon, gives Miss Nye credit for establishing, in 1930, the pattern on which our home economics extension work has been based. For one thing, she changed the policy for utilization of specialists. From that time to the present, the main function of the home economics specialists has been serving as state project leaders to aid home demonstration agents in program development.

Positions for specialists in foods and nutrition and in clothing and textiles had been established in 1920. Miss Nye saw the need for additional specialists in housing, home management, and child development. In New York State, she had developed extension programs through organized groups of women known as Home Bureaus, loosely affiliated with the county Farm Bureaus. Miss Nye outlined plans for organizing the work in Oregon on the basis of neighborhood or community groups of women who would meet regularly throughout most of the year and who would select their programs in consultation with the state leader and her specialists. These community groups became identified as Extension Units, and representatives from them were named to constitute an overall County Extension Advisory Committee.

One of the pioneers in carrying out Miss Nye's plans in the counties was Mabel Mack, a recent OSC graduate with many original ideas, who served as home demonstration agent in Jackson County for twelve years. Mrs. Mack felt at first that she was wasting time and taxpayers' money attending group meetings of women who gave primary attention to luncheon preparations, business meetings, and quilting bees. She tactfully persuaded the homemakers that if they were to make the best use of the flow of information and ideas available through extension channels they needed to separate instructional sessions from other activities. As the program developed, she was able to turn her attention in the direction that it has taken since—spending her time in the training of volunteer leaders from the community who, in turn, carried on the teaching program in smaller groups. In New York State, Claribel Nye had worked through Home Bureaus with paid leaders in the communities, but such an arrangement did not seem feasible in Oregon, and the effectiveness of the unpaid volunteers has shown that the Oregon plan has worked well. When Mrs. Mack came to the central office on campus as an extension administrator, she had an opportunity to coordinate similar organizational schemes in other counties.

In the 1930's Claribel Nye helped organize home economics radio programs for the state-owned station KOAC. Some of the scripts, modified for local purposes, were broadcast by the home demonstration agents in their communities through the cooperation of local commercial stations. Here, again, Mabel Mack pioneered in Medford at station KMED. The programs have continued and are a part of the weekly programing in nearly every county in the state. With the coming of television, stations throughout the state cooperated with home demonstration agents in broadcasting visual programs for homemakers.

Before Miss Nye's time, home demonstration agents had received no regular classroom instruction in extension work. She arranged for

a course called Methods in Home Economics Extension in summer
school in 1930 and since that time several courses have become
a regular part of the training program. Miss Nye also established the
policy of employing promising candidates for county home agent
work as extension agents-at-large, giving them an opportunity to
serve as assistants to specialists, to assist in emergencies or overloads
in the counties, and to relieve the state leader of some detail. This
experience proved to be an excellent training feature.

To Claribel Nye goes much of the credit for laying the foundation for the State Home Economics Council which grew out of a
statewide Family Living Conference held in 1931 as a follow-up of
the White House Conference on Children's Health and Protection.
An annual series of similar conferences on home interests continued
for nine years and gradually evolved into the annual meeting of the
State Home Economics Council. Through this Council, homemakers
of the state have had an opportunity to carry out programs of local,
state, and even national significance through affiliation with the
National Home Demonstration Council and the Associated Country
Women of the World. One committee of the State Home Economics
Council helped determine research needs. It suggested investigating
the nutritional needs of rural children, the large incidence of dental
caries among Oregon youth, and the design of work clothing for
mature women. Another committee proved quite effective in appealing to the state Legislature for financial support for research when
other sources could not be found. One committee of the Council
raised $57,760 within the county units to make possible the con-
struction of Azalea House on the Lower Campus, a cooperative
living group for girls with academic ability but limited income.

Miss Nye remained in charge of home economics extension
until August 31, 1935, when the University of California took her
from Oregon. Although she had been with us only a little more than
five years, she made a lasting impression.

Thelma Gaylord, a home demonstration agent in Clackamas
County, served as acting state leader for seven months until she
resigned to be married. Then came Azalea Sager (for whom Azalea
House was named). A former clothing specialist, she became state
leader on April 1, 1936, and served until October 1, 1952. When she
took office, the state was just beginning to recover from the Depression. Extension had an excellent opportunity to develop a diver-

sified program sensitive to community needs. Through unsettled times when the work was geared to helping families recover from the Depression, to assisting them in meeting emergency conditions brought about by World War II, to aiding them in recovering from that war and in adjusting to another national emergency during the conflict in Korea, the firm hand of Azalea Sager guided the home economics extension program. When Miss Nye left in 1935 there were four home demonstration agents, three specialists, and the state leader—a staff of eight. By the time Mrs. Sager retired eighteen years later, financial support had increased sufficiently to maintain a staff of thirty-nine home demonstration agents working in the counties, ten specialists, the state leader, and three assistants—a staff of fifty-three. This marked increase in staff provides one measure of the growing support received from the counties, from the state Legislature, and the federal government to make an expanding program of service possible.

Frances Ann Clinton (Hall), who had been a home demonstration agent in Multnomah and Umatilla counties and Mrs. Sager's assistant for several years, served as state leader from 1952 to 1958. Esther A. Taskerud, who had been a home demonstration agent and 4-H Club leader in South Dakota and Iowa and a Club leader and regional supervisor in Oregon for more than ten years, became state leader in 1958.

In recent years, home economics extension has developed in philosophy and service by shaping its program to meet changing requirements. "The responsibilities of the family in the increasingly complex world," says Miss Taskerud, "are greater than ever before. The process of rapid social and economic change and the changing status of women make necessary programs for adults and youth designed as prepartion for family and community living in modern society."

In continuing to focus its attention on the family as a fundamental unit in community and nation, the home economics extension program epitomizes the finest principles of the home economics movement as adapted to late 20th-century America. Because it reaches homes not otherwise touched, or inadequately touched, by other educational programs of schools and colleges, it has a unique opportunity and responsibility.

Extension people place primary emphasis on problems that threaten stability of the home—early marriage, changing values, poverty, mobility and anonymity, changing roles of family members, and the pressures and tensions of a technological society. The loss of independence and transference of what once were family functions to the community require adjustment in the pattern of family living. Home economics extension seeks solutions to problems of adjustment and at the same time strives to maintain the stability of the home.

Aware of the fact that consumers in this country spend more than $1 billion each day and that eighty percent of our families use consumer credit, the extension people feel that a great deal needs to be done to develop what they call "consumer competence"—ability to purchase wisely and to handle budgets and credit intelligently.

Family housing problems today differ from those in the early decades of the 20th century, but they are just as real and vital to wholesome homelife as they were then. Extension home economists work toward the development of competence in purchasing, building, and remodeling; understanding of financing; and skills in managing, equipping, and decorating the home. They give special attention to the housing requirements of young families, the disadvantaged, and the aging.

Home economics extension provides leadership in encouraging good practices in family health, safety, and protection. It assists in community resource development for the mutual benefit of home and community. Through 4-H Clubs and cooperation with other youth groups, it assists in preparation for adulthood and responsible family membership. Touching many homes, home economics extension has a vital role in achieving the goals of the home economics movement.

7. Two Deans

Oh, wonderful new day, unfolding to the children
    of men!
Bring us afresh the vision of beauty;
Show us anew the path our feet must tread.

                —DEAN SARAH LOUISE ARNOLD

EARLY IN MY TEACHING CAREER I became acquainted with two deans who influenced the course of my life—one as an administrator, the other as a source of inspiration. Dean Henrietta Willard Calvin helped shape the School of Home Economics of which I later became dean. Dean Sarah Louise Arnold helped shape my philosophy of life. These two women came from quite different backgrounds and worked in different spheres, yet professionally they had one goal in common—the improvement of society through improvement of home and family life.

Mrs. Calvin came to Oregon Agricultural College as dean of the School of Domestic Science and Art in June 1912. A widow with five children—the two youngest of whom were still with her—she knew both theory and practice in the household sciences. She had been born in Anna, Illinois, in 1865 and had lived as a child in Kansas. She attended Washburn College in Topeka and graduated from Kansas State Agricultural College in 1886. She married John H. Calvin, a Kansas State graduate, and soon after their first child was born they moved to New York City where Mr. Calvin entered law school in Columbia University. Mrs. Calvin read law and political science with her husband and as their family grew, studied—in a practical way—dietetics, pediatrics, child care, health, and home nursing. At the time her husband died in 1898, she had a family of four boys and one girl. She moved back to Topeka, became librarian

in the children's room of the city library, and later took a similar
position at Kansas State College. In 1903 she became professor of
domestic science on that campus and in 1908 moved to a similar
position at Purdue University in Indiana. When she came to Oregon
she brought a wealth of experience and a knowledge of what was
being done in home economics in other parts of the country.

Dean Calvin found that enrollment in the School of Domestic
Science and Art had jumped forty percent the year before she came.
It received another increase of twenty percent (from 213 to 265) in
the fall of 1912, and she estimated that in the following two years the
increase would again be twenty percent annually. Consequently, she
prepared for expansion and guided the school in new directions. Her
recommendation that the school's name be changed to the School of
Home Economics was accepted and it became effective on September 1, 1914. In her first formal report, Dean Calvin phrased another
recommendation bluntly and forcefully in this manner:

> The School of Domestic Science and Art is divided in
> portions of three buildings . . . second floor of the Agronomy
> Building . . . The Dean's office and classroom are on the second
> floor of the Agricultural Building, while all food preparation is
> done in the basement of Waldo Hall. All these various rooms
> are greatly crowded and are occupied almost continuously from
> eight in the morning until six in the evening. The rooms in the
> basement of Waldo Hall are difficult to ventilate, ill-lighted and
> inconvenient, while the long standing upon the cement floors
> is detrimental to the health of both the teachers and students.
> As the number of students in these laboratories is greatly in-
> creased, the gas plant is so wholly inadequate that much of the
> time it is impossible to keep the full number of flames alight. . . .
>
> The need of a building devoted entirely to the School of
> Domestic Science and Art is so apparent that there is no need
> of entering into a discussion. It is impossible to carry on effec-
> tive work under these conditions which are menacing to the
> health of both student and teacher.

Dean Calvin got her new building. President Kerr, fully realizing
the need for it, had already put an architect to work drawing plans.
It was designed to be built in three sections. Construction on the east
wing started in 1913 and the departments moved into it in the fall

of 1914. It not only provided more room and better equipment, but also brought the cookery laboratories up off concrete floors. "Oh, those hard concrete floors!" one instructor exclaimed years later. "My arches were never the same afterwards." It has never been clear to me why many home economics laboratories have been located in basements—often with uncovered concrete floors. In home economics instruction we point the way toward improvement of facilities for the housewife; yet in colleges and high schools in many parts of the world, I have found students and teachers standing for hours at a time on bare, cold, crippling concrete. We were grateful for wooden floors in the new building.

"This excellent structure," Dean Calvin wrote, "adds greatly to comfort and convenience of both students and teachers. No better accommodations are afforded any school of Home Economics west of the Mississippi River and no school in the entire United States has better or more suitable equipment." We may excuse Mrs. Calvin's over-enthusiastic description of the new facilities in the flush of excitement over the accomplishment. With mounting enrollment and addition of new course work we soon filled the new building.

Dean Calvin could see opportunities opening for women capable of solving the problems of good food service for large numbers of people, as in restaurants, school lunch rooms, college residence halls, hospitals, institutional homes, asylums, and social centers. "More and more," she once wrote, "the life of the modern community is dependent upon institutions. Women are rapidly taking their places as executive and administrative leaders in the important functions of these institutions. . . . Facilities for specializing in this work at the College are therefore given special attention."

Significant curricular changes took place in Dean Calvin's administration. The two-year preparatory course became a Home Maker's Course, from which Laundering was dropped and new courses, Care of Children, Sanitation and Care of the Home, Personal Hygiene, and Home Nursing and Invalid Cookery were added. In the degree curriculum in foods, new courses in Experimental Cookery, Methods in Demonstration, Catering, and Institutional Management were added, as were two new graduate courses in Special Research in Cookery.

Ruth McNary Smith added a new type of course when she returned from a year's graduate work at Columbia University. In

Teachers College she had taken especially interesting courses in Housewifery and Household Administration. The course she introduced in Housewifery at OAC—and incidentally also at Iowa State when she accepted an appointment there in 1917—dealt with "efficient care of the house from the chemical, economic, and practical points, including . . . treatment of floors, walls, and woodwork; removal of stains; cleaning of rugs and carpets; laundering of household linen and clothing, and selection of cleaning apparatus and machinery." Basing her teaching on what she had learned in Dr. Benjamin Andrews' class at Columbia, Ruth put new vitality into the course in Household Administration. In this favorite course of hers she taught "the order and administration of the house, the proper division of the income, with a study of the budget, the maintenance of standards of efficiency; and a study of the domestic service problem." New graduate courses called Modern Problems in Household Administration were also added.

In the Department of Domestic Art, the course of study was similarly upgraded during Dean Calvin's administration, although that department did not move into graduate work as soon as we did in Domestic Science.

Dean Calvin encouraged the dissemination of information through publications. She had the assistance and encouragement of Ralph Hetzel, the energetic Extension Director, and Edwin T. Reed, the new College Editor. Both men saw the possibility of reaching more people through pamphlets and bulletins than could be reached in person. In home economics the staff had written only three publications before Dean Calvin came. In 1911 Miss Van Liew and Miss Van Deusen had prepared a small bulletin called "A Suggestive Two-Year Course in Cookery for the Schools of Oregon with Suggestions for Installation of a School Kitchen for Twenty Students." Miss Tobin and Miss Ewing had prepared for publication similar "suggestive courses" for sewing and for domestic art in high schools. The first edition of "Camp Cookery," the booklet which Ruth Smith and I wrote, came out just before Dean Calvin arrived. With Dean Calvin, Mr. Hetzel, and Mr. Reed working together, a whole series of home economics publications came into being during her administration.

The first and bulkiest of these was "Recipes for Use in Freshman Cooking Classes" by Mrs. Calvin, a 56-page bulletin published in

1913. Then came a series of little extension pamphlets for short-course classes, to hand out at demonstrations, to distribute to boys' and girls' clubs, and to mail in answer to inquiries. Mrs. Calvin wrote "Principles of Bread Making," "The School Luncheon," "Fruit and Vegetable Canning," and "Essentials of Bread Making." I wrote "Principles of Cake Making," and "Principles of Jelly Making." Ruth Smith wrote a bulletin on "Methods of Cleaning," in which she points out the limitations of the carpet sweeper and goes on to say, "Recently a large number of so called 'vacuum cleaners' operated either by hand, water, or electric power, have been offered for sale. . . . Some of these cleaners . . . are not worth buying because they are not based on a correct mechanical principle." Later, Anna Turley, Helen Cowgill, and I revised and expanded "The School Luncheon" into a 24-page bulletin.

In her pamphlet on school luncheons, Dean Calvin had stressed the need for quantity and quality of food for growing children and for variety and attractiveness to lure appetites. She had pointed out objectionable features of the typical luncheon—children eating alone without companionship of home people and eating hurriedly to permit time for play. Mr. Hetzel suggested we divide the expanded edition of "The School Luncheon" into three sections: (a) suggestions to the housewife on what to prepare and how to pack it; (b) suggestions for teachers in rural schools on making the noon meal more palatable and pleasant; and (c) suggestions for large schools.

Replies from teachers in rural schools to whom we had sent questionnaires indicated that those who served hot lunches found that better work resulted in the afternoons. Menus they served included cocoa or soup, baked potatoes, steamed pudding, and macaroni and cheese. The school children normally prepared the meal, served it, and cleaned up afterwards, thus gaining useful experience. Teachers said that at first parents and school boards sometimes questioned whether or not serving hot lunches was a proper function of a school, but after the program started, they became enthusiastic about it.

As an aid to those teachers already serving hot lunches, and to encourage those not yet doing so to begin such a program, we made a number of suggestions about selection of foods, choice of recipes, setting of tables, table etiquette, and dishwashing. The bulletin gives me credit for having designed the chest illustrated in it for the "storing of home economical equipment." According to my figures, for $13.20 a box could be constructed and equipped with pans, utensils, bowls, plates, and napkins for use by twelve children for their daily hot lunch.

Other states have gone through a somewhat similar experience in pioneering with school lunch programs. In this day of federally assisted school lunch programs, we take the benefits of hot lunches almost for granted. Most housewives no longer have the daily lunch-making chore to perform. Children do better schoolwork; they have better balanced meals, better digestion, and a social experience. As the home economics movement spreads around the world, we find many countries, however, that still need to apply the simple practices we have found beneficial in the school lunch programs in this country.

In 1912-13, in place of the nutrition courses I had taught the first year, Dean Calvin assigned me to teach several courses outside the regular curriculum for girls. I had a day class for college boys who were "batching" or who wanted to learn principles of nutrition and practical cookery. In my night class in camp cookery, one of my students was Kenneth Scott Latourette, a Yale graduate, who had been teaching in Yale-in-China but had come home to Oregon City because of illness. I had an evening class for wives of the men who came for the Agricultural Short Course and added one for unmarried farmers and orchardists who were doing their own cooking at home. The night classes became so large they had to be divided, giving me classes four nights a week. In one group were a number of young bachelors who had come west to make their fortunes raising fruit in the Hood River and Rogue River valleys. In answer to questions about making yeast breads, I explained that yeasts are plants that require food, moisture, and warmth, that they use sugar to produce gas which causes dough to rise and become light, and that like other plants yeasts can be killed by too much heat. In the laboratory session, I found one Armour Institute graduate kneading his bread dough with undue gentleness and asked him why. He explained that he was being careful not to kill the little yeast plants.

AT THE END of my third year at OAC, I decided to go to Cleveland at my own expense to attend the annual meeting of the American Home Economics Association. I had been thinking about Ellen H. Richards and the association she had helped form and I had been devouring every issue of the *Journal* she started. She had died while I was still in graduate school, but I wanted to meet other leaders in home economics. Dean Calvin encouraged me to go and mentioned some of the people I would probably meet. Consequently, soon after school was out in 1914, I started east.

In Chicago I stopped to visit a Foster Hall friend, Lillian Francis, who had just graduated from the University of Chicago. Since Lillian had been hostess and helper to her father following her mother's death, her father thought it was time for her to take a vacation and suggested that she go on to Cleveland with me. We readily agreed, and he made reservations for us on a passenger steamer from Chicago to Cleveland.

In Cleveland we got to the auditorium at Western Reserve University in time to hear the University's famous president, Charles W. Thwing, welcome the group and to hear the opening address by Dean Sarah Louise Arnold, the president of the Association. I had not met Dean Arnold, but I had used her book, *Stepping Stones to Literature*, when teaching grade school in Missouri. I was prepared to enjoy her as I had enjoyed her writing. I found her to be a gripping personality, and I hung on every word she spoke.

Now as I write of Sarah Louise Arnold, I open the December 1914 issue of the *Journal of Home Economics* and recall her opening words:

> *Doctor Grenfel, in lecturing to the students at Harvard University, chose as his subject "What Life Means to Me." It was probable that his lectures, interpreting his conception of life, gave to the students the best he could have possibly given; for the utmost that we can do for another is to interpret life as we have seen it. . . . The chief contribution of any individual is to render back in some fashion, for the service of others, the picture of life as it seems to him. I therefore shall not apologize for using the pronoun "I," or for giving as my last message to you a statement of the essentials of Home Economics as they appear to me. . . .*

Miss Arnold went on to point out that home economics means various things to various individuals but that "it will probably mean something finer and better to each and every one of us in the years to come." She described homemaking as a primitive, dominant instinct that "will never depart from the human race. One of the functions of Home Economics is to make clear that this instinct expresses the law of God, who himself has put into our hearts to make homes, to shape them, and maintain them. One purpose of ours, then, should be to take hold of hands with all the agencies which are at work doing this fundamental thing."

As might be expected of a person who had been a teacher of teachers of literature before she became a home economics educator, Dean Arnold sprinkled her addresses and writings with allusions to great writers. She often quoted poetry, sometimes from other poets, sometimes her own. Illustrating the step-by-step process so necessary in education she quoted this little verse:

> We build the ladder by which we rise
> From the lowly earth to the vaulted skies,
> And we mount to its summit round by round.

To illustrate her point that "once we have realized what the home is for and what its richest gifts may be, we shall make different decisions as to comfort and convenience" she told this story:

> A young friend of mine married but did not set up housekeeping. She and her husband "boarded." Perhaps you do not know what that means. I once asked a small boy in school where he lived, and he replied, "I don't live: I board." These people "boarded" because they wanted to "save." The wife became a saleswoman and liked it so well that she would not go to housekeeping. "I like to spend what I earn."
> "What do you buy?" I asked.
> "Oh, clothes, suits, hats, ribbons, and gloves."
> "Let us keep house," said the husband.
> "Oh, no," she replied," "We can have so much more if I earn too."
> So the days were spent for hats and clothes and the great and beautiful thing which these two might have had in their lives never came. Should we not try to find out, first of all, why the home is worth while and what things are worth while to do in the home, instead of multiplying recipes and adding mere conveniences? Shall we not come to understand what it means to "spend" our days in the home so that the lives of all who

*share its shelter shall become great and beautiful? What a rare
income that would bring us!*

Dean Arnold concluded her address that day in Cleveland by
saying,

*I hope we shall not change for the thing called efficiency
the real treasures of our home life. . . . I trust that we shall not
exchange hospitality for convenience and comfort. I trust that
we shall have such vision as will reveal to us what homes are
for and that we shall come to understand that no peace can
come to any home of ours unless we help to bring peace and
fullness and worth and comfort and understanding to all homes
in this beloved land of ours.*

That was my introduction to Sarah Louise Arnold. Over the
years, as I came to know her better, I developed a profound admiration for this remarkably versatile, interesting, active person. She had
been born in Abington, Massachusetts, in 1859, and spent her early
life in that quiet little town. Something of a child prodigy, she read
Caesar's Commentaries in Latin fluently by the time she was eleven
and had graduated from high school at thirteen. Too young to go to
college, she "stayed home to help mother" for four years, never
dreaming as she said later that this precious time "was a vital part
of my education and training." When she was old enough to go on to
college, she spent two years at Bridgewater Normal School and then
taught in various towns, mostly in New England. At twenty-nine
years of age she became supervisor of primary schools in Minneapolis
and six years later primary supervisor in Boston. As a result of her
intense interest in instruction in English, she developed a system of
phonetics illustrated in her books in the "See and Say" series and
in *The Mastery of Words* and *Stepping Stones to Literature*. She also
collaborated with Harvard Professor George Lyman Kittredge on
books related to reading.

In Boston, she helped found Simmons Female College in 1899.
When it opened in 1902, she resigned her position with the public
schools and became the first Dean of Simmons College. She also had
charge of teacher education and the work offered in household
economics. She read her first paper in home economics at the fifth
Lake Placid Conference in Boston in 1903. She made a statement

then that has for many years been exactly in keeping with my
thoughts on the subject:

> *The relations which are established between home economics,*
> *the sciences, literature, history, human life, go to show that the*
> *first foundation for the teacher of household economics is a*
> *liberal education, which will enable her to recognize these*
> *relations. . . . Without such an education, she must fail to*
> *comprehend the true relation of her province to the knowledge*
> *of the world.*

From that time on, Dean Arnold was active in the home economics movement. She was a charter member of the AHEA and was
elected its president in 1912 and 1913. Her first presidential address
contains the oft-quoted sentence:

> *The time will come and come soon when we shall be absolutely*
> *sure that the sanity and safety of our state institutions depend*
> *upon the sanity and the safety of our homes.*

Although we met only briefly at that Cleveland meeting, Dean
Arnold and I became well acquainted in later years when I often saw
her at meetings. During World War I, she served on the Food Administration Committee with Herbert Hoover, who sent her all over
the country to encourage housewives to conserve food and to help
with European relief work. In that connection she came to Oregon
to see me, since I had state responsibilities along the same line.
Unfortunately, I was confined to bed with a deep cold the day she
arrived in Corvallis, but she came to my house, declaring she was
unafraid of my cold. At the door, my sister Lora and her year-old
daughter, Elinor Hanson, who were with me at the time, greeted
her. When Miss Arnold came to my room and embraced me, she said,
"The loveliest thing just happened to me. That beautiful little baby
held out her arms as I came into your home and came right to me."
Miss Arnold was that kind of person. People held out their arms
to her.

She spoke to our staff and students and explained how "Hooverizing" in homes and institutions could conserve food, especially
wheat and sugar. She had lunch at our home management house,
Withycombe House, and left copies of her poem:

Grace at Table

Here we gather, dear All-Father,
Round thy table to be fed.
'Tis Thy gift—our daily bread.

As we gather to be fed
Nations plead for daily bread,
Fighting son and anguished mother,
Orphaned children—all together
Pray to Thee for daily bread.
At Thy common table, Father,
Ask we all for daily bread.

God, All-Father, hear our prayer!
Move our hearts and minds to share
With Thy children at Thy table
This Thy gift of daily bread—
Sacred gift of daily bread.

Lest they perish, swift and eager
Share we now our daily bread.
Give through us, O great All-Father,
to Thy children, daily bread!

Her visit was short and she soon dashed away on her round of one-night stands. Later in the spring Miss Arnold wrote from Washington D.C., discussing some minor problems I had brought up at the time of her visit. "Don't worry," she said. "The only thing is to 'heave in' our very best, every day and every hour, and trust God for the rest. Many others will be striving to help—some wise and some otherwise. In the end the spirit of their work will count. The veriest child can carry the coal that will light the fire. And in the end it all helps—even if none of it is perfect. In this big school of the nation (it is a 'mixed school,' as we used to say) all grades of understanding assemble and the volunteer teachers are of various capacities. But that is true in every college also. So cast in your pearls—and do not worry. The old Chinese proverb helps me: 'Do good and throw it into the sea. Though the fishes may not know it, God will.'"

Shortly after the war she retired from the deanship of Simmons College and took up a new career. While working with Mr. Hoover, she and Mrs. Hoover had become good friends, and partly through this connection she succeeded Lou Henry Hoover as national president of the Girl Scouts of America in 1925. After the Hoovers moved into the White House, Miss Arnold was an occasional guest there. "She was certainly a great and loyal woman," ex-president Hoover wrote in 1954 at the time of her death, "loved by everybody with whom she came in contact."

Epilogues

I

After our trip to Cleveland, Lillian Francis and I kept in touch with each other, and in 1915, when the opportunity arose, she accepted a position on our campus as half-time YWCA secretary and half-time instructor in domestic science. She and W. A. Jensen became good friends; the following year they were married. Lillian gave up her career as a teacher of home economics for a career as homemaker for Oregon State's long-time executive secretary and for their daughter Frances, who in her time would herself become a home economist.

II

Dean Calvin stayed in Oregon less than three years. She resigned to go to Washington, D.C., to become, with Carrie Lyford, one of the first two specialists in home economics in the U.S. Bureau of Education. In 1922, Mrs. Calvin became supervisor of home economics in the Philadelphia public schools—a position she held until her retirement in 1936, when she moved to California to be near her youngest son George in Oakland. Kansas State College awarded her an honorary Doctor of Science degree, and the building she helped plan for that campus is still known as Calvin Hall.

Margaret M. Justin, dean of home economics at Kansas State College for 30 years and a former student of Mrs. Calvin, paid her this tribute at the time of Mrs. Calvin's death in May 1947:

Mrs. Calvin shared with other pioneers in home economics certain attributes: ability, high courage, deep conviction, and certitude of objectives. Beyond and above that possessed by most people she had enthusiasm, zest for living, and a merry heart. The world is better because she lived.

III

A few years after her short visit to Corvallis, Dean Arnold wrote that she would like her niece and namesake, Sarah Louise Arnold, who had graduated from Sweet Briar College and who was teaching home economics in Brockton, Massachusetts, to come to OAC as a student. We were delighted when she arrived for the spring term in 1922. The niece and I became good friends and have corresponded and visited each other across the continent several times. The last time she came to Oregon, my husband and I took her to Crater Lake. On visits to her lovely colonial home filled with interesting antiques —including a canopied bed in which Lafayette is supposed to have slept—we always talk rapidly to make each moment count. The niece resembles the aunt, even to quoting poetry and expressing beautiful thoughts in the finest language. In her lifetime—and to some extent still through her niece—Dean Arnold has had a profound influence on my life and thought. As a person of high ideals and vision and as an effective writer and inspirational speaker, she had no peer.

The Home Economics Building at Oregon State University as envisioned by the architect before the east wing was built in 1914. The center wing was completed in 1920 and the west wing in different architecture in 1952.

8. *Tearoom at the Fair*

All this leads to the newest reason for keeping our
heads bandaged to keep them from swelling.

—ANNE SHANNON MONROE

THE BATTLESHIP *Oregon* and the State of Oregon helped make the
World's Fair in San Francisco in 1915 a huge success. The *Oregon's* speedy yet dismally slow circuit of Cape Horn, which took
two months at the beginning of the Spanish-American War, drama-
tized the need for a waterway through the Isthmus of Panama. Even
before the U.S. Congress approved the canal project, San Francis-
cans began making plans for a great exposition in 1915 to call attention to the West Coast and the Pacific Ocean area—a region that
would suddenly become much closer to the East Coast by water.
Oregonians saw the possibilities offered by the Panama-Pacific
International Exposition for showing off their products, promoting
their land, and enjoying cultural benefits.

Oregon was the first state to select a site for its exhibit building.
In March 1912 a party of 228 Oregonians headed by Governor
Oswald West (for whom West Hall on our campus is named) went to
San Francisco to break ground for the building. A fir pole from
Oregon was raised, and the chief gunner from the battleship *Oregon*,
which the U.S. Navy had agreed to station in San Francisco Bay for
the duration of the Fair, ran up a flag. The president of the Exposition
handed Governor West a deed to this bit of what he termed "Oregon
soil."

The Exposition grounds lay along what is now the Marina on
the north shore of San Francisco. The Oregon Building stood on the
bay front directly north of the Palace of Fine Arts, the huge, domed

structure built for the Fair that remained standing afterwards until rebuilt in permanent form in 1967. The Oregon Building, shaped like the Parthenon of the Athenian Acropolis, had 48 huge logs of Douglas-fir replacing the doric columns of the original. The frieze was a fretwork of pine and fir bark. At the main entrance stood two incense cedar logs each more than eight feet in diameter. Plantings of salal and Oregon grape fringed the building. A 222-foot Douglas-fir, floated from Oregon to San Francisco through the ocean, was erected as a flagpole in front of the building.

The main floor of the interior had a reception area in front of a huge stone fireplace but was mostly filled with exhibits of Oregon products—vegetables, cereals, lumber, fruits, hops, dairy products, woven woolens, stained glass windows, pottery, and paintings. The OAC forestry and poultry departments sent displays. Professor James Dryden's hens from the flock that had produced a world's egg-laying record with an average of 303 eggs in one year astonished many fairgoers.

Guides for the Oregon Building were young men, mostly seniors, from the University of Oregon and Oregon Agricultural College. They, with some members of the Oregon Commission, and other workers known as "the Oregon family," had living quarters in the building. Rather late in the construction it became evident that the Oregon family would have to be fed. The Commission approached President Kerr and President Kerr approached Dean Calvin with the proposal that the OAC Department of Domestic Science open a small kitchen and dining room in the Oregon Building to serve three purposes: to provide breakfasts and dinners for the workers in the building, to provide meals for the guests of the Commission, and to serve luncheons for the public. The income from the noon luncheons, at seventy-five cents apiece, was expected to pay the cost of food for those meals, travel expenses for the girls and instructors to San Francisco and back, and incidental costs such as laundry, table decorations, and concession expense. Dean Calvin accepted this opportunity for laboratory work in quantity cookery. She saw the possibility of giving seniors a new type of training and at the same time giving them the opportunity to see the Fair. By rotating them in teams through the 288 days of the Fair, quite a number of the seniors would have a chance to participate.

To cover the Fair, the Portland *Oregonian* sent Anne Shannon Monroe, a journalist who later became well known as an author of western books. She proved a good friend of the Tearoom. In one of her early dispatches Miss Monroe described the fine impression the young men from the University of Oregon and OAC were making as guides in the Oregon Building. She went on to say:

> Well, all this leads to our newest reason for keeping our heads bandaged to keep them from swelling. Proud of our college men guides, more than proud of our splendid young women from Oregon Agricultural College who with such womanly dignity and sweetness are teaching us all the beauty of service in the home economics department—proud as we have been of these girls we did not quite realize that we had so much more to be proud of than other states, until prominent club women of San Francisco visiting our building and our school exhibit, told us in amazement that in California they had nothing to compare with Oregon's showing of practical results.
>
> In fact, upon investigation I find no state can compare with Oregon for practical results in home economics. . . . The girls receive not a cent for this service. They are part of Oregon's demonstration of her home economics school training; they are as much of an exhibit as our manufactures, our timber, and our grains. They do their work so well, and with such charm and grace, that they are a credit to the state.

Miss Monroe wrote such an excellent feature article for the *Sunday Oregonian* that I am going to let her tell the story of our Tearoom at the Fair in her own words by reprinting much of that full-page article here.

CORVALLIS GIRLS' COOKERY MAKES BIG HIT AT SAN FRANCISCO FAIR

DOMESTIC SCIENCE DEMONSTRATION ESTABLISHED BY OREGON AGRICULTURAL COLLEGE IN THE STATE BUILDING AT THE PANAMA-PACIFIC EXPOSITION HAS PROVED SURPRISING SUCCESS AND LUNCHEON MAIDS ARE BESIEGED WITH PROPOSALS

By Anne Shannon Monroe

OREGON BUILDING, PANAMA-PA-CIFIC INTERNATIONAL EXPOSI-TION, July 24 — (Special) — In private theatricals and on the legitimate stage it frequently happens that the scheduled "hits" don't hit, while the unexpected combinations create a furor. Something of the kind happened to the Oregon building when as a sort of tacked-on afterthought the Oregon Agricultural College put in a home economics lunchroom with the idea of demonstrating the practical nature of the girls' training. . . .

After the Oregon building was finished and the space pretty well laid off for various exhibits a place had to be found in which to tuck the lunchroom. Many people daily exclaim in astonishment as they walk along the balcony of the Oregon building and look out upon San Francisco Bay, lapping at our very feet: "Why under the sun wasn't the lunchroom located on the north side of the building, where it would have a water view?"

The answer is it came too late and had to be put in where it could be gotten. It was the "hit" that came all unscheduled, for no one dreamed that this "afterthought," this demonstration by the college girls, was to prove the great big feature of the Oregon building, so far as the general public is concerned.

The objective point toward which the Oregon Agricultural College has worked consistently and persistently has been

practicability; to make the young men scientific farmers, to make the young women of the home economics department scientific housewives. Whether they were to use this housewifery in their homes, in larger homes of an institutional character, or in schools where they would train other young women in scientific housewifery made no difference. They must be able to plan and prepare correctly balanced meals; they must be able to serve them happily, and they must have an appreciation of restful, quiet atmosphere pervading their activities. They must always be neat and wholesome in appearance. . . . Daughters of the best families of Oregon—young women who represented the power to shine socially and intellectually, and who came from well-to-do homes, would cook and serve a meal without losing caste, and with dignity and self-respect. . . .

No better place could have been selected to demonstrate the simple idea of scientific service than the exposition, where people from all over the world stream daily through the gates, and a settled colony is maintained, made up of people from every state and nation.

The Oregon home economics lunchroom has but one fault—it is not large enough to serve the entire exposition. It was planned merely for demonstration purposes, and but a small space could be given it. There is a scientifically equipped kitchen, where everything is as white and clean as a surgeon's operation-room. Large panes of glass are the only separation between the public and this kitchen, so that you can watch your dinner being cooked if you wish to do so. Every process is open at all times to public inspection. "That's what I like," I heard a spic-and-span military man say as he pointed out with his cane the laboratory-like kitchen open to view.

The dining-room seats 40 people ranged about six small tables, every one of which is immaculate with good linen, nice large homey napkins and shining silver. Flowers always decorate the tables—not withered flowers dropping their petals, but flowers fresh from gardens with the bloom of youth still on them. The colors of the lunchroom are a soft mingling of tans and grays, restful and unobtrusive. Deep French windows open onto the balcony, affording abundant light and air, and soft silk curtains shut out the public during the lunch hour. You eat unobserved by the crowding throng, which is a point of importance at this big fair, where it often is difficult to get a seat at a table.

Within the home-economics lunchroom you have an impression of quiet and aloofness, of the privilege of taking all the time you need for lunch, of no one being in a hurry and no one being fussed. The atmosphere is as big an achievement as the food.

At noon the college women can serve but 85 people. At the beginning the girls wondered if—at 75 cents apiece—they would get enough customers to fill the tables. They had not been serving many days before everyone seemed to have heard about it, and while there was absolutely no advertising, no cards or literature of any kind, the crowds began to come. Everyone seemed to have passed the word along that here was a real place to get real food. They came in such numbers that admission had to be regulated. One of the OAC guides was stationed at the door to give out luncheon tickets to the first comers. When 85 had

been given out the rest were turned away. The result was that the luncheon people began to come earlier and earlier. Then they had to make it a rule to begin giving these tickets at 12 o'clock sharp. People then began to send in requests by phone and by messenger for tickets. This did not seem fair to those who had traveled the tiresome length of the grounds to be there by 12 for a chance at the lunch-room, so the rule was made that they must line up for their tickets and none could be given out in advance.

High and Low Satisfied

Every restriction but added to the room's popularity. Now, by 11 o'clock each day, men and women begin to form in line, and they stand there an hour to get one of the tickets that entitles them to a seat in that quiet, restful room where they are served the best American food. Governors from half the states, foreign commissioners, artists, authors and actors have all tried the home-economics cooking and pronounced it good.

Many get angry because they are turned away. Most people, however, are delightfully sweet about it as soon as they understand, and appreciate the democratic spirit that governs the lunch-room. The guide on duty repeats the story over and over again to the new-comers—that it is a college demonstration of home-economics training and not a restaurant in the general acceptance of the term; that the capacity limits the number to just so many, and this is the very best he can do. He is extremely sorry for their inconvenience; and if they can't wait—why, right across the street in the California building is a very good cafe open to everyone.

And the blessed college girls. How do they manage it? Five months now in the dining-room—they have served the Oregon family consisting of between 30 and 40 at breakfast and dinner daily. Quiet, sweet, unostentatious service and the best-cooked food in the most generous quantities is the rule. They show they have college appetites in mind.

Nine girls are on the job all the time. Seven do the actual work of preparing the food. There is one permanent buyer, Miss Inez Bozorth, the senior, who will be in charge till the end, and one permanent manager of the dining-room, Miss Anne Russell.* The duties are so apportioned that each girl, during her term, has experience in creating each dish and in doing each task. The girls make out the menus, which are approved by the instructor in charge. The instructors change each month and a new set of girls comes in every three weeks. Each set remains six weeks, but it is so arranged that there are always three experienced girls on hand when the new ones come in. They are chosen from the college seniors in Corvallis for their scholarship, their health, and their general efficiency.

All Rotate on Duty

Two girls are detailed each morning to rise at 6 and go on duty to prepare breakfast for the Oregon family, which is served promptly at 7:30. They are assisted by three dining-room girls, who come on duty at 7. They rotate in this early rising, so that one does not rise at this hour two mornings in succession. The full force is on duty for luncheon, and each girl is responsible for one particular problem. Each girl manages each problem for one week, and as there are six household problems, when her term is ended she has gone through all the problems.†

Three girls serve luncheon, each one being responsible for 12 people. They rotate on the dishwashing. The only service hired about the establishment is the laundry. All else, from cleaning to the preparation of the most dainty and intricate desserts, is done by the girls. For dinner, two girls are detailed to do the cooking and three to do the serving. Two who are off duty wash the dishes. Always there are four girls who may doff their uniforms and white linen, wear street clothes and be guests at the breakfast and dinner tables.

All three meals are of three courses. For luncheon there is always a salad, a big, fat, generous salad, a soufflé, a vegetable, a dessert and tea, coffee or milk. It is similar for dinner, save that a roast generally takes the place of the soufflé. For breakfast there is fruit, breakfast food, and eggs in some dainty form, or ham, or bacon. Simplicity is the keynote and excellence the rule. For the many special luncheons given in the Oregon building, the same luncheon exactly is served; there are never any extras, the only difference between these luncheons and the every-day ones is that the former are served in what is known locally as the "Governor's Suite," the pretty blueroom adjoining the public lunchroom. The service of the two is identical.

Money Goes to State

The money made by the college girls is used to defray their own expenses and their transportation to and from the fair. All money taken in by the guide at the door is turned over to the Oregon state bookkeeper, Mr. Williams, who pays all bills and deposits the balance with the Commissioners. . . . Economy of management is part of the college training, and there is no waste, either of materials or in buying.

How do the girls like it? The work itself they love. They have grown fat on the regular hours and close work. Every girl has improved in appearance by the close of her six weeks' term of service. Some of the experiences have been trying till they got far enough away to see them as funny; for instance, there are people

---

* Miss Bozorth and Miss Russell and a woman to supervise dishwashing each received $50 a month in addition to their expenses for the ten months of the Fair.

† In order that the time the seniors spent at the Fair would not keep them from graduating and that they receive adequate credit for the course of training, each girl was granted six term hours of college credit.

The Oregon Building at the Panama-Pacific International Exposition

so ingrained in the habit of fixed thought that when they see a young woman don an apron and cook a dinner, or serve it, she becomes a maid in their minds, regardless of her education, circumstances or family. A few have had this attitude, and it was not pleasant for the recipient. Then the visitors have insisted on tipping, though a sign plainly forbids it. The girls have had all sorts of sport over the men and women who are accustomed to saying "thank you" only in silver. They know these are college women, they know it is a college demonstration, and still they push coin into their hands or leave it under their napkins. Part of the daily gymnastics of the dining-room girls is chasing up these people to return the money with which they insist on saying "thank you."

The majority of people are embarrassing in their appreciation. They stop the girls to tell them how lovely they are, how good everything is, and to ask if any are free—this from the men. The daily joke is the daily proposal. Usually it comes to the maid who creates the Parker House rolls. Those rolls are as famous as Butler's pigs.‡ Every girl has had one, as they rotate on the rolls. All the professions are represented in these proposals, with a preponderance of the clergy. The girls can't get through a luncheon without writing out recipes for someone, or promising to mail them to the women who stand before the glass windows of the kitchen and watch.

Girls Benefit by Training

The girls are learning a great deal besides the preparation of foods. They are learning to meet the public, and the value of manner and appearance. These girls are finding that preparation for life means more than the ability to grind at their books. A pleasing personality, a pleasant manner, responsiveness without obtrusiveness, a quiet low voice, a cheerful expression, a human sympathy with difficulties —all these things they find score high in making a success of housewifery. . . .

‡ Miss Monroe here refers to a popular short story of the day, "Pigs is Pigs," by Ellis Parker Butler.

We had some problems in operating the Tearoom that Miss Monroe did not know about—or at least did not choose to tell her readers about. Mrs. Calvin made arrangements for setting it up and went to San Francisco to supervise it at the opening of the Fair but left shortly thereafter for her new position in Washington, D.C. and turned the Tearoom over to the rest of us. We also had our regular classes on the campus to teach and had to fill in there for each other while we took turns at the Tearoom. Since its operation was the responsibility of my department I had some anxiety over whether or not it would be a financial success, and I had some decisions to make that I had not bargained for.

Once while I was the instructor in charge at San Francisco, one of the Oregon Commissioners made a suggestion that we permit smoking by guests in the "Governor's Suite." I questioned the propriety of this suggestion and put him off until I could write President Kerr. Quite characteristically, Dr. Kerr assured me that he had confidence in whatever decision I would make. I therefore informed the Commission that we would not permit the air to be contaminated —and that ended the matter.

Food technologists on the campus in Corvallis had been experimenting with the juice of the popular new loganberry. They sent us several cases of this flavorful juice, which we stored in a room above the business office. Alice Butler (Marsh) reminded me in recent years of this incident: "One morning one of the men from the business office rushed up all excited and yelled, 'What's happened? Blood is running down our office walls!' We dashed into the storeroom so fast that we were sprayed with fermented loganberry juice. What a sight—all over our white uniforms and aprons!"

Our customers kept the menu from being a problem. We had thought at first that we would have considerable variety so that the girls could gain experience in quantity cooking and in serving many different dishes. Parker House rolls, the soufflé, and baked potatoes became so popular, however, that we had to serve them as a standard part of the luncheons. We varied the first course and dessert and varied the soufflé with cheese, tuna, tomato, or the ground remains of the previous evening's roast, but kept a rather standard menu. This practice permitted us to concentrate on quality and effective timing and kept us free from having to experiment with a new menu every day or two.

The tiny crowded rooms where the girls slept in double-decked beds (Tumble Inn, All Inn, Dodge Inn, Three Weeks Inn, and Sleepy Hollow) looked as if they might be a problem, but the girls took the situation with such good grace and humor that none developed. The girls did not spend much time in their rooms. They worked a strenuous schedule six days a week but they had free time in which to see the Fair—and what a Fair it was to see! Dignitaries referred to it as "the university of the world," "a university of current information," and "an encyclopedia of human progress." Prominent men and women of the time and those later to become prominent came to the Fair. President Woodrow Wilson did not come because of the war situation in Europe, but sent Vice President Thomas R. Marshall. Ex-Presidents Taft and Theodore Roosevelt were there. Future presidents Herbert Hoover and Franklin D. Roosevelt and their wives had a hand in the proceedings. William Jennings Bryan spoke to the largest audience (121,288) he ever addressed. Thomas Edison showed Henry Ford one of his new inventions. Barney Oldfield and Ed Rickenbacker drove in the car races. The girls on duty in the Tearoom ran to the windows daily to see Aviator Art Smith write his name in the sky.

The girls loved the frequent concerts of John Philip Sousa's band and the Navy band from the *Oregon*. Camille Saint-Saëns, Paderewski, Fritz Kreisler, and Victor Herbert came for recitals. A group of the girls went into San Francisco to hear Madame Schumann-Heink sing in the unfinished Civic Auditorium. Carrie Jacobs Bond lunched at the Tearoom and was so pleased she gave a private recital in front of the fireplace one evening for the whole Oregon family, playing and reading some of her compositions.

Anne Shannon Monroe took a group to see an exhibition of dancing at the National Dancing Masters' Convention at the Claremont Hotel in Berkeley. Bill Hanley, the Central Oregon cattle king about whom Miss Monroe later wrote a book,* took a group to the St. Francis Hotel for a roast beef dinner. Mrs. Clara Waldo took another group to see *Peg O' My Heart* at the Geary Theater. President Kerr chartered a launch and took a group for a spin around the bay and out through the Golden Gate. After a track meet in Berkeley,

---

* *Feelin' Fine*, published by Doubleday, Doran, and Company, Garden City, New York, 1931.

the OAC team invited the girls to see the Gay Way with them and came back afterwards for refreshments in the dining room.

When Ruth Smith was the instructor in charge of the Tearoom, guests included Ernesto Nathan, the former mayor of Rome; Thomas Lamont, the industrialist, who came back at least once and thanked the girls in person; and a group of Japanese dignitaries who wanted to see the kitchen and seemed especially interested in the ovens in which soufflés were baked. Two of the Olds brothers, founders of the Olds, Wortman, and King department store in Portland (now Rhodes), came many times and one of them told me the last day he was there that if he were going to be in San Francisco any longer he would gladly get in line every day to be served in our Tearoom. The Governor of Michigan called me aside one day to ask questions about our school and college and how we had been able to put on such a fine demonstration so far away from home.

About the middle of July we came to the conclusion that we were going to be solvent. After covering all expenses we would be able to reimburse the Oregon Commission for their expenses in connection with the Tearoom. In the end, when I went back to San Francisco in November to help in closing, we found that we had cleared about $2,000. In accordance with our agreement, the Commission received $1,000 and the School of Home Economics received $1,000. Our share went into the college student loan fund. Later the Commission returned $700, which we used to buy furnishings for the first home management house.

The Commissioners also sent us a framed, illuminated wall plaque which hung in the corridor of the Home Economics Building for many years:

AN APPRECIATION . . .
   of the service and womanly dignity of the senior girls of the Domestic Science Department of the Oregon Agricultural College who, under the direction of Miss Ava B. Milam, Miss Sarah L. Lewis, Miss Ruth M. Smith, Miss Bertha Davis, Mrs. Alice M. Dolman, Miss Christie Moore, and Miss S. Hadwen, made for themselves a lasting place in the affections of the thousands whom they served at the Oregon Building, Panama Pacific International Exposition, 1915, and particularly in the hearts

of the "Oregon family," the members of which had the greatest opportunity to observe them at their work and to note the results favorable to the state, the institution they represented, and to themselves.

FOR MANY YEARS we kept hearing compliments from people all over the country who had visited or heard of our demonstration project in San Francisco. Three articles I wrote about our experiences were published in national magazines. At the Fair, a representative of the *Ladies' Home Journal* asked me to write an article on the Tearoom. I offered to help *her* do it, but she insisted that Editor Edward W. Bok wanted it to come from me. I agreed finally and wrote an article entitled "College Women Dignifying Service," the motto over our lunchroom door in the Oregon Building and sent it in. When the galley proof came back, I found the editors had changed my introduction, rewritten parts of the article, and given it a new title: "Where Baked Potatoes Took First Place." Embarassed about these changes, I tried to withdraw the article, but Mr. Bok wrote a saucy letter saying I had no right to stop its publication. I talked with Mrs. Kidder, the Librarian. Since she did not see anything I should complain about, I dropped my objection, and the article was published in the February 1916 issue of the *Ladies' Home Journal*. Mr. Bok sent me a check for $50, the first money I had earned by writing, and I sent it to my mother as a gift. Later the *Industrial-Arts Magazine* ran an article as I had written it and kept the title, "College Women Dignifying Service." The May 1916 issue of the *Journal of Home Economics* carried a somewhat similar article under the title, "A Unique College Exhibit."

Participation in the Tearoom had a lasting effect on the young women who took part in it, on the underclassmen back on the campus, and on the development of institution management in the School of Home Economics. Ruth McNary Smith resigned her OAC staff position to become manager of the diet kitchen of a large hospital in San Francisco. Inez Bozorth, one of the student managers of the Tearoom, joined our staff as secretary and instructor for three years, served as director of dormitories at the University of Montana for a few years, and then was appointed manager of the Lawyers' Club at the University of Michigan, a position she filled with efficiency and distinction until her retirement.

Katharine McDermott (MacCosham), one of the first group of girls to go to the Oregon Building recalls, "The thing that helped me most was learning to cook and serve in large quantities—and meeting the public through serving." The week Lorene Parker (Whelpton) made the Parker House rolls, the other girls took delight in pointing out "Miss Parker" to patrons who asked who made them. "The experience I acquired," Lorene once told me, "has been invaluable to me. Planning meals for a church supper, PTA harvest supper, reception, or bazaar has never seemed a problem." Mylius L. Shoemake said, "We made a reputation all over the Fair grounds and even downtown San Francisco. One of my tasks was to cut down time in preparing Parker House rolls, thus saving time on motions. I used details of this and other projects many times in the thirty-six years I taught in Fresno high schools and junior college." Edna Mills (Ricker) wrote, "I gained much to help me later in my teaching career, both in handling quantity cooking and in learning to live in a community of people. To be honest, I think serving the 'Oregon Family' stands out more in my memory than the noon lunches we served the public." Edith Crockatt (Strain) said, "We participated with pride and dignity, as we tried to make each part of the project as perfect as possible; we felt a keen sense of satisfaction in the finished product."

Other girls on the campus who had not had the opportunity to go to San Francisco became enthusiastic about this field of work. Agnes Redmond (Miller) is a good example. She was a freshman in 1915 and heard the seniors tell tales of their adventures at the Fair. Here was a way, she said to herself, to combine interesting work with good financial reward. In World War I she volunteered for hospital work and became a dietitian at Letterman Hospital, adjacent to the Fairgrounds in San Francisco. Her supervisor was one of the seniors she had listened to, Ierne Ahern. After the war, when what she calls "the tearoom craze" hit San Francisco, she and another dietitian opened their own business—and sold it five years later at a good profit. She went into a variety of other institution management positions after that, as did many of our graduates in the coming years.

At the close of the Fair in San Francisco, we asked that the kitchen equipment used for the Tearoom be shipped to the campus, and eventually we got it as starter equipment for a campus Tearoom of our own.

9. New Horizons

D EAN CALVIN'S RESIGNATION in March 1915 left the School of
Home Economics without a dean. A telegram from President
Kerr came to me in San Francisco asking me not to accept any new
position until he had talked with me. When we had a chance to talk,
Dr. Kerr said that he and the Board of Regents had agreed that
I should be the new dean. Surprised and stunned, I replied that I
would not consider such a promotion. I felt I was too young and
inexperienced. There were other women in the school older than
I, and I had all I could do in my present position.

He asked me to suggest someone else. I knew that Edna N.
White, head of home economics at Ohio State University, would
make us a fine dean and recommended her. Edna declined, but in
later years proved a great help to us in another way—as head of the
new Merrill-Palmer School in Detroit.

President Kerr appointed a committee of three to administer the
School of Home Economics until a new dean could be found. Mrs.
Mary Fawcett, Dean of Women, was made chairman; Mrs. Helen
Bryce Brooks represented Domestic Art, and I represented Domestic
Science. Togther, we took care of whatever matters needed attention
while President Kerr continued his search.

Early in 1915, I decided to build a home of my own in which
to live and to entertain students, faculty, and other friends. When
my parents came for an extended visit that summer, Father helped
me choose a lot a few blocks from the campus. Mother helped me
develop plans, while Father talked with the carpenter. In a time
when large houses were the custom, many people thought I was
building a doll's house when I built one just large enough to accommodate myself, a college girl to live with me, and a guest or two
from time to time. I have since enlarged and remodeled this house,
but it still remains my home at 127 North Twenty-Sixth Street.

For their stay in Oregon, Father and Mother rented a house in another part of town, where we had a family reunion that summer. All of my sisters except Ada, who was with her husband in Puerto Rico, came in July. Several years before, the younger twins, Lottie and Lora, had come West after teaching school for a year in Missouri. Lottie had come to OAC to finish work for a degree in home economics in 1914. Ada, who was then teaching geography at the Los Angeles Teachers College (which later became UCLA), was joined by Lora who received her degree there. Nell, who had been teaching most recently at Pomona, California, brought her fiance, Robert Scott Miner, Sr., a graduate of the University of Illinois who traveled for the American Book Company, to Corvallis for the family reunion. I refer to him as "Senior" because there are now also a Robert Scott Miner, Jr., and a Robert Scott Miner III. Nell had met Scott Miner a few years before while she was teaching at Monte Vista, Colorado. On July 14, 1915, they were married in our parents' temporary home in Corvallis.

Lora, who had taught one year in El Centro, California, but liked Oregon, found a teaching position in Salem. On one of her frequent visits to Corvallis she met Jess Hanson, a graduate of the University of Missouri, who had come to Corvallis to study poultry husbandry with Professor James Dryden at the same time that I came in 1911. After he and Lora were married in my new home in the summer of 1916, Jess began to develop his own strain of White Leghorn chickens—a venture which became notably successful.

Lottie, too, eventually made Corvallis her home. After high school teaching in Oregon, 4-H Club work in Kansas, and extension work in Montana, she moved to Modesto, California. There she met Ernest V. Vaughn, a history professor in the junior college. They came to Corvallis to be married in her twin sister's home in July 1924. It was on this visit that Dr. Vaughn met the Dean of the School of Basic Arts and Sciences at Oregon State College, Dr. M. Elwood Smith. Dean Smith subsequently brought Ernest to the OSC history department where, in later years, he served as department head until his retirement. Hence, for many years I had the good fortune of having two of my four sisters living near me.

Uncle Roz could not come for Nell's wedding in 1915, but after he had heard about the Tearoom at the Fair, he wrote that he would open a tearoom for me in Kansas City if I would manage it. I told him, "No thank you." I liked what I was doing and was convinced by this time that the compensations of working with college youth were much more appealing to me than the prospect of greater financial returns from the management of a business.

Being a member of a college faculty with the opportunity to meet many interesting people also appealed to me. The staff member I enjoyed most in my first ten years in Oregon was Ida A. Kidder, the Librarian. From the first day on campus, when I lunched with her and others who gave me a sense of reassurance, I admired her, and as time went on I found her a helpful, sympathetic, clearheaded confidante. When I went to her for advice, she did not give snap judgments; she listened carefully to all sides of a question before giving her opinion. Because of her advanced years and the sympathetic way she treated others, students and faculty alike knew her affectionately as "Mother" Kidder.

Although Mrs. Kidder looked somewhat like Queen Victoria, and—I suspect—dressed her hair to heighten this resemblance, she was not regal in her manner. She seemed a close friend to hundreds of people of all ages. A former student wrote from France in World War I, "Don't you dare call yourself 'old'! That applies only to people who have ceased to be interesting . . . not to such dynamos of kindness, sympathy and understanding as you. . . . You will never get too old for the companionship of your boys and girls. The immortals that live on your bookshelves have endowed you with a personality that defies the March of Time."

Mother Kidder was rather heavy set and partially crippled by arthritis—and perhaps other ailments. As time went on she became almost office bound. One of the engineering professors helped to keep her mobile. When the World's Fair closed in San Francisco, he arranged to have one of the electric carts visitors had rented to carry themselves around the grounds brought to the campus. Mrs. Kidder soon learned to operate it and once more became a familiar figure on the campus as she rolled about on the walks, pausing now and then to chat with faculty and students.

One of the students whom Mrs. Kidder took under her wing when he first came to the campus was Eric Englund. A young man of exceptional ability, Eric had been born in northern Sweden and at an early age had moved to England and later to Texas and eventu-

ally to Portland. Alone in the city, with only a sketchy knowledge
of English, Eric was "discovered" by the YMCA leader Robert C.
French, who suggested that he prepare for college. "I don't have
any money," Eric told him. "How fortunate," Mr. French replied,
"You are going to college at Corvallis." With Mr. French's assistance,
Eric completed preparation for college by evening study in the
educational department of the Portland YMCA and came to OAC in
the fall of 1914. He had not been on the campus long before Mrs.
Kidder also discovered him. Forty years later in a recorded interview,
Eric paid this tribute to her counsel and guidance:

> *The library was on the second floor of Benton Hall. [Mrs.*
> *Kidder] had no office but a desk in the corner, which suited her*
> *very well because she could survey her whole domain, the*
> *reading room and many of the files, just by looking around. She*
> *saw us all as we came and went. Not far from her desk was a*
> *table on which she had a sign with large letters that said*
> *"INTERESTING"—that is all it said. There she would put the*
> *books of a cultural, broadening character for students to pick*
> *up, and she noticed those who came to that table and browsed;*
> *others, she tried to encourage to go there. It always pleased her*
> *immensely to be asked by fraternities, sororities, and other*
> *student groups to come to their homes and read to them. It was*
> *the best entertainment for her. She loved it, and so did the*
> *students. One day, the home economics practice house [Withy-*
> *combe House] was snowbound, and the girls were practically*
> *all of them at home—we were all snowbound. Mrs. Kidder was*
> *invited there to read to them, and she read from Emerson's*
> Society and Solitude.

Eric Englund also related how he and Mrs. Kidder liked to
read aloud to each other, especially in Emerson, and how she had
been an inspiration to him throughout his later life.

One of the greatest accomplishments of Mother Kidder's professional career was the planning, design, and construction of a new
library building, completed in 1918. An elevated walkway 100 yards
long was constructed from the second floor of the old building to a
second story window in the new one and faculty and students who
pitched in to help move books might be seen at all hours of the

day carrying armloads of library materials over the walkway. Not
to have been seen in the line of march was to evoke the jibe: "Carried
any books yet?" Mrs. Kidder took great pride in the new building.
"From its simplicity, harmony, and adaptability to service" she once
said, "I cannot but consider it the most artistic building on the campus." In her twelve years as Librarian, she saw her enterprise grow
from 4,264 volumes in one room to 35,814 volumes in a handsome
new home. From a single librarian, she saw the staff grow to eight
full-time persons, five of whom were professional librarians, and one
half-time worker. In cooperation with the faculty of the School of
Home Economics, she built a fine collection of books and periodicals
in home economics and related fields.

AFTER TWO YEARS of administration by a committee, the School of
Home Economics still did not have a dean. In the spring of 1917,
Mrs. Clara Waldo, the only woman on the Board of Regents, came
to see me. She told me that the Board and the President still agreed
that I should be the new dean. After we had discussed the matter,
I agreed to accept with one stipulation—that I be given time to visit
departments of home economics across the country before my appointment became effective.

A short time later, before I knew the matter had been settled,
Eric Englund called at my office. Since he was a varsity debater and
orator, YMCA cabinet member, and president of the student assembly, I did not know at first in what capacity he had come to see
me. His conversation soon revealed that he had come as editor of
the *Barometer*, the student newspaper, to interview me about becoming dean. When he noted my reluctance to talk about the proposed promotion, he laughed and said, "It's all right. President Kerr
sent me."

The Board not only agreed to my stipulation, but also granted
me a travel allowance. After making arrangements for my classes,
I started off to learn what I could through observation and conversation. At meetings of the American Home Economics Association, I
had met some of the deans and department heads and heard others
speak; I knew others by reputation. For the most part I had stood
in awe of them, but on this trip they treated me so graciously that
I began to look upon them as friends and colleagues. At the Uni-

versity of Wisconsin, Abby L. Marlatt, whom I found stimulating, invited me to stay with her in her apartment. At Iowa State College Catherine MacKay said, "Don't you think it is about time for you to come back to Iowa and finish the job you started here?" At Kansas State College, Dean Mary Pierce Van Zile told me how much they still thought of Henrietta Calvin. At Chicago, my former teachers were pleased to hear of the advancement of one of their alumnae. Isabel Bevier of the University of Illinois had always seemed an awesome figure to me. She was so closely associated with Ellen H. Richards in the AHEA and so important a person at meetings that I called on her a bit timorously, only to find my fears entirely unfounded. She was friendly and hospitable and we had a congenial relationship from that time on. At Purdue University, I met Mary L. Matthews and enjoyed my stay there. At Ohio State University, Edna M. White and I "hit it off" well and became close friends. At Cornell University, I was the house guest of the co-deans, Martha Van Rensselaer and Flora Rose, in their campus home. At Columbia University I met a group whom I had many occasions to consult in the future—Henry C. Sherman, Benjamin Andrews, Cora Winchell, Mary Swartz Rose, and others.

In Washington, D.C., I called at the offices of former Dean Henrietta Calvin and OAC Alumna Carrie Lyford, the specialists in home economics for the Bureau of Education. Miss Lyford was away on a trip, but I had a good chat with Mrs. Calvin. She suggested that while visiting different types of institutions I should see the facilities for preparing teachers of home economics for Negro schools at Hampton Institute in Virginia. Miss Lyford had been providing assistance to the staff there, and Mrs. Calvin thought it would be well worth my while to take the trip. She suggested I take the night boat down the Potomac and arranged for a young man who was in war-time government service in the Bureau of Education as a $1-a-year man to go along. His home was in Old Point Comfort, not far from Hampton Institute. He proved to be a congenial escort and even invited me to his family home for breakfast the next morning. His mother, a fine Southern gentlewoman, had quite a surprise, I can assure you, when we dropped in on her at six a.m. But that is another story.

The purpose of this trip was to see the home economics facilities at Hampton Institute. I was impressed with the pleasant manner and friendly attitude of the faculty and students, the effective arrangement of their laboratories, and especially, with the efficiently operated home management house which also served as a guest house for campus visitors. It was such a purposeful atmosphere that I could readily understand why Carrie Lyford gave up her position in Washington a few years later to go to Hampton as Dean of Women and head of home economics.

Everywhere I went I sensed a feeling of tenseness and foreboding because of America's entry into the World War, but otherwise it was a thoroughly delightful trip. I made many friends and gained insight and information. Having picked up pointers on how to administer (and how not to administer) a school of home economics, I entered the deanship on October 1, 1917, with a feeling of greater adequacy than I would have had otherwise.

The clouds of war that swept up from the horizon in 1917 engulfed the campus in the early months of my first year as dean. Many of our men students went to training camps, preparing to go overseas. Some of our women students entered work related to the war effort. The ASTP (Army Student Training Program) brought hundreds of young men to the campus for training. The School of Home Economics became involved in another way. In September 1917, I received a letter from the United States Food Administration in Washington, D.C.:

> *Miss Ava B. Milam is hereby appointed Home Economics Director in the State of Oregon. It is understood that her activities, as far as the Food Administration is concerned, are to be under the general supervision of the Federal Food Administrator in the State of Oregon.*
> *(Signed)* Herbert Hoover
> *Food Administrator*

A call came also to come to Washington for a meeting of State Home Economics Directors. The assembled group included familiar faces—Martha Van Rensselaer, Sarah Louise Arnold, Isabel Bevier, and others. Mr. Hoover made an inspiring and effective presentation of the hardships and suffering the war had brought to the peoples of Europe and the Near East and explained what we could do to help. Our job, as he described it, was to persuade housewives to

conserve clothing and food, especially wheat and sugar. He wanted
us to show homemakers how to keep nutritional needs in balance
while using substitutes so that more food would be available for
overseas shipment.

W. B. Ayer, a Portland philanthropist who was the Federal
Food Administrator for Oregon, had various assistants on his committee. Mr. Childs, manager of the Portland Hotel, where we held
committee meetings and lunched as guests of Mr. Ayer, was in charge
of the conservation program for institutions. My task in the food
conservation program was to marshal the facilities of the School of
Home Economics to stimulate "Hooverizing" in the homes of the
state.

Our phase of the program consisted of five principal activities:
(1) In our regular courses we included instruction in remodeling old
clothing and conserving food so that the students could carry this
information into their own homes and communities. (2) We added
short courses for homemakers and students not registered in home
economics. (3) The home economics extension staff and the resident
staff gave talks and demonstrations at women's clubs, teachers' and
parents' meetings, high schools, Red Cross units, fairs, and other
meetings. (4) We sent out information to newspapers and distributed
pamphlets. (5) We arranged food and clothing exhibits for use not
only on campus but also at fairs and meetings throughout the state.

Much of the material published by the Food Administration
was distributed through my office. The heavy correspondence averaged nearly 400 outgoing letters a month during the busiest year. It
was a crash program that had to be accomplished rapidly if it were
to be successful. In addition to the campus and state-wide responsibilities, the work required me to make two more trips to Washington,
where I arrived late at the meetings because of the difficulty of train
travel in wartime.

ANOTHER CLOUD on the horizon in my first year as dean grew black
and ominous. My mother had not been her usual vigorous self for
a time, although she made no complaint. In the spring of 1918 word
came that she had become critically ill. Both President Kerr and
Mr. Ayer agreed that I should go home, and arranged for others to
take care of my duties during my absence.

Our family physician, Dr. Miller, could not diagnose the extent of Mother's illness. Uncle Roz insisted on taking her to Kansas City. The doctors there found a tumor on her spinal cord and recommended surgery, although the hope for recovery was not great. All the family, except Nell, whose son had been born only a few days earlier, assembled to be with Mother in this crisis. The surgeon was Dr. Arthur E. Hertzler, who later became well known as the author of a book on pioneering medicine entitled *The Horse and Buggy Doctor*. As Mother was wheeled into the elevator to go up to the operating room, I kissed her and told her that Ada's husband Ted would go into the operating room with her. She whispered, "And God, too." After what seemed an interminable time, she came down again. She smiled wanly at us and whispered, "God was with me," and lapsed into a coma. At daybreak the next morning we stood around her bed as she breathed her last. The stillness was broken by Uncle Roz, who said, "A great woman has gone. She taught us how to live."

I felt that Father needed someone with him at this difficult time and offered to give up my position in Oregon to make a home for him, but he protested, "If anyone gives up his work, I should, for I have almost finished my life and you have just started yours." I did stay through the summer to help him sell our large house and dispose of belongings not needed by him or his daughters. Father finished out his term as postmaster in Macon and then went to live in Springfield, Missouri, with Ada and Ted and their small daughter, Mary Louise, named for Mary Louisa McGinnis Milam.

After I returned to the campus, Mother Kidder's illness confined her to her rooms in Waldo Hall. In the evenings, groups of students often came to play musical instruments or sing under her window. Her colorful life came to an end on February 29, 1920, when the influenza epidemic was at its height. Because public gatherings were restricted, no funeral was held. Mother Kidder's body lay in state in the vestibule of the building that had been the crowning achievement of her career. An ROTC honor guard stood beside the bier as students, faculty, and townspeople filed by to pay their respects to a beloved public servant and devoted friend. Appropriately, this building—converted now to other-than-library purposes—bears her name: Kidder Hall.

Mrs. Kidder left her personal copy of Emerson's *Society and Solitude* to Withycombe House. The remainder of her set of Emerson she willed to Eric Englund. "There is a touch of affection and inspiration in an experience of that sort," Eric later said. "I have that set of Emerson with me in London now [1956]. I had it with me in Stockholm when I was on assignment in the foreign service there; it has been with me since it arrived at Wisconsin, when I was doing graduate work there, and will always be with me."

Kidder Hall

10. Expansion

Home wasn't built in a day.

—JANE ACE

THE SIX DEPARTMENTS OF INSTRUCTION in the School of Home
Economics at Oregon State University grew out of the single
one established by Margaret Snell in 1889. When the School was
established in 1908, it consisted of two departments: Domestic
Science and Domestic Art. Several times between 1912 and 1915,
Dean Henrietta Calvin recommended dividing the two departments
into smaller units, but the only change accomplished then was giving
the old departments new names: Household Science and Household Art.

The DEPARTMENT OF HOUSEHOLD ART—which eventually became
the DEPARTMENT OF CLOTHING, TEXTILES, AND RELATED ARTS—had a
staff of one professor and six instructors at the time I became dean
in 1917. Mrs. Helen Bryce Brooks, who joined the faculty the same
fall I did, had been head of this department but resigned about the
time I became dean and soon remarried. For her replacement we
brought a truly wonderful person, Helen Lee Davis, from the Midwest. A graduate of Vassar College and Columbia University, Miss
Davis had made a fine reputation at the University of Nebraska.
Under her guidance the department developed strong areas of
coursework in design and construction of clothing, in the study of
textiles, and in applied design in house decoration. She built up an
excellent staff. Alma Catherine Fritchoff, who had been Miss Davis'
student at Nebraska and who later received a master's degree from
Columbia University, joined the department in 1918 for three years,
left for a time, and then returned in 1925 to serve until retirement.

After Miss Davis's retirement, Miss Fritchoff became department head. Gertrude Strickland, a graduate of Texas State College for Women, joined the department in 1920. She later took a leave of absence to work in a department store in Buffalo, New York, and upon her return, basing her coursework on what she had learned there, introduced commercial clothing design. Later Miss Strickland succeeded Miss Fritchoff as department head. The competence of these and other women too numerous to mention has made the department one of the strongest in the School of Home Economics. Its work has remained consistently centered, as its present name implies, in clothing, textiles, and related arts.

The DEPARTMENT OF HOUSEHOLD SCIENCE, on the other hand, became a catch-all for new areas of subject matter. When I became dean, its courses included foods and cookery, dietetics, catering, housewifery, house sanitation, household administration, institution management, the beginnings of child development and parent education, and research work. The staff consisted of eleven members. In addition to myself were Assistant Professors Alice Marks Dolman, Sarah Louise Lewis, and Alma Grace Johnson. Among the seven instructors were Sibylla Hadwen, Mary E. Koll, Inez V. Bozorth, Minnie Kalbus, and Sara Watt Prentiss. Mrs. Dolman soon took a position elsewhere. Miss Lewis left to become head of home economics at the University of Nevada. Miss Johnson became head of our new department of Household Administration.

In reorganizing the departments, we left courses related to foods, cookery, dietetics, and nutrition in the HOUSEHOLD SCIENCE DEPARTMENT and in the 1920's its name was changed to the more appropriate title, DEPARTMENT OF FOODS AND NUTRITION. Under the leadership of Jessamine Chapman Williams, who came from the University of Arizona in 1923 to become department head, a great deal was accomplished in upgrading the quality of instruction. Experimental work provided a scientific base for instruction in nutrition and dietetics. Instruction in new processes in the handling and preservation of foods was incorporated in the coursework. When Margaret L. Fincke joined the staff in 1935 with a half-time appointment in research, even more vigorous efforts were turned toward incorporating the new scientific information available.

THE DEPARTMENT OF HOME ECONOMICS EDUCATION was the first new department organized after I became dean. It had deep roots, in that the preparation of teachers for secondary schools has always been an important phase of the home economics movement. The Lake Placid conferences gave considerable—perhaps primary—attention to teacher preparation, and the American Home Economics Association has always stressed it. On our campus Dr. Snell did not teach any courses specifically for preparation of teachers, but dozens of her graduates became teachers. She sensed the importance of introducing homemaking subjects into the lower schools, and near the end of her term of active service she wrote an article for the Portland *Oregonian*, which concludes with this comment:

> *I believe the time is not far away, even in the Oregon public schools, when the household and its management will be one of the most important factors in the educational system, as it is now the most vital in national prosperity.*

As mentioned elsewhere in this book some of Dr. Snell's former students became prominent home economics educators.

The Nelson Act of 1907, which provided support for teacher preparation in agriculture and mechanic arts, led to the establishment of a Department of Vocational Pedagogy at OAC in 1909. Under the direction of the courtly Professor Edwin D. Ressler, this department broadened its scope to include preparation of teachers of domestic art, domestic science, and commercial subjects. To encourage adding of homemaking courses in the high schools, a number of us on the faculty went into communities of the state to discuss the new field with parents, teachers, and school administrators. One of my experiences will serve to show the community interest. One night when I was giving a talk in the town hall in Pendleton, the fire bell in the tower overhead began to clang, shaking the whole building. The audience dashed out to give assistance in fighting the fire. A half hour later, with the fire safely extinguished, they began to return. They wanted to hear more and kept me answering questions for an hour or more afterwards. Within the next year or so, Pendleton High School introduced a program of home economics. As other high schools followed this trend we had an increasing demand for graduates who combined technical proficiency, a knowledge of the theory and practice of teaching, and qualifications for certification as teachers.

During 1916-17, Mrs. Prentiss helped arrange an experimental program of student teaching at the Corvallis High School. Enactment of the Smith-Hughes Act of 1917 gave further impetus to the preparation of teachers in several fields, including home economics. At OAC, the School of Vocational Education established in 1917 included a Department of Home Economics Education. Staff members in the new department received appointments in both the School of Home Economics and the School of Vocational Education (later the School of Education), and the Department of Home Economics Education has continued to serve both schools as a joint department to the present time. Hatty Roselle Dahlberg, whose education had included study at Stout Institute, University of Wisconsin, Columbia University, and OAC, and Bertha Stewart Davis, who held degrees from OAC and Columbia University, were the first staff members of the new department. Lura Keiser, who had studied at Grinnell College, Columbia University, and OAC, was the critic teacher at the high school. Gladys Whipple (Goode), who had studied at Whitworth College in Tacoma and OAC, soon joined the staff as a critic teacher in household art. By 1920, we had arranged for opportunities for student teaching experience in different types and sizes of communities.

In 1924 Florence E. Blazier became head of the department, a position in which she served until her retirement in 1950. During a quarter of a century her strong sense of purpose and dynamic leadership brought recognition to the institution as having an outstanding teacher education program at both the undergraduate and graduate levels. She gave continuity to the development of public school home economics programs throughout the state. Graduates of her department were much sought after for teaching positions both in state and out. In 1939, May DuBois, a graduate and former faculty member of Colorado A & M College, joined the department as an assistant professor. Miss DuBois later received a Ph.D. degree from Ohio State University and, after Miss Blazier's retirement, served as department head from 1950 to 1968.

In 1919 THE DEPARTMENT OF HOUSEHOLD ADMINISTRATION became the second new department formed. It included the following areas of subject matter: a new course called Introduction to Home Economics; the well established coursework in house sanitation, housewifery, household management, and home nursing; and the developing new field of child study, nursery school management, and parent education—an area that eventually (in 1966) provided the basis for a separate DEPARTMENT OF FAMILY LIFE.

Alma Grace Johnson, a graduate of Indianapolis Teachers' College, Purdue University, and Columbia University, became the first head of the Household Administration Department and guided it through its early period of innovation and growth. She became widely recognized as an authority not only in household management but also in budget building and management in allied fields. Tall and gracious, almost stately, Miss Johnson sometimes awed new students with her high standards of organization and scholarship until they came to know her better and realized the advantages of working with a person of such competence. Her untimely death in April 1933 while she was passing through Salt Lake City on her first sabbatical leave cut short a promising career. Mrs. Prentiss became department head and served in that position until her retirement in 1952.

The study of child development on our campus had its roots in a series of notable visits by an outstanding home economist from England. Alice Ravenhill, Fellow of the Royal Sanitary Institute and Lecturer on Hygiene, King's College for Women, University of London, was the principal guest speaker for the six-day Home Makers' Conference in January 1916. Her lectures and short courses gave us all inspiration and enthusiasm and also an insight into international aspects of the home economics movement. She later described the first conference she attended on our campus in these words:

> The sessions were twelve in number, each of four hours. For six or seven out of these eight hours a day the hall was crowded to suffocation. The lecturers had hard work sometimes to escape from the crowds of eager questioners anxious for fuller details of various points. Extra sessions had to be held to meet the demand. The comprehensive programs given and the appreciation of its packed audiences carries at least two lessons

with it: first, the progressive spirit and the praiseworthy stand-
ards of an agricultural college which presents it and the high
efficiency and zeal of the faculty of Home Economics which can
plan and carry through to a splendid success; second, the evi-
dence thus afforded of the real craving of our home-makers for
information on a wide range of subjects.

Although Miss Ravenhill spoke on a variety of topics related to
home economics, it was her discussions of child growth and development — "Nature and Nurture," "How to Observe Children with
Intelligence," and "Recreation for Young People"—that seemed so
fresh and meaningful to us. A native of Snaresbrook, England, Miss
Ravenhill had become a popular lecturer on home sanitation and
home nursing in England. She had served as Secretary to the Royal
British Nurses Association and on the staff of a county council in
Yorkshire as a specialist in healthful home living. On her first visit
to the United States she had met psychologist G. Stanley Hall at
Clark University, which she termed "the birthplace of child study,"
and had an opportunity to see the work of Jane Addams in the slums
of Chicago. When she returned to England, she helped establish a
degree course for women in Social and Household Science at the
University of London. In one of her studies of the biology of childhood, she investigated the nature and requirements of sleep; in
another, the place of play in the educational process. She visited
many schools and playgrounds and through keen observation
amassed the information that made her lectures so meaningful.

Miss Ravenhill's visit to our campus in 1916 had such an impact
that we invited her back four times: once again for the Home
Makers' Week and three times for short courses in the Summer
Session. Each time she spurred us on to do more to provide facilities
for observation and study of the growing child. In 1917 we introduced a one-credit course called Mothercraft. Miss Ravenhill taught
it first as a three-week summer class. When added as a regular course,
it proved successful because of the character and caliber of the
women who developed the one course into a full curriculum. Many
people on the staff had a hand in its development; two of them
deserve special mention here: Sara Watt Prentiss and Vera Haskell
Brandon.

Mrs. Prentiss, a young widow with two small sons, came to
OAC to work for a degree in home economics. She had attended

the University of Washington and had taught in grade schools before her marriage. Following her husband's death, she prepared to return to teaching. After her graduation from OAC she joined our staff and was the first to teach Mothercraft as a regular course. She grew professionally with the department, taking advanced study at the Merrill-Palmer School in Detroit and at the University of Chicago, University of Minnesota, and University of California, where she received a master's degree. On sabbatical leave she studied at the State University of Iowa and traveled in Europe. She also served two years with the Extension Service in California. She became our first Professor of Child Development and Parent Education.

Twice while Mrs. Prentiss was on leave, we added someone new to the staff to teach her courses. The first of these became a permanent faculty member. Like Mrs. Prentiss, she too was a widow who had returned to college after her husband's death. Vera Haskell had graduated from our School in 1911. She taught in Portland three years, married Henry Clay Brandon, and moved back to Corvallis when her husband was appointed to develop a new department of industrial arts on our campus. When Mr. Brandon died in 1927, leaving Vera with three young daughters, she returned to college to study for an M.S. degree with a major in child development. She spent a spring term at the Merrill-Palmer School where Winifred Harley, the child specialist from England, was in charge of preschool education. Mrs. Brandon subsequently studied child development under the direction of Dr. Ralph H. Ojemann in the Department of Child Welfare at the State University of Iowa, where she received her Ph.D. degree in 1936. While Mrs. Prentiss devoted most of her time to the undergraduate program, Mrs. Brandon developed graduate work in the field of child study, and at one time had one of the larger programs of its kind in schools of home economics throughout the country.

On another occasion when a substitute for Mrs. Prentiss was brought in, we were able to add the Englishwoman, Winifred Harley, to the staff for a year to direct the nursery school. With Maud Wilson, who was in charge of Home Economics Research, and Professor Herbert R. Sinnard of the Architecture Department, Miss Harley helped design our nursery school building. The converted dwelling (Covell House) that we had used for twelve years was to be razed to make way for the new chemistry building. Instead of makeshift facilities, the new building would have a light and airy dining and inside play area. It would have suitable lockers, lavatories, and kitchen and provision throughout for areas where college students and researchers could observe and make notes without disturbing the children. A covered play shed and lawn area were to be equipped with apparatus adapted to the needs of preschool children. In addition to having Miss Harley's assistance with the design, another fortuitous circumstance helped bring the dream into reality. In a time when funds for new construction were difficult to obtain, we had a friend in an important position. Charles D. Byrne, Secretary of the State Board of Higher Education, realizing the effectiveness of this sort of training and the need for adequate facilities, worked out a financial plan whereby the construction could get under way. The Orchard Street Nursery School was completed and ready for occupancy in 1939.

In the meantime, before the first nursery school was opened in 1926, we began observation of child growth and development and practice in child care in another way. Early in 1916 the College rented and later purchased Governor Withycombe's house on Monroe Street. President Kerr called me in and told me the School of Home Economics could have it for a home management house. "Really?" I exclaimed, and Dr. Kerr laughed heartily. The Withycombe house was one of the finest in Corvallis and bordered the campus. We had reason to be joyous. We put to good use the $700 the Oregon Commission for the San Francisco Fair returned to us, using it to buy furnishings and equipment.

The next fall we began a regular schedule which permitted six senior girls and an instructor to live in the home management house for a period of six weeks. Each student took her turn a week at a time as hostess-manager, housekeeper, cook, assistant cook, laundress, and (later) child director. After two years of experience in operating the practice house we began making a baby's care a regular part of the education of our students. The mother of Patsy, our first baby, was a war widow and a graduate of our school who wanted to work toward an advanced degree and needed help with her little daughter.* The second year we had Peter, the son of a young mother and an elderly father. The marriage was not a congenial one, and

---

* When Patsy came to see me in 1967 she was a grandmother and was managing two nursery schools in California.

Peter had suffered accordingly, but he showed much improvement under practice-house care. Jimmy was in poor physical condition on his arrival but made rapid improvement. He did not remain the whole year because his parents made up their differences and took him home in March. Paul's mother and father were brilliant Reed College graduates, but the mother had suffered from influenza while carrying the baby and Paul was born prematurely. Being under-nourished, he had a feeding problem and a tendency to rickets. He, too, showed remarkable improvement. His mother died when he was six months old; the father later re-married and provided Paul with two little sisters after Paul's return home.

For more than 40 years—from 1918 to 1959—our home economics students had practical experience in caring for babies, and thereby gained confidence in their ability to care for small children. They took a great interest in this phase of their education and were grati-fied by the obviously beneficial results of their affection and care. It was not uncommon to see one of the girls pushing a baby carriage across the campus, sometimes accompanied by one of the other girls, sometimes by a young man. In later years many graduates have testified that the home-management-house experience proved of great benefit to them when their own children arrived. A further benefit of the program was that about one hundred babies received the finest care and affection. The home management house could not, of course, substitute for a normal home, but it offered far better care and more security than was possible in most baby homes, and perhaps in many foster homes.

Each baby underwent a thorough physical examination before he came to us and had the periodic care of a physician. Despite these safeguards, however, one baby died in his crib one morning just before noon. The death was found to be due to an enlarged thymus gland, and the medical authorities assured us there was nothing we could have done to save the child. The parents seemed grateful for the care given their baby and fully satisfied that death could not have been avoided. Babies who did not have homes to return to were much in demand for adoption, but we left to state officials the selec-tion of homes for them. Several were adopted by Corvallis families.

To the Covell home, purchased in 1924 as a second home man-agement house, a nursery school was added two years later. Students could then observe and work with a wider age-range of children. The

Covell unit became the nucleus for the Orchard Street Nursery School. A second nursery school, Park Terrace, was added in 1945. Nursery schools are still a part of home economics programs and a vital part of the Family Life Department. The babies, however, have gone from the home management house. All over the United States social workers seemed to oppose babies in college home management houses, on the basis, as I understood their opposition, that there was a weekly change of student "mothers." They failed to bear in mind that a faculty member kept her residence in the house and gave the baby the security of a substitute mother. It is my opinion that in contrasting the situation of home management house babies with those in large baby homes, where the nurses have little time to do other than care for the babies' physical needs, the home management house babies fared far better in development. The outcome of the opposition of the social workers, I believe, has made it impossible to continue to offer students experience in child care in home management houses in most states. I believe it has been a great loss to the program in home management houses—both to the girls who can no longer benefit from this phase of their education and to the children who might have benefited from the care.

The third new department, the DEPARTMENT OF INSTITUTIONAL MANAGEMENT (at various times called Institution Economics and Institution Management) developed gradually before its establishment in 1921. In Dean Calvin's time, we announced elective courses in quantity cookery and added new courses from time to time. For successful development we needed more than courses. We needed a laboratory—something like the Tearoom at the Fair. We could use Waldo Hall dining facilities for special banquets but could not disrupt the schedule regularly.

In January 1916, when the equipment we had used in San Francisco arrived on the campus, we put it into use on a modest scale. By remodeling space in the northeast corner of the basement of the new Home Economics Building we obtained an area large enough for a small dining room and auditorium and a partially equipped kitchen. Sometimes when President Kerr brought a group of legislators or other important personages to the campus we prepared meals for them. We also fed participants in the Farm and Home Week. We did so under difficulties, however. Once after entertaining the legislators it took until midnight to get the dishes washed and things put back in order. These occasions led to a wholesome feeling of esprit de corps among students and staff, but only because they were special occasions. It would not have been possible to carry on regular meal service with the facilities we had then.

During World War I, feeding the men of the Student Army Training Corps gave some opportunity for the girls in home economics to gain experience in quantity cookery. In 1918 Mary Elizabeth Koll (Heiner), a graduate of the University of Chicago and daughter of the chef at the South Shore Country Club in Chicago, developed a practical laboratory by operating a dining room in the first floor of a small apartment house on Park Terrace. She scheduled instruction in such a way that every girl had a turn at planning menus, purchasing, preparing meals, and serving. On a limited scale, the results were satisfactory even though the laboratory was a makeshift affair. In "The Calorie House," as some boarders called it, we accomplished a good deal at little or no expense to the college.

Not until the central wing of the Home Economics Building was completed in 1920 did we have adequate facilities for giving students laboratory experience in quantity cookery and dining room management. The third-floor kitchen, with a gorgeous view of the rolling hills to the north, was well planned and well equipped. The large open area on the south side of the top floor became a tastefully decorated, conveniently arranged Tearoom.

In 1921 when we organized the new department, Sibylla Hadwen, Director of Women's Dormitories, became its first head. Miss Hadwen, a Canadian, had received her education at Lyceé Fénélon in Lille, France; St. Luke's Training School for Nurses in San Francisco; and Macdonald Institute at Guelph, Ontario. Her assistant, Melissa Hunter, was a graduate of Indiana University and later of the University of Chicago. One of our graduates, Winifred Hazen, also served as an assistant in the early years of the department. In addition to the Tearoom in the Home Economics Building, they had the dining facilities of the new Margaret Snell Hall (now Extension Hall) to use as a laboratory.

Fern Willard Gleiser, a former Willamette University student who had received her B.S. degree from the University of Washington in institution management, took charge of the Tearoom in 1926. Under her guidance it enjoyed its most successful period. Emphasiz-

ing savory, well balanced meals gracefully and cheerfully served, it
had no lack of customers among faculty, townspeople, and students.
The department did an excellent job of preparing young women to
take responsible positions as food service managers in hospitals,
company cafeterias, hotels, schools, and private clubs. Some of them
opened their own tearooms or managed restaurants for others. Fern
Gleiser herself went on to a more important position at Iowa State
College after she left OSC, and in 1964 retired as Professor of Institution Economics and Management in the Graduate School of Business at the University of Chicago.

With the completion of the Memorial Union in 1928, new and
larger space and equipment became available for feeding students,
faculty, and guests and for putting on large dinners and banquets.
Under the supervision of Melissa Hunter, who served in a dual
capacity as the Head of Institution Economics and Director of
Dormitories, and her assistant and later successor, Georgia C. Bibee
(Peavy), the Tearoom was moved across the quad to the Memorial
Union. These facilities and the dining rooms in the dormitories
provided the laboratory experience needed. Our graduates have
accomplished wonderful results in this field. They are a great credit
to society.

WHEN I BECAME DEAN in 1917, I was enthusiastic about our prospects
and potential. "The heads of the departments," I wrote in a report,
"are women with exceptional training, experience, and executive
ability . . . They have been fortunate in drawing to their departments strong women who are devoting themselves wholeheartedly
to their work. With proper organization, with such a staff, and with
adequate facilities for the work and proper support, the school cannot do other than prosper. . . . The school is bound to grow."

The department heads and I formed an administrative committee that met frequently to discuss problems and programs. We
constantly kept before us the need for wise selection of new staff
members, since the future of the school depended to a large extent
on them. At meetings and campus visits we kept on the lookout for
staff prospects. Sometimes we brought instructors for the summer
session to observe them as possible permanent faculty members. This
continual searching provided us with fine new teachers in this period
of vigorous growth.

We realized also that we needed to provide means of refreshment and enrichment for all of us. Sabbatical leaves, under which a faculty member could receive partial salary while away for an extended period, did not become available until the 1930's. In the meantime, we encouraged staff members to take time off from their regular teaching duties, when they felt they could afford it, to travel and study.

To provide for continuing professional growth for both faculty and students, we brought distinguished teachers and lecturers to the campus—at first for the annual Home Makers' Conferences and later for the Summer Session. In this way we became better acquainted with men and women nationally active in home economics. The first of these visitors was the witty, lively, original, down-to-earth little Nellie Kedzie-Jones. She liked to tell the story of how her far-reaching career in home economics got its start. When the president of Kansas Agricultural College came to dinner at her father's home, he commented on the excellence of her biscuits and asked if she could teach college girls to bake like that. "I 'lowed as how I could," she said and then commented, "That just goes to show that presidents *then* were more interested in biscuits than in Ph.D.'s." Beginning in 1882, Mrs. Kedzie taught home economics at Kansas Agricultural College for fifteen years and then at Bradley Polytechnic Institute for a few years before marrying Howard M. Jones, a minister. She kept an active interest in the home economics movement and was a much-sought-after speaker who had success in Canada as well as in this country. She first came to our campus for a Home Makers' Conference in 1915. Although she was approaching retirement age, she was persuaded three years later by Abby Marlatt at the University of Wisconsin to take charge of home demonstration agents for that state, a position she filled with energy and diligence for fifteen years. In 1925, Kansas State College awarded her, Henrietta Calvin, and Abby Marlatt honorary doctor's degrees. I kept in touch with the remarkable Nellie Kedzie-Jones for a quarter of a century beyond that time, my last note from her being dated October 1950.

For the 1916 Home Makers' Conference, Alice Ravenhill from England was a principal guest lecturer. Anna Barrows, the first secretary of the Lake Placid group, came that year also. For Summer Session in 1916 we again invited Miss Ravenhill and added Lulie W. Robbins, another founding member of the American Home

Economics Association, who was on the staff of the Children's Bureau of the U.S. Department of Labor at that time. Mrs. Mary Schenck (Woolman) from Boston and Columbia University was also an early visiting lecturer. When M. Elwood Smith replaced E. J. Kraus as Dean of the School of Basic Arts and Sciences, Dean Smith also became director of the Summer Session. He was as eager as we were to bring the best possible people to strengthen the summer program. These included in 1920 my friend and former teacher at the University of Chicago, Alice P. Norton; Marian Birdseye and Florence E. Ward, specialists in home economics extension; and Mrs. Calvin from Washington, D.C.

For several summers in the early 1920's Dr. Caroline O. Hedger came as the principal visiting consultant in home economics. She was at that time Medical Director of the Elizabeth McCormick Memorial Fund and formerly had been on the Board of Infant Welfare Society in Chicago. In World War I, she had been the representative of Chicago Women's Clubs in Belgium for the control of the typhoid epidemic, especially among children. Her classes and lectures on child welfare gave new impetus to our developing program in child study. Dr. Hedger reminded me a good deal of Margaret Snell—tall, large, but not overweight. An advocate of hygienic living, she wore men's shoes and decried the shoes decreed by fashion for women's wear. She was especially effective in discussing health habits for children. Her success is illustrated by the fact that we invited her to teach in the summer session six different years.

Other specialists in child care and development who came for various summer sessions included several from Merrill-Palmer School—Evelyn Eastman, E. Lee Vincent, C. Winifred Harley, and Katherine W. Roberts. Chase Going Woodhouse, later a Congresswoman from Connecticut, taught courses in the economic and social problems of the family for two summers. In home economics education, clothing and textiles, applied art, household management, institution economics, and other fields we were fortunate in bringing well-qualified summer instructors. In foods and nutrition, Florence B. King of Indiana, Mary Swartz Rose of Columbia, and Belle Lowe of Iowa State came in different summers.

In one instance I invited a professor to come for the summer to give weight to my side of a controversy with the faculty of another school. A group of men in the School of Agriculture had asked me to meet with them one morning to try to persuade me to ban *Chemistry of Food and Nutrition,* by Henry C. Sherman, as a textbook in our nutrition classes. They explained that they had met with a group of county agricultural agents the evening before and had decided that what Sherman said about the use of milk, fruit, and vegetables in place of meat in the diet was injurious to the animal industry of the state. They asked that we discard Sherman's book and replace it with one they would name later.

I listened with interest, concern, and amusement. When the chairman had finished his pronouncement, I told him that at first I thought they were jesting but soon realized that they were in earnest. I told them that they must realize that no group of individuals or any division of a college can choose the authority to be used by another group, that I was indeed sorry that they felt our teachings were injuring any industry of the state, but that our responsibility in the School of Home Economics was to choose textbooks and reference material in which we had the greatest confidence and which served the best interest of the health of all consumers. I added that if we tried to teach consumption of all types of food according to the wishes of the producers the only way such consumption could be achieved would be by increasing the capacity of the human stomach. I admitted I was flattered that they felt our teachings were as effectual as they seemed to believe. I did not say so, but I felt they showed a narrow point of view not only between the two schools but also insofar as the whole of agriculture was concerned. Dr. Sherman himself foresaw a shifting in demand for foodstuffs if the dietary recommendations he described were followed. In the textbook in question he had written, "An increased demand for these foods [milk, fruit, vegetables] and a correspondingly decreased (per capita) demand for meat, so far from causing any serious 'dislocation of industry' will help facilitate natural evolution of American agriculture."

Having met Dr. Sherman several times at Columbia University and having sat in his classes, I knew him to be an excellent lecturer with a mischievous twinkle in his eye. His discussion of a proportionately greater use of fruits and vegetables was so thoroughly documented in his text with research findings and statistics that there was no question about its validity. I watched for a chance to bring him to the campus for a summer session series of lectures. He was so well received when he came that he was invited back for the next two summers also. Several of the agricultural professors attended his lectures; never did the controversy arise again.

The first summer Dr. Sherman came, we had a notable group of visiting faculty. Benjamin R. Andrews, a pioneer in the home economics movement from Lake Placid days and the first secretary-treasurer of the American Home Economics Association, taught two courses in household economics that summer. Having helped introduce home economics into Teachers College at Columbia University, Dr. Andrews was well known to most of the staff, either as a teacher or writer. He was editor of Lippincott's Family Living series, and at that time was conducting tours to Europe. That same summer we brought another Columbia professor Mary deGarmo Bryan, at one time editor of the *Journal of Home Economics*, to teach institutional economics; James R. Patterson, a specialist in house planning and decoration came from Pratt Institute; Beulah Blackmore, a specialist in clothing and textiles came from Cornell.

As I look back now, I feel that the efforts we put into developing an imaginative summer program were well worth while. With limited resources, we did a reasonably good job.

East and middle wings of Home Economics Building in the 1920's

11. The AHEA

Home Economics . . . understands the meaning of its
mission to energize, vitalize, and spiritualize the
everyday life of everyday man and woman.

—MARY E. SWEENY

IN ITS EARLIEST YEARS, the American Home Economics Association
held its annual meetings in the Christmas-New Year's holidays.
The organizational meeting was held in Washington, D.C., in December 1908 and January 1909. Ellen H. Richards served as president in 1909 and 1910, when midwinter meetings were held at
Simmons College in Boston and at the W. T. Harris Teachers College
in St. Louis. For two more years, 1911 and 1912, when Isabel Bevier
had moved up from vice president to president, the winter meetings
continued—in Washington a second time and at Simmons College
again. Then in 1913, when Sarah Louise Arnold became president,
the meeting time was changed to midsummer and Cornell University acted as host. Since 1913 the national meetings almost always
have been held in the summer, a more convenient time for most of
those attending.

As mentioned earlier, the first meeting of the AHEA I attended
was at Western Reserve University in Cleveland in 1914. The next
year, when Martha Van Rensselaer was president, the Association
came to the west coast for the first time. About 200 delegates assembled for a four-day meeting at the University of Washington,
where Effie I. Raitt was head of the division of Home Economics,
and then moved to Oakland, California, the next week for continuation. Since the Fair was on across the Bay in San Francisco, one of
the evening sessions was held in the California Building at the
Panama-Pacific International Exposition. I was so busy with Tea-

room responsibilities at the time that the meeting left little impression on me.

In 1916 while Martha Van Rensselaer was still president the Association met at Cornell University again. In 1917 it postponed the annual meeting because of wartime conditions, but met twice in 1918 at Atlantic City, New Jersey, in March and at Hull House and the University of Chicago in June. Catherine MacKay of Iowa State College was president during this period. Edna N. White of Ohio State University—who moved to the directorship of the Merrill-Palmer School in 1920—was president for the 1919 meeting at Blue Ridge, North Carolina, and the 1920 meeting at Colorado Springs, Colorado.

I had attended the meetings in Atlantic City and Chicago and for the Colorado Springs meeting had two duties to perform. Because newspapers did not often send reporters to our meetings, some of the officers felt that our programs did not receive adequate coverage in the press. For the 1920 meeting, they appointed me chairman of the Pen and Press Committee. My duty was to provide reports of the meetings to daily newspapers and a general report of the convention to periodicals. My secretary, Zelta Feike (Rodenwold), who had gone to Colorado for another meeting, joined me in Colorado Springs to assist with the reporting. We had a busy time but found being publicity agents interesting. Officers of the Association told us afterwards that we had done our work well and that our service was appreciated.

Zelta and I accomplished something else at that meeting. Before leaving for Colorado, I had talked with President Kerr and he had given his support to a proposal we intended to make—that the Association hold its fifteenth annual convention two years hence, in 1922, in Corvallis. Swampscott, Massachusetts, had already been selected for the 1921 meeting place, and we wanted to get our bid in early for the following year so that we would have adequate time to prepare if we were selected.

Several of the members of the nominating committee—Isabel Bevier and C. F. Langworthy, I remember especially—talked with me about becoming a candidate for the presidency of the Association. They felt that it would be a convenience to me in planning the program for the 1922 meeting if I had available the resources of the Association that would come with the presidency. Their arguments were plausible but not convincing. To do her job properly the president of the AHEA needed to do a great deal of traveling to coordinate the work of the Association with that of other organizations, to attend as many state conventions as possible, and to accept speaking engagements. I could not see how I could carry on my work as dean of a school of home economics on the far-western side of the continent and at the same time perform adequately the duties of the national president. Since travel had to be by train I could envision spending the next two years of my life in Pullman cars. I thanked them for their support but told them firmly not to consider me a candidate for the presidency.

The Association accepted our invitation to come to Corvallis in 1922, and we began to make plans. At Colorado Springs attendance was about 300; at Swampscott the next year about 400. Initially, we began to plan for about 400, but as the time for the convention neared the reservations rolling in indicated that we might have twice that number.

A few months before the August date for the convention, the home economics department of the University of California sent us a telegram suggesting that we give up the convention in Oregon and permit San Francisco to take over since Californians could provide better facilities and could attract a larger attendance than we could in Corvallis. As a large attendance would tax our facilities, we gave this suggestion consideration. The arrangements committee discussed it and I talked with President Kerr. We decided to reply by wire that since the Association had accepted our invitation two years in advance and we believed that we could expect a good attendance and could provide adequate accommodations we would go on with original plans.

The Great Northern Railway provided a special train at summer tourist rates to bring the delegates to Oregon. It left Chicago on July 26, picked up additional passengers at St. Paul, stopped for a two-day tour in Glacier National Park, and came on through Spokane and Seattle, arriving in Portland early in the morning of July 31.

The father of Mary Woodward, one of our home economics students, was a prominent druggist and president of the Presidents' Club of Men's Organizations in Portland. When he heard of the coming convention of home economists he became enthusiastic over the prospect of this opportunity to show the visitors something of the wonders of the Oregon Country. He asked me to come to one of the meetings of the Presidents' Club and outline our plans. As a result of these discussions, the Portland businessmen arranged to take the delegates as their guests on a trip by private automobile up the Columbia River. What we now call the Old Columbia River Highway was only a few years old then and was becoming famous as an engineering feat as well as a spectacular drive through an area of unique scenery. The Portland men were proud to show it off, and this scenic trip proved to be one of the outstanding features of the trip west for many of the delegates. The Portland restaurateur and caterer, Henry Thiele, served a noon meal in the beautiful park at Eagle Creek before the return to Portland. The Portland school board put on a banquet for the visiting home economists that evening.

The 700 delegates who came almost overwhelmed us—but not quite. We housed them in Margaret Snell and Waldo Halls—single room $1.50, double room $1.00 per night—and had some overflow into the men's dormitory. Because students in dormitories furnished their own rugs, curtains, linen, and bedding, the rooms were a bit bare, but the visitors did not seem to mind. Sibylla Hadwen and Melissa Hunter of the Institutional Economics staff rounded up enough bedding, part of it coming from the University of Oregon. Meals were $2.00 a day. Inez Bozorth, who had helped manage the Tearoom at the Fair, was on hand to help with the food preparation and service. The central wing of the Home Economics Building had just been completed the year before and our new third-floor Tearoom was in operation. The new building also provided numerous rooms for section meetings and temporary offices.

A good many of our upperclass students attended the meetings and helped in registration, providing information and serving as guides, ushers, and bellhops. It was a folksy affair, and our staff, students, and alumnae welcomed meeting home economics pioneers like Isabel Bevier, Abby Marlatt, Edna White, Mary Sweeny, and Flora Rose. The town helped entertain the visitors, too, especially the Chamber of Commerce, who invited the entire convention to a picnic one evening at the Corvallis Country Club. The delegates, so they kept telling us for many years to come, appreciated the friendliness and simplicity—and economy. The weather cooperated to make it a pleasant August meeting.

I shall not go into detail in regard to the program, but it may be of interest to outline briefly the variety of topics discussed to see what sort of problems faced home economists at that time. The Foods and Nutrition Section gave a good deal of attention to the the "Health Crusade" in the elementary schools, to the need for research, and to the content of college curricula in foods and nutrition. Jessamine Chapman Williams, who later joined our staff, was section chairman.

The Textile Section discussed (a) what the homemaker wants to know about clothing and (b) methods of textile research. The Institutional Economics Section (a) called attention to the growing opportunities for women in hotel work, employees' cafeterias, school dining rooms, and tearooms and (b) discussed the training of hospital dietitians and institutional managers. The Institutional Economics section elected Sibylla Hadwen its chairman.

The Home Economics Extension Section discussed home demonstration programs and legislative, research, and training problems that affect extension work. The Home Economics Education Section concentrated on home economics instruction as related to community service and exchanged ideas on determining the demand and preparing for it at both the secondary school and the adult-evening-class levels.

In addition to the section meetings, we had addresses of welcome from Mary E. Sweeney, president of the Association, and President Kerr and speeches by Florence A. Ward, Caroline Hedger, Isabel Bevier, and about a dozen others. Miss Sweeny concluded her remarks with this observation:

> Home Economics is preparing for its duty and responsibility; . . . it glimpses its opportunity; visions its real service; understands the meaning of its mission to energize, vitalize, and spiritualize the everyday life of everyday man and woman.

This bit from Miss Bevier's Corvallis speech has been quoted a number of times:

> The passing days emphasize the necessity for wise expenditure of time, money, and energy on the part of everybody. Whether women understand it or not, forces quite beyond their power are giving them a part in the economic and political life of the

nation. Home Economics workers need to hear and heed the command, "Enlarge the place of thy tent and let them stretch forth the curtains of thy habitation; spare not, lengthen thy cords and strengthen thy stakes."

For the main banquet, our new Tearoom never looked better. In the sparkling light of the chandeliers hanging from the arched ceiling, the windows curtained in brick red draperies and the paneled walls in light beige gave their best appearance. Cut flowers, polished silver, and shining glassware on fresh, white linen helped add to the festive air. Guests overflowed the Tearoom and some groups were served elsewhere. All were having a wonderful time and were in a gay and happy mood. As mistress of ceremonies I made the usual introductions and presented the outgoing and incoming presidents of the Association. In keeping with the jovial mood of the evening, I introduced Mary E. Sweeny as the "expiring" president and Alice F. Blood, the new dean of Simmons College, as the "inspiring" president. Miss Sweeny's appointment as the first Executive Secretary of the Association was also announced at this convention.

It was a fine time to renew old acquaintances and make new ones. Isabel Bevier was one of the officers who came early and stayed late. She roomed during the meeting at Withycombe Home Management House, but when it closed after the meeting she came to my home as a guest for a few days. Because I had to spend many hours at the office winding up convention affairs, we necessarily had simple fare as food, but the few hours I could spend with Miss Bevier I have cherished through the years. Contrary to some people's impression of her as being austere and my own recollection of her in student days at Chicago, I found her friendly and inspiring—a choice and unforgettable person.

Helen Lee Davis, head of the Household Art Department, had done valiant service for the convention by arranging the details of the program. It fell to her lot to write the School's official report of the event when she was Acting Dean a short time later. In that report she said:

The attendance was the largest the Association has ever had. . . . The alumnae were back in surprisingly large numbers. . . . Altogether splendid recognition resulted for the School of Home Economics, the College, and the State. . . .

THE MEMBERSHIP OF AHEA increased in its first fifteen years—up to the time of the Corvallis meeting—from 700 charter members to 2,117 in 1922. Attendance at the annual meeting grew from 143 at the 1908-09 meeting to 700 at the 1922 meeting. Subscriptions to the *Journal of Home Economics* had almost reached the 7,000 mark by 1922. Since that time the Association has grown remarkably. In 1966 there were 26,901 members including 4,512 graduating seniors. The attendance of 6,112 at the convention in San Francisco in 1966 broke previous records. The *Journal of Home Economics* now has a circulation of more than 33,000 and a budget of more than $100,000 annually. At its headquarters in Washington, D.C., the Association maintains a permanent staff of fifty people who assist in planning the annual meetings, publishing the *Journal* and other publications, and carrying on other projects.

As Ellen H. Richards foresaw in founding such a national organization, the AHEA serves a vital, beneficial purpose. It provides a forum—oral and written—in its meetings and *Journal*. It has established a channel to the President, the Congress, and government agencies through which home economists may voice opinions and provide advisory services. It maintains liaison with other associations with related interests; it carries on an active public relations program to keep individuals and groups informed of current issues. It publishes bulletins, books, proceedings of conferences, and an attractive series of career leaflets called "The Wonderful World of Home Economics." It has produced a variety of visual aids available at low cost to anyone who needs them. I think Ellen H. Richards would be pleased with the way in which her Association has developed.

The designer of the symbol of the Association at one time was a member of our School of Home Economics staff. The Association's

historian, Keturah Baldwin, tells in *The AHEA Saga*—one of the books published by the Association—how the design was developed:

> *In 1926, the AHEA offered a prize for the best design for a symbol for the Association, one that would "suggest the idea for which the AHEA stands: the*

application of science to the improvement of the home." The winning design, submitted by a Chicago artist, Mildred Chamberlain, did not use the classical Greek and Roman lamps which symbolize knowledge, but instead the Betty lamp, the common portable light used in colonial homes.

We had the good fortune in 1930 of adding Miss Chamberlain to the OSU faculty as an associate professor of Clothing and Related Arts. In 1932-1933 she served as acting head of the department and in many ways added new vigor to the school. Her death in 1935 brought to an end a promising career.

THE OREGON HOME ECONOMICS ASSOCIATION had its beginning about the time of the Corvallis meeting of the AHEA in 1922. At that time the national Association announced a new policy in regard to affiliation of state associations with the national, with dues to both organizations paid through the state treasurer to nationl headquarters. Sixty-four home economists made up the charter membership in Oregon and the OHEA was one of the first twenty state organizations to become affiliated with AHEA. Most of the Oregon members were OAC graduates or OAC faculty members.

Edna Groves, supervisor of home economics in the Portland public schools, served as first president of OHEA. Katherine Kooken was the second president. As third president, Helen Lee Davis of our staff encouraged homemakers to take an active part in the organization and helped raise funds for a scholarship for a Chinese student. Alice Feike Wieman served two years in 1925-1927, and for two more years in 1951-1953. Florence Blazier, Frances Wright (Jonasson), Claribel Nye, Bertha Kohlhagen (Gregg), and May DuBois were among those who served as presidents in later years.

"We are what we have been becoming," said President Dorothy Sherrill Miller at the forty-sixth annual meeting of the OHEA in 1967. "Through the years ours has been a common and dedicated purpose." On a state level the Oregon association has carried on a local program complementary to that of the national association. In a quietly effective way it has provided support for the development of home economics within the state. It has provided inspiration for its members, created better public relations, and recruited women for home economics careers.

12. China

If you would plant for a year, plant grain.
   If you would plant for a decade, plant trees.
If you would plant for a century, plant men.

—CHINESE PROVERB

FRIENDS AND COLLEAGUES had a hard time understanding why I wanted to go to China in 1922. Even the day before I left, President Kerr asked me to reconsider. He had reluctantly approved my request for a two-year leave of absence without salary, but he still had reservations about my going for so long a time. The way a local newspaper interpreted my request for leave irked me a bit. The reporter seemed to think that I was being a martyr of some sort—which was not the case at all.

Willibald Weniger, Professor of Physics, saw the newspaper account and came to see me. "Why *are* you going?" he asked. "I think friends have a right to know." I explained as best I could why—after eleven strenuous years—I wished to get away for a while. First, I felt I needed professional growth as an educational administrator. I needed time and distance in which to view the structure we had built in the preceding decade. Enrollment in the School of Home Economics had increased from fewer than 150 the year before I came to nearly 600. Degrees granted in home economics had increased from 14 in 1911 to 86 in 1922. The staff had increased from just a few on the day I arrived to a total of twenty-eight. We had outgrown the first building built for us and had added a new wing. We had two home management houses. Demand for our services had expanded. As the college had grown from fewer than 1,000 students in 1911 to nearly 4,000 in 1922, we had sought to keep pace in providing some education for homemaking for a large proportion of the women students by including nonmajors in elective courses.

Demand for our graduates, as institution managers, dietitians, teachers, and extension workers—in addition to the demand for them as wives, mothers, and homemakers—was putting certain pressures on the school.

Through all this hurly-burly of rapid expansion, I had felt an uneasiness that we might not be developing along the most effective educational lines. It seemed to me that our curriculum had become too technical and that it neglected underlying breadth. The emphasis on training technicians rather than liberally educated men and women was by no means a local phenomenon. World War I had encouraged such emphasis. Engineers and agriculturalists as well as home economists in land-grant institutions across the country were trending toward technical specialization. I wanted to have time to think about this trend. I wanted to examine my own philosophy that a strong home economics curriculum *must* be based on a strong liberal arts foundation. I needed time to think about the pressure I was receiving from enthusiastic young staff members who wanted to introduce specialized courses and new majors. Long-perspective thinking could not be accomplished while I was absorbed in the day-to-day work of a vigorous, expanding school. My first reason, therefore, for asking for a leave of absence was to get away far enough and long enough so that I could think about home economics education in general and our School of Home Economics in particular.

I have always believed in the benefits of continuing education for all staff members, and I gave consideration to returning to Chicago for advanced work in nutrition or going to Columbia University to study educational administration. At this point, however, it seemed quite clear to me that working toward a Ph.D. was not the kind of continuing education which would be best for the School, nor for me. This was the second reason for going to China.

The words of Dean Sophonisba Breckinridge still lingered in my memory: "Ava, I don't see how, in that favored section, you can teach students how the other half lives." I felt that I should get out and see for myself something of the other side of the world. If the study of home economics could contribute to improvement of home life and society in one country it could do likewise in other countries. I wanted to learn face-to-face the reaction of parents, teachers, and students to home economics as an educational force.

Ten years in Corvallis had shown me I was living in a rather provincial community. Oregon Agricultural College was alert to the needs of the state but seemed to have only a limited interest in what went on in the rest of the world. We were smug in those days. Staff members had only limited opportunity to leave for any length of time. There were no sabbatical leaves. Many of the faculty, of course, had come from other parts of the country, and a few from foreign countries, but once they became established they tended to stay put. A third thing I was seeking in my leave of absence, therefore, was to break away from provincialism.

The idea of getting away had been growing in my mind for some time when Twila Lytton (Cavert), an American who had taught in a woman's college in Tokyo, visited Corvallis. She spoke at the Methodist Church one evening, telling of her experiences in Japan and discussing education for women in the Orient. She impressed all of us with the need for workers as well as for funds to support the work of educational mission boards. I made an appointment to talk with her the next day. "Do you think a woman's college in the Orient would be interested in introducing home economics?" I asked. "If so, where would be the best place?"

She had a ready answer: "The place is Peking, China. The university is Yenching." She told me of how Dr. J. Leighton Stuart was bringing together under one interdenominational university a number of Christian colleges that mission boards had sponsored in Peking. Among them was the North China Union College for Women, founded in 1908, the first college for women in China. It had sufficient prestige, she said, both from the standpoint of being a comparatively old school and as part of the new, larger, co-educational university that if a successful program of home economics were established there, other colleges would copy it. She thought efforts expended there would have a wide-reaching influence over a period of time.

Miss Lytton described the temporary quarters of the women's college of Yenching University as occupying an old royal palace that had been built in the time of Columbus. Behind its high walls, she said, the inner courts were divided with stone walls that had round gates festooned with wisteria. She spoke of the friendliness of the people and the challenge of the work, but warned also that teachers from the Occident often encountered hardships.

Miss Lytton took the initiative with the Women's Foreign Mission Board of the Methodist Church and with the New York office of Yenching University of China. Communications began between us. When asked to outline the conditions under which I would accept an appointment to Yenching University, I presented three proposals:

FIRST, that I take with me one of our graduates, Camilla Mills from Forest Grove, who was teaching in high school at that time. She had good home and educational backgrounds, some teaching experience in home economics, good health, a pleasing personality, and an eagerness to go to the Orient. She would devote her first year in China to the study of the Chinese language.

SECOND, that I spend at least six months of my first year in the Orient visiting schools and homes and talking with teachers and homemakers in order to obtain a background that would enable Camilla and me to introduce home economics at Yenching University adapted to the *needs of Chinese homes*.

THIRD, that upon my return to the United States, Camilla would carry the leadership of the new department until a carefully selected Chinese woman could be prepared—with advanced study in the United States if possible—to assume leadership and more adequately guarantee that the work would become indigenous.

The Women's Foreign Mission Board of the Methodist Church, Yenching University, and Dr. Frank O. Gamewell, general secretary of the China Christian Educational Association accepted the proposals. All seemed enthusiastic about the plan. The Women's Foreign Mission Board agreed to pay our transportation out and back and the missionary salary of about $800 a year for each of us. Yenching University added funds to permit me to take a month-long trip to the Philippine Islands.

In February 1922, Dr. Harry W. Luce, friend and co-worker of Leighton Stuart and vice president of Yenching University, came to the campus to speak to a student assembly. When I heard him declare, "We are facing the opportunity of the ages," heard him describe the significance of China and America as the two great nations bordering the "ever-narrowing" Pacific, and listened to his outline of the steps being taken to establish the new union university in Peking, I felt more than ever that I should go to Yenching University. As I came to know the situation better in later years, I appreciated how much Dr. Luce, whose son Henry launched *Time* magazine a year later, had done in enlisting support for Yenching University. At the time he came to Corvallis in 1922, he was on his way back to China after a lecture tour of American colleges.

When I explained to Dr. Weniger why I wanted to go to China, he said, "You could not afford not to go!" He added with a wry smile, "I doubt that any other dean on the campus would dare leave his job for two years and expect it still to be there when he came back." Perhaps I was risking my job, although I really did not think so. When President Kerr asked me to reconsider I told him I felt I must go and if my going placed him in an uncomfortable position he was free to replace me. He assured me he had nothing of that nature in mind. He and I both felt that Helen Lee Davis, head of the Household Art Department, would do an admirable job as acting dean and would have the complete support of the staff.

While plans went forward in the early months of 1922 for the Corvallis meeting of the American Home Economics Association, therefore, Camilla, who was teaching in Eugene, and I were preparing to leave for China soon after the meeting. On September 2, 1922, we boarded the SS *President Jackson* in Seattle. We had rough weather the first part of the voyage, but neither Camilla nor I missed (or lost) a meal. And what meals we had! Breakfast at 8:00, beef broth on deck at 11:00, lunch at 1:00, tea at 4:00 and dinner at 7:00. We walked the decks two miles a day, played shuffleboard an hour or so, danced in the evenings, but mostly lay wrapped in steamer rugs in deck chairs, reading, talking, writing, napping. After we had crossed the international dateline, the sea became as calm as Puget Sound. We saw whales spouting, and porpoises often played alongside the ship. The assistant purser took us up to the *radio* room, where we heard a message being sent from Honolulu to Guam. Such swift communication seemed a miracle, yet we learned that we could use radio to send a message home at 28¢ a word as compared with a dollar or more per word to send a cablegram after we reached land.

When the *President Jackson* docked at Yokohama to unload cargo, we had an opportunity to spend an adventurous day in nearby Tokyo. The woman in charge of the YWCA, Jane Scott, took us around the city in her Ford. She took us to dinner in the large, attractive home of a Japanese diplomat who was at Geneva as Japan's representative at the Peace Conference and had given the YWCA use of his home. Miss Scott invited me to come back the next summer to help evaluate the "Y" program in home economics.

On our way back to the ship in the evening a woman from another ship joined us. Miss Scott told us, as she put us on a streetcar for Yokohama, how to give directions to the ricksha pullers who would take us from the streetcar to our ship. But they apparently misunderstood, for they took all three of us to the *Taiu Maru,* the other woman's ship. We tried to explain that we wished to go to the *President Jackson.* For a time they seemed not to understand; then off they took at a trot through the streets of Yokohama. Up and down and around we went on a tour that under other conditions we would have considered interesting and informative. Finally, near midnight, they pulled up beside the gangplank of the *President Jackson* and smilingly charged each of us two dollars for the tour. On board our ship, the doctor asked what had happened. When we told him, he took us across the deck and pointed to the *Taiu Maru* not more than three blocks away, where the ricksha men had taken us before they "took us for a ride."

Another stop in Japan gave us opportunity to visit Kobe Christian College for Women, where Sarah Field, an Iowa State College graduate, was in charge of the home economics program. We sailed on down through Japan's beautiful, mountain-bordered Inland Sea and out across the East China Sea. Even before we could see the mainland of China we knew we were getting close because the sea became as yellow as the Missouri River, laden with silt from the Yangtze River. Unfavorable tides and rough weather delayed us a day in docking, but we finally moved into the harbor and tied up at the Shanghai Bund.

Not until we got ashore did I know whether I was to go to Peking or Manila from Shanghai. In connection with my suggestion that I visit homes and schools in China, the Board had recommended a trip to the Philippines, where with the help of American volunteers and the U. S. government a good deal was being done to adapt vocational education to the needs of the home. The recommendation appealed to me, and I was ready to go whenever the Board thought best, although I really felt it would be better to go to the Philippines after I had some firsthand knowledge of the situation in China. And that is the way the schedule worked out. The Mission Board representatives who met us informed us that we were both to go on to Peking in the next day or two.

They took us on a drive around Shanghai. The city surprised us because it was so British-looking. They took us to two teas, to dinner, and for further sightseeing. We lodged at a missionary home maintained by the Protestant missions and managed by two elderly English women. The Chinese bellboy who took our bags up flight after flight of stairs announced in his pidgin English that he had "two piecee man for room," meaning, we found, that he had only a room for two available. This suited us very well; Camilla and I did not feel like being separated at this point.

One of the people we met at this time became a lifelong friend. Eva Hayes, wife of Rev. Egbert Hayes, came to call on us. Egbert was in YMCA work and he and Eva had learned of our coming through J. C. Clark, head of the boys' work in the Shanghai YMCA. J.C.'s brother Roy, who had married Ruth McNary Smith the year before, had told me that I should be sure to get in touch with J.C. and his family in China. I knew that at this time the Clarks were in the United States on furlough but that I would probably meet them before I left China. My visit with Eva at that first stop in Shanghai was quite brief, but on my next visit to Shanghai the Hayes were staying in the Clark home and had room for me as a house guest.

From Shanghai, on the central east coast of China, we went on up to Peking in North China; a two-day trip by train. We found the women's college campus every bit as romantic as Twila Lytton had described it. The high walls around the college, the moon gates draped with wisteria, the courtyards where dates dropped onto the hard-packed clay, the crows cawing in the trees, the long-cued, black-coated coolies moving around caring for the place and carrying our chits (notes) all seemed so quaint and so new.

Camilla began her language study almost immediately at the North China Union Language School, one of the best in the country. We had a flurry of activity the first two weeks, with luncheon and dinner engagements, visits to homes and schools, speaking assignments, and a good deal of sightseeing. On our second Sunday in Peking, we were dinner guests in the home of Dr. Leighton Stuart, President of Yenching University. We met his eighty-year-old mother, who had founded a girls' school in Hangchow fifty years before. We also enjoyed meeting his wife, a charming southern woman, who was gracious and hospitable despite her invalid condition.

It was a fortunate circumstance for us that Dr. Stuart was in Peking at the time. From the time he had started to organize the new university, he had spent a good deal of time in the United States on speaking tours and with the governing board of the university in New York City. Financial assistance from many quarters had been good. Dr. Stuart had obtained a fine site for the new campus outside the city walls toward the Western Hills, and construction had started on the new buildings.

While engaged in the bustle of sightseeing and social engagements, I also had to arrange for tickets and to get money changed in preparation for my initial trip through the country. In nearly every province, money had a different value and often one city discounted money from another except for "coppers." So it was best to get a bag of coins before starting out.

On the morning of October 9, while packing to leave, I heard the soft scuffle of a coolie's cloth shoes on the porch outside my room and then a gentle rap on the door. The messenger handed me a cablegram from my sister Ada: "FATHER KILLED IN STREETCAR ACCIDENT. NO PAIN." The blow so stunned me it stopped all activity. How thankful I was for Ada's last phrase. Father had been well in July when he was in Oregon, and his "steamer letter" was cheerful, sympathetic to what I was doing, and understanding. It was hard to realize he had gone. Indeed, he seemed near at that moment.

Impulsively, I wanted to rush home to be with the other members of the family. The impracticality of such a journey and the unfairness to Yenching University, however, soon became evident to me and I tried to dismiss the thought. Somehow I got my things together and boarded the train that night to begin the schedule of visits that had been arranged for me.

At a stop enroute to Hankow, Loy Savage, an old friend from Foster Hall days, came on board and found me in my compartment. I had forgotten about arranging to see her and, I suspect, was not very good company at that time, although I greatly appreciated the time and effort she had spent in finding me.

After visits at Hankow on the Yangtze River in central China, I went to Wuchang and then on down the river by boat to Kiukiang (Chiuchiang), Anking, and Nanking, and from there by rail to Soo-

Map of the Far East indicating places visited by Dean Ava B. Milam in 1922-1924, 1931-1932, 1937, and 1948

chow and Shanghai. Stops along the way increased my respect and admiration for the work of the missions. I talked with school groups, through interpreters when necessary, and with groups of teachers. I took every opportunity my hosts would give me to visit homes, to see homelife in action, and to talk with homemakers. I once had lunch in the home of a General Wu, who was proud of the fact that his daughter had married into the Confucius family (75th generation).

In Nanking I had a busy schedule. One day I spoke six times (three times through an interpreter) and on the same day had luncheon and dinner engagements. I also had my first visit in China with Albert N. Steward, his wife Celia, and their children. Dr. Steward was then starting the second of nearly thirty years he devoted to teaching botany at Nanking University, collecting specimens for a book he later wrote on the vascular plants of the Yangtze Valley, and serving the university and Christian higher education in many ways. Through the years I had several visits with this OAC alumnus and with his wife, who had been a student in our School of Home Economics.

On the train from Soochow to Shanghai, I realized it was Sunday and my wire to Eva and Egbert Hayes might not be delivered. A fine-looking Chinese gentleman overheard me discussing this point with an English couple and offered to have the friend who was meeting him deliver me to the Hayes home if they were not at the station to meet me. I told him that would not be necessary, but without being asked he picked up my luggage and put it in his friend's automobile.

The chauffeur drove us out to Frenchtown and at 11:30 p.m. rattled the gate and aroused a porter, who let us into the compound where the Hayeses were living in the J. C. Clark home. Later I learned that my benefactor was a philanthropist, who had given a great deal of money to assist in health education for Chinese children. When I thanked him, he said, "I have two sons studying in Boston universities and I am sure American people there are being kind to them."

Mail awaited me in Shanghai and contained notes of sympathy from those who had heard of Father's death. Mrs. Leighton Stuart sent this little verse along with an understanding letter:

The weary ones had rest, the sad had joy that day and
  wondered "How?"
A Ploughman singing at his work had prayed, "Lord, help
  them now."
Away in foreign lands they wondered "How?" Their feeble
  words had power;
At home the Christians "two or three" had met to pray
  an hour;
Yes, we are always wondering, wondering "How" because
  we do not see
Someone unknown perhaps, and far away on bended knee.

The spirit of Mrs. Stuart's letter and verse lingered in my memory for a long time and came back forcefully a few years later when I learned of her death and thought of the great work her husband had to carry on without her help.

After a side trip to Hangchow and back to Shanghai, I went on south to Foochow, where I stayed at Hwa Nan College, the Methodist women's college for South China. Here I had time to relax and reflect in a setting filled with love and compassion for one who was in need of understanding. My strenuous program before leaving Oregon, the shock of my father's death, the rapid travel in central China, and the busy schedule at each place visited had brought on great fatigue. The doctor serving Hwa Nan College ordered me to delay leaving Foochow for Canton. She and my other hostesses succeeded in keeping me there until after Christmas. What was going on in my mind at that time is reflected in one of the letters I wrote from there:

> *Service is burned into the hearts and minds of these Chinese college girls. What a future lies before them! Hwa Nan College wants and needs home economics. China is ready for home economics. At Yenching we must start slowly and build on a good foundation. At first we will be able to prepare girls for high school and elementary home economics teaching but must count on having the Chinese college graduate spend a year or two in America for preparation for teaching of home economics in the women's colleges. Our standards must be as high as they are in other subjects and the best Chinese teachers must be a part of this adaptation.*

OAC, because of its standing, because of its nearness to the Orient, and because students can go through with less expense, can play a significant part in introducing the much-needed fourth "R" (Right Living) in education if we can find some way to help finance two or three Chinese graduate students at OAC for a year or two. I have faith that some way will be found.

Western U.S. colleges, I noted, had little influence in the Orient; it was the colleges of New England that were investing money and lives in China.

On January 4, 1923, having had several weeks of relaxation and pleasant company, I moved on. After brief stops at Amoy and Swatow, the SS *Hai Hong* took me into Hong Kong and up the Pearl River to Canton. In that time of struggle among the warlords, Canton was an uneasy place. U.S. Marines from the *Helena* gave some measure of protection for foreigners, but gunboats came up the river at night and fired at the forts along the banks. At the Presbyterian school for girls where I stayed, we heard firing begin about two a.m. the first night and continue for two hours. The room where I stayed, I was told, had been hit by stray bullets a few weeks before.

We escaped damage that night, but the next morning families along the waterfront were packing their household goods and moving out for fear of looting. They had heard that the soldiers had not been paid, and they knew army commanders sometimes gave their troops the privilege of looting for a day in lieu of pay. The girls at the school had worked out plans for us in case of firing or looting near the school. I found them good sports and we had fun in spite of the anxiety. One night we heard shots in the village next to us and the next day learned that it had been looted.

Despite the upset political conditions, I went about my usual tours of schools, shops, and homes. The hordes of people fascinated me with their industry—mending women on the streets making a darn or putting on a patch while the customer waited, children making toothbrushes (for sale in the U.S.), craftsmen carving ivory, jade, and amber and doing the most exquisite silk embroidery, men on all sides cooking foods that gave off tantalizing aromas. Coming home one day, we found the street packed with soldiers. Our rickshas had to dodge guns and sabers. I was glad to have my schedule in Canton completed and to be on my way to Manila.

My principal purpose in visiting the Philippine Islands was to see what had been done in guiding vocational education toward the needs of the homes. I had come to see and hear, but the schedule prepared for me included many speaking engagements. For example, in one 24-hour period, I gave a talk to the graduating class of Harris Memorial School in the evening, got to bed at midnight, and got up at 5:30 a.m. to speak to students at Hugh Wilson Hall at 6:30. Later in the morning I talked to high school girls and young women at the YWCA before going to the normal school to observe home economics work from 10:00 to 12:00. I was supposed to take a siesta before my three o'clock visit to two Filipino homes but found that the tropics stimulated me just as high altitudes did and I could not sleep.

One of the most memorable parts of the Philippines trip was a visit to Baguio, a day's ride by train from Manila. I went primarily to see the industrial work being done among the Igorots, but in addition I saw something of the life of the people, the missionaries, and the government workers. Baguio, a resort city at an elevation of 5,000 feet, had good facilities for visitors, and I met many interesting people both native and foreign.

With my tour of the Philippines completed, I went back to Hong Kong, thence to Shanghai, arriving there on March 1, 1923. For a week, I stayed again in the Hayes home at night, but made many calls and had many engagements during the day. The Commissioner of Christian Education in China, Dr. Frank O. Game-well, gave me much encouragement. "This is one of the most needed developments in our educational work," he said, "and I predict a splendid contribution."

After spending a day with a group of Chinese women in nearby Soochow, I began traveling again on March 9. Working northward toward Peking on a new deluxe train recently re-equipped with steel cars from America, I made stops at Nanking, Tsinanfu (Tsinan), Techow, and Tientsin. In Nanking I spent two days at Ginling College, sometimes called Smith College in China. At Tsinanfu, Catherine Vance, a YWCA secretary who had served at OAC a few years before, met me and acquainted me with a new type of transportation —a wheelbarrow in which one coolie could carry six or eight people at once! Despite the slushy, slippery, muddy streets and almost continual rain, we made a number of calls; once to a very wealthy home where we were quite cordially received, and another time to a home that was in turmoil and excitement because of preparations for a wedding.

At Techow I noticed partially open freight cars, like American cattle cars, crammed with Chinese men standing. I was told that about 2,000 men like these took passage to Manchuria every day in hopes of finding work in the fields. Enroute to her home at the mission, one of my hostesses in Techow took me for a ride through the city streets, an experience I found distressing, perplexing, enlightening, and weird. Later in the day another hostess took me on horseback to a village in the country. The first house we went into had a dirt floor and thatched roof. We were invited to sit on the "kang," an elevated floor under which heat from the one stove circulated and on which the family slept. Being so honored meant that we had been invited into the bosom of the family.

After church on the Sunday I was in Techow, my hostess and her husband—who were both doctors—took me through their hospital. One chart in the maternity ward read: "14th child in 17 years. 4 children living, 9 dead of tetanus from infection of the cord, one dead of dysentery. This mother delivered herself, two days later developed great pain in hip, running a temperature." Another chart read: "9 children born, 2 living." These apparently were not unusual cases.

At Tientsin, three girls from the Methodist Mission met me in a Model T Ford. Such luxury! It looked as big as a Pierce Arrow. I found my schedule called for a number of talks as well as visits to poor and wealthy homes. I spoke to 250 girls at Chapel in the Mission's middle school, talked on training for homemaking at Nan Kai University, had conferences with girls who were interested in studying home economics, had teas and luncheons with the YWCA girls, and had a generally busy few days.

All through my home visits, one feature of Chinese life that had particularly distressed me was the custom of binding feet. Many of the women in the interior parts of China at that time still wore shoes only three or four inches long. Custom demanded that beginning at about four years of age a girl's feet must be wrapped tightly all the time to keep them from growing, presumably to make them dainty and feminine! It was so pathetic to see these little girls hobbling around on their tightly bound feet, so full of pain. Since then, education has largely eliminated this painful custom, but what a powerful thing custom is! How few of us have the courage to stand out against the customs of our culture, even though they be painful and injurious to our well being. The women and children of China, I felt, were coming into their own, and the unbinding of feet was part of a larger emancipation that included unbinding of minds.

On my trip through China, I had soon become convinced of one thing: Camilla and I could teach the Chinese little about cooking or clothing construction. We might provide insight into nutrition and balanced diets, but in preparing foods for the table the Chinese are, to my way of thinking, the best in the world (the French second). In the art of seasoning—only poorly imitated elsewhere in the world —and in the skill of preparing a variety of dishes with a minimum of utensils and delivering them to the table piping hot, they impressed me as being unsurpassed. They knew how to prepare a variety of vegetables by cooking them for only a short time at high temperatures so that they retained their color, minerals, and vitamins. They used great imagination in producing superior soups; once I had chicken soup in Canton cooked and served in a half melon and found it the best I ever tasted. The Chinese used little sugar as compared with the Japanese and Americans, and as a result had better teeth. Some health practices, although surrounded by superstitions, had a valid scientific basis. For example, they would not drink unboiled water, believing it had evil spirits in it, and in every little school I visited I saw a pot of hot water ready for making tea.

I noted that mothers appeared to nurse their babies or have wet nurses for them for a much longer time than is customray in the western world. Cow's milk, even if it were available, would not have been accepted. The Chinese thought of cow's milk as an unpalatable animal secretion. I learned of one instance when mare's milk was used as medicine, but never as food. Soybean milk and soybean curd served to some extent as a substitute for cow's milk.

In clothing construction and care, through the ages, the Chinese had devised garments which suited their needs. They utilized every little scrap of cloth. Little pieces left over when cutting out garments, for example, were glued layer on layer on a big board and set in the sun to dry and were then cut into soles for shoes. These cloth shoes could be beautiful, with exquisite handwork on them. Leather was much too expensive to use for shoes; for heavy work the coolies often wore sandals with soles of jute or twine.

Top garments for most Chinese except those of the higher income groups were made of indigo blue cotton cloth. Both men and women wore coats and trousers, the coats for women being shorter than those for men. For dress-up, men and women who could afford them wore garments of silk, the patterns in the silk changing more often than the shape of the garment. In the winter the coats and trousers were padded with fluffed-up cotton or, when it could be afforded, lined with fur. The Chinese often spoke of temperatures in the winter as being so many coats cold. Children, whose garments were patterned after those of their parents, were bundled up in the winter to resemble roly-poly dolls.

It was the style for young women to appear flat chested, a look achieved by tightly binding their chests with strips of heavy muslin. The custom was receiving harsh criticism from the health and physical education teachers because it hampered adequate breathing and impaired the girls' skill at games, as well as contributing to all-too-prevalent tuberculosis. Some of the Chinese girls were becoming interested in athletics, though in the early days when schools and YM and YWCA programs were started in China, unnecessary physical exercise was considered wasteful and undesirable, to be avoided by both old and young.

What a fascinating China was opening up to Camilla and me during these first months in the Far East! There was so much to learn of the empirical knowledge the Chinese had acquired through the ages, and so much they could share with us. When Camilla met me at the train in Peking, she was bubbling over with enthusiasm. "I'm simply wild about this place," she said. She eagerly demonstrated her newly acquired ability to speak Chinese and tried to start teaching me useful phrases. She had become so accustomed to the friendly, family-like atmosphere that she even began to call me "Ava B." which pleased me greatly. I, too, was enthusiastic at this point. After having traveled 15,000 miles since leaving America it was good to stop long enough to unpack my trunk for the first time in seven months.

We had gathered a good deal of information that we needed to digest as a basis for organizing the new department of home economics for Yenching University. Before I had gone far in my first travels the previous fall, I realized that I needed more information than I could obtain on a quick visit to a home and that I needed it in a more complete and more permanent form than the notes I could take. On the boat going down the Yangtze River from Hankow to Nanking, therefore, I had devised a questionnaire that would provide the type of information we needed in our planning. Through the cooperation of the YMCA in Shanghai, the questionnaire was translated into Chinese, printed in pamphlet form, and sent to the middle schools, colleges, and universities I had visited. The teachers eagerly cooperated and encouraged their students to complete the forms. The Shanghai YMCA collected them from the schools and sent them in big bundles to Peking, where they were waiting for me when I returned.

From the 3,500 questionnaires distributed, we received 1,270 replies which were sufficiently complete to be used in the final summary. We felt that this response was excellent. Answers to the 60 questions gave us information about (1) the type and size of family and its customs and social life, (2) housing and sanitary standards, (3) the mother's responsibilities in the home, (4) the care and feeding of children, (5) the father's responsibilities in the home, and (6) industries in the home. All of this information would be useful in designing a program of home economics adapted to the needs of Chinese homes.

Students at Yenching University, fluent in both Chinese and English, translated the questionnaires. A research assistant from the Peking Union Medical College, which was supported by the Rockefeller Foundation and was closely associated with Yenching University, helped us in tabulating and correlating the results. Camilla and I pored over them for many hours; we conferred with people with long experience in China; and gradually a pattern for a curriculum began to evolve.

The spring months of 1923 passed swiftly. In addition to studying the questionnaires, making talks on what we were learning, and working out our plans, we visited Peking schools and many types of homes. We took excursions into the country to visit the Ming tombs, temples, the Great Wall, and many other examples of ancient art and architecture. We had a round of social engagements hard to describe or imagine. I felt then, and in a way I still do, that Peking is the most interesting city in the world.

In May, Jane Addams of Hull House in Chicago came for a conference at which she stressed the evils of child labor. For many years I had admired Miss Addams from afar, but while she was in Peking, and on several occasions later, I had an opportunity to get acquainted with this great, unselfish person who had done so much for humanity.

On June 6, I had my trunk packed and was on my way again, this time to Korea and Japan. In Peng Yang (P'yongyang) in Korea I stopped briefly and made some visits. I was particularly pleased to find a building set aside for home economics work in one of the mission centers. Some of the homes were clean and attractive, but many needed the application of sanitary science. I found a cordial welcome in Songdo and Seoul and spent several days in that vicinity. Miss Addams was a passenger on the train from Seoul to Taikyu, and I had an opportunity to chat with her again and have lunch with her. When I left the train at Taikyu, she went on to Japan. After speaking to the faculty and students of the girls' school in Taikyu in the afternoon and to the whole mission in the evening, and after being fed more than adequately with a delicious Korean feast prepared by the mission girls, I caught the train to Fusan (Pusan) and the night boat to Shimonoseki, Japan.

My month in Japan was a kaleidoscope of color and movement— the brilliant green of young rice, the deep green of somber pines, the blue of lakes, the dazzling spectrum of embroidered silk, the reds and yellows of temple and shrine. Swift trains knifed through farmland, forest, and tunnels; rickshas rolled through rain-splattered streets. I spent a good deal of time walking, riding, talking, speaking, listening, and writing. Once I lost my way in a beautiful park, but a giggling Japanese maid found me and helped me get to Kyoto in time for a speaking and luncheon appointment.

In Hiroshima my hostess at a girls' school operated for 40 years by the Southern Methodists asked me to speak to the girls in the morning and to the men who were studying English at night. In Kobe I got acquainted with the Japanese bathtub—like a big barrel with a firebox underneath—and with the Japanese custom of removing shoes before entering a home. In Nara I saw the home economics facilities in the normal school and watched dainty deer in a lovely park. My memory of Osaka, the Chicago of Japan, I am sorry to say, is of mosquitoes so tiny they slipped through the netting and would not let me sleep.

Kyoto lived up to its reputation as one of the most beautiful cities of Japan with its wide streets, beautiful parks, and delightful temples and palaces. I bought a ceremonial kimono to send home to Omicron Nu and the Home Economics Club. In a school in Kyoto I saw fifty girls in a laundry class ripping up their kimonos—just as the Korean women ripped apart their waists and skirts and just as the Filipinas ripped up their camesas (blouses) before washing them. Each time they laundered them they tore the garments apart and when they were dry and ironed, basted them together again. What a time-consuming activity!

In Tokyo, Kofu, Yokohama, Karuizawa, Nikko, and Kamakura, I went into homes and schools; talked with parents, teachers, and students; went into factories and into farming communities; stood in awe in famous and sacred places; and constantly compared the cultures of China and Japan—compared homelife and customs, habits of dress and foods, use of resources, and art and architecture.

Back through Kobe to Shimonoseki, I went by train—back across the Korea Strait to Fusan, and thence by train the length of Korea, into Mukden and down along the coast to the summer resort of Peitaiho. Camilla had received my wire and was there to meet me. We had fun bathing daily in the sea, enjoying the scenery, sharing news with each other, making new friends, and learning the art of bartering with the constant stream of vendors who came to our hotel. Years later, when my husband and I were in New York, he introduced me to the mother of John Hersey, the author of *Hiroshima* and other books. We found that she too had been in Peitaiho in the summer of 1923, had lived in the house next to ours, and had gone through the same typhoon we experienced.

In the letters I had been writing home for family, staff, and other friends there is a gap between July 29 and October 20, 1923. I had been rather conscientious about writing frequently—using slack periods in ship and train travel and other times when I could get time—to share with the people at home the experiences I was having.

In the middle of the long gap in the letters, the devastating earthquakes of 1923 took place across the Sea of Japan. In Tokyo and vicinity fires swept through acres of the fragile buildings, killed thousands of people, and left hundreds of thousands homeless. My letters did not even mention this event, mainly, I suspect, because I was going through a rather difficult personal experience at the time.

First came a serious illness while I was still at Peitaiho. Although I had been careful in what I ate and my hosts everywhere had been careful to give me only boiled water and well-cooked foods, somehow I had picked up a bug. Feeling weak and weary, I stayed in bed one day in the Methodist Missionary Home. The air became sultry and oppressive, warning of an impending storm. Winds began to whip through the open French windows and I could see a funnel-shaped cloud approaching; rain began to pour. When I got out of bed to close the windows, rain drenched me to the skin. The resulting chills made me realize I was really sick. The doctor who came to see me said, "You have amoebic dysentery."

"What does that mean?" I asked.

She replied, "You must behave yourself and do as I tell you or you will die."

I assured her I would rather not die just then. As soon as she was able to find someone to go with me she sent me to the Methodist hospital in Peking. Treating me as best they knew how at that time, the doctors gave me the nauseous drug, emetine, and fed me rice water, but no other food. I promptly lost 20 pounds, but the treatment was successful. In about three weeks all tests indicated that I was cured and I am happy to say that although I have been back to Asia four times since then tests have indicated that I have had no recurrence of this infectious disease.

While I was undergoing physical examination in the hospital, a report came back from the pathology laboratory of Peking Union Medical College that there was possible indication of malignancy. The report proved to be incorrect, but for a period of days I faced the possibility of radical surgery. In the following weeks I convalesced and as soon as my appetite returned I recovered quickly. When my letters back home resumed on October 20, I appeared to be in good spirits again.

IN OUR CLASSES in the fall of 1923—the first college-level classes in home economics in China as far as we knew—we had eight girls majoring in the new subject. One girl had come from Chengtu, a trip requiring six weeks for transportation from western China. We called her Kate because of her vivacious portrayal of Katherine in a long-remembered production of *The Taming of the Shrew*.

As we began our classes, Camilla and I felt that we could give the greatest help by teaching the fundamentals of nutrition, child care and development, household sanitation, and home management. In our teaching we emphasized proper diet for resistance to disease and for general good health. We had with us Henry Sherman's and Mary Swartz Rose's texts in nutrition and many federal and state extension pamphlets to use for reference material. We also had generally used texts and reference material for the other areas. In our instruction, we tried to avoid arbitrary conclusions regarding the content of courses. Our preliminary investigations showed us that we must not be too hasty in drawing conclusions about what to teach. We built our courses slowly and with an awareness that our students should share our conclusions about the needs of homes. The great differences of economic levels and the differences in customs in family life between China and the United States made us realize that the building of these courses must be done with the aid and approval of the Chinese if home economics courses were to become indigenous. We believed that we westerners could help open the way, but for home economics to become suited to the needs of China we were truly dependent upon the fullest cooperation of the Chinese. This cooperative endeavor among teachers and students we found pleasant and satisfying. It tended to break down barriers and to bring us together in outlook and activities.

In child care and development we had the benefit of consultation with Dr. Emmet Holt, the outstanding American baby specialist and writer for mothers of young children. He had long wanted to help China and had come to Peking to help train pediatricians in the Peking Union Medical College. He took a great interest in our questionnaires and said, "This is the most interesting project I have found in China; I hope to see it published." He did not realize this hope because he died suddenly a few days later.

It was our good fortune to meet other physicians from all over the world, specialists who were spending a year or more helping train Chinese doctors at the Rockefeller-backed Peking Union Medical College. I came to know a leader in the school for nurses, and many years later encountered her again when she was in charge of nursing education at American University, Beirut, Lebanon.

In November, Yenching University and the Peking YWCA cooperated in putting on a week-long Homemaker's Conference. Nearly 2,000 adults participated. The roomy YWCA building, formerly a large Chinese residence, provided excellent facilities with rooms for displays, demonstrations, discussion groups, short talks, story telling, shadow pictures, and improvised dramas. The conference staff included progressive Chinese homemakers, nurses, our Yenching University students, and the YWCA staff. Our girls made charts, helped put up exhibits, explained them to the visitors, and told health stories. They seemed quite at ease in speaking before audiences and really enjoyed acting out their stories and plays.

Originally Camilla and I thought of the conference as a means of getting parents interested in what their daughters were studying, but we soon found that many other people were curious. It was gratifying to see obviously wealthy women with stylishly tiny feet eagerly studying the health charts showing why feet should not be bound. Men and women of different income levels studied charts on budgeting, account books, food purchasing, and books for children. This homemakers' conference proved so popular and effective that the National YWCA Assembly recommended that all YWCA's in China put on similar conferences each year. The "Y" Assembly also agreed that they would do what they could to help introduce home economics into all middle schools of China.

Later in the school year, in February, the National Association of Colleges and Universities meeting at Ginling College in Nanking organized a home economics section with about 50 women as charter members. They elected Camilla chairman. At one of the sessions, I made a preliminary report on what we had learned from the questionnaires on Chinese homelife.

On our return trip from Nanking to Peking we stopped in Shanghai. Back from their furlough in the States, Julia and J. C. Clark invited us to stay in their home in Frenchtown. We found them a charming family, eager and energetic and glad to be "back home." Sons Winston (8) and Richard (6) and daughter Emogene (5) were back at play with other children of the half dozen or so "Y" and missionary families who lived in the compound. The Clarks had many visitors and guests, and their dinner table was a place of witty, purposeful conversation. The children remember J.C. as a gifted story teller, with an anecdote to fit every occasion, though it often seemed to young Richard that his father laughed harder than anyone else at his own jokes.

One morning when I needed to go into the city, J.C. suggested that I ride with him—on his motorcycle! Although I had never been on any type of cycle before, he persuaded me to accept his invitation. Wrapped up in the fur coat I had brought from Peking, I clung to the rear seat of the motorcycle and we dashed the sixteen miles into the city in a fraction of the time a ricksha would have taken and avoided the expense of a taxi.

Camilla and I spent a few additional days in Shanghai, and then one night Egbert Hayes took us to the station to catch the train to Nanking. To save $14 apiece we rode third class, an experience we did not care to repeat! After ferrying across the Yangtze in the early morning, we caught the Blue Express, on which accommodations were better, for the two-day ride back to Peking.

By this time I had become so interested and involved in the introduction of home economics in China that I considered asking for an extension of my leave of absence. I wrote to Acting Dean Helen Lee Davis and suggested that since things seemed to be going so well at home I was not needed there but that I was needed in China. She replied that I was wrong about not being needed in Oregon and that I should come back as planned. President Kerr urged me to return in time to prepare the budget for the coming year, so I gave up the idea of staying longer in China. One thing I felt I could do to help the work along was to leave a little money. My father's estate had been settled, and although my portion of it was small, I divided it among four of the girls' colleges (Ginling in Nanking, Hwa Nan in Foochow, Yenching in Peking, and Ewha College in Seoul) to encourage them to consider the importance of training for homemaking in the education of young women. My sister Lottie added a $500 gift for the same purpose.

I reserved passage to sail on April 12. While waiting in Shanghai to board the ship, I stayed overnight with the Clarks again and J.C. took me to a luncheon of the Returned Students Club, an organization of Chinese business and professional men who had studied in other countries.

As I left China in April 1924, I felt I was leaving a second home. The people had let me come to know them, to appreciate their personality, and to share something of their culture to which we younger nations owe so much. In this present time of strained relations between our two countries, I cannot help feeling that America still has many friends among the people of China. I cannot believe that the deep-rooted affection which grew up between the Chinese and our able representatives like Leighton Stuart, his parents and brothers, the many devoted YMCA and YWCA workers, and the medical and educational missionaries has vanished. The regard in which Chinese students hold their teachers is not dissimilar to the respect and deference they show their parents. As one Chinese boy said, in one of J. C. Clark's stories, "My parents borned me, but Mr. Fitch, my teacher, completed me." I have found through the four decades I have associated with Chinese students and teachers on both sides of the Pacific that they do not forget.

13. Return from China

The ruin of a nation begins
in the homes of its people.

—ASHANTI PROVERB

THE SHOCK of seeing my own country in the spring of 1924, after twenty months in the Orient, made a lasting impression on me. I recovered in due time from changes in hair and clothing styles. ("Even old grey-haired ladies," I wrote Camilla, "have *bobbed* their hair! Who knows? By the time I see you again I may have bobbed mine.") I have never reconciled myself, however, to the contrast in cultures and living standards between China and the United States.

In China I had come to know the representatives of an old civilization, a courteous people thoughtful of guests, full of humor and good nature, energetic, thrifty in preventing waste, modest in sharing their traditions, and seemingly happy with so few material things. A weary mother in a dirt-floored hut would share her last cup of tea. A hostess would easily part with an art treasure or family heirloom for a guest who admired it. Reverence for the aged, respect for teachers, graciousness in human relations were Chinese characteristics I had grown to appreciate. The Chinese had gone through oppression and suffering and from them had distilled wisdom, cheer, and generosity.

In San Francisco, on my way home, I found myself concerned about my own countrymen. What was all our material wealth and our haste to acquire it and the shocking waste doing to us? As a people we have a good deal of natural courtesy, but are we always gracious to foreigners? We have energy, but how are we expending it? We have an interest in beautiful things, but do we really appreciate fine art? We are generous, but are we not also self-centered?

163

Do we give enough of ourselves? These were the sorts of questions going through my mind. I saw barrels of food thrown into garbage cans, durable garments tossed away after being worn a few times, vacant lots littered with rusting metal; and I thought of people in China I had seen picking through litter in search of food or usable material. In overheated homes and hotels, I thought of Chinese men leaning against whitewashed walls to keep warm. I asked myself, "Does America have too much material wealth for its own good?"

I had become aware of how desperately we needed to profit from the mistakes of the Chinese and other old civilizations who had squandered their natural resources. We must not permit our nation to follow such examples and burn up our forests, destroy our minerals, poison our flowing streams, and let our rivers wash our rich soil out to sea. The thing I began to see so clearly was how much old and new countries could learn from each other.

This line of thinking lead to a number of endeavors on my part. I was determined to do what I could in some small way to provide educational opportunities for young people of our country and those of other lands to learn from each other. As an educational administrator, I could see the path stretching out clearly in front of me. I resolved to do what I could to bring an awareness of the world in which we live into the minds and hearts of our students, yes, and perhaps into the minds and hearts of adults, too.

It seemed clearer than ever before that higher education for women in home economics must provide a broad basic, general education as a complement to technical and professional education. Our students must have opportunity and encouragement to acquaint themselves with the humanities, the arts, and the sciences upon which world culture and development are founded. They must understand principles and philosophy as well as methods and practices. They must prepare to make decisions and solve problems on the basis of reasoning rather than dogma.

On my way home from China I had developed another questionnaire—this one for the faculty of the School of Home Economics. I wanted to sound them out to see if they felt as I did about providing a broad liberal arts education as a basis for home economics and, if so, what we might do to develop the School in that direction. I did not ask for hasty replies, but handed my queries to them in May with a request that they think about them during the summer and come back and discuss them in the fall. Responses were gratifying, and through discussion we arrived at long-range decisions. We decided to curtail required home economics courses and require, permit, and encourage our students to take more courses in the humanities and social sciences. The courses in chemistry, physics, physiology, and bacteriology already required as prerequisites for home economics courses appeared adequate in these areas, and we reaffirmed our long-standing policy of relying on courses taught elsewhere on the campus for fundamental knowledge of the natural sciences instead of teaching them as part of home economics courses. Our principal change was requiring more history, art, sociology, modern languages, and public speaking or journalism and at the same time leaving room in the curriculum for elective courses. As we moved gradually toward more humanities and social sciences, we dropped or telescoped some home economics courses. Between 1924 and 1930, Household Sanitation, Housewifery, and Home Nursing, for example, were dropped from the required list in the professional curriculum. Some elements of these courses were combined with other courses; some courses were reduced from 4 to 3 credits.

We realized that requiring more courses in other schools would in time lead to fewer sections of home economics courses with a consequent possible reduction in our faculty. As it turned out, we lost no faculty time as a result of this move because concurrently with the undergraduate course reduction, graduate work increased. Other schools on the campus required their women students to take courses in home economics—Agriculture required 20 credits; Commerce 10 credits; and Education 1 credit—and as enrollment of women in other schools grew, so did our teaching load.

We encouraged both men and women students in all schools to take elective courses in home economics. By 1926 the School was serving as many students from other schools as there were majors in Home Economics. For nonmajors (according to a 1930 report), the most popular elective courses were nutrition, clothing, child training, household management, and home furnishing.

Some of us began to realize that we lacked depth in one area of education for human development. Young peoples' groups sponsored by the local churches and the YWCA encouraged spiritual understanding and development of values, but the college had nothing to offer in classroom study of religious thought and philosophy. A group of us on the faculty, assisted by Dean of Men U. G. Dubach, and with the hearty support of President Kerr, set out to establish a Department of Religion. Since no state funds were available for such a purpose, we started a drive to obtain donations. Faculty, parents, and others throughout the community and state contributed, and in the fall of 1928, Ernest W. Warrington was appointed as the first professor of religion. For more than twenty years, until his retirement in 1951, Dr. Warrington held a vital place in the hearts of students and the spiritual life of the campus. We encouraged our students to take such courses as The Sermon on the Mount, The Prophets and Their Messages, and The Great Religions of the World, and some of us staff members took them also.

Not all of the increasing awareness of peoples of the world that we were able to develop in the minds and hearts of our students came from curricular changes by any means. All of us in our teaching helped, I believe, to inculcate insight into the broader mission of home economics. We watched for opportunity for staff development through travel and graduate study. We brought visitors to the campus, and when the students from the Orient and other parts of the world began to come to our school to study, they had a profound effect. Our graduates of those years have told me repeatedly how much they appreciated the opportunity they received to broaden their horizons, both through coursework and through other opportunities to get better acquainted with the world as a whole.

For a person who tried to waive a required course in public speaking in college because she did not think she would ever make speeches, I did a good deal of public speaking in the months following my return from China. I accepted in one year forty or more engagements to speak at women's clubs, church groups, and missionary societies in various parts of the state and gave several radio talks over KOAC. My theme, constantly reiterated, was that we had much to gain from an exchange of information, ideas, friendship, and culture with women of other lands. I tried to show how we might help countries like China by providing scholarships for young women with an undergraduate education in their own countries to come to the United States to observe and study for a limited time and then return to their own lands. I still felt that they could make the teaching of home economics more indigenous than we as foreigners could. I found audiences responsive. They opened their hearts and their pocketbooks. That first fall we raised $750 to bring Irene Ho from Mukden on a scholarship. Irene had the prestige of a classical education at Yenching University, and after her study at OSC she returned to Peking to assist Camilla Mills at Yenching University and later became department head. More of Irene Ho's story is told in Chapter 19.

Irene Ho (Liu) received her Master of Science degree in 1926. Hamna Kim (Park) from Korea followed her and received an M.S. degree in 1928. Normally, we felt that our scholarship money should be used primarily for graduate work, expecting students to take undergraduate work in their own countries. Sometimes, however, when a deserving girl's background was not strong enough for her to undertake advanced study we accepted candidates for baccalaureate degrees. Lan Chen Kung from China, Poonok Kim (Kim) from Korea, and Ruth Nomura from Japan received B.S. degrees in 1929 and 1930. In the 1930's eight foreign women received master's degrees, and two, bachelor's degrees. In the 1940's, one received a Ph.D.; six, master's degrees; and four, bachelor's degrees. In the 1950's, six received Ph.D.'s, twenty-two received master's degrees, and fourteen received bachelor's degrees. The numbers increased in the 1960's.

A list of foreign students who had received degrees in home economics through 1966 indicates that most of them came from China and Canada (17 each). Eight came from Korea, 7 from India, 6 each from Japan, The Philippines, and Thailand, 5 from the Union of South Africa, and 7 from elsewhere in Africa. Other countries represented by one or two degree candidates included New Zealand, England, Finland, Greece, Iraq, Iran, Pakistan, Ceylon, Burma, Vietnam, Jamaica, and Panama.

In addition to degree candidates we served a large number of other foreign women through summer session, short courses, and partial courses.

SHORTLY AFTER MY RETURN FROM CHINA in 1924, when trunks, luggage, and boxes had accumulated in my living room at 127 North Twenty-Sixth Street, I needed help in unpacking, getting settled, and entertaining friends. Like all travelers to far Cathay since the time of Marco Polo, I had many curious and colorful treasures to display. The Dean of Women, Kate W. Jameson, who assisted women students in finding employment, recommended Ruth Gill who was then living in the home management house while working in the college library and in a restaurant downtown. She had to move soon, and needed a place to live. We agreed at our first meeting that we would live together for two weeks while getting acquainted, and if everything worked out satisfactorily she would come to live with me for a longer period. The arrangement proved so congenial that Ruth decided to remain with me while in college. Her father, who had been a pioneer missionary in Arizona and New Mexico, and her mother were no longer living. In years to come, Ruth became almost like a daughter to me and her son and two daughters seem like grandchildren. They call me "Aunty Muz," a nickname started by Ruth's eldest daughter when she was a baby and picked up by other family members and close friends. New secretaries in my outer office have sometimes been shocked to hear a caller ask, "Is Aunty Muz in?" With Ruth's help, in the first days of our acquaintanceship in 1924, I unpacked and took care of social engagements before leaving for New York for the summer.

At the office, I found things in remarkably good order. Helen Lee Davis had done such a splendid job as Acting Dean that a new position, Vice Dean, was created for her. When sabbatical leaves became possible, she was the first to avail herself of this opportunity for refreshment. She and Librarian Lucy Lewis, who had replaced Mrs. Kidder, and a group of friends took a trip around the world. For some time Helen Lee had not been well, and after her return the doctors found a tumor on her brain. She resigned early in 1930 and died in August of that year. In the hearts of fellow staff members and many generations of students, Miss Davis has a lasting place. For many years a more visible, though anonymous, tribute to her hung on the wall beside the grand staircase in the Memorial Union. Following the close of World War I, she and a group of her students in Clothing, Textiles, and Related Arts worked painstakingly on Saturday mornings to make a huge service flag with stars for all of the OAC men who had served in the war and gold stars for those who had died in service. As years passed, the stars faded, the red border mellowed, and the white center became a soft cream, but it was still cherished by alumni, relatives, and friends of those it represented and by those of us who thought of it as a memorial also to a gallant, loyal, and devoted friend and colleague, Helen Lee Davis.

Memorial Union

Some of the rest of us in the School of Home Economics also had a part in designing and equipping the beautiful Memorial Union in the 1920's. Since the new building would provide space for our Tearoom, the staff of the Department of Institution Economics assisted in planning the food service facilities. I served as chairman of a committee to plan furnishings for the lounges and main corridor. We insisted that we be permitted to employ an interior decorator not connected with any of the firms bidding on the job to pass judgment on our plans when we had completed them. One knotty problem was to provide seating for a certain number in the main lounge and corridor within the budget allowed us. We hit upon the idea of taking a Chinese design for small stools and long benches for the main corridor and thereby achieving our goal for seating and at the same time fitting the decor by having these pieces carved and constructed to match the other furniture. Well built and durable, these stools and benches are still in daily use.

One morning during vacation while the interior was being painted, I went over to the Memorial Union and found a painter high on his scaffold in the main lounge giving the ceiling beams the colors of the rainbow. "Is that just the priming coat?" I called up to him. "No," he responded, "I am using the same colors I used in the Athletic Club in Los Angeles."

"Please stop," I said, "This is a formal lounge, not an athletic club. Those beams must be the same hue as the rest of the wood paneling." Fearing that the painter might not accept my authority, I called President Kerr and told him of my concern. He hastily ordered the painter to carry out my color selection and the crisis passed.

ANOTHER INTERESTING EXTRACURRICULAR ACTIVITY I took part in during the late 1920's was a survey of land-grant colleges and universities. Directed by Arthur J. Klein, Chief of the Division of Collegiate and Professional Education, U. S. Office of Education, the survey was undertaken at the request of the Association of Land-Grant Colleges and Universities. More than 100 men and women took part in the various phases. Martha Van Rensselaer represented home economics on the National Advisory Committee. Deans of schools or professors of home economics in Michigan, Kansas, Missouri, Illinois, Tennessee, Georgia, and Oregon were on the Advisory Committee on Home Economics. My specific duties were to visit the departments of home economics in the Pacific Northwest to gather information to supplement the questionnaires sent out by the national office. I also conferred with the others in regard to the findings, conclusions, and recommendations.

Statistics collected in the survey showed that Oregon State College led all the rest in number of men (272) enrolled in home economics courses. Cornell was in second place with 227. In enrollment of girls majoring in home economics, Iowa State College led with 1,062 (82% of the women enrolled in the College). Kansas State College had 516 women enrolled in home economics, and Oregon State College, in third place, had 476 (39% of the women in the student body).

In our section of the survey we arrived at 54 conclusions and recommendations, far too many to summarize here. The report of the survey was published in two volumes, the section on home economics alone covering nearly 150 pages.

IN THE SUMMER of 1924, I went to New York and took courses at Teachers College, Columbia University. In the summers of 1925, 1926, and 1927 I registered for graduate study at the University of Chicago, where I did research in foods and nutrition and took courses in home management and household economics. I took German for reading requirements and passed the French language examination in case I decided to work further toward a Ph.D. degree.

At both Teachers College and Chicago, faculty members were interested in my questionnaire on Chinese homes and suggested that the results be published. Benjamin R. Andrews in New York offered to help me prepare the manuscript. One section of it, "Standards of Living Among Intermediate Income Groups in China," was published in the August 1927 issue of the *Journal of Home Economics*. Dr. Andrews found the International Institute of Teachers College favorable to publishing the complete study. For several summers, therefore, with his assistance at Columbia and Dr. Hazel Kyrk's help at Chicago, I worked at reducing the mass of statistics to meaningful units. It was published as a clothbound book in 1930 under the title *A Study of the Student Homes of China*.

In an introductory note, Dr. George S. Counts, representing the International Institute, wrote that the study "illustrates the modern educational principle that facts should come before action. . . . this study illustrates that transfusion of ideas between nations which Bacon rightly characterized as merchandise of light."

Timothy Tingfang Lew came to Oregon in the summer of 1928 to teach in the University of Oregon Summer School in Portland. Dr. Lew had been one of Leighton Stuart's most valued colleagues in the establishment of Yenching University and was Dean of the School of Religion there when I was in Peking. Fluent in eight languages, he had lectured at Yale and Boston universities and in various parts of this country and Europe. He had known of my questionnaire, and when he heard that my study was to be published, he offered to write a foreword. In it he made comments that even today in the time of Communist-dominated China have a solid, prophetic ring:

> The family has been the center of Chinese life in a unique way, not paralleled in other nations. Back of all the political and social forces, the family has stood as THE bulwark for peace and order, THE final authority of problems of individual and social life, and THE mainspring of devotion, inspiration, hopes, and moral idealism. For the past fifty years China has been

experiencing a great transformation. Reformers have poured out their life blood in bringing about changes in the form of government, in educational programs, and in business and industrial enterprises. All those who have had a share, however humble, in this great task have found the influence of the family system obtruding at every turn. They have found that the sacred traditions of the family system and the fine qualities they develop often aid in their new endeavor; on the other hand they have found that many of the tragic failures in the new political and industrial life have been, in their final analysis, the outgrowth of some "family considerations."

At last, however, the "changeless" family is also changing . . . . The New China is ready to learn from her foreign friends as well as her own leaders. Not by ambitious proposals of a panacea for all the evils, nor by complacent offers of theoretical platitudes, but by scientific guidance and advice, based on well ascertained facts, will China be helped, and be willing to be helped.

For the most part, in the text of the book, I restricted myself to a description of how the study was conducted and an analysis of the returns from the questionnaires. In the final chapter I spoke more broadly of the needs of home economics training and gave suggestions regarding homemakers' conferences and the joint responsibilities of home and school. After quoting Ellen H. Richards' phrase about "Right Living" being the Fourth R in education, I finished by saying,

It is hoped . . . that Chinese educators will early recognize the importance of the home economics training initiated in China; and in expanding it, will extend to men as well as women the type of training that will contribute to their success as parents and as partners in the profession of homemaking.

The editor of the book added this footnote to that last paragraph:

As this book goes to press, word has been received that the Ministry of Education of China has recognized home economics and has required that it be taught in all of the middle schools for girls in China.

I felt grateful that Camilla and I had been able to have some small part in this accomplishment.

14. Home Economics Research

Prove all things; hold fast that which is good.
—THESSALONIANS, 5:21

EVERY HOME ECONOMIST to some extent conducts research. She experiments with recipes; she tests theories of child psychology; she tries a variety of color schemes and textile patterns in clothing and home furnishings. To be of most service to others, however, she needs to perform her investigations under controlled conditions, keep her observations objective, make her measurements precise, record her facts accurately, and report her findings in such a way that they can be tested and used by others.

To Ellen H. Richards, research seemed the natural and proper means of effectively combatting the foibles, myths, fads, habits, and ignorance that governed the management—or mismanagement—of homes. A graduate of the Massachusetts Institute of Technology, a consulting chemist by first profession, she was once described by Isabel Bevier as "The consulting engineer of the Home Economics movement." She made her home a laboratory, her kitchen a test tube. She pioneered in time-and-motion studies, nutrition investigations, and design of sanitary household equipment. "Have faith in working out the destiny of the races," she said in one of the last pieces she wrote; "be ready to accept the unaccustomed, to use the radium of social progress to cure the ulcers of the old friction. What if a few mistakes are made? How else shall the truth be learned? Try all things and hold fast that which is good."

From my earliest contact with the field of home economics, the scientific approach to the acquisition of knowledge has always seemed basic. Even the title of the first course in household manage-

173

ment I took at the University of Chicago reflects the experimental approach to cooking: "The Application of Heat to Food Materials." Professor Elizabeth Sprague told us of her experiments in developing a method of precisely controlling the roasting of beef. A scientific attitude permeated the Chicago staff. It seemed quite natural to me, and I believe to others in the early days of our School of Home Economics, to use a scientific, investigative approach in teaching the various phases of homemaking. The accumulated knowledge of the past was not enough; we needed a body of new knowledge. As we took our first tentative steps into graduate work, we thought of it in terms of original investigations to help develop a store of new knowledge.

The Biennial Report for 1914-16, for example, in which we mention that graduate enrollment had increased 100% in the biennium—from 4 to 8 students—states that "graduate work is offered in household administration, house decoration, textiles, and in *research work in foods* [italics added]. . . . Experiments have been carried on to determine practical recipes for the use of English walnuts . . . the relative cooking qualities of different kinds of potatoes . . . and profitable disposal of by-products of the loganberry industry. . . . This knowledge, when collected and disseminated, will aid ... industries of the state to an extent which cannot be estimated." A beginning in textiles research at that time included a project requested by the Laundrymen's Association of Portland to determine the amount of adulterations in staple dry goods that find their way into a laundry. We were asking then for staff time to increase the amount of research work we could do, but many years passed before funds became available for this purpose.

In 1915 we completed the first master's thesis based on original research. The apple-growing industry was achieving importance in the state's economy, but there was little information available on the cooking qualities of the different varieties of apples produced. When Harriet B. Gardner, who had just graduated from Michigan Agricultural College, came to work for an advanced degree in home economics at OAC and to live in the home of her brother, Professor Victor R. Gardner of the Horticulture Department, she tackled the problem of testing different varieties of apples in five different food products. Her brother and another horticulturist, E. J. Kraus, agreed to assist and provided 71 different varieties of apples for her to test.

These men also acted as judges—as did Sarah Louise Lewis of the Domestic Science Department, Miss Gardner, and I—to rate the products made from the different varieties. Miss Gardner's study had three objectives: (1) to determine the relative value of different varieties of apples for sauce, pies, dumplings, jelly, and marmalade; (2) to determine some of the general principles underlying these cooking properties; and (3) to ascertain if differences in cooking qualities are associated with differences in gross morphology and cell structure of the fruit. Using the same recipes each time, Miss Gardner tested each variety as it reached its prime for cooking from August to April. Each time she finished a batch we five judges scored the products for flavor, texture, color, tenderness, clearness, and so forth. Using averages of our scores, Miss Gardner rated each apple variety as excellent, very good, good, fair, or poor for each of the products. Six varieties were found to give good products with any of the cooking methods employed—Maiden Blush, Tompkins King, Jonathan, Grimes, Rambo, and Northern Spy. Other varieties proved excellent for one or more of the cooking methods.

Results of this study served not only the housewife choosing apples to cook but also the nursery man and orchardist in selecting varieties to plant and the grocer in choosing varieties to sell. To give the findings wide dissemination, the Agricultural Experiment Station published the results of this study in a Station Bulletin in 1915. A food scientist told me in recent years that the findings of this study are still valid. New varieties of apples, however, have appeared since then and production problems have made some of the older ones impractical.

In the following years, we produced other theses based on research, but obviously, faculty with full-time teaching loads and other responsibilities could not spend the long hours of concentrated effort required to go far with lengthy scientific investigations. Not until Congress passed the Purnell Act in 1925 did funds become available to support full-time workers in home economics research. Inasmuch as research in home economics was a rather new field, people concerned with it had different ideas of where to place emphasis. Isabel Bevier paid us a visit in the mid-1920's, and she and I had a long talk about what types of projects we should undertake. One point clear to us was that home economics research should not try to duplicate what was taking place in other fields. Our emphasis needed to be related directly to the home and the responsibilities of the homemaker.

When James T. Jardine, the Director of the OSC Agricultural Experiment Station and administrator of the Purnell funds on our campus, asked for a proposal, we had one ready. We suggested an intensive study of standards of living in Oregon farm homes in typical communities to provide information needed not only as the initial step in projects leading to the improvement of living conditions but also as a basis for the future development of home economics at OAC. Director Jardine was much interested in this line of investigation and allocated funds for a full-time research worker. Helen Lee Davis, Vice Dean of the School of Home Economics, recommended Maud Wilson, Assistant Director of the Extension Service at the State College of Washington, for the position. Miss Davis knew that Miss Wilson was planning to leave Washington to continue with graduate study and might be persuaded to take this appointment instead. As a result, Miss Wilson joined our staff as the first full-time research worker.

Miss Wilson had an admirable background for this position. Having boarded in farm homes when she taught in rural schools in Nebraska and having been a state leader for extension work with farm women in Nebraska and Washington, she knew the problems of the rural home. "If the home of today," she once wrote, "is to be unhampered by the traditions of the past there must be a body of knowledge developed to take the place of those traditions which do not meet the needs of the modern homemaker."

Miss Wilson's first study dealt with the use of time by farm homemakers, one of the three projects suggested by the National Committee on Rural Home Studies. She carried it on in cooperation with the U. S. Department of Agriculture's Bureau of Home Economics, and the record blanks, classification forms, and rules for summarizing data were prepared by a member of the Bureau staff. Major points of interest covered in the study included variations in the time-spending patterns in Oregon rural households during weeks of normal activity in relation to (1) location of home (town or country); (2) major source of income (farm or nonfarm); (3) size and composition of household; (4) schooling of homemaker; (5) household equipment; (6) housework done by persons other than homemaker; and (7) use of commercial goods and services.

Miss Wilson found delineating patterns in the use of time a new concept for homemakers but also found women's clubs willing to cooperate. With the help of county agricultural agents, dates were arranged when she could meet with women's groups at their monthly meetings to explain the proposed study and solicit cooperators. In general the response was good, and after a few weeks she became accustomed to competing with ardent quilters, lunch preparations, and other attention-diverting aspects of rural club routine. In all, she reached about 1,200 women in this way. She made two home visits to each of the women who volunteered to keep the time records. On the first round she found that some had changed their minds since volunteering, but for the most part she was surprised to find how many were stimulated by the idea and ready to start. She asked each cooperator to keep a time record for a week in which the routine was not broken by unusual circumstances. Each volunteer kept a diary of her own activities and a record of the help she had during the week and added supplementary information on major factors that may have influenced her use of time during the period.

Miss Wilson obtained usable records in 1926 and 1927 from 513 homemakers—288 in farm homes, 71 from country nonfarm homes, and 154 from noncountry nonfarm homes. Twenty-three of the farm homemakers submitted records for two weeks. Students helped summarize the records and transferred the information to the classification charts. Miss Wilson had a chance to buy a hand-operated relic of an adding machine, built to convert pounds to bushels, and found it a great help in converting minutes to hours. Results of this study were published in various bulletins and periodicals between 1928 and 1932. (See Appendix.)

Miss Wilson found another outlet for her research. At the University of Chicago where she went for graduate study, the data were accepted as the basis for her thesis, "Time Spent in Meal Preparation in Private Households." With Dr. Hazel Kyrk (who had helped me with A Study of Student Homes in China a few years before) serving as her major professor, Miss Wilson completed her work and received her Master of Arts degree in 1931.

The second research project Miss Wilson undertook was called "The Family Home." The time study had shown that the most important factor affecting the use of homemaker's time was the house itself. She had found that little building or remodeling had been done for more than ten years, although some farms were being electrified. In attacking this new problem she assumed that livability in terms of space needs for family activities and storage was of basic importance, that minimum space requirements would take into consideration aesthetic requirements such as spaciousness and harmony in proportion, and that published results would be useful not only to families in building new and remodeling old homes but also to architects and manufacturers. A series of excellent bulletins resulted from this project.

Preparations of plans for farm kitchens had required a preliminary study to set standards for working surface heights and other space units of the house of importance to women. Data were obtained from 312 Oregon and 250 Washington women, who chose heights of working surfaces and chairs, and for whom height and depth of reach as well as certain body measurements were recorded.

During the 1930's Miss Wilson collaborated with the USDA Bureau of Home Economics in the utilization of data from its 1934 nation-wide survey, which had to do with the functions of the farmhouse and its storage requirements. Two USDA Bulletins resulted from this assignment.

In the 1940's Miss Wilson collaborated with Professor H. E. Sinnard, Professor of Architecture, in developing a series of sketch plans for houses suited to specific sets of conditions in rural Oregon, utilizing space standards determined in previous studies. The results of this collaboration were published in 1945 as a 209-page handbook for use by extension workers, "Plans for Oregon Farm and Acreage Homes."

In 1947 Oregon cooperated with other states of the western region in a field study of the housing needs of western farm families which was designed to serve in setting geographic boundaries for specific recommendations applying to farmhouse design. In 1948 Oregon's long-time project, "The Family Home," was closed.

While on leave of absence in 1936, Miss Wilson worked with the Rural Resettlement Administration. She visited open-country homes in every section of the United States and cooperated with other home economists interested in the improvement of housing for family living. She assisted architects in regional offices in planning houses for resettled families and held group conferences in ten states. On several occasions Miss Wilson taught classes in the Department of Household Administration, but for the most part she devoted her professional career to establishing standards for planning homes to meet the needs of families. Her pioneering work has had far-reaching influence and has provided assistance not only to homemakers but to the designers and builders of equipment for the home.

When Helen E. McCullough came to OSC in 1938 to work with Maud Wilson, she already had a background in housing. She had studied home economics and architecture; she had worked with architects and engineers as a housing consultant. While working with Miss Wilson, she became aware of the urgent need for research in housing, and Miss Wilson provided her with a background of philosophy and experience that later brought her national recognition. After she left Oregon, Miss McCullough worked at Cornell University with Mary Koll Heiner (one-time manager of our campus Tearoom). The two women complemented each other—Mrs. Heiner as a specialist in work simplification and Miss McCullough as a specialist in housing. Later, at the University of Illinois and in other positions, Miss McCullough continued her work. She has four books to her credit and has published dozens of bulletins and articles in professional journals. Taken all together, women connected with our staff at one time or another have made a large contribution to home economics research in housing.

In the early 1930's we were able to carry on a little research in foods and nutrition. Agnes Kolshorn devoted a term's work to a study of the baking qualities of three varieties of Oregon-grown pears; two bulletins resulted from this study. Another study on furnishing food requirements at minimum cost resulted in OSU Extension Bulletin 436, "Planning the Family Budget." Findings in a study of the Vitamin B and G content of the Bosc pear and one on basal metabolism were disseminated through the American Home Economics Association.

Nutrition research became well established as an integral part of the Foods and Nutrition Department following the appointment of Margaret Louise Fincke in 1935. Half of her time was allocated to research. A graduate of Mt. Holyoke College, Miss Fincke came to Oregon after eight years at Columbia University, where she had received A.M. and Ph.D. degrees and where she had worked with Dr. Henry C. Sherman, the eminent nutritionist who taught several times in our summer session. While Jessamine Williams was still head

of our Foods and Nutrition Department and after Dr. Fincke succeeded her, the department expanded research in nutrition, added
foods research as an established entity, and gradually acquired
additional staff and laboratory equipment.

Andrea Overman Mackey, a graduate of the University of
Nebraska, came as an instructor in foods in 1938 and later, after she
had returned from completing study for a doctorate at Iowa State
College, devoted a major portion of her time to foods research. Helen
G. Charley, a graduate of DePauw University and the University of
Chicago, joined the foods staff in 1944. Clara A. Storvick, with de-
grees from St. Olaf College, Iowa State College, and Cornell Uni-
versity and with research experience at Oklahoma Agricultural and
Mechanical College, Cornell, and the University of Washington,
joined the nutrition research staff in 1945.

Dr. Fincke's early investigations included a human-balance
study to determine the utilization of calcium in spinach and kale and
studies on the effect of blanching and quick freezing on the ascorbic
acid, thiamin, and riboflavin in certain Oregon-grown fruits and
vegetables and the losses of these vitamins in cooking. She also
investigated the intake of ascorbic acid necessary to maintain tissue
saturation in normal adults, ascorbic acid metabolism of college
students, and the vitamin value of dehydrated fruits and vegetables.

In foods research Mrs. Mackey studied the quality of frozen
meats, the antioxidant effect of edible flours derived from oil press
cakes in certain fat-containing food mixtures, and the influence of
various production and processing factors on the behavior of fats
and oils when used in food products. In later years she studied the
flavor constituents of cereal grains and the texture of fruits and
vegetables and conducted a microscopic study of batters and doughs.
Miss Charley experimented with the effects of the size, shape, heat
penetration qualities, and construction material of pans on the quality of baked products. In recent years she has investigated the chemical composition of cooking fats and how they are affected by cooking
at various temperatures and has provided data to determine a precise
method of cooking salmon. She has conducted studies of various
pigments found in fruits and vegetables and their effect on color,
flavor, and keeping qualities.

In addition to being an industrious research worker herself,
Dr. Storvick has shown a good deal of skill in the administration of

research. In 1952 she received the Borden Award of the American Home Economics Association for leadership in regional research on nutritional status. In 1955 she became the first Chairman of Home Economics Research in the OSU Agricultural Experiment Station, and ten years later when a Nutrition Research Institute was formed to coordinate the work of various scientists on campus concerned with nutrition, Dr. Storvick was named its director.

A nutrition research project that had wide-reaching results dealt with dental caries. Physical examinations of Oregon men in military service in World War II revealed what appeared to be an excessive amount of tooth decay. The Extension Women's Council helped persuade the Oregon Legislature to provide funds for an investigation of the effect of nutrition on tooth decay. Initiated by Dr. Storvick and Dr. Demetrios M. Hadjimarkos and later carried on by Dr. Gertrude Tank, this investigation provided basic data that have helped in understanding the relationship of diets and dental caries.

The dental caries investigation was expanded in the late 1940's to include samplings in Idaho and Washington as part of a cooperative research project initiated by the experiment stations of the western states. In other regional studies, about 2,000 teen-age boys and girls in nine western states were examined for nutritional status. Dietary intake was correlated with nutrients in the blood. In another phase of the project, confined largely to California and Colorado, the nutritional status of aging people as affected by age, sex, and food habits was studied. More than sixty papers based on this regional research, about one quarter of them authored or co-authored by Oregon scientists, were published in journals and bulletins between 1951 and 1958.

In textiles research, the Department of Clothing, Textiles, and Related Arts took an active part in a linen-weaving project. Flax grows well in the Willamette Valley, and it produces linen of good quality. To reduce the national dependence on overseas sources and to encourage the development of a new agriculture-based industry in the state, various federal, state, and private agencies joined in supporting extensive flax production and linen-utilization studies. Our part was to design and test fabrics using Oregon linen. The creative work of Joan Patterson showed that the fiber could be made into a variety of beautiful, colorful, durable textiles. Results indicated that household fabrics made of Oregon yarns compared favorably with those made from imported yarns. Linen weaving, however, did not grow into a big industry for two reasons: the high cost of turning fibers of the flax plant into linen yarn, and the low cost of synthetic fibers coming onto the market and to a large extent replacing linen in household use.

Other clothing and textile research projects included one suggested by the State Home Economics Council and conducted by Clara Edaburn on the design and construction of functional house dresses for the mature figure; one on changes needed in current ready-to-wear school dresses for the 7-14 age group conducted by Ida Ingalls; and one on the thermal properties of blankets of different fiber content conducted by Florence E. Petzel. In more recent years the first Western Regional Project in Textiles was launched when Oregon joined other states in studying the effects of atmospheric conditions on specific cotton fabrics. A later regional project was concerned with the efficiency and cost of laundering textiles as related to detergent type and water temperature. Other important areas in clothing and textile research include comfort factors in clothing, the nature of natural fibers, and the need for consumer protection.

In the Department of Household Administration, which later became the Department of Family Life and Home Administration, Dr. Katherine Haskell Read (Baker) came as supervisor of the nursery school in 1941, and after Sara Prentiss retired became department head. Mrs. Read carried on many investigations in child growth and development and in the books and articles she has written has pointed out what an excellent human relations laboratory the nursery school makes. Dr. Lester Kirkendall, the first man on the teaching staff of the School of Home Economics, joined the Department of Household Administration in 1949. The research for which he has become widely known across the country, and to some extent overseas, centers around his quest for a value framework to describe the importance of interpersonal relations as an approach to understanding people and helping with their human relations decisions. He is concerned with changing moral values as they affect home and family life. One of his books has been translated into Japanese and some of his articles into Dutch, Arabic, and other languages.

In all departments of the School of Home Economics some research was carried on in connection with graduate work and the writing of master's theses and doctoral dissertations. In my last two years as dean (1948-50), for example, six master's theses were completed in the field of clothing, textiles, and related arts; five in household administration; two doctoral and two master's studies in foods and nutrition; four masters' theses in home economics education. These were supplemented with voluntary staff research and the writing of articles for publication.

One of the most gratifying features of the home economics research carried on through the years on our campus has been the scientific spirit of the whole staff. They were not content to base their teachings on the worn-out or out-grown theories of the past; they continually probed for better ways of doing things, better theories on which to base decisions, and new methods to apply to the ever-changing conditions of the American home. They have benefited greatly from research in the basic disciplines, especially in biochemistry, psychology, sociology, physics, and chemistry and have exhibited a high level of scholarship in keeping up with home economics research conducted in all parts of the country. Through the journals that publish the results of investigations, through campus visits of some of the top people in the field, and through travel and advanced study they have kept abreast of national trends and have incorporated into their courses the new knowledge obtained through research.

15. Around the World

The world will never be fit for any of us
until it is fit for all of us.

— THEODORE ROOSEVERT

T HE CLIMATE OF OPINION in regard to foreign travel changed between 1922 and 1931. President Kerr agreed only reluctantly to my leave without pay the first time I went to China. Nine years later, when I submitted a request for sabbatical leave which included part salary, he offered encouragement and assistance.

Ruth Gill, the student who had helped me unpack after the first trip, agreed to meet me in Japan. After graduation, Ruth had taught two years in a California high school, had studied a year at Columbia University, and then had accepted a teaching position at the New York State College for Teachers at Buffalo. In the summers she had returned to Oregon—one year to supervise the home management house for our summer session, and other years to live with me in my home. When the President of Pomona College, who was on a committee to select a teacher to go to Canton, China, to start a department of home economics at Lingnan University, asked me to recommend someone, I thought of Ruth—partly because she had been a student for two years at Pomona before coming to Oregon State. Although I mentioned Ruth as a possibility for the Lingnan position, I told the Pomona President that I felt that she needed more than one year of college teaching experience. The selection committee chose her anyway. In the summer of 1930, therefore, Ruth started for China. I had been invited to attend the Second Pan-Pacific Women's Conference in Honolulu, but since I could not go, we arranged for Ruth to take the assignment. She therefore had an opportunity to spend two weeks at the University of Hawaii enroute to Canton.

The next summer (1931), after her first year at Lingnan University, Ruth visited Peking and then met me in Yokohama because she and I had decided to take a short vacation together in Japan. Yokohama and Tokyo were extremely hot; we therefore eagerly accepted an invitation to stay for a time as paying guests at Karuizawa* in the home of an American doctor who had lived in Japan for more than forty years. This resort community in the mountains northwest of Tokyo was a delightful, relatively cool spot. Nearby Mt. Asama put on an unusually spectacular volcanic show for us, its blazing crater shooting out boulders like skyrockets by night and plumes of gray, cauliflower-shaped clouds of smoke by day. We sometimes had to carry umbrellas to keep the falling ashes out of our hair. From our host and hostess we gained a great deal of insight into the long history of Japan. As a medical missionary, the doctor had lived close to the people and had grown to have great respect for many aspects of their culture. He kept us entranced at every meal.

After brief stops in Tokyo and Kyoto, Ruth returned to her university in Canton, and I went on to Korea. At Ewha College in Seoul, Hamna Kim (Park), one of the eight Oriental women who had come to Oregon State College on scholarships up to that time, proudly showed me what had been accomplished in the improvement of the Ewha home economics program. I, too, felt proud, not only of Hamna as a former student, but also of her creative contribution to the education of Korean women through her work with students and through radio programs for homemakers.

After six weeks in Seoul, interspersed with a visit to the Diamond Mountains and other pleasant side trips, I was ready to go to China and could have reached Peking in two days by train—traveling the same route as on previous trips in 1923—except that fighting had broken out between the Japanese and Chinese in Manchuria, and that way was closed. I had to go back to Japan, thence to Shanghai, and from there by rail to Peking. Because I had to return to Japan, I decided to stop at Kwassui College in Nagasaki, known as the oldest women's college in Japan. Partially supported by the Women's

* See map page 147.

Foreign Mission Society of the Methodist Church, Kwassui College had a small but promising department of home economics. The Japanese girls were eager to discuss their homes and to acquire a better understanding of child care and training. They had gained the impression that Americans are cruel to their children because we put the young ones to bed early at night and then go out to shop or to have a good time; whereas in Japan parents felt they should take the children along to share the outing—even if they had to strap the drowsy babies on their mothers' backs. Because of this curious difference in point of view, they thought we were robbing our children by putting them to bed early; we thought them unkind to rob their children of sleep.

Several changes had taken place in central China since my earlier visit. The J. C. Clark family had returned to the United States. Chiang Kai-shek and the Nationalists had unified the country and had made Nanking the new capital. In Nanking I had the good fortune to make the acquaintance of Pearl Buck and to have lunch in her home. She and her husband, an agricultural economist on the Nanking University staff, were giving much time and thought to means of alleviating the disastrous effects of flood and famine which Mrs. Buck had so vividly described in her recently published book, *The Good Earth,* and especially in her article, "The River," which appeared in the *Christian Century* magazine about that time. The Yangtze was still out of its banks when I was there and the devastation evident everywhere was appalling. Thousands of homeless families huddled in little sheds on top of the city wall or in other spots where they were permitted to camp temporarily. Mrs. Buck was somewhat upset at the time, not only because of the local conditions but also because a Korean reviewer had unfavorably criticized *The Good Earth!*

In Peking I found that the city's name had been changed to Peiping. Even though it was no longer the capital, outwardly it seemed its same old fascinating self. Yenching University had moved both the women's college and the men's college to a lovely new campus with its camelback bridges and peaceful lotus ponds. In what had once been the garden of a Manchu prince, five miles outside the city walls toward the Western Hills, buildings of great beauty had been constructed. The exteriors displayed the graceful curves and gorgeous coloring of the finest in Chinese architecture.

The interiors had modern lighting, heating, and plumbing. Faculty residences on the grounds harmonized with the academic buildings and residence halls for students. Overlooking all was a thirteen-story pagoda that encased the water tower.

Camilla Mills had remained at Yenching until the previous summer, when she had married Knight Biggerstaff, a Harvard-Yenching research fellow. After their wedding in Peiping, they had returned to Harvard, where Knight was working toward his Ph.D. degree.

Caroline Chen, a member of our first class at Yenching in 1923-24 and one of the scholarship women who had come to OSC, had succeeded Camilla as head of home economics at Yenching. She was assisted by another of our former students, Lan Chen Kung, who had come to us as an Indemnity Student,* took her bachelor's degree at OSC in 1929, and later received a doctorate in nutrition at Columbia University. Once again, it was good to see living proof of how successfully our scholarship program was working out.

Co-education, a new concept, had caused problems in adjustment at Yenching. The girls tended to hold their distance and insisted that young men calling for them at their residence halls wait at the entrance gate—even in freezing weather—rather than in the social rooms of the halls. One morning I heard the girls debate whether Chinese or Western customs in betrothal and marriage were better. Alhough they spoke in Chinese, a girl next to me gave me a running account in English. When they had finished, I asked, "Well, which side won?" In an almost matter-of-fact manner, the girls assured me that, of course, the Old Chinese customs had won. Parents, they explained, had their daughters' best interests at heart and were so much older and wiser than their children that they could make much better decisions on mate selection and in arranging weddings. The girls were emphatic, however, in saying that a girl should have an opportunity to become acquainted with the prospective husband the parents chose and if not happy with the selection should not be expected to marry him.

After six weeks at Yenching University, I found it difficult to

---

*The Chinese "Indemnity Students" were those who came to the United States to study, using funds which had been released by the U. S. Government from those paid by China as indemnity for damages done to the property and persons of U. S. Nationals in China during the Boxer Rebellion of 1900.

leave, not only because of my interest in the University and the fascination of the city, but also because of the great interest Chinese women students held for me and the hope I had for them.

On the way south to Canton, I had planned to stop at Hwa Nan College in Foochow, where I had spent a restful Christmas vacation in 1922, but the Japanese had already occupied part of camphor-rich Fukien Province and it was not possible to get transportation to Foochow. Canton was much quieter—as far as military activity goes —than when I had been there before. In other ways, however, it showed signs of great activity. City walls had been partially torn down and turned into elevated automobile roads. Even old temples had been destroyed to widen streets. Factories and office buildings were under construction, and sanitary conditions had greatly improved.

At Lingnan University, I found that Ruth Gill had made a good start in introducing home economics in her first year there. Another member of the Lingnan faculty at that time, incidentally, was Helen P. Hostetter of Kansas State College, who was teaching journalism and who later served as editor of the *Journal of Home Economics* (1941-46). The administration at Lingnan University wished to expand in home economics. When the Ministry of Education of China had decreed two years earlier that home economics be taught in all middle schools for girls, there was hardly any source of teachers. My principal work, therefore, was to assist the administration in designing a five-year development plan for teacher-training programs in home economics. I also visited the five middle schools in Canton that were teaching home economics and discussed coordination of teacher-training programs.

Through one of the teachers at Lingnan, Irene Ho (not to be confused with the Irene Ho (Liu) from Mukden, our first foreign student in home economics from the Orient*), Ruth and I met an interesting Eurasian family in Hong Kong. Miss Ho's father, Sir Robert Ho Tung, a British subject, was sometimes called the J. P. Morgan of China. As I understood the story, Sir Robert was the son of a Dutch father and a Chinese mother. He had married two Chinese cousins, and thereby helped them fulfill a long-time wish. As little girls, the cousins had been close friends and to remain so in

---

* See pages 248-250.

later years had decided that they should marry the same man! The first Lady Ho Tung had no children, the second had ten. Introducing his wives, Sir Robert would say of the first, "This is my wife," and of the second, "This is the mother of our children." Daughter Irene had studied at London University and later received a doctorate from that university, and had also studied at Columbia University; others of the family had studied in Europe. At a tea in their beautiful home on The Peak overlooking Hong Kong harbor and later at dinner, we had a rare glimpse into the lives of this cosmopolitan family. The Buddhist mother entertained us graciously and introduced us to some of her blond blue-eyed children, who had Chinese features and spoke both English and Chinese fluently—a delightful blend of East and West.

THE FAVORABLE RATE OF CURRENCY EXCHANGE encouraged me to plan my trip home going on around the world. For something like $459 I could purchase in Hong Kong a first-class ticket to New York on the North German Lloyd line. Since the ships sailed every month, I could leave the ship I started on, take side trips in India, the Near East, and Europe, and resume passage on a later one. The opportunity to see more of Asia and Europe appealed to me, and I found quite a number of tourists following a similar plan. I met many of them, and two women in particular, who had been missionaries in China, became traveling companions when we left the ship to go sightseeing.

The principal change I noted in Manila was continuing Americanization—new buildings, new boulevards, and flashing electric lights. After stops at Singapore and Penang, a group of us left the ship in Burma to visit Rangoon and to tour India before catching the next ship in Ceylon. When I think of Burma, I have vivid memories of the heat and glare of the sun on white walls, of saffron-robed Buddhist priests, of shrines and pagodas, shining spires, and glittering golden domes. Many of the older married Burmese women had teeth blackened from chewing betel nut—a custom purported to make wives less attractive to men not their husbands.

Through India we followed what has become a rather well-worn tourist route: Calcutta, Darjeeling, Benares, Lucknow, Delhi, Muttra, Agra and the Taj Mahal, Allahabad, Madras, and Ceylon, with a number of side visits to women's colleges. At Lucknow, we

stayed a while at Isabella Thoburn College* for women, which was
partially supported by the Methodist Church. There I saw what I
believed to be Indian college women at their best. Many appeared
to be from upper-class homes and seemed able and eager to make
the world better for their having lived. The night we arrived, the
freshman girls were having a party for the sophomores and invited
us to watch the entertainment. Their style show depicted women's
costumes from many periods in Indian history. In an amusing proph-
ecy of what college classes would be like in 1999, the girls lounged at
ease in beautiful, bright-hued saris, listening to lectures on astron-
omy by radio; in a 1999 student meeting they voted to declare a
holiday, not for themselves but for their teachers! As I talked with
these girls and listened to their extemporaneous speeches and de-
bates, I was impressed with their accomplishments. Even though
only a small number of women could be reached by these Christian
colleges scattered over India, girls like these seemed a leaven that
ultimately might affect the whole lump.

At Allahabad, I visited an agricultural institute where I had a
pleasant visit with OAC alumnus Brewster Hayes, a highly regarded
plant physiologist, and his wife, a mission doctor. She took me with
her on several house calls into hovels that did not seem fit for human
habitation but in which she was doing her best to relieve suffering,
poverty, ignorance, and superstition. When Brewster put me on the
train, I found in my compartment two ghosts with white caps and
heavy veils that reached to the waist and had holes only for eyes.
These were women in *purdah*. No men except those in their immediate families could look upon their faces. I tried a friendly smile and in
response the veils were thrown back. Mrs. Hayes had told me about
purdah and how on one occasion when treating a woman with a
heavy veil she had asked, "What good does it do to cover your face?"
Her patient had replied, "I don't know, but perhaps the men do."
How conservative womanhood is! How we hold to customs, afraid
to change! Fortunately, it seemed to me, internationalism was striking a hard blow at purdah and slowly women were uncovering their
faces.

---

*Named for the first missionary to India sent out by the Women's Foreign Mis-
sionary Society of the Methodist Episcopal Church in 1870. (See Wade Crawford
Barclaw, *The History of Methodist Missions*, vol. 3. New York: Board of Missions,
Methodist Church, 1957, pp. 502 f.)

In Ceylon I boarded a steamer again and continued on through the Arabian Sea, the Red Sea, and the Suez Canal. At Port Said, Egypt, mail caught up with us. I found sixty letters waiting for me and read avidly from one o'clock in the morning until breakfast.

Something else awaited me: a cablegram from President Kerr to the effect that the reorganization of the State System of Higher Education necessitated my return to Oregon at my earliest convenience. A letter to reach me in London would follow, he said. I knew, of course, that a reorganization of the state-supported institutions of higher education was going on. Arthur J. Klein of the U. S. Office of Education, who had been chairman of the land-grant college survey I had participated in a few years before, had also conducted a survey of higher education in Oregon. But I had not felt any particular concern for the School of Home Economics.

A few days later when I went to the office of William M. Jardine, the U. S. Consul in Cairo, I heard something that aroused my curiosity. I had met Dr. Jardine previously when he was president of Kansas State College and when he was Secretary of Agriculture. At one of the annual Land-Grant College Association meetings in Washington, he had presented us to President Coolidge at a reception in the White House. (I remember my surprise at the time in seeing that the President had *red* hair.) Dr. Jardine's brother, James T., had been Director of the Agricultural Experiment Station in Oregon from 1920 to 1931. Hence, we were not entirely strangers, but I had no reason to believe he would recognize me when I came in unannounced. "Wait, don't tell me who you are," he said. "You're Dean Milam from Oregon State College." Then a moment later he asked, "What's going on in Oregon? What's this I hear about cutting the number of deans from 39 to 13?" I told him he apparently knew more about it than I did. I had been traveling and knew little about reorganization plans for higher education in Oregon.

My reaction to this rumor was curiosity rather than concern. The School of Home Economics held a strong position on our campus and in the state, and I doubted very much that it would be reduced to a department. I had to wait, however, for President Kerr's letter to learn the details. In the meantime, the request to come home did not appear so urgent that I needed to stop my tour immediately, but I did decide to eliminate visits to Istanbul and the countries of northern Europe. Dean Marion Talbot, my former teacher at the University of Chicago, was serving as president of a women's college in Turkey and I had hoped to visit her but decided to forego the pleasure. However, after coming this far to see places in the Near East I had heard of all my life, I fully intended to see them.

One afternoon an American physician and his wife came to our hotel in Cairo to take three of us out to the pyramids. A traffic jam in the city caused by the entourage of the King of Egypt—purported to be the highest paid ruler in the world at that time—closely guarded by his Irish and English Guards on motorcycles, delayed us for a time. Our hosts suggested that we ride camels to the Sphinx from the Pyramid of Giza. Moses, the camel I rode, and the boy who led him had been licensed only recently and Moses and I did not get along well. On the long, sloping decline I found it impossible to relax and go with the motion of the swaying camel. At the Sphinx, Moses would not kneel gracefully on his forelegs and then fold his rear legs under him as he was supposed to do. When the boy struck him he came down with great force on his front knees and I dismounted unceremoniously over his head.

Because of a bruise on my knee from the fall, our doctor host advised that I not climb the pyramid with the others. Instead he suggested a drive out onto the desert to see some agate-like rocks he had found there. On the way, he drove into loose sand and got stuck. After pushing and shoving and putting paper and gunny sacks under the wheels, we succeeded only in getting stuck deeper in the sand. We saw a car coming along the crest of a dune and honked to warn it not to come too close. The driver came on, however, and he too got stuck. Neither the young Arab driver nor the Spanish girl with him could speak English, but she knew enough French for us to communicate a little. The doctor decided to go for help and leave the rest of us with the cars to enjoy the afterglow of a beautiful sunset and watch the stars come out. The air began to cool and the sand to lose its heat. Before our host returned hours later with seventeen men, the air became quite cold. Proud of their physical prowess, the laughing Bedouins in the group picked our cars up out of the sand and put them back onto a hard surface. Being thrown from a camel and getting stuck on the sands of the Sahara were adventures enough for one day! On a trip to the old city of Memphis the next day I was offered a donkey named Abraham

Lincoln, but after my encounter with Moses the previous day, I chose to walk.

From Egypt I went to Palestine. The overnight trip by train started from Cairo at four in the afternoon, took us across Suez, along the Mediterranean Sea north of Sinai, through Gaza and onto the Philistian plain the next morning. From the car windows we could see orange, fig, and olive groves. Oranges that bright-eyed youngsters held up for sale at stops along the way were finer than any I had seen in California. As the train wound its way upward through the Valley of Sorek, the Judean hillsides were splashed with the brilliant colors of spring wildflowers—scarlet poppy anemones, wild cyclamen, yellow garland chrysanthemums, and other bright-hued varieties.

The two missionaries from China with whom I was traveling knew about the pension operated by the American Colony north of the old walled city of Jerusalem. We went there for lodging for our ten-day stay in Palestine. This pleasant hostel not only provided restful beds and excellent food, but also a friendly, non-commercial atmosphere. Among the American Colony members we met were Martha Spafford Vester and her sister Grace, whose parents had founded the colony fifty years before, and Grace's husband, Dr. John D. Whiting, whose parents had been among the early arrivals. Mrs. Vester's father, Horatio G. Spafford, had been a Chicago lawyer, but after he and his wife Anna had gone through a series of personal tragedies—including the drowning of four daughters in a shipwreck off Newfoundland and their only son's death from scarlet fever—they decided to move to Jerusalem. A group of Christian friends joined them. "They came not as missionaries or preachers," Mrs. Bertha Vester once described their purpose, "but simply to find peace and to give themselves to God each in his own way, here in this arid land where Christ lived and died." Bertha was three at the time, and her sister a baby. In Turkish-ruled Jerusalem in the 1880's the little group of families and those who joined them later—including Swedish families from Chicago and Sweden—became known as the American Colony. They served all races and creeds and gained the confidence of the Moslems, Jews, Christians, and atheists. At first they lived in a high-ceilinged house inside the city walls, but as the group grew larger they moved to a former pasha's palace outside the walls, a half mile from the Damascus Gate.

Education for Moslem girls had been limited to instruction in the Koran, but when a friend of the family became minister of education he asked the American Colony to furnish a headmistress for a school to provide a broader education for them. Bertha and her governess shared the job, and a school was opened near the Dome of the Rock in the Moslem quarter. Later Bertha married Frederick Vester, the businessman son of a Lutheran missionary. She gave up her teaching post and raised six children of her own. Mr. Vester put the Colony on a sound business basis, opening a gift shop in Jerusalem and a pension in buildings adjacent to the Colony's home, installing the first telephones in Jerusalem, bringing a steam roller from Chicago to repair the streets, opening an automobile agency, starting a pig-raising and other agricultural ventures, and encouraging members of the Colony to serve as guides for tourists and to use their talents in many ways. John D. Whiting wrote articles on the Holy Land for the *National Geographic* and other periodicals. Photographers of the American Colony provided pictures for these articles and for stereopticon slides and Christmas cards. Family Bibles in many homes in the United States have pressed flowers from the Holy Land which were picked and preserved by members of the American Colony. At the time of my first visit, the Colony had opened a store in New York City. They used the income from these activities and gifts from people in many parts of the world to carry on their philanthropies.

In World War I, the U. S. Consul had urged the Colony to leave, but Bertha's mother said, "We came to serve, and this is our supreme moment for service." The Colony cared for sick and wounded and with funds provided by American friends fed as many as 2,400 starving refugees a day.

On Christmas Day in 1925, an Arab widower left a tiny baby in Bertha's arms, saying, "If I take my baby to my cave home, he will die." Bertha took the baby, named him Noel, and started a baby home and a mothercraft training center that eventually became the Spafford Memorial Children's Hospital, which so far as I know still occupies the building that was the Colony's first home inside the city walls. At the time of my 1932 visit, Mrs. Vester and her staff were caring for hundreds of children in the baby home and in a child welfare station and were helping to educate dozens of mothers. The Colony also maintained a community playground and a school of handicrafts in which girls could learn the rudiments of sewing and dressmaking.

Harry Emerson Fosdick, pastor of the Riverside Church in New York City, was an active supporter of the activities of the American Colony Aid Association. A few years before my visit, Dr. Fosdick and his wife had stayed in the Colony while gathering material for his book, A *Pilgrimage to Palestine*, published in 1927. This book helped me then and has helped me since, as I have reread it, by providing insight into what was going on in Palestine at that time.

The American Colony is unique, but another type of colonization had been going on for half a century in Palestine and was gaining momentum. The Zionist Movement to create a Jewish nation had brought in more than 40,000 immigrants before World War I and many more after the war. At the time of my 1932 visit, Palestine had a population of more than one million people, about one-sixth of whom were Jews. A good many of these immigrants had formed agricultural or industrial colonies. They had purchased land and were striving to wrest a living from it. There did not seem to be many Jews in Jerusalem, although I did see long-bearded, black-robed patriarchs facing the Wailing Wall, reading from scriptures, and swaying back and forth. Although most of the population were Arabs, there were Jewish, Christian, Moslem, and Armenian quarters within the walls of the Old City.

We went out one day to see a large farm operated by a colony of Jewish women who were partially supported by British women. We heard of other groups who had taken barren areas and, through the application of scientific agriculture and hard, purposeful labor, had developed productive and relatively prosperous communities. The country seemed peaceful at the time of my visit, but because of the colossal economic problems involved and the clash of cultural and religious differences between the colonists and the native population, I gained the impression that there was little hope for the success of the Zionist Movement.

Palestine was the Holy Land for many religions and sects. Pilgrims from many lands had been coming there for hundreds of years, some for brief visits, others to spend the rest of their lives there. One of the most interesting groups we saw were the Russians. They had fine churches, and choruses of men went through the countryside at Eastertime singing beautiful church music in their deep, resonant voices. Alms they received, I was told, helped provide a livelihood for several villages.

Palestine was a small country—smaller than the area drained by the Willamette River in northwestern Oregon. "From Dan even to Beersheba," the Old Testament extent of Israel delineated in Judges 20:1, is only 160 miles, about the same distance as from Portland to Roseburg in western Oregon. Even though the country was small, I found it so full of dramatic physical contrast and so rich in Biblical history that it never became monotonous. As Dr. Fosdick points out in *A Pilgrimage to Palestine,* one can stand on one of the mountain tops, 3,000 feet above sea level, and see almost all of the area in which many of the events of the Old and New Testaments took place. From the vicinity of Bethany, which had been the home of Mary and Martha in Biblical times, and of Bethlehem, where we went to see the Church of the Nativity, we could look down nearly 4,000 feet to the Dead Sea only 14 miles away. On the far side we could see the high plateau of the Land of Moab in Trans-Jordan. Much of the land is stone-covered, treeless, and barren—relieved in April by splotches of colorful wildflowers—but on one trip we visited the fertile Plain of Esdraelon. We could see how by contrast with the wastelands the well-watered areas looked like a "promised land" or a "land flowing with milk and honey." By western standards, however, it did not look like a productive agricultural country.

On this same trip we visited Nazareth and the Sea of Galilee and saw nearby Mt. Tabor. On trips in and near Jerusalem we were impressed by the beauty of the stained glass windows of the Dome of the Rock (Mosque of Omar); by the sacred and historical significance of such places as the Mount of Olives, the Garden of Gethsemane, and Rachael's Tomb revered alike by Moslem, Jew, and Christian; and by the dreadful bickering of Christians over the use of the Church of the Holy Sepulchre. This church had been divided among five Christian sects who held a monopoly and would permit no others to hold public worship there. Roman Catholic, Greek Orthodox, Armenian, Jacobite Syrian, and Coptic services were held in different parts of the church at the same time, but the sects were jealous of one another. Because bloodshed and even deaths had occurred as a result of arguments between worshipers, Moslem guards were stationed at the church to maintain order. This state of affairs gave me a sickening feeling. How far removed it seemed from all Christ stood for!

Palestinian women wore thick, heavy, black veils. I was told that when the Turks ordered their women to remove veils, the Palestinians had insisted that their women increase the weight and thickness of their veils as a means of showing resentment against Turkish influence.

I left Palestine with a feeling that the country had many unsolved problems with unpredictable outcomes. I also felt that I would like to return for a longer period some time to study the whole area more carefully.

From Haifa in Palestine we sailed for four stormy days to Italy. We had cabled to Naples for reservations in a pension, but by the time we had landed at Brindisi on the heel of the Italian boot and traveled by train across the ankle, Mussolini had moved some of his Alpine soldiers into the pension where we had planned to stay. When we arrived about midnight, the English proprietor had no rooms for us but permitted us to climb five long, long flights of stairs and spread out our bedding rolls on the dining room floor. We had just barely gone to sleep when in came the immigration officials to check our passports. It seemed only moments after we had gone back to sleep that the maids awakened us to have us roll up our bedding because they needed room in which to feed the soldiers. One of the girls moaned, "Now I know what they mean when they say, 'See Naples and die!'"

After quick visits to Pompeii, Vesuvius, and parts of Naples, we moved on to Rome. There we visited the Vatican, St. Paul's and St. Peter's cathedrals, memorials to Keats and Shelley, and a girls' school. We heard *Tosca* in the magnificent opera house.

In Florence, by previous arrangement, I met Alice Quigg—a friend from Oregon in whose summer home, *Grayling*, on Oregon's McKenzie River, both Ruth Gill and I had visited. Miss Quigg taught at Portland Academy in the winter, but loved to travel in the summer. At the time I met her in Florence, she was enamored of the Balearic Isles and wanted me to go to live there with her. I told her that if the elimination of deans at Oregon State College meant that I had lost my job, I might very well accept her invitation. We had a pleasant visit, went to Pisa together, and saw Caruso's home and a bit of rural Italy. I left Miss Quigg in Florence and went on to

Milan and then to Geneva where a group of us heard the League of Nations in session one morning. Paris was disappointing because of the almost continuous rain the two days we were there, but we did see some of the famous museums and art galleries, tasted delicious French cookery, and heard *William Tell* in the Opera House. Much to our surprise the trip across the English Channel was a smooth one, a blessing for which we were thankful.

In London I found among the letters awaiting me the promised one from President Kerr. In it he indicated that the School of Home Economics was to be strengthened by the reorganization. It was to be the only major school in its field in the State System, and I had been appointed Director of Home Economics for the State System, as well as Dean of the School. I could see why he wanted me to come home.

Also in London I received another surprise. I learned that Ruth Gill was to be married. When I had left her a few months before in Canton she did not even have a "steady," but A. R. Hammond had changed all that. A graduate of Iowa University who had taught for a while in Honolulu and at Bangkok Christian College, A.R. (who has no given names, only initials) was at that time manager of a business-machines sales agency in Bangkok. Through a cousin of Ruth's, A.R. and Ruth had heard of each other, and A.R. had seen her picture. They knew something of each other, therefore, when he came to Canton to meet her. After about three days he proposed marriage. She told him she did not know him well enough. He went off to Manila for a few days and then returned to propose again. Finally, she had agreed to marry him and after making arrangements to be released from the last year of her contract at Lingnan University was planning to return home.

Although I had only limited time in London, there were two people I wanted to be sure to see—Winifred Harley and Eric Ashby. Miss Harley, who had come to the United States from England in the early 1920's, had been head of preschool education at the Merrill-Palmer School in Detroit, where I had met her several times. At the time of my visit to London she had returned to England to serve for a year on the faculty of Darlington Hall. She was apparently doing some advanced study at the time also, for she received a certificate as a graduate in Child Development from the University of London a few years later. I spent a day or two with her in her home in The

Mews and learned more of her excellent work. As I mentioned previously, we were fortunate to have her come to Corvallis several times for the summer session and for the year 1937-38.

Eric Ashby, a bachelor in his mid-twenties, had come to my home with my old friend E. J. Kraus about a year before my round-the-world trip. Eric had invited me to visit him if I ever came to London. A graduate of the Imperial College of Science in the University of London, Eric had received a Commonwealth Fund Fellowship for study at the University of Chicago and the Desert Laboratory of the Carnegie Institution for 1929-31. At the University of Chicago, he came under the tutelage of Dr. Kraus, who was head of the botany department. In the summer Dr. Kraus took Eric on an extensive tour of the West, especially to Arizona, Oregon, and Hawaii. When this gay pair came to my home for dinner that day, they had an inexhaustible fund of tales about their adventures. I admired the way in which Dr. Kraus had taken Eric under his wing—as I had marveled many times before at how he had given unstintingly of his time to a student whom he thought worthy of personal assistance.

Following Eric's instructions, I had let him know that I was on my way to London. He had written me in Paris asking me to tell him what train I would be on so that he could meet me in London. He had married a young botanist from Castle-Douglas, Scotland, a few months earlier and was eager to have me meet her. I did not trouble him to meet my train, but the day after I arrived I called him and he came to take me to lunch. Later he invited me to their home for a dinner of baked salmon which he himself had prepared. I often recall that pleasant, stimulating evening with the Ashbys as I learn through newspapers and television of his advancements and writings. For thirteen years he was a professor, first in the University of Sidney, and then in Manchester. In 1950 he became President and Vice-Chancellor of the Queen's University, Belfast; and in 1956, Queen Elizabeth dubbed him Sir Eric. From 1958 to 1960 he was chairman of the Ashby Commission, which provided a blueprint for higher education in Nigeria. In 1963 he served a term as President of the British Association for the Advancement of Science. More recently, he has held the office of Master of Clare College, Cambridge University, has actively assisted developing universities in tropical Africa, has written several books and many articles, and has become one of the world's most-respected authorities in the field of higher education.

The ticket I had purchased in Hong Kong entitled me to first-class passage from England to the United States on the luxurious S.S. *Europa* at no additional expense. Among the passengers were Mr. W. B. Ayer from Portland, who had been state chairman for food conservation during World War I. Other prominent people on board whom I might otherwise never have had the opportunity to meet included Thomas Lamont, the New York banker; Max Epstein, the Chicago merchant who had provided money for the Clinic named for him at the University of Chicago; and Dr. Hugh Cabot, a surgeon at the Mayo Clinic who was formerly dean of the University of Michigan Medical School. The first morning at sea I went in to breakfast and found I was the only woman present. Among the first-class passengers, I learned, the ladies are served breakfast in their staterooms. I managed not to make too many social blunders before we docked in New York.

After I returned to Corvallis, A. R. Hammond arrived to get acqainted with me and with some of Ruth's other friends before she returned from Canton. He wanted me to cable Ruth that I approved of their marriage, but I felt that whether or not they married was something they had to decide for themselves. I suggested to A.R. that he go to Vancouver to meet her when she arrived and that they make their final decision then. If they wanted to break the engagement at that time, they should feel that it was all right to do so. If they still wanted to marry, I offered to stand "in loco parentis."

Finding they still felt the same about each other after the separation of several months, Ruth and A. R. returned to Corvallis together. My sister Lora Hanson offered her garden for the wedding to accommodate the large group of faculty, former students, and other friends who would attend the ceremonies. After a lovely September wedding, the bride and groom began a honeymoon that took them to Buffalo for six months and then on around the world to Siam, where A.R. resumed his previous position as manager of a business-machines sales agency in Bangkok.

16. Commencement

LOVELY SPRING FLOWERS and Royal Anne cherries swelling on the tree in my back yard greeted me on my return to Oregon in late May 1932. I arrived home in time for Commencement at Oregon State College, a time of unusual significance that particular year. That Commencement marked the end of one era and the beginning of a new one, not only for the sixty-nine young women receiving degrees in home economics but also for several key staff members and for higher education in Oregon as well.

William Jasper Kerr, completing twenty-five years of service to the college, presided as President for the last time. When he conferred degrees the following year he did so as Chancellor of the State System of Higher Education. At the 1932 Commencement, he conferred honorary degrees on Dean Cordley of the School of Agriculture, who had retired after twenty-seven years of service to the college; on Dean Bexell of the School of Commerce, who was retiring after twenty-three years; and on Mr. W. A. Jensen, who had been Dr. Kerr's loyal executive secretary for a quarter of a century.

Outwardly that beautiful June Commencement Day seemed happy and serene; inwardly it was a time of concern for faculty and administration—as well as for the 527 graduates going out into an uncertain future in a time of economic depression. A State Board of Higher Education had assumed the functions formerly performed by the three separate boards of regents for the University of Oregon, for the three normal schools, and for Oregon State Agricultural College. The newly formed Board set out to eliminate duplication, provide a more economical educational structure, and reduce inter-institutional competition for funds from the Legislature. It put its sweeping program of reorganization into effect on July 1, 1932. On our campus, the School of Commerce, the School of Mines, and the School of Basic Arts and Sciences were abolished; the School of

Health and Physical Education was reduced to a Division of Physical Education; certain separate departments were either abolished or brought under a school, and a new School of Science and a Lower Division of Liberal Arts and Sciences were established.

In each major field of study, one person was named Dean and Director to serve as coordinator of all work in that field throughout the State System. I, as Dean of the School of Home Economics, for example, became also Director of Home Economics to coordinate the work in home economics at the University of Oregon, Oregon State College, and the normal schools at Monmouth, Ashland, and La Grande.

The University of Oregon had long had a Department of Household Arts which offered courses in clothing, foods, and homemaking, but did not grant degrees. According to the Board's report, courses in home economics at the University of Oregon were reduced fifty-four percent, but the program of service courses was not hurt materially and in many ways strengthened. The resulting streamlined curriculum was sound and adequate for a non-degree-granting department. The head of Household Arts at the University of Oregon was leaving. One of our graduates, Mabel A. Wood, who had received a master's degree from Columbia University and had taught at OSC for several years, was appointed the new head—a position she held with enthusiasm and resourcefulness until her retirement in 1964. Our relationship was always cordial and her competence made my responsibilities as Director of Home Economics for the State System comparatively easy and pleasant.

At Corvallis, according to the Board's report, home economics courses were reduced by twenty-two percent, but the courses we lost were vestiges of another era or were nonessential. New ones strengthened and upgraded our curriculum. In Clothing, Textiles, and Related Arts, we lost Millinery, Textile Design, Historic Costumes and Textile Materials, and one summer course in Tailoring. In Foods and Nutrition we lost one of our two courses in Food Selection and Preparation, one in Meal Planning and Serving, and a food selection and preparation course for men. We gained courses in Basal Metabolism and Animal Experimentation. In Home Economics Education we gained new courses in curriculum, supervision, and adult education. In Household Administration we lost courses in Home Problems, Home Nursing, and Home Management House

Supervision, but gained new seminars in Home Management and Child Development. In Institution Economics no course changes were made.

The chief objectives of the State Board of Higher Education in reorganizing higher education in Oregon were "harmony and efficiency coupled with economy." Concurrent with the establishment of the new System, two other factors forced economies even beyond those contemplated by the Board. First, expenditure of an appropriation of $1,181,173 for higher education approved by the 1931 Legislature was effectively held up by a petition for referendum to voters of the state. The fund had been appropriated for use in 1932, but the referendum could not be voted on by the people until November; hence, the money was lost for that year. The second factor forcing economy was the loss of revenue from student tuition. The depressed condition of the economy of the state and nation had resulted in a substantial drop in enrollment. At OSC, from a high of nearly 4,000 in 1928-1930, enrollment dropped to a low of 1,870 in spring term 1934. Drastic economies had to be effected to continue to operate the college on the reduced budgets. Construction of new buildings ceased; new equipment, improvements, repairs, and painting were minimal; the number of faculty and general employees was reduced, heavier teaching and administrative duties were assumed by the retained faculty; classes were enlarged, fewer sections offered, courses eliminated; public services were curtailed, salary reductions ranging from 5 to 15 percent went into effect at the beginning of the 1932-33 academic year.

The salary reductions on our campus came about as a recommendation of the entire staff, who felt that they would rather take a salary cut than have the Board discontinue important activities serving students and the people of the state. In campus meetings when this matter was discussed, an official report states, "staff members earnestly expressed the view that as a matter of fairness to the citizens of the state, members of the college staff should accept whatever reduction in salary might be necessary in meeting the emergency. They were not unmindful of the serious disadvantage both to the work of the institution and to their individual professional futures . . . involved in salary reductions. Yet it was deemed inconsistent, selfish, and unjust for staff members to continue with full compensation when the citizens generally were experiencing reduced incomes. Moreover, reduction of salaries generally was strongly advocated rather than radical reductions of college work, thus making necessary the release of large numbers of staff members at a time when few would be able to find employment."

In the School of Home Economics in the early years of the new era, we developed three patterns of study. Each provided ample opportunity for broad cultural education as well as technical training. A student could qualify for either a Bachelor of Arts or a Bachelor of Science degree in any one of the three curricula. Curriculum A, combining general education with principles of homemaking, carried a liberal proportion of electives; it was designed primarily for students planning to become homemakers or to teach home economics in secondary schools, to do commercial work in clothing, or to enter home economics journalism. Curriculum B, a professional course of study, included technical subjects and basic arts and sciences and prepared for homemaking and for careers in institutional management, dietetics, extension work, commercial fields in foods, or teaching. Curriculum C provided general home economics training for juniors and seniors who had completed two years of junior college or lower division study.

Our philosophy as expressed in the *Catalog* at that time was as follows:

> *All problems of the home and family life fall within the field of home economics. The School of Home Economics seeks to serve, directly or indirectly, every Oregon home. Through resident teaching, the School makes its direct contribution to the life of the commonwealth. Students are trained for the responsibilities of homemaking and parenthood, for education, administration and management, for other work in home economics and allied fields. Through research and extension, closely coordinated with the resident teaching, effort is constantly directed toward the solution of home problems.*

As was the case after my return from China in 1924, I made many talks on the need for international understanding. Again I went to women's clubs, missionary societies, teachers groups, and women's professional groups. Again response was good and modest contributions continued to come in to assist with the scholarship program.

Because of the economic conditions of the time, the gifts were not large. Through radio I had the opportunity to report to the women of the state what their dollars were doing to help educate women in the Orient. My former secretary, Zelta Feike Rodenwold, who had charge of the "Homemakers' Half Hour" for the state-owned station KOAC, invited me to describe my recent trip around the world in eight weekly talks.

A new arrangement for granting foreign scholarships in home economics arose at this time. When a national officer of the American Home Economics Association asked me to continue as a member of the International Committee, I said I would rather not. "Why?" she asked. I told her that in all the years the committee had been in existence it had done relatively little to stimulate development of home economics in other countries. It had helped raise a fund in 1920 to send my former professor from Chicago, Alice P. Norton, who was then editor of the *Home Economics Journal,* to Turkey for two years to establish a department of home economics at a Constantinople college for girls. In 1930 it had sponsored a traveling scholarship for an English woman who had been teaching in India. But that was about all. It appeared to me that all the committee did was talk. My attitude had a shocking effect, and later when I pointed out that money being put away in savings accounts by the Association could better be spent to assist foreign scholars, a plan was worked out to provide scholarships on a matching-funds basis. If the institution which a selected student from another country wanted to attend would raise half the amount for a scholarship, the Association would pay the other half.

The AHEA International Scholarships plan went into effect in 1934-35. Wang Te Chin and Hu Jung Te received the first two grants to study at Yenching University. These were the only scholarships of this type granted for study at a foreign university; subsequent ones were for study at American universities. Students who came to Oregon State College on these scholarships included Takako Okada from Japan, 1937-38; Frances Wen-Yuen Fong, 1942-43, and Mei-ling Wu, 1947-48 from China; Pramila Pandit Barooah from India 1945-46; Rae P. Vernon from New Zealand, 1943-44; Martha E. Jooste from South Africa, 1949-50; and Masu Takeda from Japan, 1953-54.

A SERIES OF DELIGHTFUL SUMMER EXPERIENCES—mostly personal but to some extent professional—commenced early in the 1930's. Alice Quigg, the Portland teacher whom I had met and traveled with in Italy, wanted to sell her summer home on the McKenzie River and offered it to me at a price I could not turn down. Ruth Gill Hammond, who had spent several months one summer with Miss Quigg at *Grayling*, as the cottage was called, in succeeding years often went with me to open it up in the spring and close it in the fall. *Grayling* provided an excellent spot to entertain summer guests— family, faculty, travelers, and teachers from other parts of the country. Deep in the western slopes of the Cascade Mountains, fronting on a strikingly beautiful stream of sparkling water, *Grayling* is a place for fishing, relaxation, reading, and friendly conversation.

Here I read "Teddy" Linn's biography of Jane Addams and learned for the first time that he was her nephew. Here I caught up on reading that could not fit into a busy schedule at home. Here I have worked on manuscripts for *Journal* articles, reports that were on my mind, and chapters of this book.

Sisters, nephews and nieces, their children, and other family members have signed the *Grayling* guest book many times. Hundreds of faculty and other friends have shared this place of quiet relaxation. Marks with dates on a wall in one corner of the living room record the annual growth of many children—including Ruth Hammond's Barbara, John, and Carolyn, and Barbara's two daughters, Kelly and Sari Griggs. Growth marks for Carolyn Hammond and her niece Sari, start when each of the two little girls was only twenty-four inches tall.

The *Grayling* guest book records the visits of Abby Marlatt of Wisconsin, E. Lee Vincent of Detroit, Winifred Harley from London, Rachel Stutsman Ball and her husband from Detroit, Ruth Sun from Shanghai, LeVelle Wood from Kansas, Belle Lowe from Iowa, Lucy Chen from Yenching University, Chase Going Woodhouse from Connecticut, Mary Schwartz Rose from New York, Katherine Roberts from Detroit, Mary Rokahr from Washington D.C., Suen-i Wu Chang and H. K. Chang from Nanking, Caroline Chen from Peiping, Sarah Louise Arnold (the niece) from Massachusetts, and dozens of others.

Little Barbara Hammond helped "break the ice" on the occasion of Abby Marlatt's visit to *Grayling*. A tall, stately, large woman, positive and dynamic, Miss Marlatt was head of home economics at the University of Wisconsin. When she arrived, she took off her huge, wide-brimmed hat and placed it on the bed in the downstairs bedroom. Lee Vincent, at that time from the Merrill-Palmer School and later Dean of Home Economics at Cornell, offered to take care of Barbara and John Hammond while their mother and I fried chicken and prepared the noon meal. When little Barbara went to the bedroom to remove her hot clothing, she spied Miss Marlatt's hat and a moment later appeared wearing nothing except the hat, asking how she looked. Delighted and intrigued by the dimpled, bright-eyed child, Miss Marlatt hurried to get her camera, but Barbara was too quick for her and was gone before the camera could be found. The incident broke down whatever formality had existed up to that time.

Fifteen years later, on another visit to *Grayling*, Barbara inserted a verse in the guest book:

It Only Rhymes

Oh, where's the place you'll always find
Perfect rest and peace of mind?
Where time means naught, so clocks unwind,
And the food is good, the friends so kind?
If you, too, have wanted this kind of thing,
But your searches always end in one last fling,
Then pack the bag, friend, come to Grayling,
Relax in a hammock listening to a river sing!

Another guest in later years wrote, "Your retreat is a place to gain physical and spiritual strength as well as a place for children to grow and be measured. I went to the river at dusk. When I returned to the house, nightfall had settled like a veil around it, and the world was at peace."

Grayling at McKenzie Bridge, Oregon

17. Encounter

A S THE HOME ECONOMICS STUDY TOUR TO THE ORIENT started on its way in June 1937, alumnae of Oregon State College and other friends greeted us along the way. In Seattle, my first traveling companion to the Orient, Camilla Mills Biggerstaff, and her husband, a University of Washington professor, gave us messages for friends in China. In Vancouver, British Columbia, four alumnae came to the dock to see us off on the S.S. *Empress of Russia*. At Victoria, Alice Ravenhill, the English home economist who had been a campus visitor twenty years previously, and her sister came aboard to have tea with us. Then in the evening of June 26, we sailed west toward the Far East.

The idea for the summer tour had popped up when Paul Monroe, Director of the International Institute at Columbia University, invited me to prepare a paper to present at the Seventh Biennial Conference of the World Federation of Education Associations in Tokyo, August 2-7, 1937. Someone suggested that I form a study tour to visit Japan, China, and Korea before the conference. Alma C. Fritchoff, head of the Department of Clothing, Textiles, and Related Arts at OSC, agreed to assist in leading the tour. She had had previous travel experience, having collected textile samples and costumes one summer in Europe and having spent part of a sabbatical year in the Orient. The Director of the OSC summer session appointed her to the summer faculty (I was already on 12-months salary) and arranged for college credit to be given to all who enrolled for the tour and completed the assignments.

The Canadian Pacific Steamship Lines helped announce the tour by having a descriptive folder printed to be mailed out. The steamship company provided transportation and meals aboard the ship for Miss Fritchoff and me as leaders of the party. For what was planned to be a sixty-day tour, the others paid a fee of $765 to cover transportation, hotel accommodations, meals on board the

ship and at hotels, lectures and tours, baggage transfer, tips, and the
college registration fee of $20. We all had to pay for our own pass-
ports and visas, meals on trains, conveyances for individual trips, and
laundry and other personal items.

This seemed an opportune time for my twin sister Ada to see
the Orient, and I invited her to join our group. She was teaching high
school in Madison, Wisconsin, and she and her husband, Edgar A.
"Ted" Cockefair, had written a textbook, *Health and Achievement*,
published the previous year by Ginn and Company. Because the
prospect for royalties seemed good, they decided that Ted and their
daughter Mary Lou should take the Orient tour also. Mary Lou was
graduating from the University of Wisconsin that spring and had no
conflicting plans for the summer. When Dr. Monroe, or someone
else on the program committee for the Tokyo meeting, learned that
Dr. Cockefair was going to be in Japan, Ted was also invited to
write a paper to present at the conference.

Other OSC staff members—Lucy Case, the nutrition specialist
on the Extension staff, and Agnes Kolshorn of the Foods and Nutrition Department— joined the study tour, as did Agnes' sister, Henrietta Burton, from the Bureau of Indian Affairs in Washington, D.C.
Our group of twenty-two also included six women from California,
two others from Oregon, and six from various parts of the country,
including our cousin Dorothy McGinnis (Uncle Roz' daughter)
from Kansas City. Many of the party were OSC graduates, among
them LeVelle Wood, whom I remembered so well as a shy little
freshman afraid of everything and who in the meantime had become
a professor of Institution Management at Kansas State College and
the coauthor of a textbook. That trip in 1937, LeVelle told me years
later, opened her eyes and since that time she has taken advantage
of every opportunity she has had to travel.

Another group of ten, led by Benjamin R. Andrews of Columbia
University, boarded the ship at Victoria. They were going for somewhat similar purposes but with a different itinerary. They joined us
occasionally for our daily lectures and discussions aboard the ship.
One day Dr. Andrews gave a lecture on the values of travel. The
Tokyo YWCA had arranged to have placed on board the ship a
set of books on Japan for the use of both parties. The ship's route
carried us far enough north to see some of the Aleutian Islands. The
weather on deck was not pleasant and we were glad to have tours

of the ship's kitchen and storage plant and other parts of the ship to supplement our study periods.

When we arrived in Japan, the Japanese greeted us eagerly and treated us hospitably. Reporters and photographers came out in a launch to meet us at Yokohama. A radio broadcast the night before had announced our arrival. Women from Tokyo's Women's University and the YWCA had prepared a luncheon for us, but because of the ship's having docked hours late in a dense fog, the luncheon turned into a "high tea" at five o'clock. We missed meeting Kagawa, the great Japanese social worker, and hearing his talk because he could not wait for our late arrival. At a sukiyaki dinner later, many of our travelers encountered for the first time the Japanese customs of taking off shoes indoors and sitting on mats before low tables.

On the following extremely hot July day, we toured Tokyo and called at several homes before returning to our ship at Yokohama about eleven o'clock. This time we had adequate guides and did not get "taken for a ride" as Camilla and I had on our first visit 15 years before. As the ship sailed between the Japanese islands enroute to China, a wireless message came from Program Chairman Paul Monroe asking me to prepare a second paper for the World Federation meeting, but I declined with thanks. I had enough to do without writing another paper. The ship stopped long enough at Kobe for us to visit the women's college where we found Sarah Field still serving as head of the Home Economics Department and had a glimpse of her laboratories and home management house. At Nagasaki, where the ship stopped for coal, the head of home economics at Kwassui College came aboard and dined with us; later we went ashore to see her department and a demonstration of the formal, graceful tea ceremony. From the deck of our ship we also watched the laborious coaling process in which men and women passed hundreds of tons of coal by hand from barges into the ship, finishing at four o'clock in the morning.

Enroute to China we looked forward eagerly to two days in Shanghai, one in Hangchow, one in Nanking, and a week in Peiping. Therefore, the advice we received from American Express representatives in Shanghai caused dismay. They advised us to take the next ship, a French liner to sail in four days, back to Japan. The "China Incident" at the Marco Polo Bridge, which led to the outbreak of the Sino-Japanese War, had occurred on July 7, 1937, while we were approaching Japan. By the time we reached Shanghai, the Japanese had invaded North China. The American Express people had charge of our travel arrangements in China, and they said they could not assume responsibility for meeting our schedules if we continued our plan to go to Peiping.

I had been in touch with President Leighton Stuart at Yenching University; he had been expecting us to visit Peiping and Yenching University. I wired him in regard to our situation, and he replied that in spite of the disturbed conditions in the North he thought it would be all right for us to come but to remain a few days longer in Nanking than planned. Miss Fritchoff and I called our group together and discussed the situation. We told them we were willing to go on to Peiping if they wanted to go but that they must not blame anyone but themselves if for any reason our return to the United States was delayed. They voted unanimously to go ahead when Dr. Stuart thought it safe to do so.

With this decision behind us, we began getting acquainted with the country—sightseeing, shopping, visiting schools, factories, and homes, and dining on delicious multi-course Chinese meals. We spent three days in Shanghai and one in Hangchow, and then went on to Nanking, which was still the capital at that time. Albert N. Steward, the OAC graduate whom I had met on previous trips, and his daughter came to see us. Irene Ho, daughter of Sir Robert Ho Tung, whose Eurasian family Ruth Gill and I had visited five years before in Hong Kong, was on the Ministry of Education staff. Dr. Ho directed our schedule for the two days we spent in Nanking. She showed us a number of schools and other projects being sponsored by Generalissimo and Madame Chiang Kai-shek.

When we boarded the train for Peiping we were surprised to find a car reserved for us and the Assistant Traffic Manager, a Chinese graduate of the University of Michigan, on hand to accompany our party north. He explained that we were to be guests of the railway and need not pay for our meals. He helped make our day-and-a-half trip to Tientsin quite comfortable. A few hours before reaching Tientsin, officials received a message that we should stay overnight in that city because martial law was being observed in Peiping and the gates of the city were closed at night. Local educators in Tientsin learned of our arrival, and a large delegation met us and took us to the Astor House hotel for a good night's rest. We were called at

5:30 a.m. and by 7:30 we were back on the train moving toward Peiping in a heavy downpour of rain.

Except for occasional barricades of sandbags we saw little evidence of hostilities as we entered Peiping. There was some unrest and tension in the city, but for the most part life was going on as usual—except in one respect. Peiping normally prepared for a large influx of tourists in the summer but this year hardly any had come. Our party, therefore, received more than its share of hospitality. In accordance with arrangements made through the American Express months before, we stayed at a pension operated by Mrs. Chien, an American woman who had married a Chinese man and had opened one of the fine old Chinese homes as a stopping place for visitors. She served excellent meals, provided comfortable rooms in a delightful Chinese setting, and gave expert assistance in many ways. She knew our planned itinerary and had rickshas awaiting us whenever we needed them.

In Hangchow and Nanking we had seen two of our OSC girls— Letty Warrington, daughter of the head of our departments of Religion and Philosophy, and Betty Chandler. Here in Peiping we ran into them again. They had spent the previous year as exchange students at Lingnan University and were now touring the country.

One afternoon we went out through the western gate of the city to Yenching University. All of the party were delighted to see the beautiful campus that they had heard so much about—especially from me. School was not in session in the summer, but we saw the women's college and home economics facilities.

Miss Chen I (Caroline Chen), a member of the first class in home economics at Yenching, was Chairman of the Home Economics Department as she had been at the time of my 1931 visit. During the previous school year, Mabel Wood, on leave from her position as head of home economics at the University of Oregon, had assisted her. In a quietly effective way, Miss Wood had provided the strength to hold the department together. She had run into a problem that is not unknown to many home economists in colleges and universities. I shall let her tell the story in her own words:

> *Quite unexpectedly, I found myself in the midst of a plot, scheme, or effort of some sort to place Nutrition and Foods*

under Chemistry and to put the Nursery School under Educa-
tion or Psychology and leave only the few clothing classes to
be known as Home Economics.

The greatest tension was in Nutrition, where the instructor
wished to be identified as a chemist rather than as a home econ-
omist. The Chemistry proposal was to change all Foods and
Nutrition course numbers to Chemistry numbers and to list the
nutrition teacher as a professor of chemistry. They did suggest
that when home economics grew strong enough to offer gradu-
ate work, the nutrition courses could be returned to Home
Economics. My argument, briefly, was that this did not sound
like a good way to develop strength in the Home Economics
Department and that if the Chemistry Department could give
the nutrition teacher a full load of chemistry courses, I would
take over the nutrition courses. After many tea sessions lasting
into the dinner hour, the chemistry professor said, "We'll forget
it for this year and leave things as they are." I'm sure that I was
more diplomatic than this brief statement would indicate, but
I did literally talk them down. . . . It was only my devotion
to home economics which made me hold out.

Although Mabel Wood sometimes felt that her one year at
Yenching was too short a time to accomplish what she wished to,
she performed a significant service in keeping the Department of
Home Economics from being fragmented. When Martha M. Kramer,
on leave from Kansas State College, replaced her the next year, the
war situation brought more urgent problems. Dr. Kramer did a fine
piece of work at Yenching under trying conditions. She remained
there until the University was closed by the war in 1941 and was
interned with others of the Yenching faculty until repatriated.

Among the students and faculty we saw that summer of 1937
there was fine spirit and enthusiasm. One of their accomplishments
was publication of a pamphlet entitled "Department of Home Economics, Yenching University, Peiping, China, 1936-37." It had a
full-color photograph of their college building pasted on the front
cover and black-and-white photographs on the inside. In it they
told with pride about the opening of the department in 1923, the
Home Economics Club organized in 1929, scholarships program,
home management house, and two nursery schools (one for children

of Yenching faculty and the other in the Cheng Fu village nearby).
The booklet also showed illustrations of their work in nutrition research, textile design, house planning, and clothing construction.

Leighton Stuart, his same gracious, charming, brilliant self,
greeted us at Yenching, took us through part of the campus, gave
a tea for us, and brought us up to date on the development of the
University. He told us how happy he was that we had made the effort
to come to Peiping and that he hoped we would not be inconven-
ienced in so doing. A faculty member, Dr. Y. P. Mei, also spoke to us.

For six days we visited shops, markets, universities and colleges,
the dietary and medical social service department of Peiping Union
Medical College, the Summer Palace, famous temples, homes,
orphanages, and theaters. Caroline Chen held a tea for us in her
home and introduced us to her father, a picturesque Chinese gentleman who had taken up painting after the age of forty and had become a leading Chinese painter of bamboo.

One evening Mrs. Chien planned a moonlight picnic on a boat
in a lake called the Pei-Hai. Our English-speaking ricksha boys had
not been busy all day—we had gone by bus for that day's trip—and
they were well rested and ready to run. They knew we were late
and raced through the city with passengers and ricksha pullers alike
in a jolly mood, bantering with each other and trying to see which
could reach the Pei-Hai first. In the balmy summer evening we
enjoyed a delicious chicken dinner. Nearby, Coal Hill and its beautiful pagoda and the Forbidden City with its lovely Imperial yellow
tile roofs came into view in the light of the rising full moon while a
young musician on board the boat sang songs to fit the occasion. The
American Ambassador and his wife came alongside in his launch
and called up to us, "How are the adventurous school marms getting
along?"

One afternoon the Mayor of Peiping extended us special courtesies for being the one party that had succeeded in reaching his
city despite advancing Japanese troops. With Dr. Y. P. Mei and
other members of the Returned Students Club acting as guides, we
were admitted to parts of the Forbidden City long closed to the
public. They conducted us through a labyrinth of courtyards and
rooms housing some of China's most valued art treasures and at the
end served a high tea in the Imperial Gardens.

In the business district, our party made quite an impression. Shopkeepers took heart when they saw two of us coming and asked, "Where are the other twenty members of your party?" Our activities appeared to be newsworthy and were mentioned several times in the local newspapers.

On what was supposed to be our last evening in Peiping, Dr. Stuart invited me to come out to Yenching University to have dinner with him. There he told me of some of the impending problems he faced. He had to decide what would be best to do if the Japanese advanced further into the country and took control of the city. After the moon had risen we drove back to Mrs. Chien's and Leighton came into the garden where the rest of the party were enjoying what they thought would be their last evening in this exotic city. They were glad to have this opportunity to say how much they appreciated the encouragement he had given us to come on to Peiping and that they thought the visit to this city the high point of our whole tour.

In order to get an early start the next morning, we were called at four o'clock. After breakfast we left for the train, which was scheduled to leave at six, and deposited ourselves and our luggage —numbering about 60 pieces by this time—in an air-conditioned car. The locomotive had its steam up; we settled back ready to depart. Six o'clock came but the train did not move. Chinese friends who had come to see us off began to make inquiries. They learned that fighting had taken place in the night, and the railroad and telegraph lines between Peiping and Tientsin had been cut. The stationmaster could not tell when the train would leave. At nine o'clock our car was detached and the air conditioning went off. We were advised then to go to the Wagon-Lits Hotel in the Legation Quarter, a few minutes' walk from the station. There we were marooned awaiting orders, but no train ran all day.

The second morning we were called at five in readiness again for the six o'clock train, but when we came down to breakfast, a war correspondent told us no train would run that day. The city gates had been closed and no motor cars or airplanes could leave Peiping. A newsreel cameraman made several attempts to get out, but at the end of the day he was still with us. Rumors began to fly. We heard that the night before about 150 Japanese soldiers, posing as Legation members, had gotten inside the Chinese city, but their ruse had

been discovered and twenty of them had been killed. We heard that
the Japanese had given an ultimatum that the Chinese withdraw
their troops by noon or the city would be bombed. We heard that
Tungchow had been bombed and five hundred people killed.

We were comfortable in the famous, first-class Wagon-Lits
Hotel, but were confined to the Legation quarter and not permitted
to go far to shop or to sightsee. The first day we were almost the
only guests in the hotel, but the second day refugee Chinese families
began to arrive. They carried with them only a few personal belongings—including their most valued art treasures. We passed the time
by having lectures on Chinese art and Chinese child life. One day
Ted Cockefair and I read the papers we had prepared for the Tokyo
meeting but which we now feared we would arrive too late to
present at the conference. Haldore Hanson, Associated Press correspondent for China, and other speakers discussed the political
situation and gave talks on subjects of general interest. One factor
that lessened the strain of waiting was the philisophical attitude of
the whole group toward the delay.

At night we often heard gunfire and explosions. One morning
we heard reports that wounded soldiers and civilians were being
brought into the hospitals slowly but many still lay outside the
gates unable to receive attention. According to reports, the Red
Cross ambulances were not allowed to go outside the gates to bring
in the wounded. Only those able to crawl inside could be picked up
by coolies waiting to help them into trucks to be taken to hospitals.
We heard that thousands of dead lay just outside the city gates.
Some of the newspaper reporters and moving-picture cameramen
who had seen the dead and wounded came back to the hotel much
upset. Some days it rained all day. It was devastating to realize how
many wounded were still out there on the wet fields receiving no
help.

All American citizens in the city had been ordered into the
American Embassy grounds, where a bustling tent city sprang up.
Some Americans did not come in because they preferred to stay
to protect their homes and businesses or schools and were staying on
in their compounds with their Chinese associates and servants.

Our dining room became quite cosmopolitan. Colorful Chinese,
many distinguished-looking, predominated, but there were also
quite a number of Americans and a sprinkling of English, Irish,

German, Swiss, Italian, French, Russian, and some Japanese. Nobody waited for introductions. Any new information passed swiftly around the room. We kept our bags packed ready to go at a moment's notice.

After a few days the fighting around the city died down and we were permitted to travel about. On a second attempt we got out to see the Temple of Heaven, which we agreed must be one of the most impressive places in the whole of China. Just before we reached the Temple, a Japanese airplane circled over the field and dropped newspaper propaganda, which our ricksha boys ran out and picked up for us.

On the evening of August 4, I recognized Dr. Henry S. Houghton, Director of the Peiping Union Medical College, when he came into the Wagon-Lits Hotel, and I spoke to him. He and the British manager of the railway had just come from Tientsin on the first train to get through in more than a week. The American Express man informed us that the Japanese officials—who were now operating the railway—had given their consent to our leaving the next day. At seven o'clock the next morning, ten days after our original departure date, we went to the station in pouring rain and crowded onto the train. Much to our surprise, we left the station at nine—on schedule! The 86-mile trip to Tientsin usually takes about two and one-half hours. That day it took nine. At every station the train had to wait for instructions—by radio, since telegraph wires were down —to proceed to the next station, and we had to wait many times for trains carrying troops, ammunition, and trucks. We saw much devastation caused by war—destroyed buildings, wrecked trains, and damaged crops.

The Japanese soldiers who crowded the Tientsin station looked far from friendly, but after war equipment had been unloaded we were permitted to pick up our luggage and go to the Astor House in the British Legation. All about were signs of fighting and devastation. An Englishman told of seeing hundreds of dead bodies pitched into the river and then washed back again with the tide. A Russian, who had stood on a rooftop, told of seeing a mass of humanity— like a river, relentless in its movement—flowing along the streets with children and old people trampled underfoot. Some of the American soldiers had given their month's pay to the refugees.

Boarding our train the next morning was a difficult undertaking. Hundreds of Japanese soldiers surrounded the station, but not one Chinese coolie was to be seen to help with the baggage. We were not allowed to leave the taxis until time to board the train, and then we passed singly between double rows of soldiers with fixed bayonets. Normally, the trip from Peiping to Mukden took about fifteen hours. We anticipated that it would take longer this time but never dreamed it would take three days! We left Tientsin about eight-thirty in the morning and reached Shanhaikuan, where the Great Wall comes down to the sea, about six-thirty in the evening. We were informed then that the train would go no farther. We were told that our car might go back to Tientsin, and since the hotel at Shanhaikuan was full, we would have to stay all night in the station.

We objected to being put out of our car. We showed our first-class tickets. After much conferring the officials agreed to set our car off the main tracks and let us spend the night in it. We were offered bed sheets at 7 mex (about $2) per sheet but decided to do without them. We needed no blankets because of the heat. We expressed a desire to have our meals at the hotel, but a petty official said that Japanese maidens were not permitted on the streets at night. He finally conceded the point, however, and we had a good dinner at the hotel. Our jolly crowd met the situation in good spirits.

After breakfast the next morning our car was picked up and we started again for Mukden. We had no dining car the whole day, but we managed to survive until we reached Mukden about midnight—a few minutes too late to catch the last train that would make it possible for us to reach Yokohama in time for the embarkation of the *Empress of Japan,* on which we held reservations for the trip home.

The Japan Tourist Bureau tried to help us find a possible route to Yokohama. The way we were going appeared the only one available, not only because of the congestion caused by troop movements but also because of floods caused by the heavy rains. We investigated air travel from Mukden to Yokohama and were offered passage for one by a woman who had chartered a plane. This seat we gave to Henrietta Burton, whose home and work were in Washington, D.C. The way things looked at that time it was possible that we might have to divide our group further in order to obtain passage home on the crowded ships.

The Japanese tried to make our stay in Manchukuo as pleasant as possible and to leave a favorable impression of the wonderful things Japan had done for that country. The country was quite beautiful and crops seemed abundant. Both in Mukden and in Dairen, where we finally caught a boat for Japan, we had a chance to visit shops and factories.

The little *Ural Maru* took us in four days down through the Yellow Sea and across to Kobe in Japan. As we disembarked with all our luggage, cameramen and reporters surrounded us. We realized that to discuss the "North China Incident" frankly while on Japanese soil would offend the Japanese and possibly would be unsafe. We did our best, therefore, to evade direct questions both from newspapermen and educators.

The World Federation of Education Associations committee entertained us in Tokyo. At a luncheon at the New Grand Hotel they served us delicious lobster and excellently prepared ice cream and gave us the little silk U.S. flags and packets of folders which they had presented to the delegates at the convention. The Harvard man who introduced me at the luncheon hinted that I should talk of our experiences in North China, but instead I centered my attention on expressing gratitude for their hospitality and our regrets at having missed the conference. The committee assured us that if we would leave the manuscripts we had prepared, they would be included in the published proceedings. This promise they kept and when the handsomely printed, cloth-bound set of five volumes of the proceedings appeared the next year, Volume III included my picture and Ted's and the text of our papers in the Science and Science Teaching Section. Ted's was entitled "Suiting Biological Instruction to Human Values." Mine was "Education for Family Living," in which I reiterated a familiar refrain: "For most persons, family living is a continuous experience, and the results of that experience are largely carried over into society. Therefore, improvement of the quality of family living is basic to the betterment of society." Ben Andrews' paper printed in the proceedings is entitled, "Is War Ingrained in Human Nature?"

Fortune smiled on our voyage home. A Canadian Pacific ship had been commandeered by the British Fleet to go to Shanghai, pick up 1,400 refugees, and take them to Hong Kong. The ship could not return to Shanghai a second time to pick up its regularly scheduled

passengers because its fuel supply was too low and it had to go to
Nagasaki for coaling. From there it was rerouted to Canada and had
plenty of space for us since it had not picked up its Shanghai passengers. On board was Ben Andrews' party, which had not taken
the Peiping trip, and individuals and remnants of other parties returning from the World Federation meeting. LeVelle Wood, who
was beginning a sabbatical year, and Agnes Kolshorn, also on leave,
remained in Japan. The rest of us arrived back in Victoria on September 11, all in good health, without loss or damage to a piece of
luggage, and with no additional expense to members of the party,
even though we had been gone nearly three weeks longer than the
original agreement provided for. We were all back home in time to
resume our regular fall jobs. As the party broke up, the members
told me that if Miss Fritchoff and I ever planned to take another
study tour group anywhere they wanted to go along.

MISSIONARIES, TEACHERS, and others who stayed in China did not
have so easy a time of it. When the Japanese occupied North China
there were fourteen institutions of higher learning in Peiping. Three
months later only four remained. The new military governors regarded them as the "hotbed of anti-Japanism," and soon forced most
of them to close. Then began the first of the massive migrations out
of Japanese occupied territory into Free China areas to the south
and west. The second began in the winter of 1937-1938 from the
Shanghai-Nanking area, where buildings of both Chinese-owned
and missionary universities were either leveled to the ground or
occupied by Japanese forces. The third occurred the next fall when
Canton, Wuchang, and Hankow fell to the invaders. In successive
migrations students and faculty, with such books and equipment as
they could transport, moved westward, most of them eventually
into Szechwan Province. Two colleges I knew well, Nanking University and Ginling College in Nanking, were among the earliest to
move to Chengtu in Szechwan. Cheeloo University in Tsinan joined
them soon.

In the fall of 1937, Dr. Stuart's immediate problem was whether
or not to follow the other universities in a hasty withdrawal to Free
China. No one could predict what the Japanese would do, but he
decided to stay in Peiping. He wrote later in his autobiography:

We had incidents almost daily, usually minor ones but always with the possibility of becoming serious. This was especially true because of linguistic limitations on both sides and the natural suspicions of an occupying army in unfriendly territory. . . . Japanese were never permitted to enter the gate [at Yenching University] except by special arrangement and were always escorted over the grounds by my secretary or someone else. I soon discovered that the secret of dealing with them was a blend of firmness and friendliness. Their military power and the brutal use they made of it caused the Chinese to cringe before them. On the other hand, they met with little more than forced compliance. Despite their blustering they were not too sure of themselves and stood in a certain awe of the unrevealed American attitude. Courteous treatment was all the more appreciated by them under these conditions. To show no fear of their armed might while heartily cordial in manner enabled me to meet their truculence or break their nervous reticence in many a delicate encounter.

Individual Yenching students slipped away through the lines to Free China for patriotic or other reasons, and Dr. Stuart assisted them. He kept the University operating and to a considerable extent continued other personal responsibilities throughout the country— until December 1941. The weekend of the Pearl Harbor attack he had gone to Tientsin to meet with Yenching alumni. Early Monday morning as he was quietly planning to return, two Japanese military policemen took him into custody and escorted him back to Peiping. Although they were polite, they evidently had strict orders not to let him out of their sight. He was held prisoner, at first with two hundred marines in their barracks, then in comparative comfort for four months in the home of Dr. Houghton, the Director of Peiping Medical College, and finally until the end of the war, in the bare rear quarters of a house once owned by a British businessman. Through this confinement he had as companions Dr. Houghton, Dr. I. Snapper, and Mr. Trevor Bowen, members of the Peiping Union Medical College staff.

Dr. Stuart never did know for sure why the Japanese gave him this sort of treatment or why these particular men had been singled out. He later wrote:

I think we now understand one reason at least for [our strange incarceration]. In the impossible event of the Japanese Army having to surrender I would have been used as a mediator for peace with Chiang Kai-shek. Dr. Houghton would have had the responsibility of keeping me physically fit for this, and we two being administrative officers for our respective institutions, Bowen was held as a third hostage.

Yenching University in Peiping, of course, had to close during the war. Foreign staff members, other than Dr. Stuart, were placed under guard but were permitted to remain in Peiping for more than a year after Pearl Harbor. In March 1943, they and other enemy nationals of North China, principally British, American, Dutch, and Russian—totaling about 2,000—were herded together and shipped to a crowded internment camp in Shantung Province. A young Harvard graduate, Langdon Gilkey, who had joined the Yenching faculty in 1940, was among them. I had known Langdon's mother before she was married, when we lived in Foster Hall at the University of Chicago. His father, a prominent Baptist minister, was Dean of the Chapel when I went to Chicago for summer study in the 1920's and I heard him preach many sermons. The son, Langdon, kept a journal while interned and from it later composed a vivid description of the life endured in internment. His book has received many favorable reviews for the insight it provides into the lives of people of diversified backgrounds when they are forced into such an unnatural situation.*

A group of what Dr. Stuart called "splendidly loyal Chinese teachers" organized Yenching University in exile. "They had about 400 students in borrowed buildings," he said in describing the situation he found at Chengtu in 1945.

The boys were housed in an ancient and charmingly picturesque Confucian temple, infested by rats and crowded to the limit. The chief complaint of the girls was the bedbugs which no way could be found to exterminate. But the spirit was wonderful. . . . I felt it worth the nearly four years of imprisonment to experience the rebound, to see how my beloved colleagues and their

---

Shantung Compound: The Story of Men and Women Under Pressure by Langdon Gilkey. New York: Harper and Row, 1966.

*students had been bravely carrying on in the face of so many
difficulties and to revel in their hearty welcome.*

After returning from Chengtu, Dr. Stuart paid a surprise visit
to the internment compound in Shantung, "making possible another
delightful reunion [with] Yenching faculty and colleagues and many
friends and acquaintances." As soon as arrangements could be made,
with assistance of the U.S. Navy, he returned to the United States to
get plans under way for reopening Yenching University in Peiping.

18. Turbulent Decade

Man must enlarge his heart as he has his intellect.
—Yale University Chaplain

THE TEN YEARS from 1938 to 1948, for me, were filled with a variety of adventures, both personal and professional. After the study tour to the Orient in the summer of 1937, the school year 1937-38 went smoothly. Enrollment in home economics passed the 600 mark for the first time. The 609 undergraduates, 25 graduate students, and 4 special students made a total of 638 students. In addition, we had a large number of nonmajor students, both men and women, in our classes. The increase in majors made it necessary to rent the Dolan House and put it into operation as a third home management house.

As mentioned previously, C. Winifred Harley, the child specialist from England and the Merrill-Palmer School, supervised the nursery schools that year. She also taught in the summer sessions in 1937 and 1938. Other visiting faculty in the summer of 1938 included Rachel Stutsman Ball and Katherine Roberts from Merrill-Palmer, Helen Hunter, a specialist in adult education from Iowa State College, Bess Steele, a textile design specialist from the University of Nebraska, Eleanor Maclay, a nutritionist from the University of Cincinnati, and LeVelle Wood, back from her round-the-world trip.

In the fall of 1938, I made arrangements to be gone from the campus for winter and spring terms. I took sabbatical leave to do what I had been encouraging other members of the staff to do—to take time for advanced study or purposeful travel. I started for New York to continue the graduate work I had begun in the summer of 1924 at Columbia University. Enroute east, I stopped along the way—as usual—to see friends and relatives. After a brief visit with my sister Ada in Madison, Wisconsin, I went on to Chicago where my elder sister Nell and her husband lived close to the campus of the University of Chicago. Their son, Robert Scott Miner, Jr., at that time was a junior in the University. In Ann Arbor, I stayed overnight with Inez Bozorth, manager of the Lawyers' Club at the University of Michigan. Inez drove me to Michigan State College where we had a good visit with Mary Lewis, one of our graduates in the Foods and Nutrition Department, and other members of the staff. An interesting experiment going on in the home economics curriculum at Michigan State included, among other changes, required courses for freshmen in music appreciation, art appreciation, and drama appreciation.

In Detroit I stopped at the Merrill-Palmer School. Because I have mentioned this unique school several times in previous chapters and expect to do so later, and because its unusual contribution to home economics may not be familiar to all readers, I am going to pause at this point to tell a little about it.

As one provision of her last will and testament, Mrs. Lizzie Merrill-Palmer of Detroit wrote:

> *I hold profoundly the conviction that the welfare of any community is divinely and hence inseparably dependent upon the quality of its motherhood and the spirit and character of its homes and moved by this conviction, I hereby give, devise and bequeath all the rest, residue and remainder of my estate for the founding, endowment and maintenance of a school at which girls and young women shall be educated, trained, developed and disciplined with special reference to fitting them mentally, morally, physically and religiously for the discharge of the functions and service of wifehood and motherhood and the management, supervision, direction and inspiration of home.*

The Board of Trustees appointed to administer this provision of Mrs. Palmer's will selected Edna Noble White, head of home economics at Ohio State University, as the founding director, and the Merrill-Palmer School of Motherhood and Home Training opened its doors in 1920.

To Miss White, who guided the destinies of the school for twenty-seven years, from 1920 to 1947, must go a great deal of credit for the remarkable achievement of this pioneering endeavor. As leaders in education for home and family life, she and her school have had a dramatic impact on the whole field of home economics. She instituted in this country the use of the nursery school as a laboratory for advanced study, first mainly for college women in home economics but later also for both men and women in psychology, physical growth and nutrition, child development, sociology, and education. She thought of the nursery school also as a laboratory for parent education. She saw clearly the necessity of an interdisciplinary staff for a center of human development and human relations study and brought in specialists in many fields.

Housed at first in a former residence and gradually expanding into other residences nearby, the school developed in three areas of responsibility: (1) service to the metropolitan community which had been Mrs. Palmer's home—to parents, children, and community organizations and institutions; (2) service to other educational institutions, especially to schools of home economics and departments of social sciences all over the country, and to faculty and students from all parts of the world; and (3) extensive and intensive research programs in subjects and problems of interest to the school. The Merrill-Palmer School has been of great service to our School of Home Economics. It opened its facilities to our staff members, to selected junior and senior students for a term at a time, and to our graduates who desired advanced study. It provided us with excellent summer and short-course instructors. Its staff produced books and articles on physical and mental measurement of preschool children, on nutrition for children in nursery schools and in the home, on standards of physical and mental growth, and on many other topics —basic studies of value to all teachers and researchers in the field. Every time I visited Merrill-Palmer I came away inspired by what I had seen and heard.

At the time of my 1939 visit, Edna White, then in her twentieth year as director of the school, arranged a lovely luncheon for me with a group of her staff in a spacious dining room. I had a good visit with Lee Vincent and Katherine Roberts and other staff members. In New York state at Buffalo State Teachers College I saw other friends before going on to Ithaca. Ada's daughter, Mary Lou Cockefair, was there at Cornell University doing graduate work in home economics and serving as director of one of the home management houses. Following the summer tour to the Orient, Mary Lou had come to Oregon State College and completed work for a B.S.

degree in home economics in 1938, and had accepted the Cornell position for the next two years. Martha Van Rensselaer had died several years earlier. Flora Rose, now Director of the College of Home Economics, had an Oregon dinner party at her home and we all had a grand visit around her fireplace.

At these stops along the way and in New York City, the country for the most part seemed outwardly calm. The national economy had made a strong recovery from the Depression of the early 1930's. Schools, shops, stores, theaters, and other businesses seemed to be going about their work with energy and enthusiasm. Yet beneath the outward calm lay a feeling of uneasiness. The sounds and news from overseas caused one to wonder what was coming. In late-night radio broadcasts from Europe we could hear the hoarse shouting of Adolph Hitler and the unison cry of "Heil, Hitler!" by a hundred thousand massed Germans. Without bloodshed, Hitler had united Germany and Austria and had taken over the Sudeten fringes of Czechoslovakia. Prime Minister Chamberlain of Great Britain, after making three trips to see Hitler, had not seen fit to oppose the German expansion and had announced "peace in our time."

Cora Winchell of the Columbia University faculty took me one morning to Carnegie Hall to hear John Gunther's talk, "Inside Europe and Inside Asia." Gunther said he believed there would be no war in Europe that spring. He said Hitler needed a "digestive interlude" to assimilate what he had bitten off Czechoslovakia. He said that England's reluctance to try to stop Hitler showed the Japanese that the British Lion had no real teeth—only "bridgework"— and would not do anything to stop the Japanese conquest of Canton.

A few weeks later Miss Winchell and I went to a University of Chicago dinner party at Delmonico's. Dr. Edward Benes, the President of Czechoslovakia whom Hitler had forced out of office and who had joined the University of Chicago faculty, was one of the speakers. Another speaker asked the audience to take a long view of the present crisis and contrasted the strength and poise of the calm voices of the democratic nations with the raucous voices of Hitler and those cheering him. He seemed to reflect the same attitude expressed by John Gunther a few weeks previously, that the British are known for losing all battles—except the last one.

News from the other side of the world disturbed us even more. The Japanese invasion of China, which we had seen at its beginning at Peiping in July 1937, had rolled on relentlessly. Shanghai, Nan-king, Hankow, and Canton—cities whose people I had known—were all in Japanese hands. At a meeting of the Foreign Policy Association at the Hotel Astor I heard a discussion of the question: "Can Japan Conquer China?" One of the speakers was Haldore Hanson, the Associated Press correspondent who talked to our study-tour party in Peiping. He had just returned from China where he had been with guerrilla armies and had been held by the Japanese as a spy for ten days. He described the guerrilla warfare being conducted by the Chinese as a "pin-pricking" process. He said the guerrillas' pur-pose was not to destroy the Japanese but to control the political and economic areas in occupied territory. Japan does not hold a block of China, he said, but only lines and points, and seventy percent of the territory in North China is in the hands of the guerrillas. He felt that the Japanese could go on for some time but that they were reserving their trump card for their greatest enemy—Russia. All of the speakers seemed confident that China would win in the end.

A short time later I went to a dinner in a Chinese restaurant with about one hundred people who had lived in China. Bishop Gowdy from Foochow told how that city had been saved from the invasion because the Chinese filled the river mouth with granite slabs that prevented the Japanese from bringing their boats into the harbor. Of the 108 counties in Shantung Province, he said, only four were actually under Japanese control. He and others recently re-turned from China shared an optimism that China would win in the long run despite the destruction and devastation. All of these assurances of eventual victory did not seem at all satisfying when one visualized the misery and suffering the Chinese people must be going through.

At International House and in various gatherings in New York I met a good many people who had spent time and energy trying to improve living conditions in the Orient. All of us who had served in the Far East wondered whether or not our efforts would have lasting benefits. We knew they were appreciated at the time, but with the world in turmoil it was hard to assess our contribution. A speaker at Teachers College Chapel one day, Dr. Henry P. VanDusen of Union Theological Seminary, helped put the missionary effort in perspec-tive. He had just returned from a 470-delegate Christian world fellowship conference in Madras, India, where 200 different languages were spoken. He told of a skeptical international lawyer who had gone out to the meeting and admitted that the question in his mind was, "Can any good come out of the Christian church for mankind?" He came back convinced that no nation or union of nations can endure unless grounded on the principles laid down in the Sermon on the Mount and found himself questioning whether or not any good for mankind can come out of any corporate body other than the Christian church.

New York provided opportunity to hear some of the great ministers of the time. Harry Emerson Fosdick at the huge cathedral-like Riverside Church adjacent to Columbia University, was my favorite and I went there frequently for Sunday services, sometimes for the Wednesday evening services, and for several of Dr. Fosdick's Lenten sermons. John D. Rockefeller, Jr., often helped pass the collection plate. On one windy, rainy February morning, when the harmony of the stained glass windows and the beauty of the church and the music gave one a sense of gladness for being there, Dr. Fosdick was at his best. His sermon was "The Most Satisfying Happiness Known to Man." He pointed out that Peter, James, and John were common people, but greatness grew out of what they espoused. He quoted President Wilson, who said he would rather devote his services to a cause he knew would fail but would ultimately win, rather than devote his services to a cause he knew would win but ultimately fail. Dr. Fosdick referred to the tendency to seek happiness for *impressions*, which he called second-rate happiness; whereas first-rate happiness comes only through *expression*. What's wrong with family life, he said, is that there is too little creativeness put into it; that it takes infinite patience, wisdom, and creativeness to make family life a success. "Creativeness," he said, "is the greatest happiness known to man."

At the weekly noon to 12:30 p.m. chapel at the university one day, Rabbi David DeSola Pool, regularly heard over the radio, spoke on Judaism. He attempted to interpret his religion for his audience composed of people of all faiths and closed by saying that the love of God and love of neighbor provide the most concise summing up of the faith of the Jew. At lunch one day at the Union Theological Seminary cafeteria—which had the reputation for having the best food in the neighborhood—several of us were invited to go next door to the Jewish Seminary to hear one of the professors an-

swer questions which had been put to him by one of the Columbia
University classes. The elderly scholar, sitting at his desk in his
library, analyzed these questions and impressed us with his wisdom,
learning, and tolerance. He appealed to the group to sense that
teaching Christ's crucifixion to young children at the most im-
pressionable age has contributed to anti-Semitism all through
Christendom. The young ministerial students in the group questioned him about the Zionist movement, through which the Jews
were colonizing Palestine. The point that impressed me most about
this experience was that traditional barriers seemed to be tumbling
down when Jews and Gentiles could ask questions of each other and
answer them with candor and poise.

For my stay at Columbia University, I was able to obtain an
apartment at Seth Low Hall on Morningside Drive near the campus.
At first I feared that living in the same apartment house with many
professors I would not get to know students well, but I found my
fears ungrounded. An American woman, Miss Harriet Howey, whom
I had met at Kwassui College in Nagasaki, Japan, came to the Hall
about the same time I did. She recognized me and invited me to join
her as a partner, or "cooking mate," in preparing some of our meals
in the kitchen on a lower floor of the Hall. About eighty women living
in the Hall, mostly graduate students, availed themselves of the
opportunity to use the kitchen and dining room at any time of day or
night. They called themselves "The Skilleteers." Storage space for
each of us was assigned in the cupboards and large refrigerators.
Having become weary of restaurants, I found the companionship
congenial. At first I thought there would be too much confusion and
noise, but the arrangement proved superior to cafeterias. Our group
had a feeling of "belonging," and like a group of undergraduates in
a college residence hall we were thoughtful of each other and shared
extra coffee and packages of cookies from home.

Almost every state was represented among us. Our group also
included two girls from Puerto Rico, a public health nurse from
Denmark, a recently naturalized German woman, and a Chinese
playwright, one of whose plays had just been produced at one of the
University theaters. Our conversation centered around courses,
theaters, operas, and political problems. As soon as any of us donned
an apron, we received a welcome "Hello." As a rule, not more than
twelve or fifteen were present at the same time, but one evening the

president of the group, a public health nurse from Texas, called us all together, served us Sanka and cookies, and told us what to do and what not to do. I had a good deal of fun observing the dynamics of our politics—make a complaint, and you got appointed to a committee at once!

This scheme of living seemed to me to have merit for every college. We had splendid markets a block away, with delivery to kitchens, and we learned to use frozen-pack foods. Many of us found it a relief to create a batch of biscuits or cook a steak or toss a salad after being in class or in the library for three or four hours. We went out for meals often, but just having the facilities available for cooking if we wanted to use them gave us a friendly feeling for the place.

My principal purpose in coming to New York was to take studies that would help me as an educational administrator. By arriving on campus while the winter semester was still in progress, I had an opportunity to audit several courses and panel discussions before registering for the spring semester. In this way I saw in action more than a dozen of the top Teachers College professors—some of the leading men and women in education in the country. In February I registered for a full load of seventeen points in Teachers College and in addition audited a course in masterpieces of Biblical literature in the Theological Seminary. The courses I took for credit included student personnel administration, rural sociology and economics, educational foundations, problems in higher education, and techniques in teaching the social studies. Most of the courses were taught by several professors. The leader of the course in problems in higher education was Donald P. Cottrell, a capable instructor whom I came to know very well nine years later after he had become Dean of the College of Education at Ohio State University. Dr. Cottrell had conducted many educational surveys and brought us glimpses of educational systems of the Soviet Union, Sweden, Denmark, and other countries. Since our class included a number of experienced educators with well established viewpoints, our discussions sometimes reached fever heat, especially in the battle between the conservatives and progressives. Dr. Cottrell demonstrated his skill as an alert referee, without espousing either cause.

Other instructors included Ruth May Strang and Esther Lloyd-Jones, who taught the courses in personnel administration with constructive imagination; George S. Counts, who had provided an introduction to my book on student homes in China when it was published nine years before; and Edmund deS. Brunner, a rural sociologist, whom I felt was a great asset to Teachers College. While many of the professors knew only metropolitan America, Dr. Brunner knew rural America and drew into his courses students from all over the world. John L. Childs also gave our class some excellent lectures in the foundations of education course.

Outside of the classroom I had the opportunity to renew acquaintanceship with many faculty members I had known for a long time and others I had known only by reputation. The famous William Heard Kilpatrick had retired but lived in the same apartment house where I was—as did Dr. and Mrs. Cottrell and their two children, Dr. Brunner, and others. Dr. and Mrs. Benjamin R. Andrews, who were among the first to greet me, had a Sunday dinner for a group of Oregon friends and included Mary Swartz Rose and her husband and Cora Winchell—all of whom had come to OSC for summer sessions. Mary de Garmo Bryan, another sometime-member of our summer faculty, was president of the Faculty Women's Club and invited me to join the club for my stay on the campus. She and her husband, a ship builder, also invited a group of us for dinner at their Greenwich Village apartment. Dr. Rose and her husband called for me and we had a beautiful drive to the southern part of Manhattan and a delightful evening with the Bryans.

Not only was New York a crossroads metropolis but its Columbia University was a stopping-place for people whom I had met in various parts of the world. Mrs. Dass, president of Isabella Thoburn College in Lucknow, India, where I had spent several days in 1932, lived a while in Seth Low Hall. She wore her lovely, graceful native dress and impressed all as an astute leader of higher education for women in India. One day at the Faculty Women's Club, Mary Beard, wife of historian Charles Beard, gave a talk. She and her husband and daughter had been on the steamer with Camilla Mills and me as we went to China in 1922, and I had seen them a number of times later in Peking. We renewed our acquaintance, and I enjoyed hearing what Mrs. Beard had to say concerning the collection she and her husband were compiling of the lives of great women of the world.[*]

---

[*]*Woman as Force in History: A Study in Traditions and Realities* by Mary R. Beard (New York: The Macmillan Company, 1946) grew out of the writing Mrs. Beard was doing at that time.

New York also seemed to harbor a number of Oregon State College graduates. The first Sunday I went to Riverside Church I saw four of them. Julia Fuller Clark and J. C. Clark, whom I had first met in Shanghai in 1924, had returned from the Orient more than ten years before. J.C. was still with the YMCA and had recently become the director of the Seamen's House on the waterfront. The Clarks lived at White Plains, New York, and invited me to visit them before I returned home. Two girls from Corvallis, both of them daughters of faculty members, were there that day also: Frances Jensen and Letty Warrington. The last time I had seen Letty was in Peiping in July 1937.

One night in March I had dinner with two of our graduates, Pauline Paul and Mary Ellen Turley. Pauline was doing research work for General Foods Corporation and Mary Ellen was at St. Luke's Hospital. At another time, we three had a curry dinner together and went to see the play, *Outward Bound*. Gladys Miller and Bernice Chambers, on the staff of New York University, asked me to come one day for lunch at the Picadilly Hotel to hear a reading of the play *The Little Foxes*, in which Talullah Bankhead was starring on the stage at that time. Gladys' book, *Design in Decoration*, was to be published in September. Bernice had written a book on clothing while on the staff of New York University.

Florence Merryman Lewis, one of the girls who had lived with me while she was going through college, returned on furlough from Buenos Aires with her husband, Phil Lewis, who worked for Texaco. They had many exciting tales to tell of their adventures in South America. They planned to be in America ten months before going back again. It was delightful to observe Florence as hostess at a tea she and Phil insisted on giving for me.

Mary Lou Cockefair came from Ithaca at Easter time, and we went to see *Family Portrait*, in which Judith Anderson played the part of Mary, the mother of Jesus. Also about that time I took advantage of the opportunity to see and hear Lauritz Melchior for the second time, this time in *Parsifal*, and to see Raymond Massey in *Abraham Lincoln*, a play which had just received the Pulitzer Award.

One Sunday in early May I accepted the Clarks' invitation to go with them to New Haven, Connecticut, where their younger son Richard was a sophomore at Yale University. We attended services at the Yale chapel where the minister said that man must enlarge his heart as he has his intellect. After the services we met Professor Kenneth Scott Latourette who, as a young missionary returned from China, had been in one of my first classes in Camp Cookery. He and J. C. Clark had known each other from their college days when J.C. was attending OAC and Kenneth Latourette was attending McMinnville College in Oregon. Dr. Latourette, at this time Professor of Oriental History at Yale, was a prolific writer of scholarly books. He produced so many that eventually he had one of the longest entries in *Who's Who in America.*

Richard Clark showed us around the campus, and we had dinner in his college dining room. For the first time I had a good look at the Yale campus—its Gothic architecture, wide lawns, and pleasant walkways. Several libraries and the gymnasium were open on Sunday and we were able to take a look inside. Following graduation from high school, Richard had gone with his father on one of the World Y Tours to Europe and afterwards had spent a year in Germany, learning the German language, living part of the time with a family in the Black Forest. He had also visited Y families in Europe. As an exchange, Richard's father had brought a German boy to the United States and had assumed responsibility for his schooling. Upon his return to the United States, Richard received a scholarship at Yale which paid his tuition. He earned his board by cataloging German publications in the Yale library.

A significant story leaked out, illustrating the relationship that existed between Richard and his father. One Saturday night two of Richard's college friends invited him to join them for a drive to New York City to see a show. After the performance, his friends decided to stay in the city for the weekend; consequently, Richard was driving home alone when he was picked up for speeding and was confined to jail because he did not have enough money with him to pay the bail. Realizing the lateness of the hour, he decided to spend the night in jail rather than disturb his father in the middle of the night. The next morning when Richard called his father, J.C. did not have sufficient cash on hand. Since it was not easy to find a store open on Sunday morning, he decided to go to church first and get one of the ushers to cash a check. J.C. finally reached Richard, paid his fine, and brought him home for dinner. When Julia had an opportunity to ask her husband if he had scolded their son, J.C. replied:

"No, I just took one look at poor Richard and decided he had suffered enough."

THE SPRING SEMESTER at Columbia ended in late May and I returned home in time for the 1939 Commencement at OSC. Ruth Gill Hammond, who had been teaching part time in the Household Management Department after she and her family had returned from Bangkok about three years before, was moving to Portland. To replace her I thought of Edna Van Horn, whom I had met in Dr. Cottrell's class. We found it possible to expand the position to full time, and after a bit of correspondence, Edna agreed to come. She stayed only a year at that time, because in June the next year she accepted a position as Executive Secretary of the American Home Economics Association and moved to Washington, D.C., for three years. Following her AHEA assignment, she returned to OSU and remained on the staff until her retirement.

In 1939, the war that John Gunther predicted would not come in the spring arrived in late summer. On September 1, Hitler sent his troops crashing into Poland. The next summer (1940) France fell, and the following winter the fiery Battle of Britain raged. The Japanese continued their conquests in the Far East and on December 7, 1941, attacked the American base at Pearl Harbor, Hawaii, and drew the United States into the global conflict.

Once again, the School of Home Economics did what it could on the home front to ease the burden of war and speed the peace. My principal war work this time was as chairman of a large statewide committee responsible for the Nutrition for Defense Program. The committee's principal function was to coordinate the efforts of about twenty groups concerned with maintaining acceptable standards of nutrition for the people of the state and at the same time providing a maximum amount of foodstuffs to support war and relief programs. We surveyed geographically and socially the coverage of the various agencies and afforded them an opportunity to become familiar with each other's work and responsibilities. Dr. Margaret Fincke, head of our Foods and Nutrition Department, and Dr. Ernest Wiegand, head of the Food Technology Department in the School of Agriculture, were also campus representatives on this committee.

For all of us, opportunities for further graduate study and travel for enrichment were gone for the duration of the war. Opportunity for another type of adventure, however, arose in the prewar and war years. Editors of several journals asked for articles, and I found compliance with these requests an interesting diversion. Among others, my articles in this period included reports on the 1937 Study Tour to the Orient for *Omicron Nu, Practical Home Economics,* and the *National Magazine of Home Economics Clubs;* "Oregon State's Nursery School" for *Nation's Schools;* "Administering a School of Home Economics" for the *University Administration Quarterly;* and three articles for the *Journal of Home Economics.* One of the latter dealt with the character and contribution of the late Effie I. Raitt, for many years head of home economics at the University of Washington. Another was entitled, "The Challenge of China." The third, a response to a quip in the *New Yorker* magazine, resulted in a series of letters to the editor.

The August 5, 1944, issue of the *New Yorker* contained the following comment:

> **Homemaking** reared its chintzy little head the other day when the ladies of the American Home Economics Association decided that maybe the Home should rate a Cabinet position, to be called the Department of the American Home. . . . Home was quite a place when people stayed there, but Home Economics is just another in the long line of activities which take ladies away. Of the home economists we have met in our lifetime, all had one trait in common: not one of them was home.

The *New Yorker's* witty remark ruffled some feathers. Helen Hostetter, editor of the *Journal of Home Economics,* prodded me into making reply. She published my article, "Strengthening Home Economics Stakes," a short time later. It gave me an opportunity to support the contention that the study of home economics prepares both for homemaking and for a career. At OSC we had recently completed a study of our graduates and had data showing that two out of three graduates married within three years after leaving college; five out of six eventually married and became homemakers. Only one out of eight married graduates was employed outside the home. Thirteen out of fourteen unmarried graduates were in earning positions. Our study indicated that nearly all of the wives of men in the armed forces planned to return to homemaking after their husbands returned to civilian life.

Immediately after college, I pointed out in my article, most home economics graduates go into teaching, dietetics, extension work, journalism, commercial foods work, nursery school teaching, or other earning fields, but only a small percentage continue as wage earners beyond three years. I outlined our OSC curriculum in which every student studied a broad liberal arts course and a home-making core of instruction that included child development and family relationships, household management, foods and nutrition, clothing and textiles, and home furnishings.

"This program permits no narrow specialization as undergraduates," I wrote. "We have no so-called [departmental] majors . . . and have not had for more than 20 years. We have, instead, home economics majors who are equipped first for the job of homemaking and second for an earning job. Our program seems in no way to handicap these graduates for wage earning but gives them a broad base on which to build if they continue wage-earning careers beyond the average of three years." I pointed out also that when alumnae write back to the school expressing a wish that they had taken more work in a particular field, the courses named are almost invariably in a field other than the one in which they had primary interest as undergraduates.

This article when published created a ripple of reaction—not from the *New Yorker,* of course—but from readers of the *Journal.* Marion Talbot, University of Chicago, wrote the editor praising "a return to the real meaning of home economics rather than an emphasis on ascorbic acid, nicotinic acid, riboflavin, and vitamins. . . . Family life must be stressed if your AHEA is to fulfill its real function of developing and retaining and strengthening family life."

Not all reactions, however, were complimentary. A home economist for the National Livestock and Meat Board in Chicago wrote:

> Dean Milam . . . says that five out of six of her graduates marry. Isn't this number likely to drop after the war? . . . Her curriculum seems to be a little of everything. . . . Wouldn't such a curriculum boost dietetics training to six years instead of five? . . . Many of us wish for *more* specialized training rather than less. . . . I cannot agree that home economists have focused too much attention on technical subject matter. Home economics *is* a body of technical subject matter!"

This last letter required an answer, and I wrote to the editor pointing out that our graduates qualify for student dietetic work in institutions approved by the American Dietetics Association at the end of their four years and that they qualify for commercial home economics jobs in four years—and we had no difficulty in placing them. I took this opportunity to say again:

> Oregon State College is convinced that it has a dual responsibility to all of its students, training them for the home and for a profession, and that those who remain in the profession are the better for the breadth of their undergraduate program.

In addition to letters published in the *Journal,* I received comment from others, most of them in support of the point of view that education for homemaking comes first in the education of a home economist. The flexibility and versatility of our graduates in facing changing conditions and fitting themselves into positions of service and leadership in times of national emergency and of personal tragedy have certainly borne out the validity of this viewpoint.

In the turbulent 1938-1948 decade, the School of Home Economics did not have as much disruption as did other schools on the campus. The School of Engineering, for example, which had been enrolling more than 1,000 students annually dropped to fewer than 300 in two of the war years and then zoomed to more than 1,800 in the postwar influx of men released from military service. The School of Home Economics reached a high point of enrollment in 1940-41 with 754 students then dropped back to the 600 level where enrollment remained fairly constant. The number receiving baccalaureate degrees in home economics yearly ranged from 87 to 114 in the decade but remained fairly close to the average of 100 a year.

The staff fluctuated somewhat as members participated in the national effort in various ways. Some took leave for special assignments, others resigned for better positions, but the majority continued to serve in college and community. When advanced study could be resumed and travel became possible we were ready. My first opportunity for overseas travel came early in 1948.

19. Ambassador

A PRINCIPAL PURPOSE of my 1948 trip to the Orient was to help conduct a survey of the Christian colleges in the Philippines. Since the survey was not scheduled to begin until July, I took the three preceding months to see how the women's colleges in the Far East had fared during the war years, to see what could be done to assist with reconstruction, to see our alumnae, and to interview candidates for scholarships. At a recent meeting of the Association of Land-Grant Colleges and Universities Dean E. Lee Vincent of Cornell University and I had been named co-chairmen of the Committee on International Education in Home Economics and I had duties to perform in connection with that appointment.

Two features of my 1948 travels stand out most distinctly—the speed and ease of getting from place to place by air and the joy of meeting old friends. A few hours out of Seattle on April 10, our Northwest Airlines plane landed at Anchorage, Alaska, and before long I was talking with a young friend: Frances Jensen (daughter of W. A. and Lillian Frances Jensen) called by long distance telephone from Fairbanks, where she was teaching at the University of Alaska, to wish me well on my trip and to tell me she planned to study the next year with our one-time Tearoom manager Mary Koll Heiner at Cornell University.

Out over the Aleutian Islands, our pilot learned by radio that our next scheduled stop to refuel and change crews at Shemya on the far tip of the island chain could not be accomplished because of fog. We would have to stop at Adak for twelve hours to give our crew the required rest. Even though the airline had just fed us an adequate dinner on board the plane, the men at the Army Air Base at Adak prepared for us huge steaks, French-fried potatoes, and dessert. We did the best we could to show our appreciation. The stewardess, the one other woman passenger, and I spent the night in the Red Cross living quarters for nurses, while the other six passengers and six crew members bunked with the soldiers. We all regretted this delay because it would mean missing appointments in Japan and, in my case, missing plane connections for an appointment in Korea. On the other hand, we appreciated the opportunity to see how soldiers on our northern frontier had to live in lonely little spots like Adak and Kiska, surrounded by cruel-looking mountains and icy seas.

The 2,400-mile run from Adak to Tokyo took about 13 hours, and we arrived in Japan at nine-twenty Monday night. Despite some minor discomfort in the more than 5,000 miles I had flown since leaving Corvallis, I felt ready to commend flying as a mode of transportation. Pleased that I did not have to spend three weeks on a crowded steamer, I still had difficulty comprehending the speed of air travel. It had taken less than a day and a half to fly from Seattle to Tokyo!

Instead of catching the Monday plane for Seoul, I had to stay in Japan until Thursday. Lula Holmes, an educational specialist on the staff of SCAP (Supreme Command for the Allied Powers—MacArthur's headquarters) took me in tow for two days and scheduled meetings with groups of teachers and others interested in higher education for women. My interpreter was a young Japanese home economist, who had studied at Washington State College and was now working with Dr. Holmes. The Japanese women, I found, were heartened by the way higher education for women was being advanced by SCAP. My last night in Tokyo I went to a movie at the Ernie Pyle Theater with the Northwest Airlines crew and sent my first letter home with the stewardess, who mailed it in the States.

In Korea, I had an unusual opportunity to see the outcome of our program for bringing Oriental women to America to study home economics. So often in education we do not have adequate follow-up to see the results of our teachings. We turn out graduates year after year and can review their progress during their years on campus, but in too many cases we never really know how effective we have been in preparing them for their subsequent years. In Seoul, I could talk with three of the first Korean women we had brought to our campus for advanced training and see how they had fared in their professional and homemaking careers.

Hamna Kim (Park), our first Korean home economics graduate (B.S., 1927; M.S., 1928), who had so proudly shown me her accomplishments at Ewha University when I visited her in 1931, had left Seoul after that visit. At the insistence of her brother, she had been married to an older Chinese man, who—in spite of the objections of the Ewha faculty—had taken her to Canton, China. Hamna and her husband suffered severely during the war but gradually worked their way northward through China and into Korea. Under the Russian occupation of North Korea after World War II they lost everything, and they and their two sons, fifteen and nine years of age, returned to Seoul destitute. Hamna could not have been more than 45 years of age, but she looked to be 65. Yet, after walking two hours from her home into the city to see me, she still showed the same indomitable character she had exhibited at OSC. When urged to do something she did not want to do she would respond, "It is better so" and stand pat. Helen Kim, the competent president of Ewha, in my presence once repeated an offer she had made earlier for Hamna to come back to the home economics staff. Hamna protested, "My mind is so old." Dr. Kim's quick retort was, "Dean Milam will treat it." I could see Hamna was not well, probably suffering from some deficiency disease. I gave her my vitamin capsules, some clothes, and a little money, but she still had hard days ahead of her.

About three years later, after I had forwarded a small gift to Hamna, she wrote to me from Pusan, where she was working in a U.S. military facility during the Korean conflict. "These days," she said, "I really am having some experience in my life. It is easy to be discouraged for any one at present situation in Korea. Nothing else, but too much suffer—too much terror and misery. Lost families and friends and all the possessions what we have to have for the daily life. I imagine you would hardly recognize Seoul if you be there now. About 60% of the houses are burned in Seoul and left only posts of the brick buildings and broken windows. Even though I had a very hard situation, I am getting along all right. . . ."

At the time of my 1948 visit, E Soon Choi (M.S., OSC, 1938) was head of Home Economics, the largest department at Ewha University, but this was only one of her major responsibilities. She was raising a daughter and son (six and three years of age), assisting a busy and cooperative husband, and caring for a paralyzed 82-year-old mother. E Soon had worked in the fields during the war, and in speaking of the future, she looked up and said calmly, "Now, Miss Milam, I know I can meet anything that comes." Tears welled in her eyes when I presented her with a gift from one of the OSC staff members. Although she and her husband both were employed, their combined incomes covered only the cost of simple Korean food for a family of five—so bad was inflation. Still using a traditional Korean kitchen because they could not afford electrical appliances, she gave a dinner party for a group of us. Although the group was small, the meal must have played havoc with her food budget. Living through troubled times, E Soon had matured gracefully, and there was a gentleness, kindness, strength, and beauty about her that had grown through meeting life's big problems with courage.

Poonok Kim (Kim), (B.S., OSC, 1930) whom I remembered as a shy, soft-spoken young lady, had also developed remarkably under the burden of responsibilities. After her return from America, she had married a Reed College Korean and by the time I saw her in 1948 she had five children, the eldest of whom was seventeen. Two years before, she had announced to her husband and children, "I have given all to my family, but now I must also help my country." She had accepted an appointment as head of the Department of Women and Children in the Bureau of Police. One day while I was there, she came to tea in her smart-looking uniform with an assistant and several American governmental officials. "She is doing a fine job," the officials told me, "in reclaiming women and children." Who would ever have expected this from shy Poonok? I was reminded of the adage, "So long as the material is human, there's no such thing as finality."

During the two weeks I spent in Seoul, I saw several other OSC alumni, both Oriental and American, and heard of still others who were helping South Korea establish itself as an independent country after long occupation by the Japanese. I also met the three young women who were to be our next Korean graduate students. Sang Won Woo invited me to her home for dinner. Along a street that looked more like a narrow, unpaved alley, a gate opened into a courtyard with plants in the center, and Miss Woo introduced us to her home. We slipped off our shoes as we entered the matting-floored room and sat down on the floor around a narrow table. Her mother, dressed in a white jacket and black plaited skirt, with her hair parted down the middle and drawn back into a knot low on the neck, greeted us and thanked us for coming. The father came in, welcomed us in a few English words, and then departed. Sang Won, in bright jacket and skirt, helped her mother serve a delicious Korean dinner. I had high hopes for Sang Won, and our faith in her has been repaid many times over. The two other girls who were to be our students also invited me to their homes, but I was unable to go.

E Soon Choi and her family took me to the airport on the morning of May 2. President Helen Kim of Ewha sent us alone in her car because she had been advised not to go out of her guarded house herself. She had been persuaded to run for the Legislature in the election the following week and her advisers thought she might be in personal danger; several other candidates had been assassinated within the last few days. One of her dogs had been poisoned and another's throat slashed a few days before my arrival. There were many demonstrations and all sorts of Communistic activities to intimidate the Koreans and discredit efforts to achieve a fair election.*

As the plane took off, I could see E Soon, her husband, and their children waving farewell with their handkerchiefs. My thoughts were of their future and what there was in store for that truly fine little family with such wonderful potentialities for good.

As to that future—the husband died several years later, but E Soon continued her professional career. It was especially gratifying to all of us who know her that the Faculty Senate of Oregon State University saw fit, in the fall of 1965, to present E Soon Choi with a Distinguished Service Award. Her citation reads, in part:

> *Distinguished Korean educator, administrator, and home-maker . . . professor of home economics and child nutrition and dean of women at Yonsei University . . . former dean of*

---

* President Kim, I later learned, successfully survived that election campaign and provided many more years of leadership. In May 1968, I received an invitation—which I unfortunately could not accept—to attend a banquet in Seoul in honor of Dr. Helen Kim, who was then Chairman of the Ewha Board of Trustees, in recognition of her fifty years of service to the university.

home economics at Ewha University . . . ardent representa-
tive of Korean women on half a dozen top-ranked Ministry
of Education and Ministry of Agriculture committees . . .
national officer of the YWCA in Korea . . . self-sacrificing
donor of inexhaustible time, effort, and devotion to the
service of her government, her nation's homes and children,
and her own family . . . one of the great women leaders of
the Far East.

IN CHINA in 1948, inflation had devastatingly devalued the currency.
The 500 U.S. dollars I deposited with the Associated Mission Treasurers in Shanghai was credited to my account as $264,000,000 in
Chinese money. I drew out $10 million for expense money in Shang-
hai, $20 million for a trip to Nanking, $50 million for a trip to Peiping, and a like amount for a trip to Chungking. The plane ticket
from Nanking to Tsinan alone cost $11,500,000!

China had become quite air minded, more so than the United
States, or so it seemed to me at that time. In addition to the cost,
however, obtaining a flight reservation and ticket took some doing.
As someone described the process: you have to have somebody start
getting a ticket before you arrive, start additional activity as soon
as you arrive, fill out blanks, present photograph and inoculation
records, make a down payment by check, add to it as inflation in-
creases, and the day before you are to leave you go to get the ticket
—perhaps again paying more. But when a ticket could be obtained,
air travel had advantages. The trip from Shanghai to Peiping, which
previously had taken two days by rail, was only a three and a half
hour flight. As a disadvantage, I no longer had long trips by rail in
which to catch up on diary letters and other writing. Some of the
passengers, unfamiliar with air travel, became airsick, but fortunately
I did not.

One of the people who gave me assistance in managing currency
and arranging transportation was Bessie A. Hollows, who was in
charge of the Methodist Woman's Division of the Associated Mission
Treasurers. She and Irene Ho (Liu) met me at the airport when I
arrived in Shanghai. My, that was a busy city! Traffic clogged the
streets and everyone seemed in a hurry. Pedicabs—bicycle-powered
rickshas introduced by the Japanese during the occupation—had

reduced the amount of human labor involved in transportation and seemed to be everywhere.

Irene invited Miss Hollows and me to meet her family and have dinner with them the following evening. As the first home economics scholarship student to come from the Orient to OSC, Irene had completed study for her master's degree in 1926. She had returned to Peking to assist Camilla Mills at Yenching University and later became head of the home economics department. She married an Iowa State College Ph.D., Homer Liu, an agricultural chemist. Together, as Irene once expressed it, they "had a great deal of achievement." When Dr. Liu went to the North-Eastern Provinces to promote machine farming, Irene resigned her Yenching position. Taking their year-old daughter, she went with her husband to Mukden—which had formerly been her home—and accepted a position teaching home economics at North-Eastern University. Two years later with two daughters they returned to Peking, where their first son was born. Next they moved to Hangchow, where Dr. Liu became head of the Department of Agricultural Chemistry and Irene taught home economics at the National Chekiang University. He wrote two university texts on soil science. He invented and patented two methods of treating fertilizers but was unable to put them into manufacture because of lack of capital. Irene wrote textbooks on home management, nutrition, and child care for college students and served for a while as domestic science editor for a publishing house in China. In 1935 Chiang Kai-shek's Minister of Finance, Dr. H. H. Kung, placed Dr. Liu in charge of a large project in reclamation of alkaline lands in North China. The family moved to Tientsin where Irene became head of the Department of Home Economics at Ho Pei Provincial Girls Normal College. When the Japanese occupied Tientsin, Dr. Liu followed the government to Chungking in western China, and Irene joined him a year later with four children, the second son being only a few months old at the time. In the western capital of Nationalist China, Dr. Liu became chief of the Bureau of Sulphur and Saltpeter Control, and succeeded in supplying more than the required amount of basic materials needed for black powder and dynamite. Since he was much in need of less strenuous work and because his salary was insufficient to support his family, he resigned from government service and turned to farming and manufacturing. To avoid possible bombing from

Japanese war planes, they moved from Chungking to ten acres of rice paddies and mountain slope. They built houses to accommodate refugee friends, planted two hundred fruit trees, and raised livestock, including chickens to provide two eggs apiece for each child each morning and a whole chicken for the family once a week.

As more refugees came, more houses were built, and before long, the place developed into a village. The refugees, though devoid of property, were people of high culture—artists, dramatists, players, musicians, and literati. Schools flourished and the village became a cultural center. Irene's children, associating with these talents, began to learn painting, playwriting, and acting. The girls learned to imitate two of the most renowned female impersonators of the Chinese stage.

The family was very nearly self-sufficient, but in order to have a cash income, Irene's husband began to manufacture a pipe tobacco he called "Ireana" in her honor to sell especially to British officials attached to the government. They also produced Virginia country-cured ham that became popular with American military and naval personnel stationed in Chungking.

At the time of my arrival, three years after the Japanese had surrendered, the Lius had moved to Shanghai. They reserved a private dining room in a restaurant near the Cathay Hotel, where they took Miss Hollows and me for a delicious and memorable Peking Duck dinner. The beautiful, striking-looking daughters were sophomores in college. One of the handsome boys was taller than his sisters; the other had snapping dark eyes. All of them demonstrated their talents, showing us their paintings, singing for us, and doing dramatic imitations. It was gratifying indeed to feel that we in Oregon had some small part in the development of this fine, wholesome family which had gone through the vicissitudes of war with such poise and courage.

In Nanking, I called on Albert and Celia Steward, who had suffered privation and long separation during the war. Celia's guest book records my presence in their home on May 7 and again on June 6, 1948. On one of these visits it was pouring rain and going up the steep road to the Steward home was so difficult that the driver could not pull the pedicab alone. Dr. Steward, seeing our plight, came down the road and got drenched to the skin helping the driver deliver me safely to the Steward home.

Also in Nanking I saw Dr. Leighton Stuart in his new capacity as American Ambassador to China. After being released from incarceration at the close of the war in 1945, he had gone at once to Chungking and Chengtu to prepare the way for Yenching students and faculty to return to their campus in Peiping. Despite his heavy schedule of meetings with associates and visits with Generalissimo Chiang Kai-shek in Chengtu, he had found time to send me a beautiful, hand-painted silk and bamboo scroll, which I still treasure, and to write briefly of the trying time he had undergone. Then as soon as he could—with the assistance of the U.S. Naval Air Transport Service—he had flown to the New York office of Yenching University and met with the Board of Trustees.

To assist the Board in raising funds for rehabilitation of various campuses in China, Dr. Stuart set out on a trip across the United States. In March 1946, he spent three days in Portland. I helped arrange a luncheon for him with prominent businessmen and lumbermen. "What does your university need?" Aaron Frank, one of the owners of Meier and Frank Company, asked. Dr. Stuart quickly pointed out that he was not speaking for Yenching University alone and that he was not asking for anything specifically; he was there to describe the situation and they could do whatever they felt they should do. Fine support in the form of building materials and cash donations resulted from this Portland visit. Dr. Stuart seemed in excellent health despite the hardships he had endured, and I had a feeling then that he was about to do some of his greatest work.

About the time that Dr. Stuart arrived in the U.S. from China, President Truman announced that General George C. Marshall had agreed to leave retirement to go to China as his personal representative in an effort to find a solution for ending the civil strife between the National Government and the Communist Party.

When Dr. Stuart returned to China in April 1946, Philip Fugh, his long-time private secretary and confidant, suggested that he go to Nanking before returning to Peiping and call on Generalissimo Chiang Kai-shek, who by that time had returned the capital to Nanking. At the suggestion of the Generalissimo and Madame Chiang, he also called on General Marshall. From this time on, General Marshall seemed to appreciate Dr. Stuart's advice and suggestions, and after Dr. Stuart returned to Yenching University, Marshall called him back several times for conferences. At the close of one such visit, on the Fourth of July 1946, General Marshall amazed Dr. Stuart by asking if he would be willing to become U.S. Ambassador to China. Dr. Stuart remonstrated that at the age of seventy he should be retiring from active duties rather than taking on new ones. General Marshall knew that Leighton Stuart had unusual qualifications to serve in this period of extreme crisis. Although his father was from Virginia and he had been educated in the United States, Leighton had been born in China and had lived there more than forty years. He spoke the official language, Mandarin, as well as a native—better, Dr. Sun Yat-sen's son once told me. In his childhood Leighton had attained a good command of the Wu dialect used in Hangchow, Shanghai, and Nanking. He knew the leaders of both sides in the civil war. In Chungking the previous September, the Communist leaders Chou En-lai and Mao Tse-tung had greeted him as an old acquaintance and had taken him and Philip Fugh to lunch. Although his work had centered in education, Dr. Stuart had known the leaders of China from the time of Sun Yat-sen.

When Dr. Stuart agreed to accept the appointment, General Marshall, President Truman, and the U.S. Senate acted swiftly, and on July 10, 1946, his appointment was confirmed. Dr. Stuart tendered his resignation as President of Yenching University, but the University refused it and gave him leave of absence instead. He had agreed with General Marshall to serve for only a year or less. By the time I arrived in Nanking, however, he had completed nearly two strenuous years and had more ahead of him. "The style of living [as an ambassador]" he wrote later, "the emoluments, the prestige, were all very different from the simplicity to which I had been accustomed." His office was in his residence, an imposing, tastefully decorated building. The decorator had used Dr. Stuart's beautiful Chinese scrolls, vases, and pictures so skillfully that in the Embassy he had a touch of home.

I stayed in Nanking only a few days on my first visit. The people at Cheeloo University in Tsinan had asked me to visit them, but when I told Ambassador Stuart of the invitation he advised against my accepting it. He felt that Tsinan was uncomfortably close to Communist-occupied territory and that travel congestion might create obstacles when I was ready to leave. The Cheeloo people would not take "No" for an answer, however, and appealed again for me to come. Dr. Stuart finally agreed and sent word to the Governor of the Shantung Province that he wished me not to remain in Tsinan beyond May 16, thus facilitating departure to Peiping.

Mary K. Russell, a Kansas State College home economist, and Dr. Martin Yang, a Cornell man of the Cheeloo staff, greeted me so warmly in Tsinan that I could sense how hungry the community was for outside contacts. I had not visited Cheeloo previously but knew about it. Students and faculty migrated to Chengtu early in the Japanese invasion. After the war they had returned to their old campus and now exhibited remarkable spirit and courage. Even though the Communist troops were only seven miles away—on the far side of the Yellow River—the university staff were hoping to finish the semester before evacuating again—if they had to. In the meantime, they carried on with energy and enthusiasm.

They had a full schedule for me—breakfasts, lunches, teas, picnics, and dinners. One evening I spoke to about 1,000 women of a teacher's college and a higher middle school, and I scheduled half-hour conferences with many of the professors. One morning an eminent archeologist, educated in an English university, came and told me of the prehistoric black porcelains he had discovered. We also discussed the political situation. He felt strongly that the only hope for China was through trained Christian leadership but said he realized it might take fifty years to effect great change. Fifty years in Chinese history did not appear to be an inconsiderable time to a thoughtful Chinese educator.

To my great delight I found the campus of Yenching University in Peiping unmarred by the war. Once again it seemed the loveliest campus I had ever seen. The Japanese had used it as a military hospital and stripped it of equipment as they left. They also left unsightly concrete structures, part of an unfinished alcohol plant, but these western-style buildings, which the Yenching staff were converting into engineering laboratories, were sufficiently hidden that they did not mar the beauty of the Chinese architecture.

Dr. Stuart was appreciative of the financial support we in Oregon had found for Yenching University. Early in 1946 at the time when he had come to Portland to describe China's needs, I had received a telephone call from Dr. Frank E. Brown, a physician in Salem, who told me he knew where there was a modest sum of money available to improve child life in China. Later he came to talk with me. He was convinced, he said, that the best way to improve the life and health of a people is through influencing child life and through the training of women and men for Christian family living. This he believed could best be accomplished through higher educational leadership. As a result of our conversations he agreed to provide $5,000, if it could be matched by a like sum, to be used in the rehabilitation of home economics facilities at Yenching University. Dr. Stuart agreed enthusiastically to this proposal and would have undertaken the raising of funds to match the gift. It seemed to me possible to raise the money in Oregon. Alma Fritchoff and I set out to do so. We spent Saturdays and Sundays and weekday evenings calling on friends, clubs, and businesses and in the end raised $6,403.25 from 228 contributors to add to Dr. Brown's $5,000 for the rehabilitation of home economics at Yenching University.

How good it was to see old friends among the Yenching staff members! Chen I (Caroline Chen) one of the first eight girls to take home economics at Yenching in 1923, had taught at Yenching continuously except for a few war years and for the time she had spent in the United States, and was now head of the Home Economics Department. She had studied at OSC twenty years before and had received a master's degree from Columbia University. She handled my ten days' program in Yenching quietly, efficiently, and joyously. She saw to it that all applicants for scholarships had ample time for conferences with me. Never once did she say she would like to go on for further study herself, but I knew it would mean much both to her and her department. At the end of my stay, I said, "Caroline, I should like to assign a scholarship to you." A light of joy impossible to describe came into her face. Accepting the scholarship, she later came to our campus for refreshment and advanced study.

In addition to Caroline, there were three other home economists on the staff who had studied at OSC—Mrs. Y. P. Mei, Hsi-Hsuan Yu, and Li Keng. Yenching had 855 students (542 men and 313 women), all purposeful and studious. Much in the spirit of those at Cheeloo University, these students and the faculty were going along calmly as though the Communist troops were not just on the other side of those very visible Western Hills.

The day I left Peiping Caroline Chen and Mrs. Mei took me to the airport in the LaSalle automobile which a departing Japanese general had left for Dr. Stuart. It was then being used by Dr. Mei, the acting president of the University. As the plane took off in early afternoon the pilot circled and I had my last look at the yellow tile roofs of the Forbidden City, my last glimpse of the Summer Palace and the Jade Fountain, my last view of the city which I still believe to be the world's most fascinating.

The plane circled down over Shanghai in the late afternoon, awaiting clearance to land at the busy airport, and we had an excellent view of that city of four million people. Because of travel difficulty in the city, Caroline Chen had written her brother, an architect (University of Pennsylvania graduate), asking him to meet me. This he did and insisted on calling for me the next morning to help arrange for tickets to Chungking and Chengtu for the following day. He could not see me off but again insisted on sending his driver and car to take me to the airport at five o'clock in the morning.

Our DC-4 Skymaster crossed China in a matter of hours and landed at an airport ten miles out of the city of Chungking. We passengers squeezed into a bus with hard wooden benches and bumped along a rough road filled with hairpin curves down into the city. The only other westerner among the passengers, a young woman going to visit her husband at the American consulate, had gotten off before the bus stopped at an office where everyone else seemed to be getting off. I asked the driver if I should get off here and he said, "Yes, office." It was the place to reclaim checked baggage, however, and not the main office. Mabel Nowlin of the Methodist Mission had written that someone would meet me but I found no one there. The Chinese banker who had sat next to me on the plane came to my rescue. "Have no fear," he said, "I shall get you to your friend." After our luggage arrived an hour later he arranged transportation to the Methodist Mission and insisted on paying for the ricksha.

After I had relaxed with a cup of tea, a piece of spiced cake, and a nap, along came another pleasant surprise. The woman who called to take me out to dinner was Wu Sung Chen (Li), another of the "First Eight" home economics students at Yenching University in 1923. She had gone to the main airline office to meet me but had finally discovered that I had by-passed it. I remembered Sung Chen well as a beautiful, strong girl who spoke excellent English. Her father had been consul in Panama during her high school days. Now she was married to a professor of engineering and had become head of home economics at the government normal college in Chungking. We had a delightful visit.

The DC-3 on which I was to go to Chengtu was small enough
that it could take off from a smaller airport on an island in the Yangtze River. An ancient little boat took us across to the island early the
next morning and we were soon flying over the rich plains of Szechwan, sometimes called the "Texas of China." At Chengtu I had five
wonderfully interesting and pleasant days at the West China Union
University and the Government University. The friendly people I
met gave me not only good insights into their home economics departments—their limitations, problems, and possibilities—but also an
opportunity to interpret for them home economics as I saw it and
its future contribution to China. I spoke to the staffs and students
of both universities and to a group of principals of schools in Chengtu. President Fong of West China Union University seemed eager to
have the work in home economics expanded. It had been started at
the time his university was playing host to Nanking, Ginling, Cheeloo, and Yenching universities six years before but had much room
for improvement. For one thing, I tried tactfully to persuade the
administrators to bring the home economics laboratories and classrooms up out of the basement and to help them realize that using
cast-off or inferior facilities does much harm to a field of education.

The foods class prepared a dinner one evening for about thirty
guests and served it outdoors in the courtyard. As I sat down at my
placecard, I found at my side another guest who had just arrived.
She looked up at me and in soft-spoken English said, "I think you
were my teacher." I looked into the eyes of this gentle, rather delicate little woman and saw Chang Chung-Ying, the beloved "Kate"
of the First Eight to study home economics at Yenching. How we
laughed when we recalled the dramatic portrayal of Katherine in
Taming of the Shrew that had won for her this nickname. She was
the one who had spent six weeks traveling from her West China
home to Peking so that she could study home economics. Now she
was principal of the Methodist Middle School in Chengtu, and her
husband, a Yenching graduate, was also in educational work. The
couple had two daughters in the University and a younger son.

In all, I met four of the original First Eight girls who started
the study of home economics at Yenching University twenty-five
years before. The fourth one, Kwan Suen-Chen, was in charge of the
home economics department of the Nanking Theological Seminary
and formerly had been chairman of the Home Committee of the

National Christian Council. She was helping train young people for missionary and church work, especially in counseling parishioners in family-life problems.

One morning in Chengtu, when the Commissioner of Education had asked me to speak to the principals of the middle schools, "Kate" was in the audience. After my interpreter finished speaking, she arose and asked the Commissioner if she might speak. With permission granted she turned to me saying, "Miss Milam, I wish the privilege of paying tribute to you and your teaching. May I speak in Chinese?" Of course, I consented. My interpreter translated her heart-felt explanation of what home economics had meant to her personally and to her home and family. A reporter for an American newspaper later quoted me as saying, "It cost me three hours' flying time and 1,000,000 inflated Chinese dollars to call on a former student . . . but the satisfaction I felt was worth $2,000,000—normal money!" With a feeling of satisfaction that I had undertaken these visits in Korea and China preceding the survey in the Philippines, I left Chengtu on June 5, stayed overnight in Chungking, and flew back to Nanking for my second visit to the capital.

A girl born and raised on a farm in Missouri might dream of being entertained like a princess in Oriental splendor. She might fancy herself, dressed in her finest apparel, whisked away along a flower-bordered driveway in a magic carriage. She might imagine herself at a formal dinner chatting pleasantly with the personal representatives of the heads of the great nations of the earth. She might dream of such things—but she would not really believe they could happen to her. Yet—they did happen on my visits to Nanking.

On a flower-scented spring evening, the long, black Lincoln limousine of the American Ambassador to China drew up before the women's dormitory at Ginling College. A liveried Chinese chauffeur stepped out and held open the door of the immaculately polished automobile. A bevy of smiling students and faculty well-wishers watched my departure as the impressive vehicle swung around the driveway and out into the street with the flag of the United States flying from one front fender and the flag of the United States Ambassador flying from the other.

As the other guests and I entered the Embassy, attendants showed us the diagram for seating, which made it easy not only to find our places at the long table but also to see who the other guests were. We were ushered into a spacious reception room, where Ambassador Stuart, looking remarkably vigorous and in good spirits, greeted us and introduced us to the other guests. The dining table had beautiful candelabra and flowers for centerpieces. The place settings of silver-and-gold-banded Lenox china were embossed with the Seal of the United States, like place settings in the White House.

Dr. Stuart invited me on two such occasions. In fact, he invited me for a third, which I declined because of "a previous engagement." It was only after his secretary tactfully informed me later that for an Ambassador's invitation there are no engagements that take precedence that I realized the Missouri farm girl had made a faux pas!

At the first dinner I sat across the table from Ambassador Stuart. On one side of him sat Mrs. Edward Clark, the guest of honor, who was on a world tour with her husband in the interests of World Government. On the other side sat the wife of the Russian Charge d'Affaires, Madame Fedorenko, who spoke no English but whom Leighton appeared to keep well entertained. On one side of me sat the President of the Legislative Yuan, Sun Fo, the son of the late Dr. Sun Yat-sen; on the other side His Excellency Dr. Chu Chia Hua, Minister of Education. The second evening the Ambassador seated me between the Swiss and Indian ambassadors, who were having a heated discussion of the ills and advantages of imperialism. I thought for a while I would have to referee their bout. Dr. Stuart told me later that was exactly the reason he had so seated us.

Several other times on less formal occasions Leighton and I lunched or dined together and he took me on several drives through the city and surrounding countryside. He seemed to enjoy his work, yet at times he felt the futility of some of his efforts. The outcome of the devastating struggle between the Nationalists and Communists was impossible to foresee in the spring of 1948. He clung to his hopes and worked hard to achieve them. I think he appreciated having someone he could talk with and confide in. Both in conversation and in his letters he spoke frankly, and that is one reason I destroyed all of his letters to me. I wanted to make sure that the confidential matters he discussed would forever remain in confidence.

Dr. Stuart served as Ambassador to China from July 10, 1946, to December 31, 1952. By the time he resigned, the Communists had taken control of mainland China, and the Nationalist government had moved to Formosa.

20. Survey

THE COLLEGES AND UNIVERSITIES of the Philippines had no "far western provinces" to flee into as the Chinese colleges did when the Japanese occupied or destroyed their campuses. Some groups of faculty and students evacuated into the mountains and jungles and stayed together to some extent, but the interruptions of guerrilla warfare, the need to help with civil government affairs, to say nothing of the demands of faculty, family, and visitors, tended to take more of their time than did educational programs. While the war was still going on, Protestant mission authorities in the United States began to make plans for postwar rehabilitation of their educational institutions. In 1944 the Philippines Committee of the Foreign Missions Conference of North America created a subcommittee under the chairmanship of Dr. Arthur L. Carson to study probable needs. The subcommittee recommended forming an association of Christian schools and colleges in the Philippines and sending a survey commission from the United States. The Association was formed immediately after liberation in 1946. Dr. Donald P. Cottrell, my one-time professor at Columbia University who had become Dean of the College of Education at Ohio State University, Dr. Frank W. Price, a specialist in theological education, and I were selected as the three members of the Survey Commission. Dr. Price found that he had urgent commitments in China that would prevent him from joining us. He planned therefore to conduct his part of the survey separately. To Dean Cottrell and me fell the responsibility for making the initial survey and formulating recommendations. We planned to start our work in the Philippines in mid-July, 1948. I arranged my itinerary in China accordingly.

In South China, after visiting Lingnan University in Canton, I intended to fly to Foochow to visit colleges there, but heavy rains had put the airfield in Foochow out of use and I had to cancel that flight. Dr. Frank E. Brown, the Salem physician who had helped rehabilitate home economics at Yenching University, had given me $500 to use in any way I saw fit to further my work in the Far East. Cancellation of the Foochow trip provided time to use his gift for a trip to Siam. For the six-hour flight from Hong Kong to Bangkok, I chose a BOAC (British Overseas Air Corporation) flying boat. Before we started, a steward explained the life belt and how to inflate it. "Should we have to make an emergency landing and injure our craft," he said, "we have to get up on top of our ship. Should you fall off into the water, here's a whistle—blow it and we will come after you." I thanked him and laughed, for I could not imagine myself having the presence of mind to find the whistle attached to the life belt, much less to blow it, if I actually fell off the ship.

Fortunately, I had no need for the whistle. We had a smooth flight along the South China coast and over Hainan and the Gulf of Siam. I had cabled for reservations at the Trocadero Hotel in Bangkok and went there upon arrival. The next day I called Walter A. Zimmerman, whom Ruth Gill Hammond had mentioned many times. A member of the World Service Staff of the International Committee of the YMCA, Mr. Zimmerman had gone out in 1930 to assist leaders in Siam in establishing and developing a YMCA organization and program in the country. In the early years of their married life in Bangkok, Ruth and A. R. Hammond had been close friends of Mr. and Mrs. Zimmerman. Walter greeted me cordially even though we had not met previously and came to the hotel at once to see me. "You don't need to stay here," he said and insisted on moving me to the YWCA. When I told him the purpose of my visits to colleges in the Orient, he offered to introduce me to the Rector of Chulalongkorn University. First, however, he wanted me to meet a Simmons College alumna, who could open other doors for me.

Walter had many places for me to see and many people for me to meet. He took me to see the house that had been the Hammond home and the place where the Hammond children, Barbara and John, had been born. On the Fourth of July, he took me to a mid-day reception in the beautiful grounds of the American Embassy where there were about 250 people, consisting mostly of Americans but also including prominent Siamese, diplomats from other countries, and colorfully dressed French priests.

I found the Simmons College graduate, Mrs. Swai Tongchua, a charming and beautiful woman. She took me to see Mom Luang Pin Malakul, Under Secretary of State in the Ministry of Education, and his assistant. Both men, having been educated in English universities, spoke excellent English. When I told them of the effect the study of home economics was having in other countries of the Orient, they seemed quite interested and receptive to suggestions.

The next day, Dorothy Ward, one of the two competent representatives of the United States Information Service in Bangkok, called for me and took me to the USIS offices to discuss cultural relations and scholarships for Siamese women to study in America. While I was in this conference, the Rector of Chulalongkorn University sent word he would like to see me, and Mrs. Tongchua and I went to meet him. We had tea with him and his male secretary—an elaborate tea with chicken sandwiches, pastries, fruitcake, and coffee. The Rector and the secretary had also studied in England. They explained why they were so receptive to the idea of introducing home economics into Chulalongkorn, the only university in Siam at that time. Of the 2,000 students, about half were women, they said, but the women were not permitted to take engineering; only a few could take medicine or science, but the Arts College was ninety-eight percent women. The officials felt that women should have some other fields open to them and asked many questions about staff, equipment, required courses, and opportunities in professional fields in home economics. Before I left Siam, these men and the others I had talked with indicated that they were considering sending some of their women to the United States to study home economics. Later that fall (1948), after I had returned to Oregon, I received a letter from Mom Luang Pin Malakul saying that as a result of our discussions the government had created three graduate scholarships to send women to America to study home economics. Two were to come to Oregon State College and the other one to Kansas State College. That is how Prachuabchitr Vadhanasevi (M.H. Ec. '51) and Pratin Kutranon (M.H. Ec., '52) came to our campus. They returned to Thailand, as the country had been renamed by that time, and started courses in home economics. With the establishment of Kasetsart University near Bangkok, a department of home economics was planned and it has developed since that time. Both Margaret

Fincke and Agnes Kolshorn of our staff later spent several months there at different times as advisers to the department.

After the short visit to Siam, I had a few days of rest and relaxation in Hong Kong. As I was about to board the Pan American plane for Manila on July 13, I received a cablegram. What now? I thought. I was much relieved to find that it contained a message of welcome from Mrs. Benitez, the president of the Women's University in the Philippines, inviting me to attend a reception in their University the following day.

Arriving in Manila, I found much of the city still in shambles. Wartime bombing, street fighting, and uncontrollable fires had left many business, government, and school buildings a mass of rubble or gutted, empty-windowed skeletons. Streets had received some repairs but were filled with chuckholes and loose gravel. Hulks of rusting ships dotted the once beautiful Manila harbor.

Dean Cottrell, I learned, had been delayed for visits to mission colleges and schools in Japan and China, and we could not start our visits to the Christian colleges in the Philippines for about two weeks. This intervening time gave me an opportunity to review materials that had been prepared for us, to get acquainted with people we would be working with, to give talks at schools and at an Extension Center about 200 miles out in the country, and to see how home economics had fared since my first visit in 1923.

Home Economics had gotten a good start in the Philippines following the Spanish-American War when American or American-trained Filipino educators had assisted in developing the educational program. These volunteers have been called "America's First Peace Corps."[*] In later years, the development of an educational program in home economics had not lived up to its early promise. The central government had established a Division of Home Economics in 1923, but it had been placed under the Bureau of Plant Industry and in 1936 merged with the Division of Plant Utilization. In this setting the home economics section had a limited function in research and extension activities related to food and fibers; *production* rather than *improvement of homelife* seemed to be the chief objective. At the college level, home economics was concerned almost exclusively with training of teachers and was confined to

---

[*]Willis P. Porter, "America's First Peace Corps," *Saturday Review*, June 20, 1963, p. 45.

departments of education. Improvement of the home was not considered of paramount importance, and there was little provision for preparation of dietitians, nutritionists, hotel and restaurant managers, and home demonstration agents. The remedy for these defects, I believed, was to establish independent departments of home economics within the colleges. An agricultural mission from the United States the year before had recommended establishment of a Division of Home Economics in the government but it had failed to materialize by 1948.

In my talks as Dr. Cottrell and I went about the country in 1948, in our final report, and in an article in the Manila *Times,* I kept pointing out the need for improvement of education for homemaking. In an editorial in the Philippine Normal School magazine, *The Torch,* a writer took me to task for my attitude. He pointed out that "There have been appreciable changes in home conditions since the introduction of [home economics] in our schools in 1904. . . . We fail . . . to understand how any impression could have arisen that the training in home economics afforded in our schools has failed to reach hundreds of thousands of Filipino homes." He was right, of course, to a limited extent, but he failed to see how much more could be done. Here was a country suffering a heavy mortality rate as a result of disease and malnutrition, much of which could have been prevented through the application of principles of home sanitation and nutrition. I had another chance to say a word—not the final word, by any means—on this subject in an article called "Functional Homemaking," published in *The Philippine Educational Forum.* The Filipinos had made a start but it seemed to me they needed to move ahead much faster.

Late in July, Dean Cottrell arrived and we began a series of planning conferences. As Commissioners for the Protestant Missions we had a dual responsibility: (1) "To assist the Filipino and American educational authorities of the member institutions of the Association of Christian Schools and Colleges . . . to analyze their problems and to profit by such wisdom as might be forthcoming from conferences . . . with the Commissioners," and (2) to write a report to be presented at a meeting of the Philippine Committee of the Foreign Missions Conference of North America in Columbus, Ohio, on October 4-5, 1948. The newly formed Association had 52 member institutions, spread from southern Mindanao to northern

Luzon. Sixteen of them offered work above high school level, and three had four-year collegiate programs. We realized early that we would have to plan our time carefully to accomplish our purpose. The Conference needed up-to-date, first-hand information directly from the schools and needed our recommendations to help shape their policies for the coming years. Heads of the member institutions of the Association gave every assistance. They provided us with copious background information, usually supplied us with a guide to assist with air tickets and accommodations, and discussed their problems with us freely. Dr. Arthur Carson spent a great deal of time with us. He had been inaugurated as President of Silliman University, the largest of the Protestant universities, in 1939, had evacuated to the hills with students and faculty when the Japanese occupied the campus, and had been taken off by submarine to the United States in 1944. He had been active in developing plans for rehabilitating the schools and colleges after the war and was therefore a mine of information for us. It became obvious to us that we could not visit all institutions in the time available. We therefore laid out an itinerary that would include about one-third of them.

Before departing from Manila we conferred with the Under Secretary in the Ministry of Education and the Director of Private Schools and learned from them that the government had rather rigid control of both public and private schools. We met with members of the U.S. Embassy staff, with a member of the U.S. War Damage Commission, with administrators of various schools and colleges in Manila, and with officers of the missions and evangelical churches.

In addition to gathering information, Dr. Cottrell and I were called upon a number of times to speak to various groups. I met with home economics and alumni groups. One afternoon while I was speaking at the University of The Philippines, a storm came up and the noise of the rain on the improvised metal roof made too much competition for me, even with a loud-speaker. Girls in the audience sang songs for about fifteen minutes until the storm subsided and I could finish my talk. Both Dean Cottrell and I found meeting with all sorts of groups worthwhile, but when such meetings began taking too much time from our principal job for the private colleges, we had to draw the line and accept no more speaking invitations.

The day before we left for the southern islands of the archi-
pelago, we had an interview with the President of the Republic,
Elpidio Quirino. We arrived at his offices in the Palace promptly a
little before eleven o'clock and were ushered into the cabinet room
to wait until he was ready to see us. My thin voile dress was quite
comfortable for street wear but provided insufficient warmth in that
air-conditioned room; I was covered with goose pimples before we
were admitted into the President's office an hour and a half later.
President Quirino, a large man immaculately clad in a white shark-
skin suit, received us courteously, discussed our project, made some
suggestions, and indicated his approval of our commission.

The next morning we took off early for a five-hour flight in a
Philippines Air Line (PAL) plane to Cotabato on Mindanao, the
southern-most of the large islands. Although it was the rainy season,
we had a beautifully clear flight, in sight of forested islands and
emerald water all the way. After one stop to refuel, we arrived at
Cotabato about noon. An open jeep was there to pick us up and
take us through a long straight cut in the jungle inland about 35
miles to the village of Pikit. We stayed overnight in the home of a
Filipino doctor—the only house in the town that had not been destroyed in the war. After visiting Union Institute, talking with the
Director and his wife and other men and women operating the
school, and seeing the students and something of the community in
which they lived, we made several recommendations. It seemed to
us that the Institute should revamp its formalized liberal arts curriculum to meet the needs of this rural community. We felt, and the
staff agreed, that this institution could prove to be a very significant
one by establishing a demonstration high school. As we visualized it,
the school should have a model homestead with a house that would
represent improvement over typical houses, yet would be within
the means of at least some of the families of the region. It would have
a model farm demonstrating the use of mechanized equipment and
good agricultural practices. We felt also that it should have an adult
education program for both men and women in agriculture, homelife,
recreation, health, and religious education. We suggested the formation of a non-stock corporation to operate the school to assure a
base of community support in the event that the Director or the
staff should at any time be withdrawn from the institution. The staff
heartily agreed with these recommendations although the staff

members realized that in fields such as agriculture and home economics trained instructors would be needed and a different pattern
of financial support would be necessary for buildings and equipment.

Working back northward, we stopped at Pilgrim Institute at
Cagayan and at Silliman University in Dumaguete in Negros Oriental. Dr. Carson, the Silliman president, called for us in his car one
morning about six-thirty and took us around the island to visit Hib-
bard Institute at Guihulngan and West Negros College at Bacolod.
It was a long, hard trip over rough roads but took us through beautiful country. To save time at one point we walked across a raging
river on a swaying bamboo bridge where a jeep met us on the far
side while our car took a round-about route and caught up with
us hours later.

At Iloilo on Panay Island we found Central Philippine College
—which had been founded in 1905 by the Baptists—a most promising
institution soon to develop into a university somewhat along the
lines of Silliman University. From Iloilo, Dr. Cottrell flew to Cebu
and then took a small boat on an overnight trip to Leyte. "Tropical
calm prevailed," he later wrote, "with sufficient tropical heat to drive
some of us out on deck with our pads to sleep—that is, until about
3:00 a.m., when the seas rose with brisk winds. It was still dark
at 5:30 a.m., when we were to have pulled up at the dock of a little
port town, but our craft could only throw over the anchor and transfer us—very precariously, with 16-foot waves — to an oar-driven
lifeboat to move in toward the beach. Even then, our sailors would
not try to beach the small craft but put each of us and our suitcases
on the back of one of the men to be carried ashore. We drove on up
the island after recovering our claims to dignity, to Tacloban where
MacArthur and Romulo came ashore on their famous 'return' and
viewed the monument which had been erected there."

I caught up with Dean Cottrell again in Manila. After a week
of conferring with officials, making notes, and beginning to shape
our preliminary recommendations, we took off on our northern trip.
Plans called for only one day at Tuguegarao, but five days later we
were still there, grounded by a typhoon. The first day, a missionary
minister who had been trained as an engineer at the University of
Florida took us by jeep for a wild two-hour ride to a meeting at
which we were to speak. When Dean Cottrell's hat blew off, the
driver whirled around in the middle of the road. A barefooted Fili-

pino boy carrying a hoe over his shoulder thought we were after him and dashed for the bushes. The driver swished alongside the hat and, bending over, picked it up polo-fashion, hardly reducing his speed. He was such a buoyant, jolly person that he kept us in gales of laughter. It was easy to see why he had been successful in teaching the Filipinos both Christianity and the rudiments of sanitary engineering.

When we found that the stormy weather prevented us from making our planned visits to schools, Dean Cottrell and I made good use of our time by working on our preliminary report so that we could have it ready to discuss at a round-up conference for representatives of the 52 members of the Association on September 10 and 11. One distressing thing about education in the Philippines was the way in which private schools, some of them calling themselves colleges, were springing up with hardly any facilities for instruction and with inadequate staff and financing. A multitude of stock companies had been formed to operate schools, with the idea of making money for the stockholders. Some had run up deficits and were trying to persuade church groups to take them over. We could recommend discouragement of this trend among evangelical schools but could do nothing to stop the unjustified spread of stock-company schools.

When planes were able to get through from Manila, we helped the wife of the engineer-missionary who had taken us for the jeep ride and in whose home we were paying guests, to take the first plane out. She was about to give birth to twins and needed maternity care. Dean Cottrell and I obtained passage on the second plane. For an hour we flew over flooded areas where tree tops were almost the only things showing. A local storm forced us to change course and fly out over Bataan and Corregidor as we came in to land. We found Manila streets had been under water for days.

Dean Cottrell and I went to work in earnest getting our notes and recommendations ready for the round-up conference. We had interruptions, however. One day we had to spend three and a half hours filling out forms, being fingerprinted, and paying various fees for our exit permits. In Seattle, on the way over, we had paid a $12.50 fee; on arrival we had paid an $8 head tax; now to leave we had to pay more fees—about $50 in all, just to enter and leave the country! "It is difficult," I wrote at that time, "not to grow impatient at what seems to us to be such waste and inefficiency, but we must remember that it is a very young republic and surely will ultimately evolve a better system!"

Everything went well at the round-up conference. Dr. Carson, as chairman, had a good agenda planned. Dean Cottrell and I presented seven principal recommendations:

1. That the Association of Christian Schools and Colleges continue as an independent organization, strengthening itself through a ten-year program of continuous study of educational problems.

2. That within the membership three union universities be planned, one at Dumaguete using Silliman University as a base, one at Iloilo using Central Philippine College as a base, and one in Manila drawing several Christian colleges into one institution and adding a College of Medicine and a School of Social Work. (In making this recommendation, I was influenced by Leighton Stuart's success in Peking in combining several colleges into Yenching University.)

3. That the proliferation of junior colleges that had sprung up since the war be discouraged in favor of strengthening four-year colleges.

4. That the general education curricula of both schools and colleges of the Association be guided more directly toward the needs of the people for improved homelife, health, agriculture, and industry rather than toward purely academic studies as had been true in the past.

5. That in financing these institutions a larger share of their support be obtained from the Filipinos themselves.

6. That a limited number of demonstration centers be set up to show what could be done rather than undertaking vast programs of mass education.

7. That in the evangelical tradition, the development of Christian character continue to be a primary aim.

After hearing our recommendations, the conference divided up into seven groups to discuss them. For the most part they found our suggestions entirely acceptable but made modifications, additions, and suggestions, to most of which we readily agreed. After the conference Dean Cottrell and I went into seclusion to write our final report. Dr. and Mrs. Carson took us up to the Tagaytay Club on a ridge overlooking Lake Taal an hour out of Manila where we could work easily in cool air without interruptions. By going on a rigid schedule—beginning at eight o'clock in the morning and continuing some days until ten or later in the evening—we were able to convert our notes into a 95-page final draft and have it ready for the typists in a week's time. Back in Manila, elated that the job was completed, we decided to relax a bit and went to an air-conditioned theater to see and hear Jeanette MacDonald and Nelson Eddy in *Rose Marie*.

How MUCH OF LASTING VALUE we were able to acomplish in the Philippines is hard to measure. Silliman University has continued in a position of leadership among the private institutions but has held its enrollment in the collegiate division to slightly more than 2,000 students as at the time of the survey. We recommended strengthening work in home economics and agriculture and Silliman University has moved somewhat in that direction through a department of agriculture and a Community Development Program. It now offers a Bachelor of Science degree in home economics.

Central Philippine College at Iloilo City on Panay Island became Central Philippine University in 1953 and today has more than doubled the 1,575 enrollment it had when we were there. It now has a College of Agriculture and offers a few master's degrees.

When we met with the Philippine Committee of the Foreign Missions Conference of North America at Columbus, Ohio, in October 1948, our report was well received. The committee appreciated having the opportunity to discuss with us the problems the colleges faced and the recommendations we had formulated for their future. The manuscript we had written at the Tagaytay Club on the ridge overlooking Lake Taal was published by the Foreign Missions Conference of North America under the title *Schools and Colleges in the Philippines: A Report*. In the spring of 1967, when Dr. Cottrell was preparing to retire from the deanship of the College of Education at Ohio State University, we learned from Dr. Carson in Quezon City that our report "still has influence in the Philippines" and that he planned to quote from it at a forthcoming meeting of the National Council of Churches and visiting Mission Board representatives.

21. Alma Mater

ONE SATURDAY MORNING in the 1940's two young men called on me in Corvallis. They said their mother had asked them to stop to see me on their way home to California after a summer working in the Oregon forests. They told of their educational plans and talked of the woods, of literature, of international affairs, and of course of their mother, father, and older and younger brothers at home. As I listened to these fine-looking young men, I could see Helen Gardner in their features and their enthusiasm. They did not seem to mind spending an hour with their mother's former teacher and friend. When they left, I wrote to Helen, "They are just the kind of sons I would have expected you to raise."

In Helen Gardner Thayer's reply, which proved to be one of her last letters, she commented on how difficult it must be for us in the School of Home Economics "to keep in touch with the more than 3,000 graduates reported in this year's news letter." She continued,

That very informal call [of my sons] was, in a way, my answer to that letter. There is nothing very professional in my life these days, but there is a "heap o' living" with a husband and four sons and many friends and relatives coming and going. While daily life with five men is something vastly different from the nice precision of a home economics course, still I appreciate to this day many of the experiences there, without which life for my family would have been much poorer.

That was one reason I asked the boys to call upon you. I wanted them to know you who had been such a good friend and adviser during my rich years in school and I wanted them to see, even superficially, the great work that is being done for the advancement of human living. While we did not discuss it in those terms, I feel sure from the light in their eyes as they told me of the call that it was a rich experience for them.

271

Teachers find their most gratifying rewards in the accomplishments of their students. We in home economics are especially fortunate because the accomplishments of our students include marriage, homemaking, child rearing, community leadership, and adventures in career fields. In their achievements as mothers, wives, scientists, business women, designers, teachers, authors, and civic leaders we like to think we can see reflected to some small degree the results of our efforts. We may be justly accused of having a selfish motive in keeping in touch with our alumnae, because we gain a good deal of personal satisfaction from seeing our girls make good and perhaps in helping them over rough spots in their later lives.

As I look back on it now, I can see that policies and practices we inaugurated through the years have helped to foster a close association and a feeling of mutual respect among students, faculty, and alumnae. Having all been poor little lost souls on a big new campus at one time in our own lives, we realized how important it is to help frightened freshmen find themselves and regain their composure. Both from the standpoint of the individual and of the School we felt it important to provide new students with the information they needed in choosing courses. We believed also that getting to know students personally and sharing some of their problems would help both them and us as we started our work together. The personnel program which evolved helped us achieve these aims. Having received from the Registrar the names of prospective students, we mailed out form letters or pamphlets providing information not to be found in the *Catalog*. For several years we had beautifully illustrated booklets written by Zelta Feike Rodenwold entitled "Woman's Career" and "What Can a Woman Do?" describing the broad scope of home economics opportunities. We invited students to write for more information or to come to the campus for conferences and to bring their parents if they wished.

The Registrar sent us records for incoming freshmen showing high school preparation and test scores. Each new student was assigned a staff adviser and, usually, a senior or graduate student to serve as a Big Sister. One evening of Freshman Week the faculty and new students had an opportunity to meet each other and mingle socially at a reception in the Home Economics Building. In the first month of the school year the Home Economics Club gave an informal dinner for the freshmen in home economics followed by entertain-

1924

Upper left: A moon gate in the North China Union College for Women, Yenching University, Peking, China.

Above: Camilla Mills and Emogene Clark in Shanghai.

Left: J. C. Clark and Ava B. Milam in Shanghai.

Below: The first eight girls to study home economics at Yenching University, Peking, China.

1932

Above: Ruth Gill with a class in cookery at Lingnan University, Canton, China.

Left: Ruth Gill Hammond and A. R. Hammond at their September wedding in Corvallis, Oregon.

1937

Above: The two sets of Milam twins at the beginning of an overseas trip. *Left to right:* Ava B. Milam, Ada Milam Cockefair, Lora Milam Hanson, and Lottie Milam Vaughn.

Below: The Home Economics Summer Tour to the Orient at the entrance of a tea merchant's summer villa in Hangchow, China.

1919 and 1950

Dean Ava B. Milam at her desk in
the School of Home Economics, Oregon State College.

ment, such as a Chinese fashion show. These functions helped the students get acquainted and begin to form lifelong friendships.

The first term, each freshman in home economics registered for Introduction to Home Economics, a course I usually taught or at least helped teach. Taking my cue from the medical profession, which attempts neither diagnosis nor advice until family histories are studied, I took freshmen into my confidence and told them at our first meeting of my desire to know more about them in order that I might serve them better as they came to me in the future— both as students and as graduates—seeking advice, assistance, or employment. At the first meeting I also gave a resumé of my life and recounted some of my trials and errors, successes and failures. I found this approach effective because it helped put us on a personal basis. When I asked them to write me a letter giving a sketch of their own lives as their first assignment, they felt free to discuss their personal lives with me. I made clear that this first assignment was not mandatory and that it would have no effect on their grades in the course. I asked them to make the sketches informal, just as though they were sitting in front of my fireplace telling me about themselves. I assured them that only my secretary and I would read their letters and that their files would remain confidential. All freshmen had conferences with me early in the year. The letters served as a helpful introduction not only for these early contacts but also as a basis for my better understanding of the girls through succeeding years. My secretary helped condense the letters to a typed resumé to which I could refer before the initial interview. The students whose letters revealed the most pronounced problems were scheduled for the earliest conferences.

At the beginning of the experiment, I was impressed by the influence these letters had on me; they deepened my faith in and respect for youth, though I had not really been aware that I lacked either. They helped me to think of students as individuals. Often I could help other staff members in interpreting students, without divulging any information given in trust. The self-analysis required by the letter also helped the student. Looking at herself in light of what she was and what she wished to become at this time of psychological change in her life seemed to stimulate and give release. Some students gave little information about their homes or themselves, but not one of the letters failed to reveal something helpful in interpreting the student's personality.

Soon after I became dean, the staff decided that we needed a permanent, more personal, and more definitive record of a girl and what she did in a course than the cold, bare A-B-C-D-F grades. We began writing descriptive comments and recording them on 9-by-12-inch cards. These records often began with my remarks following my first freshman conference with a student and continued with spontaneous comments (not checklists) by instructors whose courses she had taken. These comments proved valuable in counseling a student while she was in college. They provided a broad base for evaluation to be used in placement and in writing letters of recommendation. This record became known as the "personality file" and after graduation was continued as the beginning of the alumnae file.

We found that Commencement did not necessarily become a permanent parting of the ways between students and faculty. The girls wrote to us and we responded. They came to see us when they came to the campus, and we sometimes went out of our way a bit to see them in their offices, places of business, schools, and homes. Correspondence grew so bulky that we could not keep up with all of it adequately and individually. First as a Christmas letter, and later at any convenient time of the year, we began an Alumnae Newsletter. Beginning in the late 1920's and continuing fairly regularly at two-year intervals, it gave news from the different departments—changes in staff, promotions, sabbatical leaves, travel, and continuing education—and news of the School as a whole—changes in curricula, remodeling, building plans, and so forth. We mailed the mimeographed letter to all alumnae for whom we had addresses and to other former students and staff members who wanted to receive it. The response encouraged us to continue this means of keeping in touch. The mailing list at present numbers more than 5,000 names.

A good many of the letters received in response to the Alumnae Newsletter have gone into the file envelope kept for each alumna. These files also include clippings from newspapers and magazines, copies of letters of recommendation we have written, photographs, notes, Christmas cards, and various other pieces of information. Each file contains a human interest story—the story of a timid, uncertain freshman whose personality developed through her college years and who made her first tentative venture into adult life—as home-maker, teacher, home demonstration agent, or business woman. They show how she moved forward in her career, and they record her changes of address as she moved about the world. They describe honors won and distinctions achieved; sometimes disappointments and tragedies. They tell stories of courage and resourcefulness, ambition and enterprise, inventiveness, and ingenuity. They provide examples of "late blooming roses," students who received mediocre grades in college, who did not impress their instructors as particu-larly promising, yet who have gone on to remarkable achievements. Perhaps we should take a peek into some of these files and follow the development of examples from several career fields.

When we open the envelope for HELEN MILLER (ARMSTRONG), we find a note on top of the packet: "Selected Woman of the Year by the Women's Medical Society of New York State, May 1965." How, one wonders, did a girl born before 1900 in the village of Corvallis, who attended high school only two years, and whose grades in a little western college were not at all outstanding, ever rise to such an achievement? Records in the file show that Helen Miller entered OAC in 1913 at the age of 17 and graduated in 1917. Her early positions—one year teaching in the tiny community of Glendale, Oregon, and three years with the Tillamook Testing Association in another small town, Cloverdale—did not appear especially promis-ing. In the fall of 1922, however, Helen entered the University of Oregon Medical School in Portland. Putting to use what she had learned in some of her home economics courses, she worked as a dietitian in the medical school hospital to help pay her expenses. Four years later she received her M.D. degree. For a two-year in-ternship she chose the Infirmary for Women and Children in New York City. There in the big city Helen found her niche. She estab-lished three prenatal clinics in settlement houses for the Department of Health. As her private practice grew she specialized in obstetrics and gynecology, eventually moving her office to 375 Park Avenue. In 1937 she married Alexander F. Armstrong, a manufacturer of paper and paper containers, but continued her medical practice. She bought an abandoned schoolhouse in the country for a weekend retreat and added to it and modernized it into a year-around home.

When the suburbs swept out to her area, she built the Kinnelon Medical Center on adjoining property to serve the bustling new community. In addition to her regular work at the New York Infirmary, Doctor's Hospital, and her New York office she undertook supervision of the Cancer Detection and Research Center at Kinnelon. Her colleagues throughout the state elected her president of their society and then selected her as "Woman of the Year 1965." That's how it happened.

MAREN GRIBSKOV, Class of 1918, made her career decision early and stayed with it for half a century. As a member of a Scandinavian family in Junction City, she inherited a love of good food. In college she gained experience in quantity cookery in her home economics courses and while working in a faculty boarding house. At the senior breakfast which President Kerr and I attended she revealed her inner personality when she announced that her ambition was to be worthy of the sacrifices that had made college possible for her. After graduation she helped feed the men of the Student Army Training Corps at the University of Oregon. Then she and Martha Becken ('17), who had been a home demonstration agent serving three eastern Oregon counties during World War I, went out to look for a good location to start a restaurant. They toured much of the West in a Ford car and finally narrowed their search to Bend, a lumbering town in Central Oregon which seemed in need of a good eating establishment. It took some persuasion on their part to obtain financial backing, but in 1919 they rented a building across from the livery stable, cleaned and polished it, and announced the opening date for their lunchroom. One of the men who had counseled against the project brought a group of businessmen on the opening day and before the end of the noon hour all their food was gone. With Martha handling contacts with the public and Maren preparing the meals they got off to a good start. A five-foot snow the first winter stayed on the ground for two months, but businessmen, teachers, lumberjacks, and travelers beat a path to their door and by the end of the first year they could pay off their $1,200 mortgage. They moved the lunchroom several times as they needed more space. When Martha married Sid Conklin she withdrew from the partnership. In 1936, Maren established the now-famous Pine Tavern, a restaurant noted for its distinctive decor and tasty, nutritious meals graciously served. The late E. R. Jackman, Oregon author, wrote in 1966, "The Pine Tavern in Bend is still regaling the traveler with fine food. . . . I have seen many restaurants start with high hopes and crisp lettuce, only to allow the lettuce to wilt. Not so this place. . . . It is one place where even today anticipation is no better than realization." The last time I visited the Pine Tavern, Maren was serving more than a thousand meals a day and pleasing a wide clientele through her catering service. One year the people of Bend named her Citizen of the Year, the first woman so honored. *Maren's Pine Tavern Menus and Recipes* has become a popular cookbook. After appeasing appetites for fifty years, Miss Gribskov sold the Pine Tavern in 1967 and prepared for retirement.

LeVelle Wood, the "shy little freshman afraid of everything," turned out to be quite a courageous woman and an extensive world traveler. After graduation in 1921, LeVelle taught in the little town of Wasco in Central Oregon for a year, supervised the limited home economics work at Oregon Normal School in Monmouth for five years, went to Columbia University to earn a master's degree, and then settled down in a teaching and food service position at Kansas State College with Dean Margaret Justin. Out of her classwork in institutional management grew a textbook, *Food Service in Institutions,* of which LeVelle is coauthor. Now in its fourth edition, this book is a standard in the field. As mentioned previously, our summer home economics study tour to the Orient infected her with wanderlust. On sabbatical leave the next year she remained in Japan to provide technical assistance for the YWCA and then went on around the world. In World War II she served with the American Red Cross in North Africa and Italy and took vacation trips to other parts of Europe. She came to our campus several times to teach in the Summer Session but would never take a full-time position. At Ohio State University she became Chairman of the Division of Institution Management (the second one of our graduates, incidentally, who was a department chairman at Ohio State at that time; Minnie Price ('11) had been State Leader of Home Demonstration work in Ohio since 1923). In 1958-59 LeVelle Wood was president of the American Dietetic Association and along the way acquired dozens of honors including listing in *Who's Who in America*. Upon retirement in 1965, she left almost immediately for a dietetics meeting in

Sweden and for a nine-months tour that covered 52,000 miles. Her Christmas letter that year came from India. Post-retirement activities have included teaching or consultative appointments in the University of Washington, in a university in New Zealand, and the University of Tennessee. The comment of one of her instructors for the "personality file" was incisive and perceptive: "Seems young and inexperienced but has the prospects of a fine professional woman."

GLADYS MILLER ('22) was once described in a Chicago trade paper as "a teacher, author, reporter, editor, lecturer, columnist, radio broadcaster, decorator, retailer, government adviser, lighting expert, furniture designer, stylist, colorist, coordinator, consultant, critic, and contributor to our industry for years." The report went on to say, "In her student days at Oregon State University, she was the sole official female football scout in the Pacific Coast Conference." Gladys' file does not tell of this latter activity but it does give the picture of a young woman who "has good ideas and is not afraid to work. Lots of enthusiasm and interest." Gladys was born in Nebraska but came to Oregon in her early years and finished high school in Portland. She was a little older than most freshmen when she entered college in 1918 and this maturity may account somewhat for the comments of her instructors about her excellent judgment, good art foundation, and being "set in her opinions," but these comments are also full of references such as "excellent work . . . pleasant to work with . . . contributions to the class." After graduation in 1922, Gladys taught for two years in Arizona then went to New York University for advanced study. Her creative ingenuity led her into many fields of work related to home furnishings and interior decorating. She has edited or published three magazines—*Building Products Guide, New Home Guide,* and *Home Modernizing Guide*—has written four books on decorating, and has written a syndicated newspaper column. In 1942 and 1943 she redecorated the Blair House and Lee-Blair House in Washington, D.C., to be used as diplomatic guest houses by the U. S. government. In wartime Washington she supervised the furnishing of 22,500 rooms in 36 government buildings. She purchased and installed the furnishings for 8,000 WAVES at Arlington Farms. "It is now called Girls' Town," she wrote in 1943. "Twenty-eight acres of girls! That is mass production any way you look at it." In her field Gladys has received many recognitions, including an honorary Doctorate of Fine Arts from the Moore Institute of Art, Science, and Industry in Philadelphia. She has traveled extensively abroad and occasionally comes back to the campus for lectures, conferences, or visits.

JEANETTE CRAMER pioneered in home economics communications in a day when men dominated journalism even more than they do today. "Cooking for our good sized family," she wrote once about her homelife in Grants Pass, "canning literally hundreds of jars of fruit and jellies and vegetables, working in the orchards, sewing for myself and neighbors, all the entertaining and camping and church activities and club work that I ever did have each fitted right in when I needed them most." After high school Jeanette attended Oregon Normal School, taught in a one-room school and in Grants Pass schools, and entered OAC as a sophomore in 1919. Her instructors found her, "A strong, capable girl. Has opinions but cooperates well." After graduation in 1922, she went back to her high school in Grants Pass for another year of teaching, then began the newspaper and radio assignments in Portland that made her life's work distinctive. Broadcasting, writing for *The Oregonian,* and lecture demonstrations took up most of her time, but she also gave talks to women's clubs and first aid to homemakers by means of telephone. She once said, "Knowing that anyone, at any time of day, may call up and ask any question bearing even remotely on home economics and that an answer is expected, certainly keeps one on the alert." At one time these calls averaged 50 a day with many more at holiday time. In 1933 Jeanette married Arthur Mason but continued with her career. She joined the home service staff of the Meier and Frank Company in Portland two years later. Eventually, the steady pace began to tell on her and she withdrew from business to devote herself to homemaking, garden club, and community work. She died in January 1965 but left behind a pattern of home economics communications work that has been widely adopted elsewhere.

Comments in OLGA P. BRUCHER's file include such phrases as "conscientious . . . high standards . . . well poised . . . a splendid student and a fine girl . . . likable . . . good ideas." Olga had done her preparatory work in Iowa before coming to us in 1919. She stayed out a year after her freshman year and then returned to graduate with a good record in 1924. She was so dependable and useful to us by that time that we kept her as secretary for the School for two years and then as an instructor in Foods and Nutrition. From 1929-1942 she served on the facutly of the College of Home Economics at Cornell University and then became Dean of the School of Home Economics at the University of Rhode Island, where she remained until retirement in 1962. In 1952 the American Home Economics Association urged President-elect Eisenhower and Secretary-designate Ezra Taft Benson to appoint a woman as an Assistant to the Secretary of Agriculture in the new administration. The Association nominated "six of the nation's top-flight home economics administrators"—including two of our former staff members: Olga Brucher and Claribel Nye, one-time head of our home economics extension work. Although neither was selected for the position, the nominations show how highly they were regarded by home economists nationally. Among many national recognitions, Olga was elected to three offices in the American Home Economics Association. She served as Secretary from 1945 to 1947, as Vice President from 1949 to 1952 and from 1956 to 1959, and as President from 1960 to 1962.

PAULINE PAUL, a girl from McMinnville who had attended Willamette University for a year, set out to be a winner when she entered OSC in 1932. She tried out for women's debate and made the squad. She sang in the Madrigal chorus. In her nine terms on our campus she averaged 18 credits a term, receiving one credit of C (in Physical Education), 16 credits of B, and all the rest A's. She also worked part time to help support herself. Instructor's comments sound like rave notices with many comments about her brilliance as a student, but also with cautions that she needed to be considerate of slower learners and to realize the need for social contacts. At one of my conferences with her, I cautioned her about the undue use of slang, but I do not believe she paid much attention to me in this regard; all through the years her letters have been full of chatty conversation and bubbling good spirits. She prepared for research work in foods and nutrition and after receiving her B.A. degree in 1935 went first to University of Minnesota, then to several positions with General Foods. She took her doctorate at Iowa State University and held appointments with Swift and Company in Chicago and at

Michigan State University before moving on to the University of California at Davis where she became head of the Department of Home Economics. At this writing she is professor of Foods and Nutrition in charge of foods research at University of Nebraska.

"Quiet, reserved, but an attractive personality" is the theme that runs through the instructors' comments on MERCEDES BATES. She entered as a freshman from Portland in 1932 and graduated in 1936. For a time she had a good deal of interest in nursery-school work and spent the spring term of her junior year at the Merrill-Palmer School. She accepted a fellowship in our nursery school for one year after graduation, then moved into business. In 1938 she joined the Home Service Department of the Southern California Gas Company and later served as department head until 1945. She then started her own company, a firm of food consultants for television, photography, and recipe development in Hollywood. For four and a half years Mercedes was Senior Editor in charge of the Food Department of *McCall's Magazine* before becoming the new Director of the Betty Crocker Kitchens of General Mills, Inc., in charge of a staff of more than fifty professional workers in Minneapolis. In June 1966, she became one of the vice presidents of that huge food processing and distributing corporation — the first woman officer in its history. Gracious, sincere, competent, Mercedes Bates exemplifies the finest type of achievement of the home economist in business.

KATHLEEN ASTON showed promise right from the start. After my first interview I characterized her as "tall . . . strong . . . fine looking . . . pleasant mannered . . . cultured"; after the second one, "real refinement and ability." Others wrote of her "charming manners . . . enthusiastic criticism in class discussion . . . willing attitude . . . original ideas . . . outstanding energy . . . meets people well . . . has never disciplined herself to do anything very hard but has the capacity to do so . . . high standards of scholarship." Kathleen had been born in England but had moved to Oregon at an early age and graduated from St. Helen's Hall in Portland. She stayed out of school a year before entering college. In addition to making mostly A and B grades in college she was also the campus fashion authority and wrote a weekly column, "Katie's Komments," for the *Barometer* (student newspaper). In the summers she worked in Portland stores. After graduation in 1938 she held several buying and reporting jobs and did advanced study at New York University. In 1943—the year she married Jack Casey—she joined the Conde Nast Publications as Chicago editor for *Vogue* and *Glamour*. According to Hope Chamberlain (Corso), another of our graduates who went into journalism and who interviewed Mrs. Casey after she had been in the new position a year, Kathleen pioneered as a woman executive in the Chicago offices of that publishing company, for up to that time only men had held the top positions. In 1953 she moved to New York and became editor-in-chief of *Glamour* magazine, a position she has held with the same sort of imagination, poise, good taste, and dependability that she exhibited in her early years as a student.

Before leaving the "personality files" let's look at one more example of a graduate who succeeded in a particular career field. MARION DONALDSON grew up in an Extension-oriented family. Her father was in agricultural extension work in Montana at the time Marion was born in Helena. They moved a good deal when she was a child: to Washington and then to Enterprise, Oregon, and later to Corvallis. She took part in 4-H Club work, became a 4-H leader, and won a 4-H Club scholarship. After my first conference with her, I characterized her as "nice looking . . . wholesome . . . not self-conscious . . . exceptionally good home background." Her instructors found her "neat . . . reticent . . . phlegmatic." Although appearing strong, she fainted in class one day and the instructor thought that "illness may be responsible for her listlessness." Although she did not do especially well in some of the courses related to dietetics, she never lost her determination to make dietetics her career field. After completing requirements for graduation in the summer of 1938 she obtained an internship at the Duke University Hospital and afterward was a hospital dietitian in Cincinnati and in Medford, Oregon. The outbreak of World War II provided a new demand for dietitians, and Marion went into Army hospital work in North Carolina, England, Africa, and Italy. After release from the service she tried home demonstration work in Yamhill County, but when the opportunity came to return to military service she accepted it. She was commissioned as a Captain in the Women's Medical Specialist Corps, which brought her assignments in the

Office of the Surgeon General in Washington, D.C., in Japan, and elsewhere, culminating in her promotion to Lieutenant Colonel. She served as chief of food service at the Tripler General Hospital in Honolulu and received the Legion of Merit award for her outstanding work. She married Robert Douglas, a retired major, and after her retirement in 1964 took up the responsibilities of homemaking in Kailua, Oahu, Hawaii.

The files contain so many stories of human interest and achievement that one hardly knows where to stop. They would make a book in themselves. Being true-life stories they do not always seem to have happy endings. Some heart-rending ones seem to close all too abruptly; yet they also illustrate achievement in character, service, and gallantry. We have never stressed education for adversity, but in many instances our graduates have faced disaster with amazing serenity and equanimity.

MARY LOUISE ARMSTRONG's instructors described her as alert, enthusiastic, responsive, bright, dependable, and attractive. Her excellent 4-H Club record had led to her selection as representative of the Oregon clubs at the 4-H Club Congress in Chicago in 1938. She had worked a year in the Portland Public Library before coming to college. In addition to working part time in college she made a remarkable scholarship record and won many honors (Mortar Board, Phi Kappa Phi, Omicron Nu, Alpha Lambda Delta, Mu Beta Beta). Her analysis of the benefits of the Danforth Summer Fellowship, which she received in 1942, is one of the finest in the files. Following graduation in 1943 she became home service consultant for a company in Seattle and then accepted an appointment with the National Livestock and Meat Board. As regional home economist for eight western states, and later for ten northeastern states, she gave meat cookery demonstrations and lectures for schools, homemaker groups, and service clubs. A New York *Herald-Tribune* news story about her work began, "Give Mary Lou Armstrong a chunk of meat from either end of the cow—tongue or tail—or what lies between—and Mary Lou will cook you a dish in superlatives." One of her employers described her as "making friends wherever she went . . . diplomatic, using excellent judgment on all occasions." This brilliant beginning, however, was not to flower. Incurable cancer caused her

to resign and return to Oregon. She directed women's programs on
KOAC for a time but had to give that up also. Confined to bed in
her home in Portland, she showed a poised, uncomplaining selfless-
ness and gallantry difficult to match. She died in December 1946,
two months after her twenty-sixth birthday. She had taught us much
by her example and made for herself a lasting place in the hearts
of those who had the good fortune to know her.

ARDYTHE WILSON's brief career was equally valiant. From her
home in Hood River she had gone to Reed College in Portland a
year before coming to OSC. Attractive, poised, and capable, she
impressed her instructors with having ability to become a strong
professional home economist. After graduation in 1938, she enthusi-
astically taught in junior high school and managed a school cafeteria
in Oregon City. The next year she returned to Corvallis as the bride
of Dr. Robert W. Dougherty, a member of the OSC Veterinary
Medical faculty. We enjoyed having Ardythe near again and seeing
her happily settled as a homemaker. At the beginning of World
War II, her husband Bob was called to active duty as an officer in
the Veterinary Corps. Because it was not feasible for Ardythe to
accompany him, she took a part-time position on campus and entered
graduate school. After receiving her master's degree in 1942, she
taught the following year in Bend. "Remember me and my sewing?"
she wrote. "You would be surprised to see me now. I sew and I like
it. And I really enjoy teaching clothing. Honestly, I never knew that
day would come to pass!" Her spirit was gay, but physically she was
failing. I had noted at one of my last interviews with her; "She looks
so thin." She underwent an operation in Chicago for removal of part
of a tumor on her brain. Removal of all of it, the doctors believed,
would have ended her life then. They felt she had a chance for recovery, and she began to inquire about employment possibilities
while convalescing in Florida. In the spring of 1944 she visited her
parents in Hood River and friends in Corvallis. Although we did not
realize it at the time, she was saying goodbye to us. Sweet and gentle,
despite her failing eyesight, she showed consideration for everyone
and uttered no word of complaint or bitterness. She returned to a
hospital in Chicago to fight for her life as long as strength remained.
Bob was transferred to an assignment nearby where he could be
with her much of the time to help feed her and provide companion-

ship. "Her spirit and cheerfulness have been wonderful," Bob wrote me, "and have made her the pet of the ward." In Chicago for a meeting, I visited them five times and came away impressed with their strength in facing one of the most difficult of life's realities. They were teaching us a great lesson—the two of them together. Never once was there evidence of self-pity, fear, or weakness — always courage and good humor. Ardythe passed away in July 1944 in her twenty-eighth year. On her last trip to Oregon she had selected a plot where she wished to be buried in the foothills of Mt. Hood in view of the mountains and valleys she loved so well. It was a simple, intimate service in a pine grove which her gracious personality seemed to pervade, rising above the evidence of sadness.

WE ON THE School of Home Economics staff enjoyed seeing and talking with our graduates so much that we arranged special events occasionally to entice them back to the campus. Those who lived near came for home interests conferences, short courses, and visits. Some came at Commencement time for class reunions and when they had daughters, sons, or grandchildren graduating. On two special occasions we invited them to come for programs of several days' duration.

Dr. Margaret Snell had taught her first classes in Household Economy and Hygiene at OAC in the fall of 1889; the year 1939-1940, therefore, seemed a good time to celebrate the 50th anniversary. We arranged a program and published an illustrated booklet, not only to review the past to see how far we had come in half a century but also to outline the present status and take a look into the future. We found a convenient time when the 10th Annual Conference for the Study of Home Interests sponsored by the Home Economics Extension Council could be combined with a 50th-Anniversary celebration. Speakers of national prominence invited to participate included Helen Judy Bond, Head of Home Economics at Columbia University and President of the American Home Economics Association; Edmond deS. Brunner, the rural sociologist who had been my teacher at Columbia University; Claribel Nye, our former state extension leader, from the University of California; and Louise Stanley, Head of the Bureau of Home Economics in Washington, D. C. Home economics leaders from western states— Gladys A. Branegan from Montana State College, Christene B. Clayton from Utah State Agricultural College, Velma Phillips of the State College of Washington, Effie I. Raitt of the University of Washington, Margaret Ritchie of the University of Idaho, Helen Thompson from UCLA, and Mabel Wood of the University of Oregon—also took part in the program.

On a Tuesday morning in late February, Dr. Stanley, Dr. Bond, Dr. Brunner, and I launched the program with a coast-to-coast broadcast from radio station KEX in Portland. That evening OSC President George Peavy, former President and Chancellor W. J. Kerr, and graduates representing the five decades of home economics at Oregon State spoke at a banquet in the Memorial Union. The following morning, Oregon Governor Charles Sprague and Mrs. Beatrice Walton Sackett, a member of the State Board of Higher Education, continued the program which ran through three more days of lectures, demonstrations, panel discussions, and exhibits.

At the banquet, alumnae selected to represent each of the decades reviewed the School's history in ten-year segments. MARY EDNA GROVES, Class of 1898, whom I had first met in one of my evening classes my first year on campus and who had later served as supervisor of home economics in the Portland public schools and with the Indian Bureau, represented the graduates of the 1889-1899 period and spoke of Dr. Snell's early struggles in starting the department.

DR. ALICE L. EDWARDS ('06) represented the 1899-1909 decade. Members of a pioneer family that helped establish the community of Bellfountain in the hills south of Corvallis, Alice and seven brothers and sisters had graduated from OAC. She was teaching biological sciences when I first came to the campus in 1911. Later she received M.A. and Ed.D. degrees from Columbia University, taught at University of Minnesota, and was Dean of Home Economics at Rhode Island State College. For ten years—from 1926 to 1936—she was Executive Secretary of the American Home Economics Association. She wrote a book, *Products Standards and Labeling for Consumers,* published in 1940. After participating in our 50th-Anniversary celebration she became head of home economics at Mary Washington College in Fredericksburg, Virginia, where she remainded until her retirement and return to Oregon.*

---

*Miss Edwards died in Salem on July 5, 1962.

DR. VERA HASKELL BRANDON ('11) described as "adolescence" the 1909-1919 period when the School had three deans—Greer, Calvin, and Milam. It was marked by the changes, rapid growth, and frustrations that accompany the similar period of human development. Dr. Brandon knew about adolescence; she had raised a family of three girls (all of whom studied home economics) and was Professor of Child Development on our staff at that time. She told of her experiences as a freshman on our campus.

> *"When I walked into the Registrar's office, which was then a corner of Professor J. B. Horner's history classroom, there were no crowds; a few people were about but no one seemed hurried. I approached Registrar Horner, and with my weak and uncertain freshman voice told him I had come to register. He asked me what course I planned to pursue. My reply was that I wanted no specific course but just some art, music, and literature. The response on Professor Horner's face told me he was not pleased. After some deliberation he shook his head and said, 'That is all right for elective work but what you need is Domestic Science.' Domestic Science, thought I. what could that be? 'Well,' said Professor Horner, 'I will not register you today; go home and think it over and come back tomorrow and register.' My lack of information about this new high-sounding course made it impossible for me to weigh values. If Professor Horner (the experienced and well-informed man he seemed to be) thought I should enroll for Domestic Science, then I was willing to take his judgment. . . .*

By taking this advice, Mrs. Brandon said, she had gained the background on which she later built a lifetime career.

MAUD MUELLER WALKER (STEPLETON), Class of 1927, who believes that "homemaking is the greatest profession of all," represented the 1919-1929 decade. She had married soon after graduation, but two and a half years later her husband had died, leaving her with a small son to support. She came back to Corvallis, enrolled her son in nursery school, and received a teaching fellowship on the nursery school staff as she undertook graduate work in child development and psychology. She received her master's degree in 1934 and then became the first full-time Parent Education Specialist for our

Extension Service. A few years later she married a widower, State Senator Dean Walker, and met a new challenge in family living—that of putting together two families. Her message to the alumnae at the 50th-Anniversary Banquet was formulated around her basic philosophy, which she later phrased in these words: "Experience has taught me how important the homemaker's role in family life can and should be: To run the home so that each member of the family feels welcome and proud to bring friends home, to gather into the home the friends and acquaintances who enrich the lives of one's husband and children, and to so plan family occasions that they leave happy memories of stimulating discussions and sharing experiences are the challenge of the homemaker." Several years after Mr. Walker's death, Maud married Kenneth F. Stepleton and moved with him to Chicago, where she established a new home and enjoyed visits to and from her three granddaughters.

AMELIA SANSOM (B.S., 1930, M.S., 1942) represented the 1929-1939 decade. Exhibiting the same winsome, vivacious personality that had made her a campus favorite in her college days, she spoke from a broad background in home economics. Her mother had studied under Margaret Snell. Following her own graduation, Amelia had taught for a year and then had become a home economist on the staff of the Homemakers' Bureau for Safeway Stores, doing test kitchen and cooking school work. She then went to work for the *Oregonian,* where she became director of the Homemaking Institute known to her readers as "Nancy Morris." She came back to the campus to manage one of the home management houses for two years while working for her master's degree. Shortly thereafter she joined the Extension staff of the University of California and at the time of the 50th-Anniversary program was Assistant State Home Demonstration Leader for the University of California at Berkeley.

JUNE MORSE represented the first class of the second half century. The program committee thought we should have a look into the future through the eyes of a senior. They chose June, who had been Queen of the Junior Prom the previous year, because they agreed she was an outstanding student in every way—although the instructors' comments in the personality file for her last few months in college indicate that her class work slumped a bit because of "too many honors falling her way." After college, June lived up to her early promise. Following a year of teaching, she went on to graduate work at Syracuse University where she received her M.S. degree. She joined the staff of the General Mills Test Kitchen in Minneapolis in 1944 and later that year married Captain Truxton Ringe of the U. S. Marine Corps. Subsequent moves have found her in Virginia, North Carolina, Pittsburgh, California, Baltimore, and Seattle.

The attendance of alumnae at this 50th-Anniversary celebration, their appreciation of an opportunity for a short refresher course, and their enthusiastic responses were so encouraging that we watched for an opportunity to schedule a similar conference. After World War II, we decided that the 60th Anniversary would provide a good excuse for inviting the alumnae again. We published another illustrated booklet, this one entitled "Sixty Years of Growth in Home Economics." On a Friday and Saturday in mid-March 1950, we held a condensed version of the program given ten years earlier.

By 1950, the country had become international minded. The program committee chose for keynote speaker Mrs. Raymond Sayre, president of the Associated Country Women of the World. She spoke on "The Challenge of Women in the International Field" and "Home Economics—A Need in Germany." MABEL WOOD ('25) added to the international theme by making reference to her experiences at Yenching University in her talk on home economics as a part of a liberal-arts education. At the request of the program committee I talked on the need for home economics in the Orient. EUNICE HEYWOOD, ('29) a field agent for the Federal Cooperative Extension Service who had recently returned from Europe, described "What American Home Economists are Doing in Germany." Eunice had long been in home economics extension work and later went to the top in her field. She had worked in New York and New Hampshire before joining the central office in Washington, D.C. In later years, she became Assistant Director (1955) and Director (1959) of Home Extension Programs for the Federal Cooperative Extension Service and in 1960 received the USDA Superior Service Award for outstanding leadership as the culmination of a gratifying career.

As another speaker for the 60th Anniversary conference, WINIFRED HAZEN ('21) came from Salt Lake City to speak on "Reaching the Homemaker Through Family-Life Programs." The combination of an excellent mind, executive ability, genuine sincerity, a conscientious interest in children, and graduate study in Toronto University and Columbia University had resulted in an interesting career for Winifred after her graduation. She had supervised our campus Tearoom, had been director of dormitories at Rhode Island State College, had engaged in adult education work in Michigan, had been Director of Emergency Nursery Schools and Parent Education in the state of Washington, and, at the time of the conference, was Consultant in Family Life Education for the state of Utah, where she remained until her retirement. The alumnae enjoyed hearing her views based on varied experiences.

Radio had become a potent force in disseminating homemaking information by 1950—although television would supplement it in the next decade—and one of our graduates, ELEANOR SELOVER WILKINS ('19) had become one of the most influential homemaking commentators in the Midwest. Eleanor Selover had taught in Washington and Arizona before her marriage to F. Scott Wilkins, an agronomist who joined the staff of Iowa State College. Following his death in 1936 (when Eleanor needed to go into an earning position to support herself and two children), she pioneered in radio programs for women. She did not have an easy time getting started; women were not popular on the air in those days. Their voices were said to be too high or too soft to be effective. Eleanor proved the critics wrong. Her friendly personality and competent homemaking advice as "Martha Duncan," Women's Radio Editor for station WOI in Ames, Iowa, won a tremendous following—which was still continuing when she began partial retirement in 1966, after what she described as "thirty wonderful years of friendship with families of the Midwest." At the 60th Anniversary Banquet her subject was "Homemakers Learn by Radio."

The "Review of the Decades" features of the 50th Anniversary program had proved so interesting and popular that the committee decided to have something similar for the 60th-Anniversary program. Another group of exemplary alumnae were chosen for the occasion and at the Friday evening banquet, following greetings by OSC President A. L. Strand, Mrs. William Jasper Kerr, and several others, the decade speakers were presented—this time in reverse order with the most recent decade first.

BERNICE SCHAAD (WORTH), Class of 1945, represented decade 1939-1949. As a member of a large family (seven boys and four girls), Bernice had grown up on a farm near Newberg. Backed by a mother who encouraged each of her children to work to capacity, she came to college with the remarkable record of never having received a grade below "A" in high school. In college her grades were good. She worked to help support herself and was president of Omicron Nu in her senior year. She received her internship in dietetics at the Massachusetts General Hospital, where she graduated in 1946 at the head of her class. Her record there includes such comments as "Takes ordinary confusion in her stride . . . definite executive ability . . . thoroughness, dependability . . . willingness to see tasks done . . . happy disposition." She had been dietitian in several hospitals, and at the time she represented her decade at the celebration she was teaching dietetics at Emanuel Hospital in Portland. In September following that visit to the campus she married Wayne Thomas Worth, and subsequent Christmas greetings in the file indicate that she has been enjoying putting to practical use her college courses in child development.

In her three-minute talk, the representative of the 1929-1939 decade, MARY FERGUSON THOMAS (MEISEL), Class of 1939, stressed the advantages of "the broad scope of preparation received at Oregon State." This background had given her confidence that she could build an interior decorating department for a large retail store in Salem when she found it necessary to support herself and her daughter. Mary had married soon after graduation but had been widowed. Although she had not originally planned to be a career woman, she found having the foundation on which to build a career useful when she needed to become a wage earner. Mary later remarried and now has another daughter. Her elder daughter came to OSU, graduated, married, and became a homemaker.

IRENE BRYE CARL ('20), representing the 1919-1929 decade and radiating the same "happiness and vitality" her instructors had noted in her many years before, pictured the "roaring 20's." She asked:

> *Do you remember 1919? We lived in the cadence of "Good-bye Broadway—Hello France." Most of our boys were overseas; the SATC boys were on the campus. The YMCA hut stood where the Memorial Union now stands. The Home Economics Building*

was a single wing. Enrollment of the School of Home Economics was third in the nation . . . Our dresses were six inches from the floor with sloping shoulders and flat figures; our hair was long . . . The night the news of the Armistice came our hearts soared . . . only to find it was a false report . . . Finally the boys returned and we breathed again . . . Dean Milam and Camilla Mills left for China . . . Our dresses became short. We cut our hair. The tempo of the nation was the Charleston. Installment buying swept the country . . . Home Economics research became possible through funds from the Purnell Act . . . The first nursery school was established. Radio broadcasts from the college station started . . . The name Oregon Agricultural College was changed to Oregon State College. We really were growing up! Our dresses were now to our knees. Our waists at the hip line—our hair very short . . . walkathons . . . flagpole sitting . . . Lindbergh . . . miniature golf . . . This decade had a tempo all its own. It was gay, turbulent, and rebellious. We find ourselves grown up. Do you remember?

Irene had other things to remember that spring of 1950—both gay and tragic. She had the once-in-a-lifetime opportunity to be the official chaperone for the Portland Rose Festival Queen and her court. Her fellow Directors elected her that spring the first woman President of the Oregon State College Alumni Association. She had lost her husband several years before but had enjoyed the companionship of her son (Robert Wilbur Carl '50) and daughter (Marion Carl Eaton, '45) and Marion's daughter Carol Anne. Loss of two-year-old Carol Anne in a drowning accident in May was for all of them a great shock, one that was somewhat alleviated a few weeks later by the birth of Marion's first son—she now has three more. Mother, homemaker, enthusiastic civic leader, Irene Brye Carl was an excellent person to represent her decade.

MARTHA BECKEN CONKLIN ('17), who had been one of the first residents of the Withycombe Home Management House and who had helped Maren Gribskov open the lunchroom that became the Pine Tavern in Bend, represented the 1909-1919 decade. After her marriage she became a farm homemaker for her husband, their son, and her deceased sister's daughter, whom Martha raised as a daughter. The Conklins opened a guest house on their ranch and Martha continued to use her skill in meeting and entertaining visitors. She spoke to the alumnae from the standpoint, therefore, of business-woman and homemaker.

JULIA FULLER CLARK ('06), whom I had first met in Shanghai in 1923, was a bit reluctant to accept the invitation to represent the 1899-1909 decade because of her health, but she wanted very much to come. Her husband, J. C. Clark, felt she could make the trip from Wisconsin all right by air and sent his regrets that he could not come also. We held an alternate in readiness, in case Julia did not feel well enough to make the presentation, and the way the program worked out, her sister, Etta Fuller Howard ('04) took her place and made the three-minute talk at the banquet.

CARRIE A. LYFORD ('96) came out of retirement at Elgin, Illinois, to represent the 1889-1899 decade. As mentioned in a previous chapter, Miss Lyford had been one of the first specialists in home economics at Hampton Institute, and Supervisor of Indian Education in the U. S. Bureau of Indian Affairs for 16 years. Hers had been the path of a pioneer and we were all grateful to have her with us for this occasion. Later in the year she moved from Illinois back to Washington, D.C., where she had lived many years, and died from a heart ailment at her home in Chevy Chase, Maryland, in June 1954.

ABOUT TWO MONTHS after the 60th Anniversary celebration, near the end of spring term, 1950, the Home Economics Club invited me to meet with them one evening, presumably for the purpose of awakening the seniors to the importance of becoming members of the national and state home economics associations. At the close of the meeting, President Mary Williams (Lovvold) said, "There is another matter which we wish to take up at this time," and brought out a beautifully wrapped gift box. In it I found a leather-bound book of more than 100 letters from alumnae to me, with an introduction by Mary Heumann Adams, former president of the Club. This priceless gift came as a complete surprise and so filled me with emotion that I could not speak for a while. Later at home, Mickey Drawn, the freshman who was living with me then, was so excited she would hardly let me look at the snapshots in the book. She sat by my bed and read all the letters aloud. It was after midnight before she finished. The book, of course, contained many personal messages to

me, but the descriptions they provide of what college training in
home economics meant to former students and the glimpses they
give into home and family lives make up a volume of lasting value.
Spanning half a century, these human-interest vignettes present a
rare glimpse into the lives and thoughts of homemakers and career
women in many parts of the country and in many walks of life.

In her letter to me, Ruth Kennedy Tartar, Class of 1920, commented, "I am told that now you too are becoming an Alumna." Yes,
it was true in a way. I was about to "graduate" also. Having reached
my 65th birthday the previous November, I was required to re-
linquish administrative responsibility for the School of Home Economics at the end of June. A committee of the faculty of the School,
under the chairmanship of Mrs. Sara Prentiss, was formed to assist
in the search for a new dean. To serve during the interim period,
Dr. Vera Brandon became Acting Dean on July 1, 1950, a position
she held until the arrival of the new dean, Dr. Miriam G. Scholl,
in 1954.

Since Margaret Snell's class of 1892 received the first ten Bachelor of Home Economy degrees, more than 5,000 baccalaureate
degrees have been awarded to majors in home economics on our
campus. Before I came in 1911, 264 had been graduated, averaging
12 a year in Miss Snell's time, and 18 a year in Dean Greer's. Between 1911 and 1917, when I became dean, 319 more degrees, an
average of 53 a year were awarded. In my first two years as dean
they averaged 63 a year, in the 1920's 83 a year, in the 1930's 70 a
year, in the 1940's 108 a year, in the 1950's 86 a year, and in the
1960's 111 a year. In my term as dean from 1918 through 1950, 2,854
baccalaureate degrees in home economics were awarded. In addition, hundreds of other women who did not stay to graduate, who
graduated in other schools, or who received advanced degrees
through the Graduate School, have loyalty to the School of Home
Economics as to an alma mater.

22. Syria

A good effort, into which one puts one's heart,
is never lost.

—F. T. WAHLEN

ABOUT THE TIME of my retirement as Dean of the School of Home
Economics at Oregon State College in June 1950, my doctor
gave me a thorough physical examination and pronounced me in
excellent health. I felt vigorous and active and sought an outlet for
energy. Acting Dean Vera Brandon suggested a part-time teaching
appointment, and I saw in it an opportunity to develop a seminar
for seniors and graduate students on the meaning of the home economics movement. Requests from several states had asked me to
come for speaking engagements. I intended to accept some of them
to use my time constructively and satisfyingly.

I spent a good deal of time in the summer of 1950 at *Grayling*
on the McKenzie River—writing, thinking, planning. In preparing
for the seminar, I wrote to the University of Chicago for biblio-
graphic assistance. A librarian with a remarkably long memory, who
remembered me from my student days, compiled a list of books that
I might find useful in organizing a history of home economics. In
the fall, the seminar got off to a good start, and I felt at the time it
would be worth continuing in succeeding years. Other activities
interrupted, however, and I never returned to the classroom except
as a guest lecturer for the Introduction to Home Economics course
and for special occasions.

Earlier that year I had received an inquiry from the Food and
Agriculture Organization (FAO) of the United Nations, which had
temporary headquarters in Washington, D.C., as to whether or not
I would be interested in going to Egypt under the new FAO technical

assistance program. The terms of that particular proposal did not
appeal to me but I did not rule out the possibility of accepting another foreign assignment. Soon another proposal came—one that I
suspect was initiated by Margaret Hockin (Harrington), Chief of the
Home Economics Branch in FAO, whom I had first met when she
was in YWCA work in Toyko. Margaret thought my background,
both in the administration of home economics educational programs
and in the investigation of home needs in Asian countries, a particularly desirable one for assisting in the development of home economics education in Syria.

The FAO staff warned me that the assignment would not be
easy. They pointed out that the cloistered status of women in Syria,
the inaccessibility of Arab homes, and the newness of technical assistance and lack of support of its objectives would make satisfying
results difficult if not impossible to accomplish. I decided, however,
to accept a one-year assignment to Syria as the first technical assistance home economist to be sent out by FAO.

As I made preparations and set out on the new adventure, everyone along the way gave me assistance and support. On January 15,
1951, my sisters Lottie and Lora and Ruth Hammond and her children saw me off. At Chicago, my niece, Mary Lou Cockefair Holt,
and her husband came to the airport to add their word of encouragement and to have a brief visit in 26° weather. Upon arrival in Washington in balmy, spring-like weather, I found that Margaret Hockin
had worked out a briefing schedule that would make maximum use
of the next two weeks. At that time, the home economics activities
of FAO were being developed within the Rural Welfare Division.
Dr. Horace Belshaw, Director of this Division, said to me, "Before we
appointed you I was fully convinced that if anyone can do this job,
you can. If you do not achieve all you would like to achieve, do not
think you have failed. Take a long view of it." Later in a meeting he
said to a group of us ready to go out to our assigned countries, "Your
success will depend on your going as true missionaries, with the realization that you have much to learn as well as much to give."

The United Nations' program of technical assistance to underdeveloped countries, I learned in early briefing sessions, represented
a pioneering effort for which few guidelines had been established,
especially in the education of women for homemaking. FAO officials
and others realized that the welfare of the peoples of the Near East

was being retarded by inadequate, inappropriate, and poorly equipped educational facilities for girls and women. Research and improved teaching methods were being used in agriculture, but comparable assistance in homemaking lagged far behind. Improved agricultural practices usually resulted in higher incomes, which made possible a higher standard of living, but often the increased income was not used effectively to improve personal and family welfare, due largely to the contrasting position and education of women and men.

The fourth conference of FAO, in 1948, had approved the expansion of the work of the Rural Welfare Division to include home economics education and extension services to member countries. In 1950, Margaret Hockin, as the first home economics officer for FAO, visited the Near East to survey needs and to recommend ways of providing assistance to the local governments. Subsequently, the Government of Syria, through its Ministry of Agriculture, requested FAO to provide the services of a home economics adviser. The purpose of my assignment, in the language of my instructions, was "to supply advice and assistance to the Government [of Syria] in the development of a program of education in home economics, including the institutional training and extension services for rural areas . . . [and] to advise and assist voluntary rural organizations in the development of educational programs related to homemaking and the general improvement of living conditions."

I began to get acquainted with the country by reading books and reports. I called on the Syrian Minister and Secretary at the Legation in Washington; I had tea with the sister of the president of the University of Syria; I talked with Syrian students attending Georgetown University. One day in a hallway I met Eric Englund—who as a student reporter at OAC in 1917 had come to interview me as the new dean of the School of Home Economics for a press announcement. Dr. Englund and his wife had just returned from Sweden where he had been Agricultural Attaché in the U.S. Embassy. The night before I left Washington, Eric and his wife gave a dinner party, where we discussed problems and possibilities of overseas assignments.

Because Cornell University has a long history of international service, my advisers thought a visit to Ithaca, New York, would increase my store of information. I did not see my friends of longest standing at Cornell—Dean Flora Rose had retired to California to live with Claribel Nye, and the new Dean of the College of Home Eco-

nomics, E. Lee Vincent, was out of the state — but other friends
greeted me. Acting Dean Catherine Personius met me at the Ithaca
airport. Former Oregon State staff members Mary Koll Heiner and
Veterinarian Robert Dougherty, alumna Frances Jensen, and Dr.
Glenn Bakkum, professor of sociology from OSC, were among those
who added their word of encouragement for the coming mission.
Dr. Bakkum was also being briefed for an overseas assignment and
would leave for Cairo a few days after my departure. Conferences
with Lebanese and Syrian students and with faculty members who
had lived in Syria or had conducted surveys there proved fruitful. It
was cold outside and snow swirled about our plane as we left Ithaca,
but I had a feeling of inner warmth.

In New York City I found further assistance. In the new, glass-
sided, many-storied Secretariat building of the United Nations I
conferred with the husband of Lorene Parker Whelpton ('17), the
well-remembered "Miss Parker" who once baked the Parker House
rolls for the Tearoom at the San Francisco Fair. Dr. Whelpton was
a specialist in population studies. One evening he and Lorene took
me to meet Alice Cosma and her husband. Mrs. Cosma, a Syrian
serving on the Status of Women Commission of the United Nations,
told me of the struggles and problems of women in her country and,
further, kept me from having any illusions as to the coming mission
being an easy one.

I called at the Syrian Consulate in the Empire State Building. I
met members of the staff at the Institute of International Education.
I went to see Dr. D. F. Milam, director of the New York Heart Association, who had spent two years in Lebanon and Syria. I had met
Dr. Milam—who may have been a distant relative—many years
before when we were both working in Herbert Hoover's food conservation program during World War I. He discussed frankly the
difficulties one encounters in the Near East in programs of health
and education involving change. He said that at times I would feel
as though I had come up against a stone wall, but he urged me not
to give up.

A Syrian man studying our rural schools—whom I later met
again in Damascus—pointed out, "When you go into our country
you will be able to understand human suffering for you have a
woman's heart." I called on Dr. Frank Laudermilk, a forester and
soil scientist, whom I had met previously at Nanking University in

China and again when he had come to Corvallis to lecture on what deforestation had done in the Near East. He vividly described again for me how areas that in Biblical times had been food-producing regions had been turned into empty miles of sand through deforestation and soil erosion. As we parted he invited me to visit him and his wife in Berkeley, California, when I returned to the West Coast. He promised to make flapjacks for us as he had learned to do years earlier as a forester in Arizona, using our manual, *Camp Cookery*.

Family members rallied 'round to give me support and encouragement. Niece Elinor Hanson McKee and her family at Larchmont, New York, devoted one Sunday to me. Uncle Roz' son, Donald McGinnis, and his wife took me home to New Jersey with them one evening, and nephew Robert S. Miner, Jr., and his family took me to LaGuardia International Airport on the cold, blustery 31st of January. To fortify me for the trip, they gave me two beautiful orchids which were just right for my coat and hat, and a supply of vitamin and calcium tablets, penicillin, and other pharmaceutical supplies which a doctor friend of Bob's knew I would have a hard time obtaining in the Near East.

Because of the inclement weather, the huge TWA Constellation loaded inside the hangar, and when all was in readiness we rolled out onto the runway and took off at six-twenty in the evening—more than an hour later than scheduled. About midnight this "non-stop" flight to Paris stopped at Gander, Newfoundland, and some of us got off in the 3° weather and stretched our legs in the waiting room. After leaving Gander, our plane climbed to 30,000 feet to avoid icing conditions. As the heaters were inadequate, for about two hours we had a chilly time of it. Later I went to sleep to awaken as breakfast was being served at about noon Paris time.

When I arrived at the Hotel de Stockholm in Paris, I found a cablegram indicating that my appointments at the United Nations Educational, Scientific, and Cultural Organization (UNESCO) were to begin at three o'clock that day. It was already later than that time before I received the message, but when I arrived at UNESCO headquarters I found three men—two Englishmen and Dr. Matta Akrawi, author of a new book on education in Arab countries—patiently waiting. They expressed appreciation for the objectives of home economics. They invited me to see UNESCO projects in Cairo and to attend the UNESCO conference in Teheran in October.

At the hotel I left a call for half past six the next morning. Following the call my breakfast of rolls, jam, and café au lait appeared. A bit later I rang for the elevator but the clerk at the desk informed me I could not come down—it was only seven-thirty and the floors were being cleaned! Fortunately, the Trans-World Airlines flight to Cairo had been delayed. Otherwise I do not know how I could have kept to the schedule.

Disruption in schedules made it necessary for me to take a "milk run" flight for Cairo that stopped at Geneva, Rome, Milan, and Athens—a fortunate circumstance that made possible crossing the Alps in daylight and seeing them in all their glory, fully covered with snow, extending up from the lower cloud banks into bright winter sunlight. Waiting rooms at the airports along the way contained tempting displays of local products for sale—Swiss music boxes, whistling birds, and yodelers in carved wood—but my luggage allowance permitted no additions. A dinner companion in Paris had given me a jar of Nes-Café, the only item I had added. At Athens, at two o'clock in the morning, we went through an hour-long examination of passports that I felt irksome and unnecessary. In the dawn of a new day the vast desert of Egypt and the green delta of the Nile spread out before us as we glided in to land at the Cairo airport.

Since the FAO regional office for the Near East was in Cairo, it was important that I stop there a short time before going on to Syria. An Egyptian member of the FAO staff met me and took responsibility for getting me through police and customs and off to the American Women's College where I stayed during my week in Egypt. Here I met Mary Frances Dawson, a graduate of Washington State College who had also studied at Oregon State. She had been teaching home economics in Egypt for 25 years and I later found her an effective assistant in our workshop in Syria. At the American Women's College, a self-supporting elementary and secondary school and junior college assisted by American teachers sent there by the Presbyterian Mission Board, I spoke one morning to the student assembly and one afternoon to an alumnae group. An English missionary nurse and two Egyptian nurses who lived in the village took us for a tour on which we glimpsed abject poverty. In a country where nearly all arable land had been brought under cultivation, we could visualize the conditions that would result if the population, as was estimated, doubled in the next 25 years. Although the government had made a few improvements, such as bringing running water into the village, I think I had never seen anything in the Far East to measure up to—or rather down to—the low standard of living and unsanitary condition of this Egyptian village. The children seemed listless, thin, and wan, and I saw not a smile on the faces of the old or the young. The wonder to me was not that they lived, but that they wished to live.

The mission schools appeared to be doing a great work in awakening some Egyptians of higher income levels to a sense of social conscience and a way of life which does not measure all in terms of self. The American University in Cairo, where Glen Bakkum from OSC was to be stationed, was building what appeared to me to be a fine and unique university. When Dr. Bakkum arrived a few days later I was in the receiving line at the American Women's College to welcome him at a reception. This college invited a number of OSC graduates and their wives to meet me at a dinner one evening. They, too, were doing what they could to assist in improving living conditions. Through some of them I was invited to visit the College of Agriculture of the Government's University in Cairo and found there an interest in introducing work in home economics. The Ministry of Social Affairs also seemed eager to have home economics introduced into the university and expressed a belief that this field was greatly needed by social workers and nurses. Graduates of the American Women's College in Cairo were community leaders in many fields. Hence, the situation was not stagnant. Much good work was being accomplished.

In Lebanon, the plane landed at Beirut, and William A. Stoltzfus, the president of the local American Women's College, met me at the airport. He and his wife invited me to be their house guest for the week I was to spend in this country. The first evening they invited about fifty guests into their home and asked me to tell them what brought me to the Near East. The next day Dr. Neale Alter, a graduate of Edinburgh University, who with his wife had established a school in the mountains above Tripoli in northern Lebanon, and I began a four-day trip through the country. At Sidon, on the coast south of Beirut, he wanted me to see the outstanding work in home economics being done by Irene Teagarden. Miss Teagarden and I recalled our previous meeting in 1924 at an American Home Eco-

nomics Association convention, when I had just returned from China
and she was soon leaving for Lebanon. At that meeting in Buffalo,
after my late evening talk on opportunities for assisting other countries, she had sought me out and asked for advice. I had shocked her
with a strong statement about not teaching *American* home economics but adapting its principles to the culture of Lebanon. She had
boarded a train soon after that meeting, she told me, and got into a
Pullman berth but did not sleep all night from excitement. She had
become quite successful in adapting home economics to home conditions she found in Lebanon in the twenty-seven years she had been
there. Her school had a fine reputation. Girls from wealthy homes
and from poor ones lived together in the home management house,
doing their own cooking and housework and gaining new concepts of
standards of living. She provided her students with a broad general
education along with theory and practice in home economics. I felt
buoyed up after that visit and found opportunity later to make use
of Irene's unique knowledge and experience.

Dr. Alter also took me to see fundamental education schools
in Baalbek and Biblos. Along the way we paused to see reminders
of the centuries of history of the region, including ruins dating back
to Roman times. On our way north from Beirut to Tripoli we skirted
the incredibly blue Mediterranean and drove up into the mountains
to Jibrail, where the Alters had their school. Here, in contrast to some
mission schools which stress a classical curriculum, the Alters had
geared the education of boys and girls to village life and its improvement. The boys built houses and roads and raised white rabbits. The
girls learned fundamentals of personal health, hygiene, sanitation,
nutrition, food purchasing and meal planning, cookery, sewing,
child care, and family relationships. Even more important, the girls
and boys developed a sense of dignity and worth *as persons*, without
which little progress is possible. Margaret Hockin once pointed out
an historic feature of the community the Alters had influenced.
When students in social welfare and home economics from the Beirut
Women's College and the American University in Beirut went out
to do summer field work, they found Jibrail receptive and there
started extension work with rural families.

For the journey over the mountains east from Beirut in Lebanon
to Damascus in Syria, I took a taxi-bus—an automobile which made
the trip frequently but not on a regular schedule. It started whenever

enough passengers came to fill the car. Along the roadsides, brilliant
patches of wildflowers brightened the landscape, and close to the
summit there were hummocks of snow. On the eastern slope we
passed through a contorted, dry country almost devoid of vegetation
and followed winding roads down into the oasis surrounding Damascus, purported to be the world's oldest continuously inhabited city.
It would have been a thoroughly delightful trip, except for the car
radio which the driver kept blaring in our ears.

A month had passed since I left Oregon, but what a useful,
productive, informative month it had been! Briefings and discussions
in Washington, at Cornell University, in New York City, Paris,
Egypt, and Lebanon all had one purpose—to educate me, to give me
an understanding of the country to which I was now committed for
the rest of the year, its peoples, neighbors, and friends in FAO who
were trying to help. Throughout my service with FAO I was favorably impressed with the high quality of administrators, specialists,
and other workers; the care with which they prepared people going
on assignments to parts of the world new to them; and the altruistic
yet practical approach they took toward providing technical assistance. These gave me confidence in and respect for the organization
and inspired me to become an energetic member of their team.

In Damascus, the acting head of the FAO mission in Syria,
Carrol F. Deyoe, who had arrived in Syria shortly before me, helped
me get settled temporarily in a fifth-floor room of the Semiramis
Hotel and then discussed with me frankly the local situation. Although basically an optimistic person, Mr. Deyoe seemed a bit discouraged at this point. He said he had considered sending me a
message in Cairo advising me not to come because he did not see
how I could accomplish what I had been sent out to do. After we
had talked matters over, he seemed more hopeful and we began to
plan how to proceed. He had a small office in the Ministry of Agriculture building but no space had been provided for me. He said
that he would have a table brought into his temporary office and
would share the space he had with me. There were no restroom
facilities for women in the building, but that did not greatly matter
because my hotel was within a few blocks. I told Mr. Deyoe I had
faced situations before—and not only in foreign countries—when
difficulties seemed insurmountable and the prospects of success
none too favorable; I assured him I would be patient. I reminded

him that Rome wasn't built in a day and that I had a good deal of
reading yet to do and a great deal to learn about the country before
my advice would be worth anything. He gave me a warm smile and
said, "I'm glad you're here. We'll work at this together."

In that way, our work in Syria began. A small, pot-bellied stove
in the middle of our office, stuffed with chunks of olive tree roots
several times a day, provided warmth. Books I had brought and new
ones acquired provided study material. Bright eyes of young boy
attendants peeking in through the door occasionally to see if there
really was a woman in the agriculture building provided diversion.
In a few days, the Minister of Agriculture—apparently having heard
of my arrival—sent word that he would like to see Mr. Deyoe and
me. The Minister understood and spoke English fairly well, and I
had no difficulty describing the purposes and possibilities of training
in home economics. An interpreter stood by if needed. We had a
pleasant chat, but Mr. Deyoe and I came away with a feeling that
there was no immediate solution to some of our problems.

A few days after this interview, according to the way the story
was passed on to us, the Minister of Education sent a message to
the Minister of Agriculture: "I understand you have a home economist on your staff but I do not see how you can use her. We need help
in our work with schools, and if you will transfer her to the Ministry
of Education we will give her an office, an interpreter-secretary, and
transportation so that she can go out and visit Syrian schools." The
Minister of Agriculture complied with this request. My interview
with the Minister of Education was quite favorable and his support
throughout my stay in Syria was excellent. He gave me a comfortable
office and brought in several young women to be interviewed for
the position of secretary-interpreter. Throughout Syria the second
language after Arabic was French; this area had been a French
mandate following World War I, and much of the time I would need
to converse through an interpreter. The young woman I selected as
my assistant, Khadigeh Pharaon, a refugee from Jerusalem, proved
a fortunate choice because she was an informed, energetic, enthusiastic person, as well as a competent linguist, experienced teacher,
and secretary.

We began getting acquainted with the educational system of
the country by visiting primary and secondary schools for girls in
Damascus. Some had the beginnings of a home economics program;

Syria, 1951

Right: Mr. Carrol Deyoe, Miss Khadigeh Pharaon, Dean Ava B. Milam, and the Syrian Minister of Education at a dinner in Damascus for the summer workshop for home economics teachers.

Below: The Home Economics Workshop staff. *Back row:* Syrian, Lebanese, and Palestinian assistants. *Front row second from left:* Miss Mary Frances Dawson, Mrs. Sophie Wakim Karayusuf, Dean Milam, Miss Irene Teagarden, Miss Hazel Westby, and Miss Suad Wakim.

Left: Jesse Claude Clark at the time he was leading World Y Tours to Europe in 1928.

Below: The J. C. Clark family at Kuling, China, about 1925. *Left to right:* Julia Fuller Clark, Winston, Emogene, Mr. Clark, and Richard.

Above: The wedding of Ava B. Milam and J. C. Clark with the Reverend Egbert Hayes officiating.

Right: Ava Milam Clark with her husband's grandchildren.

Ava Milam Clark, May 1968

some had none. Many were rather new schools since the number had increased from 19 in 1943 to 54 in 1951. None was very large, the largest having no more than 250 pupils. In the northern part of the country we went to the ancient cities of Homs, Hama, Aleppo, and Latakia. The Ministry of Education sent announcements of our coming to each place, and we always received a warm welcome. Teachers were courteous and students were excited at having a foreign guest. Often we found it difficult to follow a schedule because officials tried to crowd in too many school visits at each place.

Most of the schools we visited were in large old Syrian homes with courtyards secluded from the public gaze. There was a certain charm about them, but even with limited enrollment the children were packed in like bees in a hive. Usually, when we first entered a school, we climbed steep stairs to the principal's room, where Turkish coffee, cigarettes, and candy were offered. We talked of the school and the home economics program and what the school officials considered their needs in this field. Then we went to see classes at work. Sometimes the children—in black dresses and white collars and belts and with white bows in their hair—crowded into the courtyard and I was asked to speak to them from a balcony—with the aid of Miss Pharaon. In Hama and Homs, I was given to understand that I was the first American woman to visit their schools. Some of the children who had studied previously in Palestine under the British Mandate could speak English. At one of the schools in Hama a refugee child called out in good English, "We want Palestine back; we want to go home!"

In entertaining guests, almost every school, especially those with foods classes, felt that they must feed us. At first I tried dutifully to play my role as an appreciative guest and at least sample the many dishes placed before us. After one such meal, however, I realized that I would have to risk giving offense. I had great difficulty eating a dish which consisted mainly of raw lamb ground to velvety consistency in the ancient mortar-and-pestle manner and I became violently ill afterwards. It became apparent then that I could not risk my health just for the sake of being a good guest. My interpreter understood the situation, and officials who had been in other countries and had encountered difficulty adjusting to strange foods were sympathetic. Thereafter Miss Pharaon explained why I could not partake of the food they had so graciously prepared for our visits.

Homes were not as accessible as I had found them to be in the Far East. At Homs, however, we were invited into two homes, one a villa overlooking the countryside, and the other an elegant residence of a rich cotton farmer; later I did get inside homes of some of the teachers and a few lower class homes, but only a few. For the most part, we caught only glimpses from the street into the homes of the ordinary people. Like the women we saw on the streets, the women teachers in Homs and Hama wore veils out of doors. Even some of the young women who went in our car with us drew down their thick black silk crepe veils when we left the building. An American man in our party, a professor from Yale University, was not permitted to go with us and his wife into a kindergarten because of the unveiled women teachers there.

That kindergarten, incidentally, was a pitiful example of overcrowding. The 150 pupils in the school were regimented in a manner entirely alien to our philosophy of preschool education. After seeing this and other examples of mass instruction and unhealthful crowding, I knew then that one of my recommendations was going to be for facilities with greater space per student and more opportunity for individual instruction.

In Hama a groaning water wheel of ancient construction—one of the fifty or so in the city—provided sound effects for a dinner served on an outside balcony. The system of aqueducts bringing water to the city and countryside, we were told, had been constructed by the Romans and has not been excelled or replaced. On a side trip we saw a reminder of another dramatic period in the history of this ancient country. Our driver took us to where we could see perched atop a hill Krak des Chevaliers, a fortress-castle built by the Crusaders early in the twelfth century. Knights Hospitalers had raised this massive citadel where a Moslem fortress had stood and used it to protect the northern approach to the Kingdom of Jerusalem until the Saracens recaptured it in 1271.

In Aleppo, I spoke to about 150 attentive men students at Aleppo College and later to the students at the American Girls' School. In the lower schools I found strong sentiment among the men teachers for casting off the veil and permitting more women to teach in the schools. As one male Palestinian refugee teacher put it, "As Syria now stands, half of her population is paralyzed. This cannot continue. There's a great shortage of teachers and women are the best teachers for elementary boys as well as girls."

From a pleasant chat with the French- and American-trained Acting Mayor of Aleppo, I gathered that Margaret Hockin's visit for FOA the previous year had stimulated interest in home economics. He told me that he had the land and money from his municipality to build a secondary school for girls and that it would place strong emphasis on homemaking education. In other places in Aleppo I found eager support for advancing this program. I was pleased to make the acquaintance of Mrs. Sophie Wakim Karayusuf, who in 1938-40 had received one of the American Home Economics Association International Scholarships to study at Ohio University. She had assisted Miss Teagarden in Sidon for seven years but was now a homemaker. She, I thought, should be training teachers in the Teachers College in Aleppo.

From Aleppo our driver took us over the mountains to Syria's port city, Latakia. We visited government schools and a boys' and a girls' school sponsored by the Presbyterian Church. Some of these were in buildings designed as schools rather than in old residences with inadequate space and poor lighting. As we were preparing to leave Latakia for Damascus, the driver declared, "Allah willing, I will get you back to Damascus by seven-thirty this evening safe and sound." Because we had had a slight accident coming north, I asked Miss Pharaon to tell him that his steering of the car would also be a factor in our safe return. When she gave him this message, he burst into a hearty laugh, and soon we were on our way.

The trip north heartened me. Even though we were preparing to make what Gove Hambidge later termed "an unthinkable invasion of the realm of women,"* I was beginning to see that we could accomplish something. Ministry officials began calling at the office to confer with me. A University-of-Chicago-educated Arab author on the staff of the University of Syria sought me out one day. The Ministry of Education asked me what it would cost to set up two secondary schools a year with a strong homemaking training program, and I worked out a plan and estimate. Hence, at this point, which was mid-April 1951, I began to feel useful.

One day Miss Pharaon and I accompanied a group of men from

---

*The Story of FAO. Princeton, N. J.: Van Nostrand, 1955. pp. 126-127.

the Ministry of Education to see the new school of agriculture near Damascus. As we stood on the veranda looking out toward Mt. Hermon, I said, "I congratulate you on this school of which you are so justly proud," and added a bit wistfully, "When I return to Syria in ten years I hope that I will see something comparable for girls in helping educate them for better homemaking." The quick response of one of my hosts was, "But Dean Milam, that is not necessary. You see in Syria the mothers educate their daughters for homemaking all the while." To which I replied, "Certainly mothers the world over should be passing on to daughters all they can offer in equipping them to make good homes. But," I asked, "do not the farmers of Syria pass on to their sons all that they can give in helping them to be good farmers? Isn't there a body of knowledge in agriculture beyond that which the fathers are able to give their sons? Do you not believe that school training will aid these Syrian boys to deal with agricultural problems more successfully than if their education for agricultural work is left solely to their fathers? This same we hold true for home economics in the education of women for homemaking. Is not the future of your country more dependent upon the quality of its homes than upon its farms?" From that day on, these officials became much stronger supporters of a home economics educational program for Syria.

There were thirty-six secondary school teachers of home economics in Syria at the time. The elementary school teachers for girls taught all subjects, which for some included handwork and cookery, but most of them had had no formal training in home economics. In seeking a means for in-service training and refresher courses, we hit upon the idea of having a workshop. I thought that with the help of some of the home economists I had met and Arab assistants we could put together a useful series of talks, demonstrations, and discussions of various phases of home economics. I found those with whom I discussed the plan eager to try it. In Aleppo, they were interested, although at first they wanted to have the workshop held there rather than in their rival city, Damascus, the capital. It was easy to get verbal encouragement, but getting official approval and cooperation proved to be quite another matter. Maneuvering the request through all the agencies concerned—namely, the Syrian Government, FAO, UNESCO, and the Near East Foundation—could defeat all but the persistent.

One of my important jobs, as I saw it, was to make the school people and others dissatisfied with what they had, because change can best be achieved through discontent. The desire for something better, of course, had to be awakened skillfully in order not to arouse resentment. I had been doing the best I could in visits with officials, teachers, and inspectors, but no opportunity had seemed open to accomplish discontent through group meetings. So, remembering my Far Eastern experiences and knowing that "Nothing important ever happens except over a cup of tea," I inquired if the Ministry of Education thought it appropriate for me to have a simple tea in the Orient Palace Hotel with a program following. I requested that the Ministry sponsor the tea and send out the invitations in Arabic, with the understanding that I would pay the costs. Officials welcomed the idea and sent out seventy invitations to which sixty-three educators, including men and women school principals, responded. The idea of having men and women mingling at a social gathering startled some of the most orthodox Moslems, but their curiosity overcame their shock and they courageously came, entered into conversation, and stayed to hear the speeches, which, when given in English, were translated into Arabic.

A Dr. Hurbli, a Ph.D. from Columbia University who was chairman of the Ministry's Council, presided at the affair, and spoke for about twenty minutes. I spoke for ten minutes. Miss Teagarden, who had come from Sidon for the occasion, described the homemaking core of instruction in her school and the benefits students received from living in the four cottages she used as home management houses. The highlight of the program was a thirty-minute talk by one of Miss Teagarden's graduates, a homemaker with three children. Since her father was the Syrian Minister to Saudi Arabia and she spoke excellent classical Arabic, the audience attentively heeded every word she spoke as she pictured life in Miss Teagarden's school, describing its breadth in liberal education as well as its homemaking training. Several officials suggested she write her speech for publication. The tea, we felt, was a success.

Enroute to Cairo in the latter part of April, I went by taxi—this time through rain and mist—from Damascus over the mountains to Beirut. There I conferred with two women I needed for the workshop staff—Irene Teagarden from Sidon and Hazel Westby, acting head of home economics at the American College for Women in

Beirut. Miss Westby, an attractive young graduate of Montana State College who had taken a master's degree at University of Minnesota, was on leave from the University of Miami in Florida. We had a three-hour discussion, profitable because of Miss Teagarden's long experience in the Near East and Miss Westby's fresh viewpoint. We planned to have several western-trained home economists who had experience in teaching in Arab countries as main teachers, with Syrian, Lebanese, or Palestinian women, most of them college graduates who had taken a few home economics courses, as assistants.

While in Cairo, I conferred with the regional heads of FAO and UNESCO, who both assured me they felt certain their organizations would support our plans for a workshop. Also, in Cairo, at the request of the Director General of FAO, I served as consultant for the Home Economics Section at a conference of YWCA leaders from Egypt, Syria, Lebanon, Turkey, Jordan, Palestine, and Iraq. The Arab women attending this meeting discussed many topics which women of the United States would have discussed about homelife in a similar gathering. In addition they revealed other problems encountered by Arab women, such as mate selection for their children, the marrying of young daughters to much older men, treatment of servants, educated girls not being permitted by father and brothers to be usefully employed while awaiting marriage, and woman suffrage. Some of the women grew excited as they expressed their resentment that their ignorant men servants could vote but they, educated women, could not.

One evening during the conference we were taken to the YWCA camp out on the desert near the pyramids of Giza for supper. Folk dances, stunts, and group singing made it a gay party. The air grew cold and the brilliant stars came out. In the distance we could see a dozen searchlights practicing the spotting of high-flying aircraft. Also visible on the moonlit desert were the massive pyramids. I never could see those ancient tombs without thinking of the poor slaves who died building them almost 4,000 years ago—and man's inhumanity to man.

Mary Frances Dawson, the home economist on the faculty of the American Women's College in Cairo whom we planned to use as an instructor in our workshop, took me out after the conference for a 24-hour rest on a houseboat on the wide, wide Nile. It was good for a change to get out of the noise of car-honking in Cairo, to hear only the lapping of water on the side of the boat, and to watch the graceful sails skimming over the palm-fringed river.

Shortly after my return to Damascus a surprise invitation came for me to serve as observer for FAO at the Conference in Beirut on the Middle East Refugee Problem, called by the World Council of Churches and the International Missionary Council. Most of the eighty delegates from many countries who came to the conference visited refugee camps during the first three days, but having seen some of these camps earlier, I remained for these days at my job in Damascus. Top officials, who were wrestling with the refugee problem brought on by the establishment of the State of Israel and the displacement of so many Arabs, talked at general assemblies. The conference was divided into four groups to work out recommendations on (a) relief plans and cooperation; (b) rehabilitation possibilities in housing, employment, and education; (c) recent decisions and future plans of the United Nations and their effects on refugee groups and individuals; and (d) church aid. The hundreds of thousands of Arab refugees presented problems for which there were no immediate answers. It seemed evident to many that the refugees could not "go back home," that relief would have to stop eventually, and that resettlement would have to take place—but how, when, and where were baffling, solution-defying problems.

In my daily walks to and from my office and in short trips about Damascus, I had an opportunity to get acquainted with the sights and sounds of this very old yet very new and currently prosperous city. The honking of automobiles and beeping of jeeps, the clattering of donkeys and carriages, and the clang of stonemason's hammers mingled with the calls of hucksters selling fuel and vegetables and boys crying "S-Kee-Mo" to sell the popular Eskimo pies. In the city square I often passed two old letter writers who sat on stools with their backs against a wall and their clients squatting in line before them. One afternoon when I went to the Orient Palace Hotel to have a shampoo and finger wave a throng crowded the entrance. The Aga Khan, father-in-law of Rita Hayworth, the hotel clerk told me, was expected to arrive. From the mezzanine I could see a maroon Oldsmobile drive up, but the crowd surged around so close to the car that the Aga Khan could not get out into the wheelchair on the sidewalk, so the car drove away.

On another holiday, after I left a beauty shop and walked down the street, a car stopped and a young woman got out and approached me. "Dean Milam?" she asked. "They told me at the American Legation that we might find you here." Who could this be? I wondered. She introduced herself as the daughter of Nell Sykes Pearmine—the girl who had taken me for a canoe ride on the Marys River shortly after I arrived in Corvallis in 1911 and who had scolded me for nearly tipping the canoe over. What an interesting visit I had with her daughter!

After living in the Semiramis Hotel for some weeks, I moved into a pension operated by a graduate in music from the University of Wisconsin. One of her guests once facetiously remarked that our hostess could have spent her time more profitably for us in studying foods and nutrition. An American citizen of Danish parentage, she had married an Arab who was out of favor with the Syrian government. In exile in Beirut, he operated a travel agency that managed to keep his wife's pension full most of the time. The guests made a lively, cosmopolitan group of archeologists, salesmen, foresters, teachers on sabbatical, legation families, students, elderly ladies enroute to the Holy Land, and just plain tourists. We never felt at a loss for topics of conversation.

During Ramadan, the month when a good Moslem neither eats nor drinks from dawn to dusk, our FAO working hours were restricted from ten o'clock in the morning until two in the afternoon, the hottest part of the day. My secretary observed the fasting as did most of the men in our office building. Our plans had made allowance for the restricted period, and we had scheduled the workshop to begin after schools had closed and Ramadan had ended.

The two-week workshop (July 9-23) had four objectives: to give in-service training to a group of secondary and elementary teachers, inspectresses, and principals of elementary girls' schools selected by the Ministry of Education; to make the officials and teachers attending the workshop aware of what a home economics program can become when broadly conceived and executed by adequately trained leaders; to bring together the teachers concerned with home economics education and to enable them to share problems and experiences of mutual interest; and to awaken the interest of the public in this field of education through press and radio publicity and written reports. The instructors came a week early to prepare a large packet of mimeographed Arabic home economics material for each student, because home economics textbooks in Arabic were not available. Detailed records of the courses, field trips, and films were kept with the idea that they might be useful in setting up later workshops with similar objectives.

FAO provided my services and engaged five other western-trained home economists whom I selected: Irene Teagarden from Sidon, Mary Frances Dawson from Cairo, Mrs. Sophie Wakim Karayusuf from Aleppo, Hazel Westby from Beirut, and Suad Wakim. The latter, a graduate of the American Junior College in Beirut, had earned a B.S. degree at Cornell University and had taught in a village school in Lebanon, in Miss Teagarden's school in Sidon, and in the Women's College in Beirut. The Syrian Government agreed to finance eleven Arab assistants.*

We originally estimated that seventy to seventy-five students might attend the workshop without straining the facilities provided, and the financing of the travel and living expenses was agreed to by the Minister of Education. The pressure to increase the number was strong, however, and the Ministry of Education finally admitted ninety-eight to regular attendance and permitted thirty or forty additional observers to attend irregularly, paying their own expenses. Workshop members included both Moslems and Christians but most were Moslem; they ranged in experience from young women who had taught only one or two years to grandmothers with many years of teaching experience. One student was from Iraq; all others from various parts of Syria. We originally planned to follow a discussion method of teaching similar to that used in American workshops. I had found this method excellent in the Far East, but here it did not work and had to be abandoned. Once we invited discussion, everyone wanted to talk at once and the sessions got out of hand. We had to fall back on the lecture method with some controlled discussion. Student interest remained at a high level, and notetaking was vigorous.

Six days a week we held three classes of 90 minutes each (from 7:30 to 12:30) with a refreshment period of thirty minutes each morning. The five principal teachers taught two or three classes a

* Nadedeh Abbani, Anaan Menimeneh, Hermeen Razzaz, Suad Oullaby, Wadea Celeba, Sara Freije, Suad Harun, Maha Jumblatt, Daad Najim, Selwa Atulla, and Khadigeh Pharaon.

day and had an assistant for each class. Miss Teagarden taught
Foods and Nutrition and Methods of Teaching. Miss Dawson taught
three classes of Foods and Nutrition. Miss Westby taught Clothing
and Textiles in two sections at two levels and a class in Housing and
Home Furnishing. Miss Wakim taught Home Management and
Equipment and assisted in the Nursery School. Mrs. Karayusuf
taught Child Development and Family Life and directed a nursery
school with the help of three Arab assistants.

On five afternoons (from 3:30 to 6:30), we showed films provided by the British Consul, U. S. Information Service, and Cornell
University. On other afternoons the Ministry of Public Works provided transportation for field trips, three of them mostly sightseeing
trips especially for the out-of-town members of the workshop, and
others to a sewing machine demonstration, to home improvement
projects, and to a modern cotton mill directed by a Harvard graduate, a demonstration of brocade weaving and handicrafts, and a
canning factory. Although the temperature sometimes ran up to 112°
and the facilities planned for 70 had to accommodate 98 or more,
we managed to carry on instruction in an orderly manner in several
schools in Damascus. The third objective of the workshop, to bring
together Syrian teachers "to share problems and experiences of
mutual interest," was successful. Living together, eagerly conversing
during rest periods and on field trips, and hearing about the lives
and problems of other Arab women living in places in Syria
which they had never seen, the women learned as much from each
other as they did from us. Up to this time they had had no professional organization, but before the workshop closed they began to
discuss formation of a home economics association, although I am
not sure whether or not it ever went beyond the discussion stage.

During the workshop, Mr. Deyoe took moving pictures several
times. The head of the local U. S. Information Service office came
also to take photographs. Before he came into a classroom, students
were advised that they could withdraw if they so desired. At first
some of them either left the room or dropped their veils. When the
photographer brought back prints to show members of the workshop, the ones who had withdrawn became curious and wanted to
see them. Gradually, fewer withdrew each time, and by the end of
the two weeks none left the room or covered her face when he came.
Two of his photographs showing the women in their classes were

published with an article on the workshop in the *Christian Science Monitor*.

At the beginning of the workshop we held an evening party to help members get acquainted. At that time they tended to cling together in small groups with women from their own part of Syria. At the end of the workshop, when we held a farewell party, no geographical distinction was evident. This meeting—in a school courtyard lighted by colorful lanterns—included brief speeches after a delicious Damascus dinner. The Minister of Education said that this workshop had been one of the best things accomplished in his term of office. Although the workshop members from Damascus outnumbered all the rest, the group had thoughtfully chosen one of their number from rival Aleppo to be their spokesman. Poised and sincere, the Aleppo teacher expressed the appreciation of all for the workshop and for the support of the Syrian officials. She also described plans to put to use what they had learned in their own School.

SHORTLY AFTER MY BRIEFING in Washington, D.C., in January 1951, the headquarters of FAO had moved from Washington to Rome. Hence, our reports went there. Dr. F. T. Wahlen from Switzerland, Director of the Agriculture Division of FAO, read my reports carefully and sometimes responded to them. After my workshop report, he wrote, "I feel that this is one of the most worthwhile projects that has been carried out so far under our Technical Assistance Program, and I should like to congratulate you upon the manner in which you have succeeded in arousing the interest not only of the Syrian women but also of the Ministry of Education and high government officials, who seem to have given you the heartiest of cooperation. Please accept my thanks for this excellent piece of work." This came from a man who was one of Switzerland's outstanding men in Agriculture. Several years later, when I noticed in the news that Dr. Wahlen had become President of Switzerland, I wrote to congratulate him and express my appreciation for the fine leadership he had provided for the Syrian mission. His reply, in longhand, included these comments:

Those first years of the Technical Assistance Program are unforgettable, and I am sure that many of the seeds you planted in Syria and Iraq have borne fruit since, although conditions have so vastly changed. A good effort, into which one puts one's heart, is never lost.

As I had done on previous overseas trips, I wrote a letter to "Family and Friends" several times a month and sent it to the School of Home Economics at OSC where the office staff mimeographed it and sent it to a list of those interested in receiving it. The mailing list for the Syrian letters included the former President of Berea College, William J. Hutchins, whom I had first met through the Danforth Foundation, for which he was a Director. On one of his speaking tours he had come to Corvallis and had been a guest for a Thanksgiving dinner in my home. His younger son, Francis S. Hutchins, had taught in several colleges in China in the 1920's before he succeeded his father as president of Berea. As a Biblical scholar who had spent some time in the Holy Land and other parts of the Middle East and as a staunch supporter of the Department of Home Economics at Berea College during his long presidency, William J. Hutchins was particularly interested in whatever progress we were able to make in expanding education for homemaking in Syria. While I was still in Damascus he wrote me a long letter of encouragement, which ended with this memorable sentence: "I think your workshop was as great a miracle as the crossing of the Red Sea by the ancient Hebrews." He apparently passed my letters on to his son Francis at Berea and to his other son, Robert Maynard Hutchins, former President and Chancellor of the University of Chicago, who at that time was Associate Director of the Ford Foundation in Pasadena. I later learned that these letters had circulated among the staff of the Ford Foundation. They, and another letter I wrote directly to the Foundation suggesting grants for the women's colleges of the Middle East, apparently had some influence on the Foundation's decision shortly thereafter to provide assistance to several women's colleges. The American College for Girls in Cairo named the home economics center built with the Ford grant in 1954 in honor of Mary Dawson.

AFTER THE WORKSHOP Mr. Deyoe said, "You have been working hard for weeks. Why don't you take a ten-day respite?" With Dorothea McDowell, an American in charge of the YWCA of Lebanon and Syria, and Marguerite Speirs, an English woman assigned by the YWCA to the Arab refugees in this region, I started for Jordan. Miss Speirs drove us in her little English car. We stopped six times on the border between Syria and Jordan to show our visas, to go through customs, and to get information.

We arrived in the capital of Jordan at the end of the first day. Amman, on the site of ancient Philadelphia, impressed us with the enormous amount of construction underway in its little valley and up its hillsides. Black banners on buildings and the sad faces of the people told us the city was in mourning. Three weeks before—while our workshop was going on in Damascus—Jordan had lost its beloved King Abdullah. As Emir and later as King of Transjordan under a British protectorate after World War I, and as the first King of the Hashemite Kingdom of Jordan when the country was renamed and expanded to include territory west of the Jordan River, Abdullah had maintained a stable, progressive government. Other Arab countries carved out of the old Ottoman Empire had known many years of turmoil. Syria, for example, had had two changes of government in the six months I had been there and had another before I left. Much credit for the stability and comparative happiness of Jordan has been given to "The Glubb Pasha," John Bagot Glubb, a former English army officer, who resigned his commission to become almost an Arab himself. When King Abdullah had gone to Jerusalem to pray one Friday in July, he had received a great ovation from the crowds as he walked through them to the Great Mosque, but as he entered the building a man stepped out from behind the door and shot him. As commander of the Arab Legion, the Glubb Pasha had taken swift action to prevent rioting or revolution. By the time we arrived we noted no rioting—only sorrow for the loss of the King.

On the morning of August 11, 1951, after spending the night in Amman, Dorothea McDowell and I set out for Jerusalem. Since Miss Speirs was not yet ready to continue with us, we obtained the services of a native guide, who asked that his ten-year-old son be permitted to accompany us to see their former home. Before crossing to the west side of the Jordan River, we took a side trip of about twenty miles north through the Mountains of Gilead to Jerash to see the well-preserved ruins of Gerasa, famous as a well-planned city built by the Roman Emperor Pompey and later mysteriously deserted.

On the way to Jerash we noticed ahead of us a car preceded and followed by jeeps filled by soldiers. When the whole party turned around and came back toward us, drivers of cars along the road, including our own, stopped, quickly got out, and stood at attention as the well-armed procession passed. The boy sitting in the back seat of the car, our guide explained, was young Hussein, grandson of the assassinated king. Hussein's father, Talal, heir to the throne, was at that time in a hospital in Switzerland. In the next month, September 1951, Talal returned to Jordan and was crowned king but held the position less than a year before the Jordanian Parliament deposed him. Hussein, who had been studying at Harrow in England, was proclaimed king at the age of sixteen and later enthroned on his eighteenth birthday in May 1953.

At Jerash we noted another party of visitors, a man in Arab dress and his family, also there, from outward appearances, to see the Roman ruins. We recognized him as the Glubb Pasha and, as fellow tourists often do, fell into conversation with the group. We did not fully appreciate the crisis John Glubb was going through at this decisive period in his long service to Jordan. He had spent thirty years among the Arabs—a short time as a lieutenant in the British Army, then as an adviser to the government of Iraq, and later as organizer and Chief of Staff of the Arab Legion in Transjordan and Jordan. Assassinations throughout the Middle East, and now the murder of Abdullah, had caused him to redouble his efforts to maintain stability in the government he helped create. He seemed only a casual visitor to Jerash that day, but in light of what we have learned since, he must have had weighty matters on his mind. Later he continued to serve as military adviser to King Talal for a year and to King Hussein for almost four years. Then one day early in 1956, the King and government of Jordan which he had served for 26 years relieved him of his assignment and ordered him to leave the country immediately. In England, the Queen knighted him and the Army made him a lieutenant-general. Since then Sir John has devoted much energy and effort to giving the Western world an understanding of the true place of the Arabs in world culture and describing the Arab's side of the Israeli-Arab conflict. Through lecture tours and the series of books he has published, he has helped bring a clearer picture of why our involvement in the establishment of Israel has brought enmity from the other nations of the Near East.

As we continued our trip from Jerash, our driver took us down the Jordan Valley to Jericho, a winter resort we found suffocatingly hot in August. We had a thermos of cold water and kept damp handkerchiefs on the backs of our necks as we traveled. We tried to get cooled off by wading in the Dead Sea, but the water was too warm

and so heavy with salts that it felt like an oil foot bath. As we climbed
an airline distance of fifteen miles from the Dead Sea, 1,286 feet
below sea level, to Jerusalem, 2,500 feet above sea level, the air
became cooler and more comfortable. Our guide, a Christian Arab,
knew the country well, having lived in Palestine before being forced
to move. An able driver with a good car, he made an excellent guide.
He took us through Bethany where Jesus came with His disciples on
the eve of the first Palm Sunday. As we climbed up toward the Holy
City of the Jews, Moslems, and Christians, the driver's son spoke up.
"It is very hot today, but Jerusalem is a very, very, nice city," he
said, and there was a poignancy in his voice and a wistfulness in his
little face. We could understand why he and his family found it
difficult to accept Amman as a substitute for their home in Jerusalem.

As a graduate of the University of Chicago, I was eligible to
stay in Jerusalem at the American School of Oriental Research, which
was partially supported by the University of Chicago. Director and
Mrs. Douglas Tushingham made Miss McDowell and me welcome.
They had plenty of room for us because many of the archaeologists
and students who normally used the facilities had not returned in
these troubled times. Our quarters were only a short distance from
the barbed wire that marked off the No-Man's Land between Jordan
and Israel.

Our driver took us to Bethlehem the next morning. Jerusalem
and Bethlehem are only about twenty minutes apart on the regular
highway but because part of it was in Israel and we were not permitted to cross the border, we had to take a winding, steep, narrow
route that required more than an hour.

All through the country we saw sadness, and a pall of gloom
seemed to hang over Jerusalem because of the assassination. One
afternoon Miss McDowell and I went into the old walled city. When
we left, coming down the ancient steps by the Damascus Gate,
crowds were gathered around radios listening to reports of the previous day's trials in Amman. The actual murderer of the King had
been shot on the spot by guards, but ten leading Palestinian men
were accused—four of them later convicted—of plotting the slaying
of King Abdullah. Faces of the listeners showed anxiety and despair.
These words of Jesus came to me: "O Jerusalem, Jerusalem, thou
that killest the prophets and stonest them which are sent unto thee,

how often would I have gathered thy children together, even as a hen gathereth her chickens under her wings, and ye would not!"

For our stay in Jerusalem we alternated between resting, reading about the region, and going to see the historic and sacred spots open to us in this divided land. One evening we walked over to the American Colony a short distance away to see a friend and I recognized Mrs. Bertha Spafford Vester, the kindly matriarch of Jerusalem's little group of American residents. In the twenty years since I had first met her, she had become even more distinguished looking. Cheery, white-haired, and motherly, she was much beloved by all. Her baby home had grown to the point where she and her staff were ministering daily to 300 patients of all races and creeds. I also saw her sister Grace and Grace's husband, John Whiting, the author, who had been shot in the thigh by a stray bullet in the Arab-Israeli conflict and who was still having difficulty getting around. Mrs. Vester invited Dorothea and me to come for tea a few days later.

Mrs. Vester's book, *Our Jerusalem, an American Family in the Holy City, 1881-1949,* with an introduction by Lowell Thomas, had been published in 1950. I did not have time to read it carefully at the time but saved it for later reading. In addition to all the other things this woman, whom Norman Vincent Peale called "Mother of Mercy," was doing, she had taken up painting. She did not boast of it at the time of our visit, but she became so good at it that a selection of her watercolors of wildflowers has been published in book form. "In my time I have met many remarkable personalities," Lowell Thomas once wrote, "but Bertha Vester is one of the few I have ever envied." I certainly concur in his high regard for this remarkable woman and her accomplishments.

The visit to Jerusalem had its friendly, interesting, delightful aspects, but for the most part I found the Holy City a depressing sight. It was much more somber than on my previous visit. The mourning of the Jordanians for the assassinated king, and the heat and dryness of summer as contrasted with the color of the spring visit contributed to the impression, but the saddest feature was the barbed-wire-bordered No-Man's land running through the city —and no end of hostilities in sight.

Having completed our ten-day "respite"—as Carrol Deyoe called it—we were ready to return to Damascus. By starting early one morning, Miss Speirs, who had joined us in Jerusalem, made the long, hard drive with her two passengers in one day. Ten miles from our destination we had a flat tire, and we had begun to change it when along came five well-dressed young Arabs who offered their help. In six minutes they had us on our way again.

Shortly before the respite, Paul Geren, First Secretary of the American Legation in Syria, and his two little daughters, Natasha, and Juliana, had called on me and had taken me to have tea with them in their attractive home overlooking Damascus. Mrs. Geren, a graduate in home economics from Louisiana State University and Iowa State College, knew how to please an American in a foreign land. She served delicious homemade ice cream that we knew was safe to eat! As I was preparing to leave, Dr. and Mrs. Geren, whom I had not met before this day, quite unexpectedly suggested that I move out of the pension and come to live with them. They seemed such a delightful family that I eagerly promised to accept the invitation, and upon my return from Jerusalem moved into their home. Paul Geren, a man of many talents, was then at the midpoint in a notable career. He had been born in Arkansas and educated at Louisiana State University, Baylor University, and Harvard University —where he had received his Ph.D. in 1941. He left his first teaching post at Judson College in Rangoon, Burma, to volunteer as an ambulance driver for the Chinese Army and escaped from Burma with General Stillwell. After a short period of teaching at Forman Christian College at Lahore, he was commissioned as a second lieutenant in the Army of the United States for medical-officer and intelligence-officer service in the China-Burma-India theater from 1943-1946. He was decorated with the Bronze Star Medal. After the war, he ran for Congress unsuccessfully and taught economics at Berea College in Kentucky for a year before going into the U. S. diplomatic service. He had held posts in Bombay and Washington before coming to Damascus. For five years, 1951-56, Dr. Geren served in both the Legation (later raised to Embassy) in Syria and in the Embassy in Jordan. Then the family returned to the United States, where he became Executive Vice President of Baylor University for two years and Executive Director of the Dallas Council on World Affairs for two years. Returning to government service in 1961, he was Deputy Director of the Peace Corps for a year and then served as Consul General for the Federation of Rhodesia and Nyasaland, and more recently as economic counselor in Libya. In September 1967 he returned to education as president of Stetson University in Florida. Books he found time to write include *Burma Diary* (1943), *The Pilgrimage of Peter Strong* (1948), *New Voices, Old Worlds* (1958), and *Christians Confront Communism* (1962). One of the delightful benefits of living in the Geren home in Damascus was meeting the interesting guests. The State Department officials, hydraulic engineers, and labor relations representatives carried on a type of conversation different from that we had been accustomed to at the pension.

As my year of overseas assignment drew to a close, I continued to have conferences with teachers and officials, especially in planning changes and additions to their home economics programs. I helped schedule a conference for FAO staff members. I had a good talk with Margaret Hockin, who had resigned from FAO when the headquarters moved to Rome and was beginning an assignment for UNESCO when she came through Damascus on her way to Iraq. Eleanor Smyth, a home economist from England who had taken Dr. Hockin's place in FAO for a short term, came for a three-week visit and we toured schools in Syria and Lebanon and conferred with candidates for scholarships.

In October, I representd FAO at the World's YWCA Council Meeting. A total of 186 delegates from 55 countries assembled in the Grand Hotel at Beit Meri, Lebanon, on a promontory surrounded by umbrella pines and overlooking Beirut and the Mediterranean. My roommate was Mrs. William A. Stoltzfus, wife of the Women's College president. I especially appreciated this meeting because it gave me an opportunity to see old friends and to make new ones, and because one of the speeches helped me understand the Near East better than all the studying I had done up to that time.

Emma Kaufman came from Toronto as the Canadian representative. I had met her in Japan years before when she was associate secretary for the YWCA in Tokyo; she and Margaret Hockin had visited me in Corvallis and I had shared a delightful Japanese dinner with her in New York on my way to Syria. One of the teachers I had met several times at Ewha College came as a delegate from Korea. I lunched one day with a Filipina whom I had met at the time of the Educational Survey of Christian Colleges in the Philippines in 1948. In one of the group sessions I met a daughter of Dr. Harry Luce, Mrs. Maurice Moore, whom I had known about since meeting her parents and sister on my first trip to Yenching University. I made the acquaintance of many other wonderful, dedicated women. A striking young lawyer from the Gold Coast told me—with much animation—of her countrywomen's activity with the ballot and their efforts to combat illiteracy and to improve homelife. I breakfasted one morning with a group of women from Great Britain, New Zealand, and Australia, who gave me new insight into infant welfare, dental clinics, and marriage schools. Three women from Denmark told me about their folk schools, their lack of poverty or riches, and their aids to families with new babies. A group of women in colorful saris from India and Pakistan talked of the suffering brought about by mass migrations when their countries divided into two nations. It was truly a remarkable experience.

In his address to the whole assembly, Dr. Costi Zurayk, President of the Syrian University in Damascus, put the Near East into better perspective within the world situation than anyone I had ever heard had been able to do. After hearing him and thinking about what he said I could understand more clearly than ever before the geographical, historical, cultural, and political foundations of the tensions gripping the peoples of the area. On the land bridge that joins Asia, Africa, and Europe arose civilizations that have had a lasting impact on world culture; here three great monotheistic religions originated. Just as great battles of antiquity were fought on this bridge, great ideological and political forces are in mammoth struggle today. Within the countries themselves dramatic transitions are taking place as they move from a feudal-agrarian to an industrial-urban society, as they move from scant to intensive production—from man to machine production—as governments move from theocratic to secular, and as nationalism replaces otherworldliness. The transition toward nationalism expresses itself in the desire of countries to control themselves and to get free of others, but it comes into conflict with international forces. The region's resources, especially petroleum, have given it a new strategic position and a new source of conflict internationally. Dr. Zurayk interpreted the establishment of the State of Israel as a conflict between two national movements rather than a conflict between Arab and Jew. Supporting a nation by artificial means and uprooting hundreds of thousands of Arabs to give their resources to an alien state did not seem to him to be a sound idea. Christian Europe, he charged, persecuted the Jews and then tried to solve its problems not at its own expense but at the expense of others. Had there been tolerance in other parts of the world, no Zionist Movement would have been organized. Money and technical assistance, even if free from political strings, Dr. Zurayk concluded, will not change the relationship fundamentally. Today there is need for transforming the world's concept of life, for looking at ends rather than means, and for seeking real values in life—permanent and universal.

As I was preparing to leave Syria, there was quite a round of farewell parties for me. At one large dinner party the Syrian Minister of Education said, "Dean Milam, we simply forget that you are a foreigner. We would like to make a Syrian citizen of you."

23. Iraq

The quiet manner leads to God, but hurry leads
to the devil.
                                    —ARAB PROVERB

MESOPOTAMIA! "The land between two rivers"—the valley of the
Tigris and Euphrates—the eastern arc of the Fertile Crescent
of antiquity—the land of the Garden of Eden and the Tower of
Babel. In Sunday School, in the Academy, in college—all my life—I
had heard of Mesopotamia. It was the fabulous land of Sinbad the
Sailor and the *Arabian Nights,* the Biblical land of Abraham,
Nineveh, and the "burning fiery furnace." Mesopotamian math-
ematicians divided the day into twenty-four hours for us, and the
hour into 60 seconds, and the circle into 360 degrees. Weavers of
Mosul first made the cloth we call muslin. Sumerian, Babylonian,
Assyrian, and Chaldean civilizations had risen in this land, flourished
for a time, left their lasting contribution to world culture, and
withered away.

Naturally, I wanted to accept the invitation of the Food and
Agriculture Organization to go to Iraq, the country that occupies
much of ancient Mesopotamia. FAO wanted me to help set up a
teacher-training program in home economics and to help with
a survey of vocational education. But the year in Syria had been
strenuous, one of the most difficult of my life. Now that it was finished I was glad I had undertaken it, but I was tired—not exhausted
—but weary. I had agreed to come to the Near East for one year
only and had turned down proposals that I remain in Syria another
year or go on to Pakistan or India for two years. Hence, I reluctantly
also declined the invitation to go to Iraq.

But FAO cabled asking if I would consider going to Baghdad for
a two-week exploratory trip at their expense to look over the pro-

posed project, with no commitment to stay longer. "Who wouldn't?"
I asked myself. Margaret Hockin had kept writing from Baghdad
urging me to come. She sincerely believed that I had the background
to do the job better than anyone else available at the time. She
warned that it would be a difficult assignment but promised that I
would find it stimulating and challenging. I cabled acceptance of
the offer to go for two weeks.

On December 8, 1951, the Deyoes, the Gerens, Miss Pharaon,
and several other friends went to the Damascus airport with me.
They put me on a flying carpet, and I floated over the sand-covered
plateau east of Syria and swished down into the fertile valley of
the Two Rivers. An Arab country similar in many ways to Syria and
Lebanon, Iraq had been ruled for centuries by foreign powers or
had formed part of a larger political unit as part of ancient empires
and Arab dominion, and in more recent times, as part of the
Turkish Ottoman Empire. The League of Nations had given Great
Britain a mandate over Iraq in 1920. The Iraqis had elected Faisal—
a brother of King Abdullah of Jordan—as their first King in 1921.
When Great Britain relinquished its mandate in 1932, Iraq acquired
full sovereignty. When Faisal I died in 1933, his son Ghazi succeeded
him and reigned until his death in 1939. Ghazi's three-year-old son
became King Faisal II, but another member of the Hashemite family
was still serving as Regent at the time of my arrival in Iraq. The
young king was in school at Harrow in England, but came home for
the holidays, bringing two English boys with him. I met one of them
at a dinner party and learned that he was having an interesting
experience.

Iraq both *im*pressed and *de*pressed me. Its vast resources and
potential impressed me—just as it had foreign conquerors and other
visitors from the time of Alexander the Great. Ancient Mesopotamia
probably supported a population many times greater than today's
seven million. Agricultural experts I met declared that with adequate irrigation and good agricultural practices it could feed the
whole Arab world. Much of its rich alluvial soil lay barren because
of poor drainage, which results in salting, and inadequate use of the
Two Rivers of fresh water pouring into the sea. About one-third of
the world's date palms grow in Iraq. Cotton and rice grow well and
fruits such as figs, oranges, apples, apricots, and melons are productive when properly cared for. From ancient times the region had

been famous for its oil springs and in recent times petroleum production has provided a cash income of great potential.

It was depressing, therefore, to see the poverty and ignorance among the masses of the people in the midst of all this potential productivity. The lame, blind, tattered-garbed children and adults, barefoot even during the cold winter months, seemed much in need of assistance. Never had I seen a people more desperately in need of the technical help and the scientific information that could raise the productivity of the land and provide sanitary, healthful living conditions.

For a long time, outsiders had recognized the productive potential of Iraq. Ancient conquerors, after laying waste to the country, tried to put it back into production. When the area was part of the Ottoman Empire, the German allies of the Turks sent technicians to improve cotton production and later the British installed a large gin. Traders and foreign investors used their funds to influence production. Missionaries and philanthropists provided some assistance in education and health practices, but most early efforts went into increasing trade rather than improving living conditions.

Following World War I, leading nations of the world gradually became aware of their responsibilities in helping less fortunate countries to develop. Several agencies established in connection with the League of Nations began to lay a foundation for international aid. The International Labor Organization (ILO) began as an autonomous organization at the same time as the League and it provided a pattern for other agencies in international technical cooperation. The League's Health Organization undertook international assistance in malaria and epidemic control and identification and treatment of tuberculosis, leprosy, and venereal disease. The work of these international organizations, as Hugh L. Keenleyside points out, foreshadowed "the spread of an idea and an ideal. Slowly it began to be realized by others than the so-called 'impractical idealists' that in the ever-tightening integration of the modern world, poverty and wealth among nations could not indefinitely continue tranquilly or safely together."*

Following World War II there seemed to be a greater awareness of what Theodore Roosevelt meant when he said, "The world will

---

* *International Aid: A Summary*, New York: James H. Heineman, Inc., 1966, p. 105.

never be fit for any of us until it is fit for all of us." The Charter of the United Nations signed at San Francisco in 1945 states one of its responsibilities in Article One: "to achieve international cooperation in solving international problems of an economic, social, cultural, or humanitarian character." In Article 55 the member states pledged themselves to promote "(a) higher standards of living, full employment, and conditions of economic and social progress and development; (b) solutions of international economic, social, health, and related problems and international cultural and educational cooperation; and (c) universal respect for and observance of human rights and fundamental freedom for all without distinction as to race, sex, language, or religion."

On its own initiative the United States had long engaged in international cooperation, especially in Latin America—the Pan-American Union (1890), the Pan-American Sanitary Bureau (1902), President Franklin D. Roosevelt's Good Neighbor Policy (1933), the Interdepartmental Committee on Cooperation with American Republics (1939), and the Coordinator of Inter-American Affairs (1941). The Marshall Plan following World War II was aimed primarily at helping economic recovery in Western Europe, but shortly thereafter came a series of endeavors that marked the beginning of a new stage in the history of international cooperation. In his inaugural address in January 1949, President Truman outlined four courses of action which would mark United States foreign policy in the coming years. In his first three points he included (a) support to the United Nations and its specialized agencies, (b) continuation of programs for general world recovery, and (c) strengthening freedom-loving nations against aggression. It was his *fourth point* that struck the imagination of the world. It reads in part:

> *Fourth, we must embark on a bold new program for making the benefits of our scientific advances and industrial progress available for the improvement and growth of underdeveloped areas . . . For the first time in history, humanity possesses the knowledge and skill to relieve the suffering of these people. . . . . We should make available to peace-loving peoples the benefits of our store of technical knowledge in order to help them realize their aspirations for a better life. And in cooperation with other nations, we should foster capital investment in*

areas needing development. . . . We invite other countries to
pool their technological resources in this undertaking. . . .
This should be a co-operative enterprise in which all nations
work together through the United Nations and its specialized
agencies wherever practicable.

Out of this *Point Four* has grown a series of acts and appropriations, based not on dole or make-work projects but on technical cooperation, international exchange of technical knowledge and skills, and surveys, demonstrations, and training projects.

Congress debated the Point Four philosophy for eighteen months before the Act of International Development was passed and the Technical Cooperation Administration (TCA) established under the State Department to carry out its purposes. In 1951 Congress enacted the first Mutual Security Act (MSA) to coordinate all foreign aid. When President Eisenhower came into office in 1953, the Foreign Operations Administration (FOA) was established and responsibilities for all economic and technical aid were transferred to it. The Mutual Security Act of 1954 dissolved FOA and its functions were given to the International Cooperation Administration (ICA). Finally, President Kennedy again reorganized our foreign aid program under the Agency for International Development (AID).

In the meantime, other nations had launched programs. The United Kingdom pioneered with technical assistance to stimulate social and economic development in the British colonies with an act passed in 1929. This and subsequent programs provided experienced personnel for United Nations programs in later years. As former colonies of the British Empire gained independence after World War II, some, but not all, chose to retain membership in the British Commonwealth. A meeting of the Commonwealth foreign ministers at Colombo, the capital of Ceylon, in January 1950 devised the Colombo Plan to raise living standards for the quarter of the world's population who live in the region from Indonesia to Pakistan.

France began making direct contributions to the economic development of its overseas territories as early as 1935. As French colonies attained independence, this type of assistance continued. The six members of the European Economic Community—the Common Market—have provided funds for the development of overseas territories of the members. Canada has been a strong supporter of United Nations programs and The Colombo Plan. Denmark, Norway, and Sweden have provided technical and economic assistance in a variety of forms—mostly in Korea, Ethiopia, Pakistan, and India. More recently West Germany has provided model agricultural developments in Turkey and Pakistan, vocational training in Iran, and a technological institute in India. Japan has shifted some of its assistance in Southeast Asia from export promotion to economic development. Russian technical assistance has largely consisted of providing experts in conjunction with international projects such as the Aswan Dam in Egypt, the Bhilai steel plant in India, a cement plant in Afghanistan, and a sugar refinery in Indonesia.

Private organizations have also provided an increasing amount of technical assistance to underdeveloped countries since World War II. Missionary work still accounts for a substantial portion of non-governmental aid in underdeveloped countries and includes the services of experts in agriculture, education, home economics, sanitation, and small industries. Private foundations touch almost every country in the world in one way or another. The Rockefeller, Ford, Kellogg, and Carnegie foundations are the largest contributors, but smaller more specialized organizations such as the Near East Foundation and the Asia Foundation provide a highly significant contribution. Many universities, especially those of the United States and Canada, have become direct participants in various programs of international aid. In addition to these, there are perhaps two hundred other voluntary agencies, supported by private donations, working with varying degrees of specialization in various parts of the world striving to make it a better place in which to live.

The United Nations began its technical assistance programs with a $400,000 budget in 1946. By the time I reached Iraq in 1952 the UN was spending more than $20 million a year. Countries receiving such assistance had to ask for it and had to contribute a fair share of its support. To administer what was called the Expanded Program, the United Nations established specialized agencies—including agencies such as the International Labor Organization (ILO) and the World Health Organization (WHO), and new ones such as the Food and Agriculture Organization (FAO), and the United Nations Educational, Scientific, and Cultural Organization (UNESCO).

The technical assistance teams assembling in Iraq in the winter of 1952 had a spirit of idealism and determination. If anyone could accomplish what they were setting out to do, I felt that these top-notch people could. Many nationalities were represented, although English and Dutch seemed to predominate.

Henry G. Bennett, who had been appointed the first director of the U. S. Technical Cooperation Administration the year before, came to inspect the beginnings of the Point Four programs in Iraq. His wife was with him and they stayed at the hotel where I lodged. Since he was on leave from the presidency of Oklahoma A & M College, the Bennetts were pleased to meet someone who had visited their campus and who knew members of their home economics faculty. At noon on the day they left Baghdad, I saw them leave the dining room and waved as they departed. Their plane crashed in Iran that evening, killing the whole party. Dr. Bennett had provided strong leadership for the complex operation of TCA, and his sudden loss was a tragedy in many respects. He had often remarked that the more advanced countries had given the people of under-developed areas a window into the twentieth century; now they must help them to find a door. His passing made that door a little harder to find.

I was the first member of our FAO team to arrive in Iraq. Others soon followed—an English bacteriologist, an extension methods man from Austin, Texas, accompanied by his wife and son and three agricultural men trained in Turkey, and a French doctor, head of a nutrition institute in Paris. Others came later.

The UNESCO Fundamental Education team to which Margaret Hockin was assigned was preparing to go to Ad Dujayl, a large resettlement area set up by the Iraqi government on reclaimed land that had been given to the poor. Margaret was serving as an expert on women's education as well as a home economist and had an Iraqi graduate of the Beirut Women's College as her assistant and interpreter. The head of the team was a man from South Africa. Another member was an English expert on fundamental education who had come recently from Somaliland. An ILO man, a Hindu graduate of Tagore University, was their specialist in arts and crafts. A medical doctor on loan from WHO was to accompany them, and they hoped to have another doctor there to operate a clinic for the children.

The Point Four group from the United States included at first a medical specialist in child and maternal health from Harvard University, a Texas irrigation engineer, a reclamation engineer from Montana, and the resident head of the party from Washington, D.C. In addition to these were representatives of commerical concerns and engineering firms connected with road building, dams, irrigation projects, and oil. Wilbur Powers, for many years head of the Soils Department at OSC, and a team of soil scientists and engineers working for an American engineering firm engaged by the Iraqi government to develop irrigation had their headquarters in Baghdad but were out in the field most of the time.

Margaret Hockin had made a reservation for me to live in the hotel (another Semiramis Hotel—probably named for the famous Assyrian princess) where she and a good many other British workers were staying. It was not at all homelike, but I made it my residence while in Iraq. Sheikhs in flowing robes, airline crews in distinctive uniforms, and visitors from many lands gave the place a colorful, cosmopolitan air. Soon after I arrived, Margaret took me to meet Miss Emet Said, the Dean of Queen Aliya College. As Margaret suspected, meeting this remarkable pioneer, hearing what she had accomplished, and learning what she still hoped to do convinced me that I should accept the appointment for longer than the two-week exploratory period. I agreed to stay for three months. Later FAO asked me to assist with a UNESCO survey for which no other home economist was available. Hence, my "two weeks" eventually extended from early December until May of the next year.

Dean Emet Said, for whom I developed a profound admiration, was the daughter of a Syrian father and a Caucasian mother. She had received her early education in Aleppo and had gone to Istanbul for higher training. A teacher there had inspired her to devote her life to improving educational opportunities for Moslem girls. She had come to Iraq twenty years earlier as tutor for the young princess who became Queen Aliya, and in 1952 she still had close ties with the royal family, especially with the young king. "Sitt" Emet, as she was respectfully called, had studied at Columbia University in New York City for two years. When the Queen went to London for two serious operations and when she later died of cancer, Sitt Emet was with her.

Sitt Emet was a dreamer who somehow found a way to make her dreams come true. She started a girls' kindergarten and year by year added higher levels of study until finally she had a four-year college for women. It was supported by the government and after the Queen's death it was renamed Queen Aliya College. From all parts of Iraq, orthodox Moslem parents sent their daughters to this college because they felt they were sending them to Sitt Emet. They trusted her because she stood for standards they respected.

Under the British mandate, and later under their own independent government, the Iraqis had introduced education for homemaking in the lower schools, but there was no adequate source of home economics teachers. My principal assignment was to assist Dean Emet and her competent assistant, Sitt Guizine, and staff in developing long-range plans for a home economics department at Queen Aliya College. We visited schools to see what the teachers needed. We planned curricula and facilities for a foods and nutrition laboratory, a nursery school, and a playground. The college already had a good clothing laboratory staffed with teachers trained in Turkey and Paris. We made plans for a crafts and weaving laboratory that would make use of some good English looms that had been received but were not yet uncrated. Through the ILO man we hoped to get a crafts woman to come from India to teach homecrafts that would provide better products for home use and would supplement income. We searched for trained people, both Arab and American, to assist with the instruction in other areas. We found a Ph.D. in child psychology from Antioch College in Ohio to supervise the study of child development and the new nursery school. We worked with the college librarian to expand the holdings in home economics reference books and bulletins.

Because all education in the country had traditionally been dominated by men, male educators felt that they should advise in regard to education for women. At one curriculum-revision meeting of college teachers, a course in political science for women came up for discussion. The very thought of such a course was so questionable to one man that he violently opposed it. He feared it would lead to women carrying banners through the streets. Replying to objections, the women would start calmly in English and then get so excited and feel so cramped by the language that they would burst into Arabic. I could not follow all of the heated controversy, but I did gather from what they said that both men and women students were going out of their colleges with little or no study in political science, carrying with them ideas of politics gained only by hearsay. The women finally won their point, but in compromise had to accept "Introduction to Social Science" rather than "Political Science" as a title for the course.

Various men I met also tried to guide the development of home economics education. At dinner one evening the Director General in Education told me he did not want me to give all of my time to Queen Aliya College. He did not seem to realize that my contract called for that only. "I want you to help with secondary, intermediate, and elementary schools," he said, "and I want you to recommend the dismissal of servants in the boarding schools and have the girls do all of the cooking. What if a man should marry one of these girls and she doesn't know how to cook?" He seemed so serious that I could not take his comment lightly. I replied, "Certainly, the girls should know how to cook and to do much more than that, but I don't believe they need to do quantity cooking all through their school days to achieve skill in home cookery." We parted on friendly terms and I promised to work with the Ministry of Education in whatever time I could spare from my college assignment.

Following the same procedure I had used in China many years earlier and in Syria the preceding year, I set out to become acquainted with the schools of the country before developing a curriculum for training homemaking teachers. According to the 1951-52 school statistics, Iraq had 204 girls' schools and 103 mixed schools with a total of 45,586 girls in elementary school; 29 intermediate girls' schools with 4,407 pupils; 12 secondary girls' schools with 1,117 pupils; and one home arts school with 178 pupils. I visited 26 schools in Baghdad, Basra, Kirkuk, and Mosul, including nearly all of the secondary schools. At one school of 250 girls being trained as elementary school teachers, I was told that it had been built as a boys' school by the Turks a little more than thirty years before and that it was the first government school in the country. I realized that instead of dwelling on how poor the schools were at the time, we should appreciate how much had been accomplished in only thirty years' time.

As Dean Emet took me into schools of Basra, her former students gave her such a warm greeting that I was reminded of the welcome

I have received from OSC graduates as I have visited them through the years. How Sitt Emet reveled in the growth of those who had lost themselves in their efforts on behalf of others! I could see that she had left her mark on these young women.

For our stay in Basra, Sitt Emit and I registered at the Shatt-Al Arab Hotel where she was treated almost as royalty and we were given the best double room in the hotel—despite the fact that the hotel was quite crowded at the time. Scientists from all over the world had assembled to observe an eclipse of the sun which took place during our visit. The manager of the hotel gave us special attention, even inviting us to have dinner with him one evening in his private dining room. It was good to see a "queen" of education for women so royally treated. It was wonderful to see a government women's college in the Arab world and at the head of it a dynamic Arab woman who had vision, courage, and prestige. She was unafraid of men and not a bit timid about working for what she knew was right.

A short time after I arrived in Baghdad, the former OSC professor, Dr. Powers, and his colleague, Forrest Varney, called on me and invited me to come to their hotel, the Zia, for dinner. Most of the Americans seemed to live at the Zia. I was pleased to meet Mrs. Varney and a number of other Americans. The Varneys gave me news from home, including information of their daughter, Theresa, who was an OSC graduate. We enjoyed several outings together. One evening after a pleasant dinner on the lawn by the river's edge, we went to a concert given by the Iraq Army School of Music. Eighty men of the desert played Beethoven, Schubert, Tchaikovsky, Grieg, and Rimsky-Korsakoff. It was almost unbelievable.

The U. S. Ambassador to Iraq, Edwin Crocker, and his wife greeted me cordially and on several occassions invited me to come to the Embassy. In early January they introduced me to a number of diplomats and their wives at an official luncheon. Later they held a reception for the U. S. Air Force pilot, Major James A. Jabara, whose parents were Lebanese, and who was making a good will tour of the Middle East. At a Sunday dinner at the Embassy, I met Agatha Christie and her archaeologist husband. They came to Iraq from England for four months each year, he to dig and preserve ancient artifacts, and she, I presume, to dig up plots and characters for her mystery stories. She had written something like fifty books at that time. She invited me to come up to the site near Nineveh where they were digging that season, and I took this opportunity to see firsthand the precision, dexterity, and diligence with which the work of the archeologist is carried on. When we saw how hot and dusty the work was in early spring, we could realize why they came for only four months of the year.

One evening, a WHO serologist from Vienna, the South African chief of the UNESCO Team, the Indian specialist in home-crafts from ILO, a professor from Iowa State College, Margaret Hockin, and I went up the Tigris River in a rowboat to see something of the old city of Baghdad from the river. Hotel gardens, houses on the river's edge, and tumbling-down buildings seemed an apt setting for Queen Scheherazade's tales of a thousand and one nights. Our rower pulled up to the bank to rest and let us see "mes-goof" being prepared before open fires. The fishermen drew "goofa" fish from the water, split them open, propped them up on sticks, and fed the fires in front of them with fagots. A pepper-and-tomato sauce spread over the baked fish made an apparently tasty dish to sell to patrons waiting in the flickering shadows of the fire. While we were watching, two Arab women came to the river's edge with big brass trays filled with dishes balanced on their heads. They squatted down and washed their dishes in the muddy water. No wonder the death rate is high in Iraq!

On another occasion, at a luncheon garden party at the river-side home of a niece of Dean Emet Said, we saw the head of a camel coming up the bank from the Tigris into the garden. Soon the whole camel lurched into view and hanging on one side was a large banner printed in red paint: "I LIKE IKE." This idea to provide diversion for the luncheon guests came from the niece's son, an architect, and his American wife, whom he had met while studying at Harvard University.

At the luncheon and dinner table, the group of us who took the river trip together—often joined by others—frequently fell into animated conversation. A Welsh serologist with WHO enjoyed teasing me, as an American, on various points such as our lack of attention to voice training and our resulting shrill voices, our showy tourists with their ten-gallon hats, and our weird custom of putting our knives and forks down as we eat and not keeping the knife permanently held in the right hand and the fork in the left. One day our "vicious, indeed vulgar advertising" came in for discussion. I did not try to defend it, and confessed it embarrassed me also. The tormentor exclaimed, "I understand you even have college courses in advertising!"

Late in February, Sir Graham Savage, leader of the UNESCO team on which I was to serve, arrived—or as they say in the Middle East, "came out." In 1951 Iraq had requested UNESCO to send an educational mission to provide assistance with developing vocational education in conjunction with the secondary schools. The Ministry of Education had recently recommended devoting one-fifth of a girl's school time to education for homemaking in place of the two hours a week of extracurricular activity previously allocated to it. My part of the UNESCO project was to survey and make recommendations in regard to this expansion and the training of the teachers required. In addition to Sir Graham, this team also included a professor of agricultural education from Iowa State College, and the director of vocational education for the province of Nova Scotia, Canada.

Sir Graham was a competent organizer and administrator, having been Chief Education Officer to the London County Council. He was a rather formidable man—big and gruff looking—who had lost a leg in World War I and walked with a cane. We understood that before he arrived he had not known that he had been assigned an assistant from Canada and two from the United States and had expected to accomplish the mission alone. He seemed to accept us with good grace, however, and we found him an interesting addition to our luncheon and dinner tables.

As spring approached, the weather which had been quite cold at times began to turn warmer. Dust storms increased in intensity. Fine particles of dust filled the air and seeped into everything. Sometimes the visibility was so poor that incoming planes had to fly over Baghdad and go on to Basra to land. I was told that in summer, when it really gets hot and the temperature goes to 110° nearly every day, guests in the hotel, like the other inhabitants of the city, go out on the flat roofs to sleep at night. That would be a unique experience, I thought, but presumed I would be gone by then.

In my final report to FAO I made three types of recommendations—general ones applying to the whole educational system, those applying to the Home Arts School, and those relating to Queen Aliya College. I suggested that girls' schools not be patterned after boys' schools. I pointed out the need for teaching materials and equipment—texts, syllabi, reference material, films, and laboratories. I urged that more attention be given to clothing selection, dress design, and textiles and less to embroidery. A well-planned and well-equipped functional residence for a family of moderate income, I suggested, should be built on the grounds of the Home Arts School to serve a dual purpose as a practice house for students and a model for the community. For Queen Aliya College, I stressed the need for well-equipped foods-and-nutrition and clothing-and-textile laboratories and for a nursery school. I pointed out the desirability of an annual workshop for home economics teachers, various adult education programs, and a professional organization for home economics teachers. I recommended that scholarships be provided annually by the Ministry of Education in cooperation with FAO to enable college graduates who had demonstrated their ability to receive further training abroad. To what extent or how well these recommendations could be carried out no one could foresee.

The week before I left Iraq, the staff of Queen Aliya College gave a farewell tea for me to which more than sixty guests came. It was a lovely affair, and I was touched by the many expressions of gratitude for my endeavors from the American Ambassador and his wife, from other Embassy officials, from officials of the Ministry of Education, FAO, UNESCO, Point Four, WHO, ILO, and the college staff. It was a heartwarming occasion for me as I said goodbye to newly made friends. Yet, I had some misgivings about what we western nations were doing to Iraq. In response to a request from an American preparing suggestions for some Congressmen, I wrote my thoughts on the subject. This statement so clearly reflected my feelings at the time that I am repeating it here:

> As I look at Iraq, and I see the technical experts pouring in here at a rapid rate, I pray that our influence will be altogether constructive. I cannot help wondering if we may not be trying to move too fast, and may not be coming too rapidly to be absorbed, to be understood, and to be most constructive. If we try for and expect results too fast we may make serious mistakes. These people will not be hurried, and perhaps they should not be hurried. Impatience and impetuousness result usually in offense and the Arab does not forget. If the program

is not theirs *it will not* last. *I have already seen the sad result
of a loss of temper and patience from a brilliant man. He was
needed here but his organization was asked to recall him because he offended an Arab concerning unsatisfactory facilities
where he was to work. He could have handled it all tactfully
but did not and he has had perhaps a serious professional set-
back and his team has also paid a price. Brilliance and technical
expertness are* not *enough. Respect for personalities and for the
culture of the country, ability to put oneself in the place of
others, to adjust to fewer comforts than at home, ability to
control one's temper and get along with others, not being too
easily discouraged, and excellent health are all requisites for
success here as I see it from my vantage point.*

*I am favorably impressed by the majority of the people
who have been sent out here and whom I have met. However,
I am wondering at the effect of what appears to me now to be
duplication by different agencies. In some cases, I am certain
there may be room for all, but in some I cannot help fearing
the outcome. Lack of cooperation between agencies or any
effort at high pressure salesmanship may undo much good which
may have already been done or which could be done. The Arab
is sensitive and we should not forget that he does not forget.*

*I hope the international agencies and Point Four do a little
evaluating before expanding too rapidly. I fear we may be
trying to build Rome in a day. This all may sound bumptuous.
I do not mean it so. I am just one American citizen engaged in
what I felt and still feel is a very important and worthy endeavor
to aid underdeveloped countries to help themselves. I just hope
our methods may be right and the huge expenditure of funds
and efforts may bring returns comparable with the sacrifice
made by all concerned.*

ON MAY 5, quite a group of old and new friends saw me off at the
airport, trying to give me more gifts than my luggage allowance
would permit. In Damascus a letter arrived from my sister Lottie
Vaughn in Corvallis telling that she was soon to undergo a surgical
operation. I therefore changed my schedule and cut short or eliminated some of the stops I had planned on the way home so that I

could arrive in time to be with her. FAO granted me permission to finish my reports on Syria and Iraq after my return to Oregon.

Two well-known American women, Helen Keller and Dorothy Thompson, were in Damascus as I passed through. I did not meet Miss Keller but often recall a statement she was reported to have made to students at the Women's College in Beirut.

It is sorrowful to be blind, but it is worse to have eyes and not see. Soon you will go into a perplexing world. Many problems will wear strange faces and life will make unpredictable demands on you. But your responsibility will remain. You are the future mothers of your country. Your children will receive from you whatever constructive oil is in your lamps. In them your ideals will be carried forward—ideals of love and service.

At a farewell party for the American Minister who was leaving to become Ambassador to Portugal, I had a chat with Miss Thompson. We recalled our previous meeting when she had come as a Convocation speaker to our campus. She had recently visited Iowa State College and had written a column on home economics. She was especially interested, therefore, in what was being done to develop homemaking education in the Middle East.

The trip home across the Mediterranean, Europe, and the Atlantic was quite a contrast to my 1932 trip home from the Far East. Our plane carried us with swift ease over wooded Cyprus, the Isle of Rhodes, the Corinth Canal, and across Italy into Rome where I paused for several days at FAO headquarters. West of Italy we had good views of historic Elba and Corsica and cruised along the French Riviera. From Paris we hopped to Shannon in Ireland and then by courtesy of FAO I was given a berth in a sleeper plane and was served breakfast next morning in sight of the U.S. coast near Boston. Between planes in New York I telephoned Lottie that I was in the United States, called a few other relatives, and was soon on my way again.

Home again! It seemed wonderful to be in Oregon. Never had the beauties of this country, its mountains, its green fields, its roses, its abounding plenty, and its coolness seemed more appealing to me.

Epilogue

An era in the advancement of education for women in Iraq came to an end a few years after I returned home from the Middle East when Dean Emet Said died, a victim of cancer. In May 1953, young Faisal was crowned King of Iraq—on the same day that his second cousin, Hussein, was crowned King of Jordan. They were eighteen at the time. Five years later they joined their countries into an Arab Federation as a reaction to Egypt's formation of the United Arab Republic. Faisal, a few months older than Hussein, became titular head of the union. They announced that Amman and Baghdad would continue as joint capitals. The union was cut short in a few months, however, by the bloody revolt in July 1958 against Faisal's pro-Western government. In the rioting that accompanied the revolution Faisal, the uncle who had served as Regent, and other members of the royal family were assassinated. Revolutions and counterrevolutions kept the country in an unstable turmoil for some time, making technical assistance by various agencies difficult. Early in 1968, however, Margaret Hockin Harrington wrote from FAO Headquarters in Rome that the home economics program in Tahrir College for Girls (the successor to Queen Aliya College) had grown successfully over the years. The Ministry of Education in Iraq had helped establish sixteen new schools of home economics. One of the FAO representatives in Iraq had written, "Our personal experience in home economics schools is that they are actively run by generally competent and enthusiastic staff. On the whole, I was strongly impressed in Iraq by the determination which characterizes female teacher education in general and the apparent receptiveness of the pupils. These are usually girls between 16 and 20 years of age, and there is an unmistakable enthusiasm for education of all kinds as a means of emancipation. . . . Assistance that can be given to the home economics schools will pay high dividends." Mrs. Harrington concluded one of her letters, "It is encouraging to know that your initial efforts in 1951-52 and those of the FAO home economists who followed you have had such good results."

Elsewhere in the Middle East progress in improving home-life and living conditions has also been made. Some of the thrilling personal stories are too significant to pass up at this point.

Orpha Brown Spalding, a native of Kansas and graduate of Kansas State College, had been a home extension agent in Montana for fifteen years before she became home economics adviser for the Near East Foundation in Iran, the country that joins Iraq on the east. The Near East Foundation, a private philanthropic organization, had been formed as the Near East Relief after World War I to work with the displaced populations of Greece, Turkey, and Iran, known popularly in the United States as the "starving Armenians." After Near East Relief became the Near East Foundation, it turned its efforts to an expanded educational program in other countries of southwest Asia. Following the motto "Help people to help themselves through education," it has conducted educational programs in Iran, for example, in health, sanitation, and agriculture. It established training centers for rural boys to become teachers and village workers; it started a literacy program for men; it set up programs in malaria control, environmental sanitation, and water supply.

When the Near East Foundation sent Mrs. Spalding to Iran in November 1951, she found the rural people living in groups of 30 to 100 families in villages surrounded by mud walls. The houses were also made of mud with dirt floors and without windows. The only water supply was an irrigation ditch, where clothes, dishes, food, children, and livestock were washed. Because this same ditch carried away wastes, it became badly polluted after flowing through several villages. The food supply was limited and malnutrition common. "The women," says Mrs. Spalding, "were a sad lot. They were kept behind the walls and when they did go out were covered with the all-enveloping garment, the chador, a remnant of the veil of earlier days and nearly always in dark drab colors." Women supplemented the scarce fuel supply for their small brick-and-mud ovens by making patties of cow manure and placing them on the walls to dry. Few village women had any schooling, and where there were schools few girls could attend more than two years. There were no health facilities, and childbirth was attended by the village midwife who knew nothing of sanitation or infection. If the mother or baby died, the death was considered the will of Allah.

Mrs. Spalding found that the Near East Foundation had a reputation for good works and as a NEF representative she was permitted to enter the villages and homes. The literacy program for men had been sufficently successful that there was also a felt need for literacy

for women. Mrs. Spalding used literacy classes for women as the
opening wedge. Women carried their babies, papoose style, to the
classes. Because the babies were often hungry and soiled and usually
crying, it was an easy step to turn the conversation to why babies
cry and gradually to teach some child-care hints and nutrition information. She taught her native co-workers fundamental home economics, and the assistant and a village worker planned how to present them acceptably to women of the Moslem faith. After a few
months Mrs. Spalding was able to hire three other women to work
in villages. From this nucleus grew a fundamental program of education for homemaking on a level that was understandable and acceptable. Later came training centers for village girls in a rural
setting. Necessary academic subjects were taught but much emphasis
was placed on homemaking subjects. "We tried to instill a feeling of
dedication," Mrs. Spalding says, "so that they would be able and
happy to go to the villages, set an example, and gain the confidence
of the women and girls. After a year of training, the girls were placed
as teachers in village schools where they practiced what they had
learned."

One of our graduates, Dolores Bracken Fricke, Class of 1947,
joined Mrs. Spalding in 1954. In her college study, Dolores had
prepared to go into social welfare work. She spent two years teaching
home economics in a state school for the mentally retarded and then
went to Germany to work in a Red Cross club at a military base near
Stuttgart. She took opportunities to meet local people, to visit their
homes, and to compare cultures and household management practices. She came home for a short time, but the call of overseas service
was still strong. She accepted an assignment with the Near East
Foundation and after a period of indoctrination and training volunteered for duty in Iran. She and the NEF supervisor of rural education, Cal Fricke from Nevada, were married on Thanksgiving Day
in 1954. Their first daughter arrived, they announced, by "stork
freight" at the U. S. Army Hospital in Tehran three years later.
Dolores' principal work in Iran was preparing older girls who had
received at least a sixth-grade education to become teachers throughout the country. She taught the home economics part of the curriculum, which included also gardening, poultry raising, health and
sanitation, first aid, rural sociology, principles of education, and
adult education as well as the standard academic courses.

After the Frickes left Iran—for a furlough in the United States before returning to India for service with the Peace Corps—another American with whom I have been in contact, D. Elizabeth Williams of Greensboro, North Carolina, went to Iran to assist with the NEF's educational program. Miss Williams had spent about a year at Queen Aliya College in Baghdad just before the 1958 revolution. When I heard from her late in 1967, she was encouraged by the progress being made in homemaking education in Iran. Three teacher training schools for village girls were operating in cooperation with the Ministry of Education. Three colleges were including home economics in their curricula.

In the country that borders Iran on the east, Afghanistan, Dolores Moore Carter had an experience somewhat similar to mine in Syria. In 1953 Mrs. Carter, an American home economist who had been serving as a Fulbright professor in Paris, accepted an appointment to begin a pilot project in home economics in Afghanistan. She was supported by United States funds, at first from the Smith-Mundt Act and later by the Foreign Operations Administration (FOA). She found women in purdah and the male members of families resistant to any change or improvement of living conditions. She had difficulty reaching homes but hit upon an idea that proved possible to implement. With Ministry of Education assistance, she made plans for a home management house in which young teachers from two girls' schools could live in a learning-by-doing situation. Six languages were spoken by the students, but Persian was the only one understood by all. Hence, instruction was in Persian through interpreters. Mrs. Carter aroused the enthusiasm of the young women and together they rehabilitated an old cottage and refurnished it as an attractive home. After a few months they were ready to hold an open house and invited prominent women as guests. They held a reception for Mrs. Richard Nixon when she and the Vice President came through on a good-will tour. When Mrs. Carter left Afghanistan she had the feeling that the home management house had become firmly enough established that it would continue and perhaps provide a model for similar projects elsewhere in the country.

Around the world conscientious women continue to make personal sacrifices to extend the basic principles of home economics into homes and family life. They receive support from many quarters, including the United Nations. Although the United States is the largest contributor to these and other Expanded Programs of the UN, the Scandinavian countries, the Netherlands, and Switzerland contribute more on a per capita basis. My friend, Margaret Hockin, a Canadian home economist with graduate degrees from Cornell University, was the first head of the Home Economics Branch of FAO. She drew skilled people from all parts of the world to assist her and accomplished a good deal in her first short term in office, 1949-1951. After UNESCO service in Iraq in 1951 and 1952, she returned to the FAO headquarters in Rome and continued as chief of the Home Economics Branch for ten years. She married Dr. James B. Harrington, FAO consultant to the Near East on wheat and barley improvement, in 1957, and in 1962 they retired to their home in Canada. Since then they have undertaken assignments in Pakistan, Mexico, and most recently, in FAO headquarters in Rome, where Margaret was a consultant on programs in Planning for Better Family Living in 1967 and once again became Chief (temporarily) of the Home Economics Branch in 1968.

In the United States, the programs that grew out of the Marshall Plan and President Truman's Point Four sent many technical assistants throughout the world. In a quietly effective way, Katharine Holtzclaw has provided energetic, purposeful leadership. She and two other home economists from the U. S. Office of Education, Edna Amidon and Marietta Henderson, went to Germany for several months early in 1947 to assist women concerned with home economics and the education of women. In 1951, Dr. Holtzclaw became a consultant in home economics to the European area for the U. S. Regional Office in Paris. During the two years of this assignment she worked in Austria, Denmark, Germany, The Netherlands, France, Luxembourg, Belgium, Norway, and Turkey. With U.S. aid, a school of home economics on an advanced level was established in The Netherlands and a research institute in home economics started in Denmark. In 1953, Dr. Holtzclaw became the home economist on the Washington staff of the Foreign Operations Administration (FOA), which later became the International Cooperation Administration (ICA) and still later the Agency for International Development (AID). In this capacity she selected and briefed home economists to work with rural people in foreign countries. She maintained liaison with the U. S. Department of Agriculture and wrote bulletins and booklets needed in the foreign service. She conducted or assisted with surveys in six countries in South America, five countries in Africa, seven countries in the Middle East and South Asia, and six countries in the Far East. With the financial support of ICA and AID, she helped arrange meetings and workshops for both men and women interested in the improvement of homelife in many of these countries. In the twelve years Dr. Holtzclaw was in charge of the program, the number of home economists overseas varied from 16 to 40. In 1961, for example, just before ICA became AID, ICA had 54 U.S. home demonstration advisers serving in programs overseas. Among nationals working in home economics extension in cooperating countries, there were 70 home improvement specialists, 2,964 agents and supervisors, and 10,290 village-level workers serving 3,440,006 women—principally in South America, Africa, and southwest and southeast Asia. The American home economists, Dr. Holtzclaw once wrote me, "were on the job every day in their countries of assignment and could work constantly with the people and appreciate firsthand their problems. Whatever success the program attained was due in a large measure to these dedicated women of America."

The United States government has sent thousands of specialists and technicians abroad on Fulbright grants, university contracts, and the Peace Corps, among them home economists or women with some training in home economics. Missionary societies, foundations, and such voluntary organizations as the International Farm Youth Exchange (IFYE) have supported the overseas work of hundreds more. Political indifference or interference, revolutions, apathy, cultural and religious traditions, and superstitions have made their work difficult, but we can all be proud of the solid gains they have made in helping to develop within women of many nations a realization that the lot of the homemaker and her status in society can be improved.

24. J. C. Clark

A great many persons drank deeply at the fountain
of his friendship, for it was an abundant stream.

—LAWRENCE K. HALL

MY SISTER LOTTIE'S SURGERY early in the summer of 1952 was
successful, and I was able to be with her until the crisis was
over. Then at the request of the Food and Agriculture Organization
(FAO) of the United Nations, I went to Washington, D.C., to report
on my work in Syria and Iraq to a group of U.S. officials concerned
with Point Four programs. When I returned home, I completed
writing my official reports for FAO and sent them to the Rome
headquarters; both were published in English and the one on Syria
published also in French. While still under FAO assignment, I wrote
two articles on my experiences in the Middle East, one of them for
the *Journal of Home Economics*.

Someone at Cornell University suggested to Dr. David Jones,
president of a fine college for women at Greensboro, North Carolina,
that I might be available to help his college correlate its science and
home economics courses—a project for which he had a foundation
grant. When Dr. Jones invited me to come, I agreed to visit his college in October. I held time free for a vacation at the end of the
summer, a schedule that worked out well in view of what happened.

In the fall of 1951, a letter had come to me in Syria from J. C.
Clark telling of the death of Julia, his wife, from a heart attack. Her
sudden passing came as a shock to the family and their physician,
because no one knew she had heart difficulty. J.C. and Julia had
received my mimeographed letters from the Middle East and
had written to me in return. We had been good friends since Camilla
Mills and I had been guests in their home in Shanghai in 1924, and

I had visited them several times after they had returned to New York. When J.C. learned that I was returning from Iraq in May 1952, he invited me to stop in Boston enroute home to see him and his son Winston and daughter Emogene and their families. FAO, however, had arranged my air transportation non-stop to New York City and I was hurrying home because of my sister's impending surgery.

In late summer, another letter came from J.C., saying that he was driving west to meet his brother Roy and Roy's wife in Yellowstone Park and would come back to Portland with them and would be visiting other friends in Oregon. He wrote that he hoped I would not be off on another assignment before he reached Corvallis. I had seen J. C. Clark in his home, with the Returned Students Club in Shanghai, and with his family and YMCA colleagues in New York and thought of him as one of the finest men I knew. When he came to Corvallis, I was pleased to introduce him to my family and friends. The Hansons (my sister Lora's family) had heard of him in the 1930's in Berlin when they were attending the World Poultry Congress and J.C. was supervising a YMCA tour for American boys. The Hansons remembered the fine impression boys of that group had made on them in Germany and were eager to meet him.

J.C. remained in Corvallis for about ten days, and we spent a good deal of time together. I seemed somehow to know when he wrote from Massachusetts that he was coming to Oregon that someday he and I would be together. We had much in common. I knew he had been lonely since Julia's death, and as always when I returned home from an overseas trip I too felt lonely. I felt I could not adequately convey to others what I had seen, what I had experienced, what I felt regarding the contrasts between our country and the countries where I had temporarily made my home. American affluence troubled me after I had seen so much deprivation. I felt I could not make most people understand, but with J.C. it was different. He knew and understood what I had experienced. It was wonderful to talk with someone like him.

When J.C. returned to Portland to complete his visit there, I wrote him telling how much I had enjoyed my visit with him, yes, and how much I really cared for him. Why, I thought, shouldn't I? As soon as he received my letter, he tried several times to telephone me, but I was out. Then he wrote a wonderful special-delivery letter and told me he was coming back to Corvallis on a certain day. He planned to stop in Salem at ten o'clock in the morning to see Governor Douglas McKay, whom he had known since his YMCA days in Portland when young Doug was a paperboy and came to swim at the Y. I invited J.C. to come to my home for lunch when he reached Corvallis. About noon I opened the door to greet him, and he took me in his arms and kissed me and told me how happy he was. A few days previously I had slipped and fallen with my elbow under me, and cracked three ribs. So, when J. C. gave me a husky hug, I enjoyed it, although it was painful.

After we had lunched on cheese soufflé, fruit salad, and biscuits, he told me he had thought that he had sufficient funds after retirement to care for two, but inflation had caused his savings and retirement income from the YMCA to seem small. He and Julia had taxed their resources in helping their three children through Harvard, Yale, and Boston University, even though all three had worked part time to help themselves. I then gave J.C. a resumé of my savings and income and we decided we could live on our joint savings and have a wonderful life together.

As I came to know J. C. Clark better, my admiration and love for this delightful, energetic, creative, dedicated man grew. I realized what a productive, beneficial career he had achieved. I felt proud to become a part of his life and a member of his family.

J. C. Clark was born on December 28, 1881. His parents, Alvin Clark and Alice Hampton Clark of Pilot Grove, Iowa, named him Jesse Claude. As he grew to manhood, his family called him Claude, but he preferred his initials, "J.C.," and that was what most of his friends and associates called him.

J.C.'s younger brothers, Carl and Roy, were born before the Clark family moved to Oregon in 1890. Mrs. Clark's parents had preceded them to the Willamette Valley and had written back attractive descriptions of the fertile soil, wooded hills, and congenial neighbors. Since they were Quakers, the Clarks settled in the Newberg community, where the Society of Friends had founded the academy that eventually became George Fox College. Alvin Clark, a skilled carpenter, helped build the Friends church in that city.

In the wintertime, J.C. and his father cut wood for their own use and to sell as fuel. One day when they had delivered a load to the public school in Newberg two miles from their farm home, they paused at noon to eat sandwiches in the furnace room. J.C. noticed a picture on a booklet lying on the floor, picked it up, and found that it was a Catalogue of Oregon Agricultural College. Reading it, he became interested in the college in Corvallis and in the fall of 1900, instead of attending the local Quaker academy, he and a neighbor boy came to Corvallis and enrolled in the course in Agriculture.

The first year these two and another boy lived economically by "batching" in a rented room in a private home. The College charged no tuition, laboratory fees were small, and even though he had to pay $16.50 for a cadet uniform, that first year cost only $110. At the end of the year, he went home on the steamboat that carried passengers up and down the Willamette River.

In his second year in college, J.C. and the Shepard brothers, Claiborne and Ralph, paid $2.50 a week for board and room in a home closer to the campus. For his third and fourth years, J.C. moved into Cauthorn (now Fairbanks) Hall. He paid his college expenses, which ran up to $250 in his senior year, by working in the summers, by doing odd jobs at 15 cents an hour during the school year, and by handling the laundry agency for Cauthorn Hall. "I would put the laundry on the top shelf in my room," J.C. said, "and the boys would come in, take their own laundry, and leave the money. I never lost a penny that I knew of."

J.C.'s course of study included mostly mathematics, English, agriculture, and chemistry. He also took courses in history, German, shopwork, drawing, elocution, botany, military science, physical education, zoology, rhetoricals, physics, political science, horticulture, and mental science. According to the minutes of the Faculty (October 6, 1903) he was granted permission to take Latin as a senior elective.

The College had intercollegiate teams in football, baseball, basketball, and track. Other athletics included bowling, fencing, Indian-club swinging, dumbbell exercises, lawn tennis, and golf. This latter was a rather new sport in the community. J.C. once told of two new professors from the East who had brought their golf clubs with them. One fine spring day they went out on the Lower Campus to practice. "Some of us standing up on the hill," J. C. related, "wondered what they were doing. One of the boys said, 'I think they are killing gophers,' so 'killing gophers' was what we called golf for a while."

Literary societies that met periodically for oratorical and essay contests provided some social life for the students. The Young Men's Christian Association (YMCA) and the Young Women's Christian Association (YWCA) helped new students find places to live and to find part-time employment and also held regular sessions every Sunday afternoon as an aid in developing the social and spiritual life of the campus. Twice while J.C. was in college, a student-work secretary who later became one of the great leaders of the International YMCA, Ethan T. Colton, Sr., came for these Sunday afternoon sessions. At their first meeting J.C. impressed Mr. Colton as being "refreshingly honest and unsophisticated." Another young man present at that time, vividly recalled that day. Daniel A. Poling, at that time a student, class of 1904, at Dallas College in nearby Polk County and in his later life the eminent editor of the *Christian Herald* for forty years, wrote me of it: "Colton made a strong appeal for decisions that afternoon, and we were all disappointed when there was no response. At the close of the service, we were standing in the front of the church when the man who became your husband came through the front door and down to the altar. He said, 'Is it too late?' And I replied 'No.' And that was it! That was the beginning of his radiant and far-serving life."

At their second meeting, Dr. Colton recalled in recent years, "I asked J.C. how many of the students he had dealt with had made a committal to the Christian Life. He took to counting them off on his fingers. I do not recall the number but it went well into the second hand."

In his junior year, J.C. became especially interested in the campus YMCA. Clay Shepard had become part-time Secretary, and in his senior year J.C. also was a part-time Secretary. With delegates from other Oregon colleges—including Kenneth Scott Latourette, a member of the Class of 1904 at McMinnville (Linfield) College, and Daniel A. Poling of Dallas College—they held conferences in 1903 and 1904 at Gearhart, Forest Grove, and Corvallis.

Clay Shepard and J.C. started raising funds for a building on the OAC campus to provide facilities for literary societies and similar activities, for banquets and social gatherings, and for a swimming pool and showers, since the campus had no such facilities at that time. The headquarters of the YMCA in New York obtained a leading gift to get the fund started. Clay's uncle, Fred Lockley, part owner of the *East Oregonian* in Pendleton, made a generous contribution. Faculty, students, businessmen, and many others added gifts. After J.C. graduated, Clay Shepard was offered a scholarship at Harvard University but decided to remain at OAC as General Secretary for the campus YMCA. Before he had finished raising funds for the new building, he became ill and died from what was described as a combination of typhoid fever and consumption. The fund was filled, however, and the building completed in 1908 and named Shepard Hall in his memory. This hall served for many years as the campus social and recreational center until replaced by the Memorial Union. In recent years it has housed the OSU Speech Department.

Contacts with Mr. Colton and the YMCA pointed J.C. toward his life's career. After graduating in 1904, he went first to Idaho where he started boys' work in the Boise YMCA. He had a serious attack of typhoid fever in Idaho and nearly lost his life but eventually fully recovered. After two years in Boise he joined the Portland YMCA staff under the jurisdiction of Fred Lockley, uncle of the Shepard brothers, who had been the first president of the OAC campus YMCA in 1890. In Portland, J.C. again specialized in boys' club work. He helped start "Hikes to the Sea," on which he took boys down the Columbia River to Astoria by boat and hiked with them along the coast to Tillamook and then back over the mountains to Portland. He supervised construction of the first camp for boys at Spirit Lake on the slopes of Mt. St. Helens in Washington—at a time when they had to pack in all equipment. One summer he persuaded his younger brother Roy to come and help cook for the camp.

In 1907, J.C. and Julia Fuller, his college sweetheart, were married. They found a number of homeless boys in Portland who needed housing and jobs. The Clarks rented a house that would accommodate about 25 boys and moved in to supervise it under YMCA auspices. The boys did most of the housework and meals were brought in from the "Y" cafeteria. "Several of Portland's well known men of today," J.C. recalled, "got their start in that boys' home."

Meanwhile, Mr. Colton had taken a position with the International YMCA's Foreign Work Committee. When money became available for a boys' work building in Shanghai, he knew where to find the right man to supervise its construction and to operate it. Although J.C.'s co-workers in Portland regretted seeing him leave.

he accepted the appointment. In early October 1911, he and Julia
sailed for China. In Shanghai, he joined the staff of the YMCA that
had first been organized by Charles Jones Soong, the China-born
Southern Methodist Episcopal missionary, father of the famous
Soong sisters who married H. H. Kung, Sun Yat-sen, and Chiang
Kai-shek. J.C. spent most of his first year in language study and in
gaining background information to determine the best kind of
program for boys in China. He knew it could not be just a trans-
plantation of the Boise or Portland programs. For the new building
he planned a gymnasium and a swimming pool—both innovations
because traditionally the Chinese did not believe in exercising except
in connection with gainful work. He encouraged establishment of a
Boy Scout troop and started a camp in Buddhist temples on Putu
Island off Ningpo. A free school for boys supplemented the evening
courses for men. J.C. helped plan and construct a model village at
Pootung, a suburb of Shanghai, where families could live in sanitary
conditions near the factories in which they worked, instead of in mud
huts and mat sheds, and where children had a place to play other
than the muddy or dusty streets. Following the Pootung example,
the Shanghai municipal government erected more than 100 houses,
almost duplicates of the ones in the model village. Other cities in
China also used these models.

Kenneth Scott Latourette, in his history of the foreign work of
the YMCA, *World Service,* wrote of J.C.'s work in China:

> *For a time the boys' department of the Shanghai Associa-
> tion had the largest enrollment of any in the world. This was
> due to the combination of the huge population of the city and
> the imagination and creative leadership of J. C. Clark. . . .
> At one time the department had a membership of 1,814. Clark
> was placed in charge of a project for secretarial training which
> brought to Shanghai men from many parts of China. In this,
> too, he made a unique and important contribution. . . . Partly
> because of the impetus given by Clark, and partly because of
> other specialists sent from the United States and the fashion in
> which the program appealed to the Chinese, boys' work flour-
> ished. While in 1913 the only boys' department was in Shanghai,
> in 1919 sixteen Associations had them. . . .*

J.C.'s friends and colleagues have told me why he became so successful. "He was always reaching out for new knowledge, better methods of work, and greater skill and efficiency in the training of young men for leadership in their own professions," said Egbert Hayes, his fellow Y worker in Shanghai.

His liking for people was the real thing, [said Lawrence K. Hall, another colleague in Y work]. *They liked him. Many people felt they had a special place in his friendships, and I don't doubt that they did. . . . A great many persons drank deeply at the fountain of his friendship, for it was an abundant stream. . . . He was the best trainer of men that I ever knew. Using the 'project method' he helped men discover for themselves the things they needed to know. He was quick to see what a situation required, quick to foresee how to get it done, but able to enlist workers who made it their own task—not doing it for him, not because he required it, but because they saw for themselves why and how the thing needed to be done. That meant that J. C. could leave his office . . . and the work would go on.*

Lenning Sweet, who started boys' work in the Peking YMCA, once shared with me this description of J.C.'s building as he had recorded it in his diary in 1917:

. . . The boys' conference began with 137 delegates from many cities, 50 of them being taken care of in the building which is one of the best for boys in the world. It consists of 5 stories. One contains a recreation room and a small pool. Upstairs is a lobby with 9 ping-pong tables, 7 pool tables, and an office and auditorium seating about 300. Upstairs is a restaurant where you can get a meal for 10 cents; classroom, and a dormitory for 200. . . . The best thing about it all is that Mr. Clark has so managed that the whole thing is run by the Chinese. . . . The foreigners are there in the background carefully planning everything. I received a great deal that will help the work in Peking this year.

His experience with J.C., Mr. Sweet told me, had a great deal to do with his decision to spend his life in China.

George A. Fitch, who had gone to China two years ahead of J.C., said,

The securing and training of a staff of secretaries was a matter of paramount importance. In this J.C. proved a master-hand. Development of program and membership was nothing short of spectacular. . . . Under J.C.'s leadership and with the assistance of his devoted staff of trainees, a number of social service campaigns, aimed at public health, physical education, and spiritual development, created city-wide interest and were to become models for the other Associations in China to emulate.

Clifford W. Petitt, general secretary of the Foreign Association in Shanghai and later Business Manager for the New York City Y Headquarters, called J.C. "alert, outgoing, and wholly committed" and spoke of the warmth of his personality and his thoroughness in every assignment he undertook. He said:

It was easy to like J.C. He assumed no affectations. He was versatile in whatever group he found himself. He was an Internationalist. His wit and understanding were always at his command. . . . He made friends by being friendly and that was the fruit of his outgoing, buoyant spirit. He was always concerned about the welfare of others. This was the quality of his life that gave it breadth.

Sidney E. Hening, another Y Secretary who served in China with J.C. and lived in the same compound with the Clarks, said, "J.C.'s simple and unaffected personality and absolute dependability were among his sterling qualities. When a friend needed a friend he was always there. . . . We found J.C. and his family easy to live with."

In 1916 the Clarks went through a trying time as they started on a furlough year to the States. Enroute to Seattle, they planned to see parts of northern China, Manchuria, and Korea. They took a train north from Shanghai in mid-February. Two-year-old Winston developed such a high fever that they decided to leave the train at Antung on the border between Manchuria and Korea to find a doctor. A friend in Mukden had given them the name of a Danish doctor in Antung, but the problem was to find the doctor in the middle of the night. While Julia, in a room in the railway station hotel, put Winston in a bath of cool water to reduce his fever, J.C. went out to find Dr. Bye in a strange city where neither English nor J.C.'s Shang-

hai Chinese was understood. Finally he found a ricksha man who
seemed to recognize the doctor's name and started off with him over
the snow-covered streets not knowing for sure whether he was being
taken to a mission hospital or to a den of thieves. In twenty minutes
they arrived at the compound and after pounding on the gate
aroused the gatekeeper and were admitted and soon returned to the
hotel with the doctor. He found Winston had a temperature of 104°
and pronounced him "a very sick baby." He did not tell them then
what he suspected to be the cause. It was only after they had
gone on to Seoul the next day, the doctor going with them, that they
found Winston had scarlet fever.

The baby had to be placed in isolation, but J.C. and Julia, who
had the added strain of expecting another child in five months, were
permitted to care for him. YMCA friends and the hospital staff did
all they could for them during their six weeks in quarantine. As
Winston's fever mounted and the crisis neared, they called the chief
surgeon of the hospital. "The glands under his chin must be opened
tonight," he said, "or he may not be with us tomorrow." After the
surgeon had removed about a cup of pus from the swollen glands,
Winston seemed to show improvement in just a few minutes. All
three Clarks slept peacefully that night, and the next morning the
baby continued to improve rapidly. By the time they boarded a ship
for the United States in Yokohama about a week later, Winston was
beginning to take an interest in life.

Problems had not ended, however. At that time few doctors
knew how to operate on mastoids. The Clarks visited ear specialists
in several cities to try to get the discharge from Winston's ears
stopped but received little help. His injured eardrums left him with
a lifelong defect in hearing despite the fact that in later years he
received treatment from some fine specialists.

The Clarks' second son, Richard, was born in Portland in September before they returned to Shanghai. For the birth of their
daughter, Emogene, in 1919, they went to Peking to get away from
the summer heat of Shanghai and to have the services of American
doctors.

In 1922 the family took another furlough and lived most of a
year in New York City, where Julia and Winston studied lip reading
and became fairly proficient. On the return to China, their ship
arrived in Japan forty hours after the big earthquakes of 1923. The

night before they arrived they could see the light of burning Tokyo reflected against the sky. With glasses they could see the flames sixty miles away. Their ship stood by at a safe distance in the harbor and took aboard 2,000 burned and maimed people, who filled the ballroom and every available deck; the ship later left the refugees in Kobe or took them on to China. In all, nearly 100,000 people lost their lives in the earthquakes and fire, but the passengers and crew of the *Empress of Canada* had a small part in alleviating the suffering and in sharing their clothing with the destitute survivors.

It was six months later, in February 1924, that I first met the Clark family. I had been a guest in their home in the Frenchtown section of Shanghai, when Egbert and Eva Hayes were living there during the Clarks' furlough. Now the children were back with their former playmates and J.C. was back at his job. At the dinner table, both at home and when he took me to meet the Returned Students Club, J.C. was a masterful host with a store of humorous anecdotes that he could recall at auspicious moments. "Inside his suit coat," daughter Emogene recalls, "he carried a little leather case with notes he kept to remind him of stories or clippings he had collected. It took a special facial expression, love of a good story, and a dramatic sense of the right place, time, and audience to be successful with his brand of stories." In his study he had a large Morris chair with wide arms where little Emogene liked to sit—when she could get her father's attention—and hear him tell Winnie the Pooh and Br'er Rabbit stories. For generations of tiny tots, including her own, Emogene listened to him throw his voice into a quiet frenzy when he pleaded, "Please, Br'er Fox. Oh, please, don't throw me into that briar patch!" "The intent child wrapped up in his lap would unconsciously take on his expression," she says. "It was priceless to watch Father widen his eyes, wrinkle up his forehead, and create such tragic whimsey for an entranced child."

Emogene also wrote another analysis of her father that I am going to quote here because it helps gain an understanding of the sort of man J. C. Clark was.

Like the early Quakers he had a philosophy of inner peace, patience built on an understanding that God will take care of things if we will only get out of the way and let Him. He never seemed to be anxious over other people's faults or over situations beyond his control, but he never failed to execute those responsibilities that were clearly his. No man can live a life like his and not have worries, but they were always handled with the philosophy that governed the whole of his life. "Do what has to be done, honorably and righteously, and trust God; He'll do his share." He lived a happy, uncritical existence. He loved people and stood like a giant among men as a living symbol of what inner serenity can do to influence and cast a shining shadow.

Before leaving one position to go to a new one, J.C. always wrote an extensive report of his activities and suggestions for those who followed. The suggestions he wrote after 15 years in China proved so practical that the Association Press of China published them in a booklet called "Projects in YMCA Work." As an outline and guide for Y Secretaries for use in selecting and training assistants, it advocated a learning-by-doing situation called the "project method." It became a tool widely used for years to come.

After sixteen years of China service, interrupted by two furloughs, the Clarks returned to the United States. Julia was not well and the children needed to prepare for college. The family settled at White Plains, New York. Because of his hearing handicap and because he had skillful hands, Winston decided, with the family's encouragement, to go into dentistry. He helped work his way through two years at the Springfield, Massachusetts, YMCA College and four years at Harvard University Dental School in Boston, where he received his D.M.D. degree in 1942. After a year of general practice he interned a year at the New Haven Hospital and Yale Medical School. Later he completed the Tufts University School of Dentistry postgraduate course in orthodontics and since that time has specialized in orthodontics.

The second son, Richard, after graduating from high school went to Europe with his father on one of the World Y Tours and remained to live with a family in the Black Forest for a year and to visit other Y families in Europe. As related in Chapter 18, Richard received a good basic knowledge of the German language and after he returned to the United States, received a scholarship at Yale and made a fine record majoring in mathematics.

Emogene, following her talent in music, attended Boston University, met Henry Gates, another music major, married him, and after they had both graduated, began to raise the musical branch of the family.

Meanwhile, J.C. joined the Home Base Staff (the Home Division of the International YMCA Committee) with headquarters in New York City. This Division had initiated "World Y Tours" in 1924, but the plan for giving student groups glimpses of other countries, especially in Europe and South America, did not reach maturity until J.C. took charge of it in 1927. He personally supervised the early tours to Europe. He took one group the first year and two or three the second year, but after that for the eight years he directed the program he did not go himself but organized fifteen or twenty groups annually. The tours were led by teachers and ministers or others who had summers off and who could get together fifteen or twenty boys and girls. Dr. U. G. Dubach, Dean of Men at Oregon State College, was one such leader. The tours proved to be an effective way of getting young people from America into close personal touch with young people in other countries and before they ceased at the outbreak of war in Europe in 1939, some 2,500 boys and girls had taken part in the program.

In 1936, J.C. became executive director of Seamen's House at 11th Avenue and West 20th Street in New York City, the largest YMCA for merchant seamen in the world. He developed recreational programs—both physical and social—and provided a temporary home for sailors from virtually every port in the world. One of the board members donated a $2,500 rotating trophy for an inter-ship soccer league. J.C. organized other types of competition to encourage use of handball and basketball courts, swimming pool, and gymnasium facilities. At the time of his retirement in March 1944, the New York *Times* estimated that he had played host to more than a million sailors.

Early in 1944, after nearly forty years of service with the YMCA, J.C. asked for retirement in order to accept an appointment as Business Manager of the Northern Baptist Assembly to be developed on the grounds of the Lawsonia Estate at Green Lake, Wisconsin. Victor F. Lawson, publisher of the Chicago *Daily News,* and his wife had started this estate with a 10-acre purchase in 1888 and added to it by purchasing seven neighboring farms. Eventually it included more than 1,100 acres, and the Lawsons built roads, a waterfront wall, a mansion and guest houses, huge Jersey and Guernsey cattle barns (that Mrs. Lawson insisted be kept spotless), a power plant, water towers, and stables, pigeon houses, carriage houses, hog barns, and storage buildings. They had even started a tunnel—to be tile-lined—through a hill to make it easier for their prize cows to get to pasture, but the project was abandoned at the time of Mrs. Lawson's death. The Lawson heirs sold the estate to a Chicago real estate firm, whose operating company built the five-story Roger Williams Inn, a swimming pool, and an 18-hole golf course for a country club. Later the Northern Baptist Convention purchased it to convert it into a conference center for use not only by Baptists but by many types of educational and religious groups.

In planning the center, J.C. called into play his years of experience with youth groups, providing housing and dining facilities for guests, and organizing study and recreational programs. His varied experiences in construction—helping his father build houses, shop-work in college, building camps, planning and supervising erection of the Y building and model village in China—all proved valuable to him. With the support of Dr. Luther Wesley Smith and James L. Kraft, the Baptist leaders in the project, he tackled the new assignment with initiative and enthusiasm.

J.C. and Julia moved into a smaller house near the Lawson mansion on the waterfront and used it as their home and to entertain occasional guests. Julia enjoyed assisting with the redecorating of buildings and rooms. She also arranged teas, receptions, and small social gatherings. Both of them appreciated the quiet of the country life, J.C. said, "after fighting our way through the crowded streets of Shanghai and hanging onto straps in the subways of New York for many years." The Clarks made friends among the local residents, who often told them how happy they were that a Christian organization had bought the property as they had feared for a while that a gambling syndicate might purchase it and turn it into a gambling casino.

The first summer, the elegantly furnished inn and buildings that had formerly been homes provided housing for the 3,000 delegates who came for meetings. To accommodate more in later years, barns were turned into lodges. The hog barn with its concrete farrowing pens became the Rural Ministers' School. The bull barn became the first building for the Indian Village. An old home which had been vacant for twenty years became the new Music House. The old powerhouse became the Administrative Building. A storage house became the Arts Building. The pigeon house, granary, and a garage became additional living quarters. A silo became the Prayer Tower with a circular outside stairway. Mr. Kraft obtained a Canadian Indian totem pole, which may have been 300 years old, and erected it in front of the Indian Village. By the end of the fifth season, nearly 12,000 delegates and more than 50 conferences were making use of the Green Lake Conference Center annually; in recent years the total has been nearly 35,000 delegates a year.

From my occasional contact with the Clarks in this period I knew J.C. and Julia both enjoyed this work. Her sudden death in September 1951 was a severe loss. She and J.C. would have celebrated their 44th wedding anniversary that fall. Friends planted a rose garden on the grounds at Green Lake and dedicated it to Julia's memory.

J.C. began to wind up his affairs at Green Lake with a view to resigning before the next summer season. In the winter he drove to Florida alone to visit friends and relatives. In the home of his nephew, an officer at Eglin Air Force Base, he had a slight heart attack and was hospitalized for a short time at the Base hospital. After a few days, the doctors released him and told him he was fit to undertake the trip back to Wisconsin. By driving in easy stages and getting adequate rest, he made the return trip without difficulty.

In a taped interview recorded for a history of Oregon State College, J.C. related what happened next:

"I spent the summer visiting the children, came west to see my brother in Portland, and visited many friends in Corvallis. While there I met my longtime friend, Dean Ava Milam. She had just returned from two years with the United Nations in the Near East as home economics adviser to the governments of Syria and Iraq. She had rendered a fine service there, but now she had no job and I had no job, so we decided it would be much more interesting to go the rest of the journey together."

Since I had the commitment to visit Bennett College in North Carolina for an indefinite period and J.C. had friends and relatives in southern California and his son Richard and family to visit in Honolulu, we planned our wedding for January 1953. At Bennett College I found that the type of assistance needed required the full-time attention of someone for a year or longer, and since I was not

willing to undertake such an assignment, I recommended another
home economist to plan the reorganization. When J.C. telephoned
me in Greensboro and suggested that I come to California to visit
him before he left for Honolulu and to participate in a United Nations Day program in Los Angeles on October 24, I felt free to go.
J.C. met me at the railway station in Alhambra, and after we had
driven a few blocks he parked the car. "I don't see why I should go
to Hawaii alone," he said, "Why shouldn't we be married tomorrow?"
I could raise no strenuous objection except that arranging a wedding
takes a little time. He thought the delay excessive but finally agreed
to November 1, as the day.

In connection with my talk on the Middle East at the International Institute on United Nations Day, Radio Commentator Chet
Huntley asked for an interview. J.C. went to the studio with me.
Mr. Huntley explained that in this pre-election period we would not
have good reception for a live broadcast. He planned to record
the interview for release when the air had calmed down after the
Eisenhower-Stevenson contest. "My name will no longer be Milam
at that time," I warned him. Mr. Huntley gave J.C. a knowing look
and said, "We can fix that." Hence, Chet Huntley became the first
person to use my new name for public announcement and many
friends learned of the marriage through his broadcast before our
formal announcement had reached them.

Reverend Egbert Hayes, who had now retired to Southern
California, readily agreed to perform the ceremony for us. His wife,
Eva, who had welcomed Camilla Mills and me to Shanghai at the
time of our first visit, had passed away. Mr. and Mrs. Myron Longacre, with whom Egbert, a cousin of Mrs. Longacre, was staying in
Whittier, offered their fine, large home for our wedding. Lillian
Taylor, a retired member of our School of Home Economics staff,
and her sister were among the twenty guests who attended. Lillian
reported the ceremony to Alta Garrison and others in Corvallis.

*The service took place in the large living room before a
fireplace banked with flowers and a tall seven-branched can-
delabrum on each side. A son of the groom had sent tropical
Island flowers from Hawaii. . . . A pianist and a soloist provided musical background. To the strains of the Wedding
March, Miss Milam and Mr. Clark came slowly, arm in arm,
down the stairs, to stand, finally, before the minister in front*

*of the fireplace. We were all impressed by the beauty and dig-
nity of the service. Miss Milam was most beautifully dressed in
rose colored net trimmed with sequins over rose taffeta, and
was looking her very best. There was more music after the
ceremony and then came the cutting of the wedding cake,
served with strawberry punch, bonbons, and nuts. The color
scheme throughout was pink and pale green.*

The next morning we went back to the Longacres' for breakfast
before starting a leisurely drive up the Coast Highway toward Oregon. Along the way we called a few friends and lunched one day
with Claribel Nye and Flora Rose in Berkeley. When I telephoned
Helen Edwards, one of our graduates on the University of California
extension staff, I said, "I would like you to meet my husband. I
married J. C. Clark last week."

"What was that?" came Helen's startled reply. "Wait till I take
off my earring."

In northern California we tarried among the Redwoods to enjoy
the beauty of the ancient giants. In Corvallis, my sisters Lottie and
Lora, and the home economics staff had planned a reception for us
at the country club. Dorothy Gatton from the School of Home Economics and Jane Hanson, Lora's daughter-in-law, had arranged the
beautiful bouquets of chrysanthemums supplied by that expert
grower of flowers and great friend, E. J. Kraus. Ruth Gill Hammond's
daughters and Jane Hanson's daughters served refreshments. More
than two hundred and fifty guests from far and near attended and
brought us heart-warming greetings and best wishes.

When we left Portland for Hawaii, our plane was eight hours
late in taking off because of weather conditions. Even though it was
past midnight when we landed in Honolulu, Richard, his wife Mary,
and their three daughters (the youngest a babe in arms) and several
other friends were there to meet us. In typically Hawaiian fashion
they decked us with colorful leis. Mary and Richard had found a
beautiful cottage for us on Lewers Road in Waikiki—on a site now
occupied by a high-rise apartment hotel. A doctor who lived there
had gone to the mainland temporarily and made his home available
for our stay in Honolulu. We relaxed and enjoyed the flowers, climate, and each other's company. It did not become a vacation of
idleness. Richard took us to the University of Hawaii, where he

taught mathematics, and introduced us to many friends. Alumna Ruth Douglass Sulenta and her husband drove us to the Pali, fed us delicious steaks, and presented us with two orchids. Alumna Leone Rockhold Nutter took us out to her 1½-acre "plantation" overlooking Kailua Bay and when her husband Ben returned from Samoa, entertained us and some Honolulu officials at a Sunday dinner. Alumni Leome Thordarson Briggs and her husband Mark met us one Sunday at the Central Union Church and later took us to their home overlooking Honolulu. One Saturday afternoon, alumnus Webley Edwards, originator and producer of "Hawaii Calls," presented us to his nation-wide radio audience. We had delightful visits with other alumni and friends, individually and in groups, both in Honolulu and at Hilo when we flew to the Island of Hawaii for a few days.

Like proverbial postmen on holiday, J.C. went to see the Y men and I attended a meeting of the Hawaiian Dietetics Association, visited the Kamehameha Schools and Trippler Hospital, and accepted a speaking engagement at the University of Hawaii. As do all delightful vacations, this one ended all too soon, and in January 1953 we flew back to Portland and returned to our home in Corvallis.

25. Travels with J. C.

J. C. CLARK AND I readily agreed that we should spend a good deal of our active remaining years in travel. Both of us had traveled extensively but much of the time in foreign countries. Now we had the time to see more of our own country and renew acquaintanceships with friends and former associates, of which, I found, he had a vast number. I once said to J. C., "There seems to be a Y man you know in every town."

"Yes," he teased, "and a home economics girl on every street corner."

In the next four years we made four trips through the United States and into Mexico and Canada, traveling mostly by car and averaging 18,000-20,000 miles a year. Sometimes we worked speaking engagements into the itinerary, but usually our travels were free of professional responsibilities. Moving leisurely, we started whenever we wanted to in the morning and often stopped early in the afternoon. On the highway we often sang songs old and new, told stories, and exchanged ideas. In new communities we sought out interesting places to dine. J.C. could do something I never learned to do. If he became a bit weary from driving in mid-day he would stop the car on the side of the road, doze off for a few minutes, and awaken refreshed and ready to continue.

In 1953 we went by train in early February to Urbana, Illinois, where I spoke on my observations in the Middle East at the general assembly of the 52nd Annual Farm and Home Week at the University of Illinois. My sister Ada and her husband Ted joined us there and drove us to Florida in their new car. Later we came back as far as Pittsburgh with them, and saw their daughter and family, flew to Detroit, and received delivery on a new car at Pontiac. After visits in Ohio, Washington, New York, and Massachusetts, we drove home in time for Commencement. The next year (1954) we left on New

Year's Day by car for California and Mexico but returned in time to prepare for the 50th anniversary reunion of J.C.'s college class, where he was chosen as the speaker at the main banquet. Of the thirty-four seniors who graduated from OAC with J.C. in 1904, eighteen were still living; fifteen of them attended the Golden Jubilee.

Later in the summer of 1954, Ruth Hammond and her daughters Barbara, a junior in college, and Carolyn, a freshman in high school, joined us for a trip across the northern part of the country, through Glacier Park, and on to New England and down the East Coast to New York City and Washington. After Ruth and the girls flew home, J.C. and I went back to New England to spend more time with the children and grandchildren and then drove home through the middle tier of states. Our fourth long trip began in the fall of 1955 and took us through Yellowstone Park just before it closed for the season and on across the country to New England and New York and once again into the Deep South, bringing us back to Oregon early in 1956. In all we had seen 47 of the 48 states, missing only Arkansas.

Having a skilled tour director for a husband, I found, had many advantages. Whether we were alone or with others—as when we traveled with Ada and Ted or with Ruth Hammond and the girls— J.C. had our itinerary, our sightseeing, our visits, our night's lodgings planned well in advance. We saw many plays in New York but never had difficulty in getting tickets because J.C. had arranged for them before we left home. If anything went wrong with a plan or if we missed connections with someone we were supposed to meet, he had an alternate plan ready to put into effect, and we all swung into it hardly realizing there had been a hitch in plans. With what seemed almost effortless ease, our tour director managed our travels, getting us where we wanted to go on time and getting us away in time for the next appointment—with no fuss and no apparent hurry and always with adequate time for relaxation.

Between our cross-country jaunts we spent a good deal of time at *Grayling*, our summer home on the McKenzie River. J.C. really enjoyed that place and it seemed to like him and responded to his touch. He planted wildflower seeds, repaired the pathways, and put his skill in construction to use, having the house jacked up and placed on a concrete foundation and having electricity installed and other construction completed. Mostly, however, at *Grayling* we read, talked, entertained friends, and relaxed.

Guests at *Grayling* and at our home in Corvallis and the homes, schools, and places of business we visited on our trips put us in touch with many lives that had long been of interest to us. The drama of families as they grew, struggled, and prospered spread out before us. With former teachers, with former students and co-workers from many parts of the world, and with people of renown we had known only by reputation—with quite a variety of people of all ages we renewed acquaintanceships or struck up new friendships. It gave us such a warm feeling to enjoy the gracious hospitality of graduates, relatives, and other friends.

Only one of my University of Chicago teachers remained alive at this time. At Lawrence, Kansas, where she had gone as head of home economics at the University of Kansas after leaving Chicago, we called on Elizabeth Sprague. Past 90 years of age, frail in body but vigorous in spirit and alert in mind, she said to me as she had several times before, "Of all my students, Ava, you have had the most interesting life."

Benjamin R. Andrews had been a teacher of mine, and I knew him in many other capacities. Now in retirement in their home called *Ship Ahoy* at South Hero, Vermont, Dr. Andrews and his wife greeted us delightedly. Ben and J.C. struck up a congenial friendship, and the next time we passed that way, when we did not have time to see the Andrews but telephoned when we were close, those two men talked for half an hour—mostly exchanging stories appropriate for after-dinner speeches.

We had a great time seeing colleagues we had worked with in different parts of the world. The retired YMCA people in St. Petersburg, Florida, invited us to picnics and dinners where we saw many familiar faces. At the University of Miami, we found that Hazel Westby, the attractive blonde "youngster" of the workshop staff in Damascus, had returned from the leave she had spent at Beirut Women's College. Through her we unexpectedly met a couple we had long heard of but had never met. One afternoon Hazel took us for a drive in the Coconut Grove area south of Miami, and by mistake we drove into private grounds near the Fairchild Tropical Garden. As we approached the house to turn around, we saw an old man with white hair leaning on a long staff. Ada, who was with us at that time, got out of the car and asked, "Are you Dr. Fairchild?"

"I used to be," he replied, with a twinkle in his eye. Ada then told him that his cousin, Nellie Kedzie-Jones, was a neighbor of hers in Madison, Wisconsin. He invited us into the house, where we met Mrs. Fairchild, a daughter of Alexander Graham Bell. Dr. David Fairchild, for 22 years head of the Section for Foreign Seed and Plant Introduction in the U. S. Department of Agriculture, had explored many odd corners of the globe and had brought back more than 200,000 species of plants to the United States. He had written such books as *The World Was My Garden, Garden Islands of the Great East,* and *The World Grows Round My Door* and was now 84 years old. We talked of friends and places in many countries. He asked me, "Do the dogs still run on the streets of Baghdad?" and quickly continued, "No, don't tell me; I want to remember the world as I saw it." Each time we attempted to leave, Dr. Fairchild protested, and finally, when we insisted that we must go because it was past the dinner hour, he said, "I wish we had room for all of you to stay overnight with us and be our dinner guests, but unfortunately we do not." We left with the feeling that this great man, who had seen so much of the world and had contributed so much to it, and his wife were lonely. J.C. and I often spoke of that visit and how glad we were of the chance meeting. The memory of it remained fresh partly because Miss Westby presented us with a copy of Dr. Fairchild's book, *The World Was My Garden,* for our home library.

In Maine, we called on the Y. P. Meis, whom we had known in China. Dr. Mei was the Yenching University professor who served as acting president of the University during Leighton Stuart's internment. At the time of our visit he was teaching Chinese history at Bowdoin College and later moved to the University of Iowa. His wife, a Smith College and University of Chicago graduate, had studied home economics at OSC. Like other former students, she could not resist the opportunity to tease me a little about waiting so long to marry. She had sent us a note of congratulations while we were in Hawaii in which she added, "Y.P. says it is good to see you practice some home economics in a home."

Each time we passed through Washington, D.C., we went to see Leighton Stuart. Philip Fugh, his long-time secretary and confidant—almost a son—and Philip's wife and son were living with him and caring for his needs. Between our first and last visits, Leighton completed one of the finest autobiographies I have ever read, *Fifty Years in China,* published in 1954 by Random House. Although nearing eighty years of age at the time of our last visit, he was the same gracious, thoughtful, magnificent Leighton Stuart. He still spoke with a soft Virginia accent and to the end of his life maintained a remarkable personal record—as one newspaperman described it at the time he became U. S. Ambassador to China—of having "no known enemies but thousands of friends who are grateful for past help."*

In Columbus, Ohio, we found LeVelle Wood at Ohio State University in good spirits—ready to go traveling again. We found Dean Donald Cottrell of the College of Education in good spirits, too, but he had sad news for us. He had just returned from the Far East where, as chairman of an international educational commission, he had been struggling with problems of rehabilitating education in the war-torn Republic of Korea. He told us he had had no idea of ever going abroad again for one of these jobs—at least not without his wife—but when an invitation came from UNESCO, in behalf of the United Nations' Korean Reconstruction Agency (UNKRA), he had realized that there were quite a few other people who were finding it inconvenient and not too much to their taste to go to Korea to do a job when called. It seemed to him he could not refuse. He had found the assignment rugged and sobering. He said he frequently remembered the travels that he and I had taken together in The Philippines in 1948. He had talked with Dr. Helen Kim of Ewha University several times. The Ewha buildings were practically unharmed but were occupied by the military. He had hopes of getting some U.N. aid so that the faculty and students could return to Seoul. He had found that essentially the same thing had happened in higher education in Korea that we had found in The Philippines. Many fly-by-night colleges and "universities" had sprung up (42 at the time he was there) to satisfy the great urge of the people for educational advancement—or at least individually to secure the badge of it. We felt thankful after our talk with Dean Cottrell that men of his caliber were accepting assignments such as the one he had just completed.

By remarkable coincidence we encountered another friend whom J.C. had known since his college days and who had been in

---

* James D. White, Associated Press, July 28, 1946.

my early Camp Cookery and nutrition classes. Driving home from
Portland to Corvallis in August 1955 we took the highway through
Oregon City. We noticed a man walking along the side of the road.
"That looks like Kenneth Latourette," J.C. said and stopped the car.
Yale University's Sterling Professor of Missions and Oriental History
Emeritus was as surprised to see us as we were to see him. He got
into the car and we took him to the house where he came for vacations and to write in the peaceful surroundings of his boyhood home.
He had been commissioned to write the history of the foreign work
and world service of the YMCA of the United States and Canada,
a project that took much of his time for three years in research and
writing. We sat in the car and talked for some time, Dr. Latourette
asking J.C. many questions about international YMCA activities—
especially the World Y Tours. He mentions this conversation in a
footnote on page 440 in *World Service*, published in 1957.

Our travels gave us an opportunity to stop at campuses we
wanted to see—either because we had been there before or because
we had not. In the year before I retired I had gone on a speaking
tour that included brief stops at universities in Oklahoma, Alabama,
Tennessee, and Kentucky and quick visits to schools and departments
of home economics. Now, with more leisure, we had a pleasant stop
at the University of Alabama where long-time friend Neige Tod-
hunter was dean (having succeeded another friend, Agnes Ellen
Harris), and where Bessie Davey, who took her Ph.D. at OSC, was
head of Foods and Nutrition. Another time we stopped at Berea College in Kentucky. We wanted to see together this unusual, tuition-
free college which had pioneered in its work program for self-help
students in home economics, agriculture, and business and to see
Dean Florence Harrison and other friends there.

The Berea College president, Francis S. Hutchins, was not
there at the time, but we went to see his long-retired father, Dr.
William J. Hutchins, who had given me so much encouragement at
the time of my assignment in Syria. During his long presidency of
Berea College he had steadfastly supported a good home-management-house program and other facilities and staff for home economics, believing that wholesome homelife was a keystone to Christian
living. On that same trip we renewed acquaintanceships at the University of Tennessee, University of Kentucky, and Purdue University.

We had rewarding visits at two colleges in the South established primarily for Negroes. At Bennett College in Greensboro, North Carolina, President David Jones and his wife received us graciously and charmingly entertained us with a luncheon and tour of the campus. They had done a remarkable work in developing this strongly liberal arts college for women which was internationally inclined as regards teachers and students but had not yet built a strong home economics department, as they hoped to do. I had spent a week or so there shortly after returning from the Middle East and had recommended that Dr. Jones appoint someone to come and stay longer, but he had not yet obtained the qualified person needed to coordinate the work of the natural sciences with the household arts and sciences.

We delayed our visit to Bethune-Cookman College in Daytona Beach, Florida, a little too long, for its great founder, Mary McLeod Bethune, had passed away a few months before we arrived. I had never met Mrs. Bethune, but knew her by reputation as one of the leading women educators of the country. Much in the same way as Sitt Emet had developed a kindergarten into Queen Aliya College in Baghdad, Mrs. Bethune had started with five girls in the Daytona Literary and Industrial School in 1904 and gradually added to it "brick upon brick" (the slogan of the Bethune Foundation) until she had a high school. It merged in 1923 with a boys' school, Cookman Institute of Jacksonville. Bethune-Cookman Institute became a junior college and subsequently an accredited, coeducational, degree-granting four-year college. Mary Jane McLeod had been born the fifteenth of seventeen children, whose parents had been slaves. She had attended a Presbyterian mission school in South Carolina, a seminary in North Carolina, and the Moody Bible Institute in Chicago. She had married Albertus Bethune and had raised one son while teaching in various parts of the South. In addition to serving as president of Bethune-Cookman College, 1932-42 and 1946-47, she had become a widely known leader in women's and educational affairs. Presidents Coolidge, Hoover, Roosevelt, and Truman appointed her to national commissions. She served as Special Assistant to the Secretary of War, for the Women's Auxiliary Army Corps in 1942, and was a consultant at the United Nations charter conference in San Francisco in 1945. Although J.C. and I did not get to meet this remarkable woman, we did get acquainted with the institution that is her "lengthened shadow." On the Sunday we were there a band concert marked the beginning of a fund-raising campaign for a new home economics building. We were happy to be able to provide a little assistance at the start of this campaign.

In our travels we had many pleasant contacts with former students—some of them planned, some impromptu. Passing through Atlanta one time, I remembered Hortense Eppley Smith lived there but did not know how to reach her. We called the Iron Fireman Company where her husband Hugh worked and found he was out of town but the office put us in touch with Hortense. We had not planned to stop long in Atlanta, but Hortense insisted that we come out to her home. With her dark eyes snapping as they had that day in 1911 when she came to my tiny office to tell me that she and the other seniors had found me acceptable after my initial trial period, she greeted us at the door. She insisted we stay for dinner, stay with her that night, and have breakfast the next morning. We met her daughter-in-law and heard of her daughter's adventures as a member of the staff in the U. S. Embassy in New Delhi, India.

At Sanford, Florida, Mr. and Mrs. Harry Hetzel took us out to see a huge, highly mechanized celery farm, where all operations from cutting to crating were done right in the field, and to their home for dinner. Both of them were OAC graduates—Harry was the brother of Ralph Hetzel, our first Extension Director. His wife, Geraldine Newins, a home economics graduate, was the sister of Harold Newins, the forestry instructor who helped me teach my first class in Camp Cookery. At nearby Lake Wales, when we visited the Singing Tower which Edward Bok had built on Iron Mountain, I recalled my argument with the famous editor of the *Ladies' Home Journal* over my article on the Tearoom at the Fair, which he insisted on calling, "Where Baked Potatoes Took First Place."

In Ann Arbor, Michigan, we stopped to see Inez Bozorth, who at that time was still manager of the Lawyers' Club at the University of Michigan. The day we arrived she dropped what she was doing and drove with us to East Lansing to have lunch at Michigan State College with a group that included long-time friend Marie Dye, head of home economics, alumna Pauline Paul on the nutrition teaching and research staff, and a promising young woman named Betty Hawthorne, who had joined the OSC Foods and Nutrition faculty in 1946 and had taken leave to complete work for her Ph.D. degree.

In other parts of the country we called on alumnae. In Washington, D. C., my one-time secretary, Zelta Feike Rodenwold, had completed her term as Editor for the *Journal of Home Economics* and was guiding visitors through the home economics research facilities of the Department of Agriculture at Beltsville. In Greenwich Village in Manhattan and at their country home in New Jersey we were guests of Margaret Covell Kinne, daughter of OAC's first dean of engineering, and her husband Birge. In Massachusetts we enjoyed the company of Sarah Louise Arnold, Dean Arnold's niece. At the University of Rhode Island, we had a good chat and luncheon with Dean Olga Brucher of the College of Home Economics. In Salt Lake City, Winifred Hazen took us for a tour of the city and gave us the impression that this was a friendly place in which to live.

When J.C. and I stopped at Lakeport on Clear Lake in Lake County, California, to see Florence Merryman Lewis and her family, a flood of memories came to me. I visualized a little blond girl with eager eyes peeking into the principal's office in the Silverton High School and then turning away. "Why didn't she come in and talk with me about going to college" I asked the principal.

"She cannot afford college," he said. "She has to earn her own way through high school."

Florence Merryman, I learned, had been born in a dirt-floored, palm-thatched cabin in Mexico and had attended twelve schools up to that time. Because of her mother's defective eyesight she had assumed many housekeeping duties for her mother, father, and three brothers. That face I could not forget. I knew that girl should be given a chance for college. After I had returned home I arranged for her to come to Corvallis the following week and have lunch with me and the senior girl who lived with me. We talked about the possibility of her earning board and room by helping me in caring for my household duties. She accepted my offer and lived with me for four years and helped take care of my house another year while I was away on a sabbatical leave. Florence had a struggle —both financially and scholastically—but after five years of study and additional earning through babysitting and catering for faculty families she received her degree in home economics. The highlight of her college life, she once said, was a trip to Buffalo for an International Student Volunteer Convention, which several faculty members helped make possible for her to attend. After teaching and

managing the cafeteria at North Bend High School for a year, she
accepted an appointment to teach home economics at the Crandon
Institute in Montevideo, Uruguay, for she was eager for foreign
service.

In Buenos Aires, Florence met and became engaged to a Californian, a Stanford University graduate, Charles Philip Lewis. In
the three years before they were married, while Florence fulfilled
her contract at Crandon Institute, she introduced graduate courses
in preparation for introducing home economics into the public
schools of Uruguay. She introduced courses in dietetics for hospitals,
organized adult classes in foods and nutrition, conducted a radio
program on "Radio Feminina," which was owned and operated
entirely by women; supervised menus for a YMCA camp, worked
on product improvements in canned goods for Swift and Company,
outlined a basic curriculum for home economics in the public schools
of Uruguay; planned the layout and equipment for a new kitchen in
the British hospital; planned a tearoom for a department store; and
worked out low-cost menus for Good Will Industries. That girl was
a whirlwind of energy. After she married Phil and moved to Argentina she introduced waffles—in a window of a dairy lunch cafe. Since
women did not do such things in Argentina, this novelty stopped the
traffic for a block in all directions and extra traffic officers had to be
put on detail. Sixteen thousand waffles later she turned her window
over to the chain of dairy lunches and took charge of six other
kitchens. She made great improvements but felt that the operators
fell back into their old ways when she and Phil left for a year of
travel and work in the United States.

The Lewises returned to Buenos Aires in time for the birth of
their first son, a year before Pearl Harbor Day. During the war,
Florence supervised lunchrooms and taught part of the time. Two
more sons were born, but the third one died when only 3 months
old. With Peron in power in Argentina, the future did not look promising, and when passage could be arranged Florence and the two
boys came home and Phil joined them a year later. Phil had been
working for the Texaco company but in 1947 resigned to become
manager of the District Fair grounds in Lakeport, California, near
his boyhood home. Florence gained a reputation for taking care of
waifs and friend's tots and promptly was drafted to teach school.
She also organized an open house at the Presbyterian Church on

Sunday evenings for young married couples and became an Elder in the church and taught a Sunday School class. At one time she taught a junior high school class in home economics and served as a Den Mother for Cub Scouts, in addition to a full-time teaching position in primary grades.

By the time J.C. and I visited the Lewises in January 1954, they had another son, little Gordon, less than a year old. David was 13 and Stephen 10. In later years Florence and I have kept in contact. Grateful for my help and interest, she always addresses me as "Captain." After finishing high school both of the older boys, with their childhood earnings and parent's help, attended Stanford University. David graduated in mechanical engineering and went into the Peace Corps for twenty-seven months, working in the rural areas of The Philippines. After graduate study he joined the staff of Stanford Research Institute and the last I knew he was helping develop small industries in East Pakistan and his wife was teaching English to nurses of the Holy Family Hospital in Dacca.

Stephen, the second son, also took an interest in international relations and after training for Peace Corps duty in Micronesia entered graduate school and planned eventually to earn a doctorate in Public Affairs Communication Research. Young Gordon, an honor student, and president of the junior high school student body, was entering high school.

Stories of success, achievement, and service like Florence Merryman Lewis' add greatly to the joys that come from working with college students. This family provides a splendid example of influence for good in family life, in local community, and in the world at large in these sadly troubled times.

A prime purpose of our travels was to enjoy our own families and the new ones we had become a part of through marriage. My sister Eleanor and her husband lived in Macomb, Illinois, and had a fine farm nearby. Their son, Robert, had received a bachelor's degree in chemistry from the University of Chicago and a Ph.D. from Princeton University and had become production manager of a pharmaceutical plant in northern New Jersey. J.C. and I stopped many times to see him and his wife and their daughter Becky and son Robert Scott Miner III.

Mary Lou Cockefair, my twin sister Ada's only child, had taught home economics in Buffalo after receiving her master's degree at

Cornell University and then had joined the American Red Cross for two years of wartime service in the Pacific. After a year of advanced study at Columbia University she received the Omicron Nu Research Fellowship for 1948-49 to study family economics at the University of Chicago. There she met and married Charles Holt, a graduate student in economics. In Pittsburgh where Charles taught at Carnegie Institute of Technology, J.C. and I visited them first a few months after their first daughter was born. Later they added another daughter and son, moved to London and back again to Pittsburgh and from there to the University of Wisconsin.

My younger sister, Lottie Vaughn, had no children, but her twin, Lora Hanson, had two. Daughter Elinor studied home economics at Oregon State for three years and then spent her senior year and received her bachelor's degree at Cornell University. She taught at Vassar College for a year and later married F. E. McKee, who after World War II became a bank executive in New York City. J.C. and I enjoyed seeing their two sons and daughter develop from babies into fine young people.

Lora's son, Richard Hanson, after two years at Oregon State followed his sister Elinor to Cornell University, where he majored in poultry science. In Ithaca, he met and later married Jane Brown, a home economics major who also received her degree from Cornell. Dick and Jane returned to Corvallis and continued in the poultry business which Dick's father had started many years before. J.C. romped with their youngsters, two boys and two girls, and became a bright spot in their lives, and they in his.

Once after visiting sister Nell in Illinois, we crossed the Mississippi River into Iowa to locate J.C.'s birthplace at what had been called Pilot Grove. A hundred miles away across the state line in Missouri we found my birthplace at Milam Chapel near Macon. We visited a few distant relatives who still lived in Macon and in Kansas City, Missouri, and in Wichita, Kansas.

The best parts of our cross-country jaunts, of course, were the visits to children and grandchildren. Dr. Winston Clark, orthodontist, his wife Mary, and their family of four redheads and one brown-haired boy lived in Winchester, Massachusetts. Emogene Clark Gates, her husband Henry, and their family of four musicians lived in nearby Gardner. It was convenient, therefore, for us to take an apartment in the vicinity for several weeks at a time where we could be close—but not too close. J.C. played with the youngsters, fascinated them with stories, and took them on outings. Henry Gates was director of music for the Gardner schools and leader of a band for an industrial concern. Emogene sang as soloist for the Congregational Church. We had many good times with all of them. For twenty-five years J.C.'s children had called me "Aunt Ava." Their children did the same, but one day Nancy Gates said to her mother, "Where is Uncle J.C.?" Emogene replied, "You know he is not your uncle but your grampy." Then the puzzler came out. "How can he be my grampy and Ava my aunt?" One of Richard's daughters in Honolulu had solved this same dilemma by calling me, "Mrs. Grampy." By whatever names they have called me, J. C.'s family have always shown me love and affection and provided me with what J.C. often referred to as a "built-in family."

I do not think any woman could have married into a family in which the children would have been more understanding and considerate and would have accepted her with greater warmth and appreciation than J.C.'s and Julia's children accepted me. Winston once described our relationship in this manner:

> When Mom died Dad was really a lost soul, but when he married Ava Milam he found his soul and happiness again. Ava gave him comfort and security, mostly a loving companionship. I think he made Ava happy too. As Mary said, 'This marriage was made in heaven' and I really do think God and Julia connived together for this marriage. Result—one immensely happy Dad and three happy children with their spouses and numerous grandchildren because we still have a mother and a grandmother whom we love very much.

In early August 1956, J.C. and I spent some time at *Grayling* and then came home to Corvallis. On the evening of the 13th we had a simple supper and watched the Democratic Convention on television for a short time. J.C. read aloud to me for a while as he often did in the evenings, and when we retired he seemed to be feeling fine. About midnight he called me. "Ava, don't be alarmed but I am having a heart attack." In fifteen minutes we were in an ambulance on the way to the hospital. Our physician had arrived ahead of us and speedily relieved the pain in chest and arm. When the tests were completed the attack was diagnosed as a coronary thrombosis. Once during the first days when J.C. appeared to be showing signs of recovery, he said to me, "I'm not afraid to die, but I wish to live." On the third day he grew seriously ill and he was placed in intensive care. From the fourth to the ninth day, he was under sedatives. He was sometimes delirious and talked of China, the Suez dilemma, and other international matters and his concern for the peoples of the world. From the ninth to fourteenth days he seemed to improve and he asked me to read to him and to write several letters. One day he awakened himself by saying, "Thank you," and as he opened his twinkling blue eyes, he smiled and said, "I thought a little girl was handing me a rose."

At three o'clock on the afternoon of August 29th he greeted the nurse coming on duty with a "Hi!" I fed him his orange juice and told him I had written the note he requested to Green Lake. "They will understand," he said, "for Dr. Smith had a heart attack three years ago and has been an invalid since. But my attack can't compare with his." Almost immediately he became unconscious. Two nurses, the doctor, and I were with him when he slipped away into the spirit world. J.C. had lived a full, productive, exemplary life, much beloved by those saddened by his passing. I received a flood of sympathy notes from men and women in many walks of life and from many parts of the world. Thoughtful comments have continued to come in the intervening years. Less than a year before his own death in 1968, Daniel A. Poling wrote, "I admired and loved this man, and I am looking forward to 'seeing' him again." J.C.'s memory has remained bright in the minds of many, especially in mine to whose life he added extra dimensions.

26. No Place Like Home

Put the household in order and rule the state in peace.

—Chinese proverb

Home is still the heart of society, just as it was in Ellen H. Richards' day. Its traditional values are being challenged—just as they were then—but home retains its fundamental role as the basic element of the complex civilization in which we live. Home "is not only a shelter from the elements," Mrs. Richards once wrote, "not only a shelter from the curiosity and interference of the outside world, but an expression of the persons in it—of their ideals, tastes, education, and needs of soul as well as of body."

Ellen H. Richards had faith in the future—just as we must have faith today. "The past has been an iconoclastic age," she said, "but we are entering a constructive one. Old traditions are being torn up by the roots. New principles of action are being examined very closely before acceptance. . . ." A great deal has happened since Mrs. Richards spoke these words as the first president of the American Home Economics Association, but they still have a modern ring. Each generation rebels in some way against some of the values and traditions of past generations and sets up new standards to be challenged and tested by succeeding generations.

Home economics, which Mrs. Richards once defined as "the preservation of home and the economics of living," has also gone through transition, facing mental and moral readjustment. But home economics has shown a willingness to learn—an acceptance of a need to know. It has given hearty support to the acquisition of new understanding through investigation and the application of the results of research to matters of daily living. It has delved into the relationship between the social sciences and the physical sciences and the well-

379

being of household and family. At the same time home economics
has held true to the faith that the higher values of living are bound
up in intellectual, moral, esthetic, and spiritual values held by individuals within families.

The principles expressed by the founders of the home economics
movement remain as solid and vital today as at the turn of the
century. Outwardly their accouterments have changed. The principles are applied to new conditions in the physical environment and
social context, but their fundamental thesis—that improvement of
homelife is the basic means of improving society—remains just as true
now as it was then. Education for homemaking, therefore, must be
based on certain fundamental verities, yet at the same time must
remain flexible and adaptable in application. Emphasis on the
various phases of homemaking that comprise the course work of
home economics has shifted and will continue to shift, in keeping
with the environmental revolution. Millinery, basketweaving, and
making party decorations—which some of my predecessors once considered an important part of a homemaker's education—have long
since withered away. Housewifery, once of significance in maintaining sanitary conditions in the household, has changed under present-
day conditions. Home nursing, laundering, and house decoration
have a much different emphasis today than they once had. All
phases of home economics have undergone changes—some subtle,
some dramatic.

Changes in design and construction of houses and household
equipment and the availability of sanitary utilities and health services
have modified the duties of the homemaker. Today she has much
easier housekeeping tasks to perform than my mother had in preparing and preserving foods, maintaining shelter, and providing for
clothing and other needs of her family. Instead of the arm-aching
beating of batters and the continual surveillance of a wood-burning
range in an overheated kitchen, the modern housewife has partially
prepared foods, packaged blends of ingredients, refrigeration, and
mechanical appliances to speed up and simplify meal preparation.

The modern house is a joy to maintain as compared with the
rococo dust catchers of earlier generations. In our early childhood,
my sisters and I had the periodic chore of dragging carpets out to the
clothesline and beating clouds of choking dust out of them with a
broom or a twisted-wire carpetbeater. The modern housewife has at

hand mechanical devices that permit her to accomplish routine cleaning and laundering with a fraction of the effort previously required.

A skilled homemaker can still turn out durable, well-fitted, attractive garments for herself and her family—just as my grandmother
did in our home—but she does so today for economy, convenience,
and the enjoyment of creativity rather than from necessity. Skill in
purchasing based on a knowledge of textiles, design, and color is
equally as important for the modern homemaker as skill in construction.

Yes, the tasks of those who "keep" the house in most homes in
this country are easier today than they were yesterday, but the more
significant responsibilities of both husband and wife as homemakers
are decidedly more intricate and complex. Increasing urbanization
and the interdependence that modern society places on individuals,
families, and communities demand of the modern homemakers a
change in management skill, emphasis, and understanding. The new
technology, the new affluence, the new morality, and the new influence of peer groups bring pressures on each member of the family.
How well homemakers understand and utilize present-day culture
and how well they assume the role only parents can play will determine in large part whether their families form society's stalwart building blocks or disintegrate under the pressures of society.

Parents set the pattern for living by the way in which they react
to and interact with each member of the family and with the larger
community. Parents who show favoritism to one child over another
often unwittingly injure the sibling-parent relationship, resulting in
resentment and jealousy that may carry beyond childhood. Vital
patterns in family living cannot be passed on in toto to agencies outside the home. Parents must recognize the extent to which outside
agencies can assist in the development of the family but be willing
to assume responsibilities that cannot safely be delegated to others.
Babysitters and all-day nurseries, for example, have their place in
child rearing but their role should be limited. I am strongly of the
opinion that mother love is irreplaceable and that both child and
mother lose something significant in their lives if they do not spend a
major part of the child's waking hours together in the child's early
years.

Parents must see to it that grandparents, if there are any, have
an opportunity to play their appropriate role in the education of

children. As older people segregate themselves in retirement homes or villages, channels of communication with younger generations must be kept open. A grandparent should be a special friend to a grandchild—listening to the child as he talks, responding to his questions, asking him questions, tactfully disciplining him when necessary, and filling material needs when appropriate. The interaction of young and old is extremely important in transmitting cultural heritage, personal philosophy, and inspiration. One task of modern homemakers is to provide situations in which this transmission can take place.

Every child should feel that he or she is making a contribution to the family. Periodically performing certain tasks for the welfare of others as well as for himself should be part of a child's training. I believe that thoughtful parents can find daily routines that give each child a feeling that he is part of the whole and thereby help in the development of his character and the stabilization of the family. I do not believe that children should be paid for doing routine chores. They should learn the satisfaction that comes from non-paid services and courtesies. On the other hand, allowances can have a character-building influence. Learning how to handle money is an important phase of growing up. The merits of thrift, discriminating purchasing, sharing with others, and the wise use of available funds can be implanted at an early age. Here, again, the example of thoughtful parents is required.

Making life too easy for children does them a disservice. Growth comes through constructive activity; work is essential. We try to give youth an easier life than we had, but in so doing we may rob them of growth by taking away the opportunity for self-discipline and struggle. We may also rob them of the satisfaction that comes from helping others. *Large* scholarships which do not require sufficient struggle on the part of the recipients sometimes have a negative effect, robbing the learner of character development and growth by eliminating the necessity for energetic personal involvement.

Many a modern home has lost some of the virtues of the old family table with its open forums and controlled, balanced discussions. Picnicking in the family room, self-service counters in the kitchen, and meals on an irregular or cafeteria basis may encourage individual members to eat too rapidly as they prepare to rush off to other activities or to isolate themselves in other ways and thereby weaken the solidarity of the group. Wise parents will recognize this danger and do what they can to counteract it.

The speed and ease of today's transportation tend to pull families apart. Instead of spending Sunday afternoons reading and talking on the wide front porch as we did in our girlhood home in Missouri, the modern family often splits in all directions. Junior hops into his sports car to visit a pal in a neighboring university. Daughter has a date to go water skiing. Son number two has to have transportation to the hobby center to "throw" a vase on a potter's wheel. Daughter number two has to go to see a friend just back from six months in Africa, and so forth. Any parent of teenagers can add to this list—if he or she is not away on activities of his own.

All this running about does not necessarily have a negative effect on the solidarity of the family. Just as it takes members away, it brings outsiders into the home. It sometimes brings visitors with enriching ideas and tales of adventure in far places. Ease of transportation makes possible speedy family trips by air, car, and camper. My mother rarely left home, and went out of the state of Missouri only a few times, but her daughters have seen much of the world. One of them has gone all the way around it, and has crossed the Pacific seven times. Mother's grandchildren and great-grandchildren think no more of hopping from continent to continent than she did of going by train to Chicago. Such mobility need not exert a divisive force on the family. It can strengthen ties through a community of interest and bring to each member a vicarious acquaintanceship with the world and its peoples.

Communications technology provides a means for mobile family members to keep together in spirit if not in person. Air mail, tape recorder, telegraph, teletypewriter, and radio make swift communication possible between family members scattered over the globe. The telephone, which today makes voice contact possible in a matter of seconds or minutes, will be augmented in the future, we are told, by picturephone to bring families together visually just as rapidly.

In nearly every aspect of modern life, people have become increasingly dependent on one another. Sometimes dependence has come so gradually that we have accepted it without realizing a change has occurred. Let us take for example the increasing dependence the household places on services provided by persons outside the home. In my girlhood, our family was a rather independent, self-sufficient unit. It produced and preserved as well as consumed. Our gardens, orchards, and livestock provided much of our food. Some items, such as materials for shelter, shoes and materials for clothing, and kerosene for lights came from outside, but many times the materials were processed into useful products at home. In a period of emergency we could have gone for weeks—perhaps even months—with no contact with the outside world and would not have suffered materially.

Managers of homes such as I grew up in needed skill in planning work schedules, processing food products and textiles, preserving and storing foods and clothing, and maintaining a sanitary, healthful household. They relied on themselves, other members of the family, and the "hired girl" or "hired man," who became almost a part of the family, for almost everything that needed to be done. They had to be self-reliant and independent.

Gradually we became dependent on others. The U. S. government had long provided postal service to post offices in towns. When I was a girl, rural free delivery was put into effect, but even then mail did not come to our door. Ada and I frequently had the responsibility of saddling up Fanny and Belle and riding two miles to another farm, where our mail had been left by the carrier. The rural mail carrier was one of the first outsiders we came to depend upon three days a week, in all seasons, and in all weather.

Our home was one of the first in the vicinity to have a telephone —a party line to which other homes were connected and which sometimes seemed like a community forum for the exchange of news and announcements. For my father, it speeded up transactions in buying and selling cattle and widened his scope of operation. Through the telephone we lost some of our isolation—but at the same time we gave up some of our independence. We had to rely on men to build and maintain the lines and on an operator to make connections with other telephones.

On the farm we pumped water from a cistern in the back yard but when the family moved to Macon, the city supplied our water. Fuel for the kitchen range and the base-burner in the living room came at first from the woodlot, but gradually we came to depend on coal mined in nearby Bevier and hauled to our house by others. Garbage disposal was never considered a problem as long as my father kept hogs, but eventually the family depended on a man to come and haul the garbage away and a sewer to wash other wastes away. On the farm we used only kerosene lamps, or candles in emergencies, for lighting; in Macon we had gas and electricity for the first time. On the farm the men cut ice blocks on the pond and packed them in sawdust for use through the summer; in Macon a wagon brought ice to our house periodically so that we could have an "ice box" year-round in which to store foods in order to use them efficiently. Eventually, milk delivery, grocery delivery, and newspaper carriers took from us more of our independence.

My mother depended mostly on my grandmother to make clothing, but when outside services became available Mother found it both convenient and economical to call in a seamstress to assist her, and she went to a millinery shop for headgear. In town the family also depended more on skilled and professional services—carpenter, plumber, doctor, dentist, lawyer, full-time minister, and professional rather than volunteer nurses. On special occasions we even went to a restaurant for meals. To keep us in touch with the outside world, newspapers became more plentiful and frequent; magazines increased in numbers and scope, and books were easier to purchase and to borrow from libraries. Touring lecturers brought information, and nickelodeons provided entertainment. In hundreds of ways we all became increasingly dependent on others.

Today we take for granted the services provided by others. My house is connected to water and sewage pipes, to telephone, electrical, and television cables. My radio has a wireless connection with the outside world. Some of my neighbors also have gas pipes running into their homes. Tomorrow, we are told, we will have photophone and computer services. From her home office the homemaker will be able to do her banking, pay bills, store income tax information, and make calculations through use of new services.

Our society has become so urbanized, just within my lifetime, that from a state of almost self-sufficient independence the typical family has grown into a state of dependence on many segments of society for survival. Managers of the homes of today and tomorrow, consequently, require a different kind of knowledge and different skills from those required yesterday.

What effect does the changing role of the homemaker have on schools of home economics? Does it make them obsolete? Should their traditional pattern of organization be discarded in favor of greater specialization? Should they throw away accumulated past experience and start all over again? Should they take a new direction?

Advocates of the new-directions approach have in some instances tended to warp the original home economics concept out of shape and in their drive toward specialization to lose sight of the significance of education for the home. In their enthusiasm for their chosen areas of endeavor, specialists in some universities have tended to place undue emphasis on too narrow a field of interest. In so doing they may limit students' preparation for careers too much and exclude or submerge areas of subject matter which I believe are needed not only by the homemaker but also by the future professional specialist.

Discussions frequently arise over whether a school of home economics should place its primary emphasis on education for homemaking or education for a professional career. To me it is not an either-or question to be settled one way or the other. A school can do both. I can think of many a graduate who became outstanding in a particular career field who as an undergraduate emphasized a field different from the one in which she later became eminent. A successful executive in foods, for example, took her graduate work in nursery school education; a successful journalist started out to be a teacher; another to be a clothing specialist; and so forth. The breadth of their understanding of the full range of home economics undoubtedly had an influence on their ultimate achievement.

Most home economics graduates marry at some time in their lives. A large proportion go into wage-earning activities directly out of college, but practically all become homemakers at one time or another. Many will combine homemaking and a career in varying proportions and at various periods in their lives. Of the 141 young women who received baccalaureate degrees in home economics from Oregon State University in the spring of 1967, only nine expected to become full-time homemakers immediately. More than one-third of the class, however, were already married at graduation time or expected to be early in the summer. About a third of the whole group would teach home economics in junior or senior high schools or supervise nursery schools. Several expected to go overseas with husbands and find teaching positions there. Others planned advanced study in dietetics, some with internships in hospitals. Some would go into retailing and merchandising or other business careers or become airline stewardesses. Others would go into extension work, the Peace

Corps, or the Campus Crusade for Christ. I know from experience that many, probably all, will change career fields several times in their lives. The one thing they all have in common is that they will be homemakers at one time or another. Even those who do not marry will establish homes for themselves, perhaps for members of their family or others.

Education for homemaking, I therefore believe, must remain the basic core of undergraduate instruction for all schools of home economics if they are to serve best their own major students and other students across the university campus.

Preparation for homemaking today requires more than ever a broad, well-rounded education—both in the liberal arts and in the arts and sciences of the household and family living. I am not saying that every girl should have a college education in home economics to become a successful homemaker. In the education of youth we must look to the home primarily, and then to the elementary and secondary schools, to supplement the preparation for homemaking just as we do for training for vocational competence, for citizenship, and for cultural appreciation. The lower schools, however, need leadership. In all areas of home economics, they must look to collegiate schools for vision, motivation, and guidance.

Let us take one area, family life, as an example. Many high schools now provide instruction for both boys and girls aimed at preparation for marriage. Some high schools even have a child-observation program. In preparing family-life teachers for secondary schools and nursery school teachers, schools of home economics have a responsibility for synthesizing the results of research in child growth and development, for conducting experiments and observations of their own, and for helping administrators and school boards plan the organization and expansion of family life study in the secondary schools.

Departments of family life also have a responsibility for developing nursery schools both for their own use and for other disciplines. Alert universities will realize the value of the pioneering that schools of home economics have done in creating laboratories for observation of human beings. They will take advantage of the experimental and observational opportunities offered in nursery schools and encourage wider use of these facilities—and perhaps improve them. They will see the value of child observation not only for men and women students who expect to become parents but also for students going into teaching, for those preparing to become pediatricians and orthodontists, and for majors in sociology, psychology, and anthropology.

In cooperation with other disciplines, departments of family life conduct research to provide objective, experimental evidence on questions dealing with human relations in a family setting. They are concerned not only with childhood but also with adolescence, young adulthood, mature adulthood, and senescence. Faculty scholarship and research provide a basis for teaching at both the undergraduate and graduate levels and for disseminating information through off-campus teaching and writing.

In a somewhat similar manner other areas or departments of a school of home economics provide facilities, leadership, and vision. They must continually question traditional processes and test new materials. New textiles, new construction techniques in clothing, new foods and new processing of old foods, new nutritional information, new methods of teaching, and new concepts in house design, interior decoration, and the management of households and institutions must come under objective scrutiny. Trained specialists must select the best of the old and combine it with the best of the new and adapt them both to the modern home.

Home economists engaged in research must move forward with the firm conviction that we still have much to learn and in all areas probe for new understanding and seek means of motivating better use of what is now known. In research, teaching, and extension work, home economics holds a unique mediating position between the scientist who develops basic principles and the homemaker who wants to put new knowledge to daily use. Thus, much of the research conducted by home economists is carried out in cooperation with specialists from other fields, such as food technologists, chemists, nutritionists, architects, engineers, budget and management specialists, industrial designers, child psychologists, gerontologists, and educationists. Many specialists outside of home economics have an interest in research related to food, shelter, clothing, recreation, and protection, but it is often the home economists who apply their findings and recommendations to the house and family.

Among home economists across the country, there is a sense of urgency that the mass of accumulated information be put to use, especially in areas of desperate need. In the past the U. S. Department of Agriculture has provided the financial support for much of the home economics research and extension work. As a result, many projects and services have been closely related to farm homes. City homes and homes in the back country of rural America have received some attention, but not their proportionate share. The McGrath report of 1968 forcefully describes the immediate need for putting home economics practices to use in homes of the underprivileged throughout the country and especially in the cities. "How is it," Dr. McGrath asks, "that in the final third of the twentieth century, in the most affluent society in the world and within blocks of famous medical centers and educational institutions, such pitiful misunderstanding of human health and nutrition exists? How has information about food values and diet failed to reach these people? . . . Many home economists—like their associates in public health, social welfare, and counseling services—are aware of these problems and seek to overcome them. They are asking why the field of home economics cannot play a more active role in the solution of social problems."*

In the coming years, home economics extension must not only keep pace with the rapid tempo of change in our society but must also adjust to what is predicted to be a continuing shift from rural to urban environments. Extension planning, at both the national and local levels, has shown excellent flexibility and foresight in focusing attention on the home as a fundamental unit of community and nation, but means must be found to expand services to all in this country who need them. The place of home economics in the expanding role of American aid and technology in international life must also be recognized and acted upon.

From its first seemingly elementary but significantly basic beginnings, the home economics movement has spread around the world. In all countries today, I feel sure, there is some acceptance of the idea that the family is the basic social unit and that a country never rises above its homes. Enlightened leaders in developing nations realize that the improvement of homelife is essential to improvement of the national culture. Help from the United Nations, from

---

* Earl J. McGrath, "The Changing Mission of Home Economics," *Journal of Home Economics*, Vol. 60, No. 2, February 1968, pages 85-92. This article summarizes the forthcoming complete report prepared by the Institute of Higher Education at Columbia University and published by the Teachers College Press.

the governments of the United States and other countries, and from privately supported foundations, missionary groups, and other philanthropic agencies, I am happy to predict, will continue to aid in introducing or in improving the quality of homemaking education in these developing countries. Volunteers, both experienced and inexperienced, will go out over the globe, dedicating their skills and lives to making more wholesome the homes of all mankind.

I feel a deep sense of gratitude in having witnessed the beginnings, development, and world-wide expansion of the home economics movement and in having had a part in it. At this point in my adventures as a home economist, two verses I have often quoted to students express my feelings:

> Rest is not quitting
>   The busy career;
> Rest is the fitting
>   Of self to one's sphere.
>
>   .   .   .   .
>
> 'Tis loving and serving
>   The highest and best;
> 'Tis onwards, unswerving—
>   And that is true rest.

Appendix

Notes and Acknowledgments

IN ITS FIRST ONE HUNDRED YEARS the institution now known as Oregon State University had several different names. We have used four of them to refer to it in particular periods: Corvallis College in the earliest years, Oregon Agricultural College (OAC) from the time the state began to assist in its support until the mid-1920's, Oregon State College (OSC) from 1924 to 1961, and Oregon State University (OSU) from 1961 onward.

In referring to individual women, we have used either the maiden name or married name, whichever seemed most appropriate for the period under discussion. Occasionally, a young woman is identified by her maiden name followed by her later married name in parentheses. Place names are usually given as they were known at the time under discussion if different from present names. In some cases we have included the present name in parentheses following a place name that might not be identified easily otherwise. Other spellings—such as *Catalogue* and *Catalog*—also follow the orthography of the period.

Many people have provided much-appreciated assistance in preparing the manuscript for this book. Some of them and their particular contributions are acknowledged in the notes on individual chapters below. Others applied their special knowledge and skills to the book as a whole. The late E. R. Jackman read all of an early draft and gave excellent criticism and guidance for rewriting. Dean Emeritus Marie Dye of Michigan State University and Lawrence K. Hall, a former YMCA executive, read a later draft and made valuable suggestions which have been incorporated. Dr. Eunice E. Wallace and Dr. Gertraude C. Wittig read the entire manuscript with deep perception and provided detailed evaluations that helped shape the final draft. Emma B. Raymond gave early and continuing assistance. Mary de Garmo Bryan added helpful comments. Three student typists, Cheryl Nakamoto (Pershall), Cheryl Miller, and Janice Brownell, did their part with an uncommon amount of sincerity and dedication. At times this book seemed like a community project, and we are indebted to the dean and department heads of the School of Home Economics and others far too numerous to mention for their reminiscences, guidance, and encouragement.

The map on page 147 and illustrations on pages 99, 114, and 210 were drawn by Cathrine Davis Young.

CHAPTER ONE: The First Day

The late Mary Bowman Hull, Clytie May Workinger, and Ruth McNary Smith Clark, all of whom the author met her first day in Oregon, provided details and made helpful suggestions in the preparation of this chapter. Dr. Helen Gilkey and her sister Beulah also gave assistance.

393

CHAPTER TWO: Early Life in Missouri

The author's sisters, Ada Milam Cockefair and Lottie Milam Vaughn, her nephew Robert Scott Miner, Jr., her niece Elinor Hanson McKee, and Marie Blees Lohmeyer read this chapter in manuscript, made corrections, and added significant details.

The Biblical quotation written in the Testaments is from Proverbs 3:5-6.

CHAPTER THREE: University of Chicago

Sources especially useful or quoted in this chapter include:

Scholastic record of Ava Bertha Milam from June 15, 1906, to Summer Quarter 1927, provided by the Registrar of the University of Chicago, February 11, 1966.

Annual Register of the University of Chicago, 1908-09; 1909-1910. University of Chicago Press.

Milton Mayer, "Young Man in a Hurry," (pamphlet) published by the University of Chicago Alumni Association, 1957.

Upton Sinclair, *The Jungle.* New York: Grosset and Dunlap, 1906.

Catharine E. Beecher and Harriet Beecher Stowe, *The American Woman's Home: or Principles of Domestic Science.* New York: J. B. Ford and Co., 1869, p. 13.

Lake Placid Conference on Home Economics, *Proceedings* 1899-1908. Lake Placid Club, Essex Co., New York.

Isabel Bevier and Susannah Usher, *The Home Economics Movement,* Part I. Boston: Whitcomb and Barrows, 1906.

Flossie Caroline Budewig, "Origin and Development of the Home Economics Idea," unpublished dissertation accepted by the Graduate School of George Peabody College for Teachers, 1957.

Marion Talbot, *The Education of Women.* Chicago: University of Chicago Press, 1910.

Hazel T. Craig, edited by Blanche M. Stover, "The History of Home Economics," (pamphlet) published by *Practical Home Economics,* New York, 1945.

Journal of Home Economics
   "Lake Placid Conference on Home Economics 1899-1908" Vol. 1, No. 1 (1909), p. 3
   "Organization and First Meeting American Home Economics Association," including Ellen H. Richards' inaugural remarks, Vol. 1, No. 1 (1909), pp. 22-42
   Biographical sketches of elected officers, Vol. 1, No. 1 (1909), pp. 86-91
   "The Social Significance of the Home Economics Movement" by Ellen H. Richards, Vol. 3, No. 2 (1911), pp. 117-125
   "The Death of Mrs. Ellen H. Richards" Vol. 3, No. 2 (1911), p. 213
   "Mrs. Richards' Relation to the Home Economics Movement" by Isabel Bevier, Vol. 3, No. 3 (1911), pp. 214-216
   "The University of Chicago" by Marion Talbot, Vol. 3, No. 4 (1911), pp. 374-375

CHAPTER FOUR: Oregon Pioneers

Wallis Nash's tribute to Dr. Margaret Snell quoted at the chapter opening is from *A Lawyer's Life on Two Continents,* p. 207.

Much of the information for this chapter comes from publications of Oregon State University and documents in the OSU Archives. Mrs. Harriet L. Moore was especially helpful in providing source material and in reading the manuscript. Mrs. Sally Jackman Wilson screened the files for photographs and data. Lillian Schroeder Van Loan's unpublished dissertation, "Historical Perspectives of Oregon State College," (Graduate School, Oregon State College, 1959) contains helpful background and source material;

President Arnold's quotation comes from that source. Mrs. Henry Snell also provided valuable assistance for this chapter.

Wallis Nash and his wife, Louisa Desborough Nash, who stimulated interest in establishing a professorship of Household Economy and Hygiene at Oregon Agricultural College and in obtaining the appointment of Dr. Margaret Snell, had immigrated to Oregon from England in 1879. By profession a lawyer, Mr. Nash had visited Oregon years previously representing British investors who had helped finance railroad construction from Yaquina Bay over the Coast Range into the Willamette Valley. He took up a homestead in the Little Rock Creek Valley in the heart of the Coast Range a few miles from the communities of Summit and Nashville. The 1880 Census for Summit Precinct, Benton County, enumerates Mr. and Mrs. Nash, sons Wallis Gifford, Arthur Henry, and Percival, and daughter Dorothea. The family later moved to Corvallis, where sons Darwin and Roderic were born. Percival graduated from OAC in 1893. Dorothea received a Bachelor of Household Economy degree in 1895. Darwin and Roderic also attended OAC but did not receive degrees. Mr. Nash helped organize the Corvallis and Eastern Railroad Company that planned a railroad from Corvallis across the Willamette Valley and over the Santiam Pass into Central Oregon, an enterprise that became bankrupt before completion. He was active in many civic affairs. He helped build the Episcopal Church on Seventh and Jefferson streets in Corvallis and served as its organist. He was a member of the OAC Board of Regents from 1886 to 1898, much of the time serving as Secretary. He and his eldest son, Gifford, toured the valley giving musical concerts. In 1897, the family moved to Portland where Mr. Nash was an editorial writer for the *Oregon Journal* and was President of the Board of Trade from 1906 to 1909. He moved back to the ranch in Little Rock Creek Valley in 1921 and died in 1926 at age 89. Books written by Wallis Nash include:

Oregon: There and Back in 1877. London: Macmillan and Company, 1878.

Oregon: Its Climate, People, and Productions. London: Edward Stanford, 1878

Two Years in Oregon. New York: D. Appleton and Company, 1882

The Settler's Handbook to Oregon. Portland: J. K. Gill Company, 1904

A Lawyer's Life on Two Continents. Boston: R. G. Badger (The Gorham Press), 1919.

Copies of thirteen letters from Wallis Nash to Dr. Snell are contained in the Regent's Letterbook, State Agricultural College, 1880-1890, pp. 79-343.

Some records of Miss Snell's life give October 1844 as her birth date, but the date given in this chapter, November 11, 1843, is the one written, apparently in her handwriting, in a birthday book owned by Mabel Pernot.

Portrait and Biographical Record of the Willamette Valley, Oregon (Chicago: Chapman Publishing Company, 1903) pp. 1344-1345, gives what is presumably an authentic sketch of Miss Snell's life. It does not give her birth date and makes no reference to her having attended Pratt Institute. Other accounts and memories of former students indicate that she did attend Pratt Institute in New York, although they are vague as to the date. The records of Pratt Institute indicate that a "Margaret C. Comstock" enrolled for a cooking course from January to April, 1889. Since Miss Snell's middle name was Comstock, we have assumed that either the registrar failed to record her full name or that Miss Snell did not use her full name in registering.

The statement of purpose of the Department of Household Economy and Hygiene is from the *Annual Catalogue of the State Agricultural College of the State of Oregon for 1889-1890,* pp. 16-17.

The lines from Shakespeare paraphrased by V. Esther Simmons are from *Julius Caesar,* Act V, Scene V, line 73.

The quotation from Carrie A. Lyford is from her speech at the 60th Anniversary Celebration for the School of Home Economics, 1950.

A more complete description of the courses as finally organized by Dr. Snell may be found on pages 86-88 of the *Annual Catalogue of the Agricultural College of the State of Oregon for 1906-1907.*

The houses designed and built by Dr. Snell, still standing at this writing, are located at 865 Jackson Street and at 2127 Monroe Street in Corvallis. In her last will and testament, dated June 29, 1923, she gives the names of the apartments on Monroe Street as East Hillside, Lower West Hillside, and Upper West Hillside, and the two houses north of the apartments as Bryerly and Tento. These she bequeathed to nephews and nieces. The lots on the corner of Monroe and Twenty-Third Streets she bequeathed to the Wardens and Vestry of the Church of the Good Samaritan (Episcopal), who later sold them to the First Presbyterian Church of Corvallis. The Presbyterians built Westminister House, their student center, on this property. Much later, the St. Mary's Catholic Church acquired Bryerly and some of the other property for the Newman Club student center.

The quotation from *The Orange,* student yearbook, is from Vol. 2, p. 6.

Margaret Wiley Marshall's article on Miss Snell, "A Western Parable," appeared in the *Journal of Higher Education,* Vol. 25 (March 1964), p. 130.

Dean Robert C. Osborne of Pratt Institute provided information about Dr. Snell and former Pratt students and staff members who taught at OAC in letters dated April 1, April 20, and August 26, 1966.

CHAPTER FIVE: The First Year

Quotations in this chapter are from letters from Winnifred Turner Loos, March 30, 1950, and Edith Allworth Metcalf, March 29, 1950; from the OAC *Catalogue* for 1911-1912, page 22, and *passim;* and from newspapers: *Oregon Daily Journal* and Salem *Capital Journal,* December 8, 1911, and Salem *Daily Oregon Statesman,* December 9, 1911.

The first editions of "Camp Cookery" were published as OAC College Bulletins No. 65, June 1912, and No. 76, May 1913. The commercial edition was published by the J. K. Gill Company, Portland, Oregon, 1918.

The authors wish to acknowledge assistance provided by the people who helped prepare or read the manuscript for this chapter, including among others, Mr. and Mrs. Fred Plympton, Ruth McNary Smith Clark, Dr. Edward K. Vaughan, Dr. Walter Covell, Margaret Covell Kinne, Billie Reynolds Hayes and other members of the Kerr family, Dr. Helen M. Gilkey and Mrs. George Hyslop (founding members of the College Folk Club), Mrs. Irwin Harris, Miriam Macpherson Holman, and Mrs. W. E. Lawrence.

CHAPTER SIX: Home Economics Extension

Sources used in this chapter include:
Frank L. Ballard, "The Oregon State University Federal Cooperative Extension Service, 1911-1965," mimeographed manuscript completed in May 1965.
Flora Rose, "A Page of Modern Education: Forty Years of Home Economics at Cornell University," *Fifteenth Annual Report of the New York State College of Home Economics,* 1940. The quotation at the beginning of the chapter comes from page 145 of this report.

Oregon Agricultural College Bulletins No. 45 "Poultry Contest" by James Dryden; No. 72 "Industrial Contests for Oregon Boys and Girls" by H. D. Hetzel; No. 97, same title as previous item, by P. L. Griffin; No. 193 "Stitches, Seams, and Sewing Processes" by Helen Cowgill; and No 194 "Home Economics Clubs" by Henrietta W. Calvin.

Extension Home Economics Focus, prepared by the Home Economics Subcommittee on Organization and Policy, American Association of Land-Grant Colleges and State Universities, November 1966. This publication provides an excellent outline and summary of the current philosophy and policies of home economics extension.

Esther A. Taskerud, Azalea Sager, Mabel Clair Mack, and other members and former members of the home economics extension staff gave assistance in assembling the material for this chapter, reading the manuscript, and adding useful suggestions.

CHAPTER SEVEN: Two Deans

The lines at the beginning of the chapter are from Sarah Louise Arnold, "Morning Prayer," written at sunrise on Great Salt Lake, December 9, 1919.

Dean Henrietta W. Calvin is quoted from *Biennial Report of the Board of Regents of Oregon Agricultural College, 1910-1912,* pp. 31-37, and the *Biennial Report 1912-1914,* pp. 60-65.

The extension publications mentioned were published in the Oregon Agricultural College Bulletin, Series 1, numbers 57A, 58, 65, 76, 77, 83, 84, 85, 89, 151, 155, 222.

The *Journal of Home Economics* published the following articles by and about Mrs. Calvin: "Bulletins on Education for the Home," Vol. 7 (October 1915), p. 426; "Some Administrative Problems in Home Economics in the Public Schools," Vol. 9 (May 1917), p. 199; "Extension Work," Vol. 9 (December 1917), p. 565; "Philadelphia Trade Classes in Home Economics," Vol. 23 (July 1931), p. 637; "Home Economics Exhibits," Vol. 18 (June 1926), p. 321. An article in Vol. 23 (July 1931), p. 713, gives a brief biographical sketch of Mrs. Calvin, and Vol. 39 (November 1947), p. 563, carries an article by Margaret M. Justin entitled "Henrietta Willard Calvin: A Tribute."

Dean Arnold's address at Cleveland and her previous inaugural address are published in full in the *Journal of Home Economics,* Vol. 6, 1914, pp. 421-429; and Vol 5, 1913, pp. 317-325. The quoted passage comes from page 324. Her 1903 paper is entitled "Training and Certification of Teachers in Household Economics," in Lake Placid Conference *Proceedings of the Fifth Annual Conference,* Boston, 1903, p. 11. Dean Arnold's niece, Sarah Louise Arnold, read the manuscript and provided pertinent details.

CHAPTER EIGHT: Tearoom at the Fair

Frank Morton Todd's monumental work, *The Story of the Exposition,* (New York: G. P. Putman's Sons, 1921) provided a primary source for details of the Panama-Pacific International Exposition. Chapter LXI, "Oregon's Parthenon," in Vol. 3, pages 331-333, includes exterior and interior photographs of the Oregon Building and this comment by Mr. Todd on page 332: "The building contained a very fine café, conducted by young ladies of the Oregon College of Agriculture."

The first quoted dispatch by Anne Shannon Monroe was published in the Corvallis *Gazette-Times,* March 15, 1915. The long quotation is from the Portland *Sunday Oregonian,* July 25, 1915.

Letters and conversations with many who participated in the Tearoom at the Fair helped round out this chapter. Katharine McDermott MacCosham wrote on May 10, 1966; Lorene Parker Whelpton on May 23, 1966; Mylius L. Shoemake on April 28, 1966; Edna Mills Ricker on May 6, 1966; Agnes Redmond Miller on May 9, 1966; and Alice Butler Marsh and Edith Crockatt Strain in 1966. Ruth Smith Clark and W. Frank Groves provided useful reminiscenses.

The articles by Ava B. Milam appeared in the *Ladies' Home Journal,* Vol. 22 (February 1916), p. 49; *Industrial-Arts Magazine,* Vol. 5 (1916), pp. 160-163; and *Journal of Home Economics,* Vol. 8 (May 1916), p. 238.

CHAPTER NINE: New Horizons

The letter from a former student in France and other information about Mrs. Ida A. Kidder and her new building are quoted from William H. Carlson, *In a Grand and Awful Time* (Corvallis: Oregon State University Press, 1967), pp. 136-137.

A copy of the tape from which Dr. Eric Englund is quoted is on file in the William Jasper Kerr Library at Oregon State University. A transcription of it may be found in Lillian Schroeder Van Loan's unpublished dissertation, "Historical Perspectives of Oregon State College" (Graduate School, Oregon State College, 1959), pp. 266-275.

CHAPTER TEN: Expansion

Alice Ravenhill is quoted from an article cited in the *Biennial Report of the Regents of Oregon Agricultural College, 1914-1916,* p. 90. Other information on Miss Ravenhill comes from Miss Charlotte S. Black, former head of home economics at the University of British Columbia, and from Miss Ravenhill's autobiography, *Alice Ravenhill—The Memoirs of an Educational Pioneer* (Toronto and Vancouver: J. M. Dent and Sons, Ltd., 1951), especially chapter 19.

The quotations from the *Biennial Report of the Regents of Oregon Agricultural College, 1916-1918* are found on pages 51 and 56.

The quotation from Henry C. Sherman, *Chemistry of Food and Nutrition,* is from the second edition (New York: The Macmillan Company, 1918), p. 398.

An article by Elizabeth Alice Cameron, a graduate assistant in home management, in the *Journal of Home Economics* (Vol. 32, 1940, pp. 301-302) outlines one study conducted in planning a home management house.

Jessamine Chapman Williams, a native of New York State, graduated from the State Normal School in Brockport, New York, in 1901 and from Teachers College, Columbia University, in 1906. After graduate work at Cornell University and Yale University, she received a master's degree from Columbia in 1921. She met her future husband, Richard Williams, at Cornell. She taught at Sweet Briar College in Virginia, Oklahoma A and M College, and University of Arizona before coming to Oregon State College as head of the Department of Foods and Nutrition in 1923. She was an active member of the American and Oregon Home Economics Associations. She helped found the Oregon Nutrition Council, the first state council of this type in the country. She was a member of Phi Kappa Phi, Omicron Nu, and Sigma Xi. A bequest left by Mr. and Mrs. Williams made possible the Jessamine C. Williams Lecture Series instituted at Oregon State University in October 1967.

CHAPTER ELEVEN: The AHEA

Zelta Feike Rodenwold provided excellent advice on the preparation of the manuscript of this chapter.

Sources used include:

Keturah E. Baldwin, *The AHEA Saga* (Washington: American Home Economics Association, 1949) and the 1955 supplement edited by Mary Hawkins. The quotation on Mildred Chamberlain and the Betty Lamp design comes from page 108 of this source.

Journal of Home Economics, Vol. 14 (1922), gives the report of the 1922 meeting in Corvallis. Quotations come from pages 522 and 528.

Helen Lee Davis, "Report of the School of Home Economics," *Biennial Report of the Board of Regents 1920-1922* (Corvallis: Oregon Agricultural College, 1923), pp. 48-49.

Dorothy Sherrill Miller, "Highlights from the Heritage of the Oregon Home Economics Association," manuscript of a talk presented at a meeting of the OHEA in Eugene, Oregon, April 14-15, 1967.

CHAPTER TWELVE: China

Letters the author wrote home to family and friends provide the basic source material for this chapter. Some of the early editing of these letters was done by Zelta Feike Rodenwold. Mrs. Albert N. Steward (Oregon Mother of the Year, 1967) read the manuscript and made valuable suggestions.

The Corvallis *Gazette-Times* (February 22, 1922) reported Dr. Harry W. Luce's Convocation lecture.

John Leighton Stuart, *Fifty Years in China* (New York: Random House, 1954), provided useful source material on the founding and early development of Yenching University.

"A Great Man," editorial in *The Delineator* (Vol. 54, 1924, p. 1), describes the life and achievements of Dr. L. Emmett Holt, the baby specialist.

CHAPTER THIRTEEN: Return from China

The committee to plan furnishing for the main lounge, men's lounge, women's lounge, and concourse of the Memorial Union included Leo Fairbanks, head of the Art Department; Roy R. Clark, an alumnus of the School of Engineering, and his wife Ruth McNary Smith Clark, an alumna of the School of Home Economics and former staff member; Major Edward C. Allworth, alumni secretary, and his wife Peggy Allworth.

The report of the Land Grant College Survey was published as U.S. Office of Education Bulletin Number 9, Washington, D.C., U.S. Government Printing Office, 1930.

Ava B. Milam, *A Study of the Student Homes in China,* was published as Number 10 in Studies of the International Institute of Teachers College, Columbia University, New York, 1930.

CHAPTER FOURTEEN: Home Economics Research

Isabel Bevier's description of Ellen H. Richards' philosophy of research may be found in the *Journal of Home Economics,* Vol. 3 (1911), p. 214.

Biennial Report of the Board of Regents, Oregon Agricultural College, 1914-1916
(Corvallis, 1917), outlines early research work on pages 87 and 91.

Station Bulletin 124, Oregon Agricultural College Experiment Station, Department of Home Economics, "Comparative Cooking Qualities of Some of the Common Varieties of Apples Grown in Oregon" by Ava B. Milam and Harriet B. Gardner (Corvallis, February 1915), gives the details of Miss Gardner's research project.

The first quotation by Maud Wilson comes from the *Oregon State Monthly,* April 1931, page 12.

Results of Miss Wilson's first research project were published in OSC Station Bulletin 256, "Uses of Time by Oregon Farm Homemakers," November 1929. Excerpts appeared in the *Journal of Home Economics* in Vol. 20 (1928), p. 735; Vol. 22 (1930), pp. 735, 832, and 836; and Vol. 24 (1932), pp. 10 and 101; also in *Rural America,* February 1930; *Farmer's Wife Magazine,* October 1930; *Oregon Grange Bulletin,* April 1930; and seven mimeographed USDA circulars, and in an extension bulletin.

Results of Miss Wilson's research on the family home were published in OSC Station Bulletins SB 320, "Planning the Willamette Valley Farmhouse for Family Needs," October 1933; SB 348, "Standards for Working-Surface Heights and Other Space Units of the Dwelling," with Evelyn H. Roberts and Ruth Thayer as co-authors, June 1937; SB 356, "The Willamette Valley Farm Kitchen," August 1938; SB 369, "House Planning Ideas of Oregon Rural Women," with Laura Wells as co-author, February 1940; Station Circular 131, "Planning the Kitchen," January 1939; and SC 134, "A Set of Utensils for the Farm Kitchen," with Helen E. McCullough as co-author, March 1940; and Extension Bulletin 504, "Farm Kitchen Planning," August 1937.

Miss Wilson's research in standards for working surface heights was published in OSC Station Bulletins SB 445, "Considerations in Planning Kitchen Cabinets," November 1947; SB 446, "Patterns for Kitchen Cabinets," November 1947; and SB 482, "A Guide for the Kitchen Planner," September 1950.

Two U.S. Department of Agriculture publications that reported Miss Wilson's work were USDA Miscellaneous Publication No. 322, "Housing Requirements of Farm Families in the United States," February 1939; and Farmers' Bulletin No. 1865, "Closets and Storage Spaces," November 1940.

In addition to those listed above, the *Journal of Home Economics* published articles by Miss Wilson in Vol. 27 (1935), pp. 152-158; Vol. 29 (1937), pp. 361-366; and Vol. 32 (1940), pp. 321-329.

Other Station Bulletins and Station Technical Bulletins published by the OSC Agricultural Experiment Station dealing with home economics research include: SB 283, "Baking of Pears," by Agnes Kolshorn, June 1931; SB 494, "Freezing Cooked and Prepared Foods," by Ruth C. Miller and Agnes M. Kolshorn, January 1951; STB 12, "A Study of Ascorbic Acid Metabolism of Adolescent Children," by Clara A. Storvick, Margaret L. Fincke, Jeanne Perkins Quinn, and Bessie L. Davey, December 1947; STB 18, "Ascorbic Acid Requirements of Older Adolescents," by Clara A. Storvick, Bessie L. Davey, Ruth M. Nitchals, Ruth E. Coffey, and Margaret L. Fincke, May 1950; STB 19, "Dental Caries Experience Among Selected Population Groups in the State of Oregon," by Demetrios M. Hadjimarkos, Clara A. Storvick, and June H. Sullivan, May 1950; STB 45, "Variation in Dental Caries Experience Among Children of Five Western States," (A Western Regional Research Publication) by Gertrude Tank, Nettie C. Esselbaugh, Kathleen P. Warnick, and Clara A. Storvick, June 1959; STB 60, "Dough Variation and Bread Quality," by Emagene Faye Veal and Andrea Mackey, March 1962.

The principal publication of the flax research project was SM 58:1, "Weaving with Linen," by Joan Patterson, May 1958. It contains full-color illustrations of some of Miss Patterson's work.

In addition to bulletins published by Oregon State University, scientific and professional journals have published the results of OSU home economics research in a quantity too great to list here.

CHAPTER FIFTEEN: Around the World

The quotation at the chapter opening was attributed to Theodore Roosevelt by a British minister the author heard preach in Hong Kong.

A principal source of material for this chapter is the script of a series of eight half-hour talks the author prepared for broadcasting over radio station KOAC in the spring of 1933. Ruth Gill Hammond and her daughter Carolyn read the manuscript of the chapter and provided significant suggestions and additions.

Sources used include:

John Leighton Stuart, *Fifty Years in China* (New York: Random House, 1954).

Harry Emerson Fosdick, *A Pilgrimage to Palestine* (New York: Macmillan, 1927).

Bertha Spafford Vester, *Our Jerusalem, an American Family in the Holy City, 1881-1949* (Garden City, New York: Doubleday and Company, 1950).

Bertha Spafford Vester, *Flowers of the Holy Land,* with biographical sketch by Lowell Thomas and an introductory note by Norman Vincent Peale (Kansas City, Missouri: Hallmark Cards, Inc., 1962).

Bertha Spafford Vester, articles in the *National Geographic Magazine,* December 1952, p. 847, and December 1964, p. 828.

CHAPTER SIXTEEN: Commencement

Biennial Report, Oregon State System of Higher Education 1931-32 (Salem: Oregon State Board of Higher Education, 1933), outlines the steps taken to organize the new system of higher education (p. 5), elimination of courses (p. 14), fiscal problems (p. 23), voluntary salary reduction (pp. 102-103), and organization of home economics (pp. 16, 91, 105, 116-117).

Oregon State College catalogs of this period also provided useful reference material. The quotation comes from the 1934-35 *Catalog*, page 277.

Recipients of the AHEA International Scholarships, 1934 to 1955, are listed in *The AHEA Saga* by Keturah E. Baldwin (Washington, D.C.: American Home Economics Association, 1949) p. 105 and in the 1955 supplement edited by Mary Hawkins, pp. 28-29.

The quotation at the end of the chapter is from a letter from Margaret S. Munford, 1967.

CHAPTER SEVENTEEN: Encounter

Letters jointly composed by the author and Alma C. Fritchoff to friends and family at home provide the basic chronology for this chapter.

Mabel A. Wood is quoted from a letter to the author in 1966. Her article, "Teaching in a Foreign Land," and Martha A. Kramer's article, "Home Economics in Yenching University—1940," in *Omicron Nu,* Vol. 20, No. 1 (Fall 1940), provided useful background information on home economics education in China in this period as seen through the eyes of American home economists.

The Proceedings of the Seventh Biennial Conference of the World Federation of Education Associations were published in Tokyo by the World Conference Committee of the Japanese Education Association, 1938, in five volumes. Edgar A. Cockefair's article appears on page 385 and Ava B. Milam's on page 369 of volume 3.

The evacuation of Chinese colleges is recounted in *China After Five Years of War* (New York: Chinese News Service, 1942). See especially page 182.

Quotations from John Leighton Stuart, *Fifty Years in China* (New York: Random House, 1954) come from pages 127, 153, and 156.

CHAPTER EIGHTEEN: Turbulent Decade

Letters written home from New York provided part of the basic narrative for this chapter.

The *Merrill-Palmer Quarterly,* Winter 1956, has several fine articles on the development of the Merrill-Palmer School. Mrs. Palmer's will is quoted from James K. Watkins, "The Merrill-Palmer School's 35th Anniversary Symposium," pages 46-47. See also Mary E. Sweeny, "The Persistence of an Idea," pages 48-49 and the resume of Edna Noble White's life and achievements. *The Merrill-Palmer School: An Account of the First Twenty Years 1920-1940* (Detroit: Published by the School, 1940), has additional background information.

Articles by Ava B. Milam referred to in this chapter appeared in:
   Omicron Nu, Vol. 17 (Spring 1938), pp. 29-33.
   Practical Home Economics, Vol. 16 (Feb. 1938), pp. 54-55, 84, 86.
   National Magazine of Home Economics Student Clubs, Vol. 2 (Feb. 1938).
   Nation's Schools, Vol. 25, No. 3 (March 1940), pp. 28-31.
   University Administrative Quarterly, Vol. 1 (Winter 1942), pp. 106-112.
   Journal of Home Economics, Vol. 36 (1944), pp. 613-616; Vol. 38 (1946),
      pp. 199-200; and Vol. 39 (1947), pp. 205-206.

CHAPTER NINETEEN: Ambassador

The opening quotation comes from the letter in which President Truman accepted Leighton Stuart's resignation as Ambassador to China, December 11, 1952.

This chapter is based on letters from the author to family and friends and memoranda from the trip.

Irene Ho Liu provided the story of her married life in a letter to the author in 1948.

John Leighton Stuart, *Fifty Years in China* (New York: Random House, 1954) is quoted from pages 154, 175, and 286-287.

Isabell Murray Hoyt wrote the article quoted about the trip to west China for the *Christian Science Monitor,* April 20, 1949.

Philip Fugh read the chapter in manuscript in August 1967 and made corrections and valuable suggestions for improvement.

CHAPTER TWENTY: Survey

This chapter is based on the author's letters and *Schools and Colleges in the Philippines: A Report* by Donald P. Cottrell and Ava B. Milam (New York: Foreign Missions Conference of North America, n.d.). Both Dean Cottrell and Dr. Arthur L. Carson read the manuscript and made significant additions and provided appreciated advice.

Articles referred to appeared in the Manila *Times* (September 30, 1948); *The Torch* (October 6, 1948); and *The Philippine Educational Forum,* Vol. 3, No. 3 (1952), p. 41.

CHAPTER TWENTY-ONE: Alma Mater

The files of the School of Home Economics of Oregon State University provided the source material for this chapter.

The student personnel program is described in greater detail in "Administering a School of Home Economics," by Ava B. Milam, *University Administration Quarterly,* Vol. 1 (Winter 1942), pp. 106-112.

The New York *Herald-Tribune* article about Mary Louise Armstrong was published February 19, 1946.

Many people assisted with this chapter and we express appreciation to them. Nearly all of the individual alumnae mentioned or their relatives reviewed the paragraphs concerning them and made corrections if necessary. Among those whose help was especially significant are Mrs. W. M. Adrion, Mrs. Dorothea Cordley Muth, and Mrs. Lucy Schaad.

"A Food Lover's Adventures in Oregon," by E. R. Jackman, was published in the Northwest Magazine section of the Portland *Oregonian,* March 20, 1966, p. 29.

CHAPTER TWENTY-TWO: Syria

This chapter is based on letters from and to the author during the period covered. Dr. Margaret Hockin Harrington and her husband, Dr. James B. Harrington, and Miss Emma Kaufman read it in manuscript, suggested significant amendments, and otherwise provided valuable counsel.

The *Christian Science Monitor* article mentioned was published on December 22, 1951.

The books and articles by Bertha Spafford Vester listed in the notes to chapter fifteen provided useful source material, as did *The Story of FAO* by Gove Hambidge (Princeton, N. J.: Van Nostrand, 1955), especially pp. 126-127.

"Report to the Government of Syria on Home Economics," by Ava B. Milam, Home Economics Specialist, was published as Expanded Technical Assistance Program FAO Report No. 29 and as 50029-52-Syr - "Rural Training, Extension - Syria - Home Economics" 1952 in both English and French.

CHAPTER TWENTY-THREE: Iraq

Dr. Margaret Hockin Harrington and her husband read both early and later drafts of this chapter and made suggestions that resulted in extensive revisions.

Useful sources include:

Hugh L. Keenleyside, *International Aid: A Summary* (New York: James H. Heineman, Inc., 1966). Quoted matter comes from pages 105 and 121.

Doris Elizabeth Hanson, "Home Economists in Overseas Work," a report of an Ed.D. doctoral project (Teachers College, Columbia University, 1964).

Ava B. Milam, "Report to the Government of Iraq on Home Economics," Expanded Technical Assistance Program FAO Report No. 48, Rome, October 1952 (File: 50048-52-Irq-"Education-Iraq-Home Economics" 1952.)

Graham Savage, John B. McClelland, and Ava B. Milam, "Report of a Mission to Iraq," United Nations Educational, Scientific, and Cultural Organization, Paris, 1953.

Dolores Moore Carter, "The Practice House in Afghanistan: A Case Study of Pioneer Work in Home Economics in Kabul," International Cooperation Administration, Washington, D.C., 1955.

"ICA Work in Food and Agriculture," International Cooperation Administration, Washington, D.C., 1961, pp. 26-30, 31-36.

Letters from:

Orpha Spalding (Mrs. Curtis J. Spalding) from Andimeshk, Iran, December 20, 1967

Dolores Bracken Fricke from Tehran, Iran, February 16, 1955

D. Elizabeth Williams from Tehran, Iran, November 11, 1967

Katharine Holtzclaw from Washington, D.C., January 24, 1968

CHAPTER TWENTY-FOUR: J. C. Clark

Lillian Schroeder Van Loan interviewed J. C. Clark in 1956 using a tape recorder. A copy of this tape is on file in the OSU Library. A typescript of this biographical sketch may be found in Dr. Van Loan's unpublished dissertation, "Historical Perspective of Oregon State College" (Graduate School, Oregon State College, 1959).

Mr. Clark wrote a number of comprehensive accounts of his professional activities and narratives of the family's activities. These provided valuable source material.

Letters from friends and colleagues written to the author and quoted in this chapter include ones from: Ethan T. Colton, Sr., April 16 and 18, 1966; Daniel A. Poling, March 20, 1967; Egbert Hayes, April 17, 1966; Lawrence K. Hall, April 3, 1966; Lenning Sweet, April 21, 1966; George A. Fitch, April 21, 1966; March 20, 1967; Clifford W. Petitt, April 19, 1966; Sidney E. Hening, June 6. 1966.

Kenneth Scott Latourette's *World Service* (New York: The Association Press, 1957) is quoted from pages 267-268.

An "In Memoriam" in the OAC student yearbook, *The Orange, 1908*, indicates that Clay Shepard's death occurred on December 4, 1906.

Mr. J. C. Dollar, Resident Director of the American Baptist Assembly, Green Lake, Wisconsin, made suggestions and corrections on the Green Lake section.

Letters and conversations with Emogene Clark Gates, Winston Clark, and Richard Clark helped round out this and the following chapter.

CHAPTER TWENTY-FIVE: Travels with J. C.

Sources cited:

Kenneth Scott Latourette, *World Service* (New York: Association Press, 1957), p. 440. Information contained in letters from Dr. Latourette is also included in this chapter.

Rackham Holt, *Mary McLeod Bethune: A Biography* (Garden City, N. Y.: Doubleday, 1964).

CHAPTER TWENTY-SIX: No Place Like Home

The quotation in the opening paragraph is slightly paraphrased from *The Cost of Living* by Ellen H. Richards (New York: Wiley and Sons, 1900), p. 56.

F. Caroline Budewig, "Origins and Development of the Home Economics Idea," an unpublished dissertation (Graduate School, George Peabody College for Teachers, 1957), pp. 200 and 250-296, discusses the philosophy and leadership of Ellen H. Richards. See also "Mrs. Richard's Relation to the Home Economics Movement," by Isabel Bevier, *Journal of Home Economics*, Vol. 3, 1911, pp. 214-216.

The verses quoted at the end of the chapter are from "True Rest" by John Sullivan Dwight in *The Library of Poetry and Song* compiled by William Cullen Bryant, Vol. II, pp. 557-558.

Home Economics Faculty
Oregon State University
1889-1950

Adams, Tina Feigenson. Graduate Assistant in Household Administration, 1943; Instructor, 1943-1946.

Aller, Florence Dorothy Snowberger. Instructor in Household Administration, 1948-1949.

Anderson, Wilma Hazel. Assistant Director of Dormitories, 1929; Instructor in Institution Economics, 1930-1932.

Angell, Rose Zander. Instructor in Home Nursing, 1910-1911.

Arnold, Mildred Marguerite. Instructor in Foods and Nutrition, 1939—; Assistant Professor, 1943-1946.

Ashe, Maude L. Instructor in Foods and Nutrition, 1943.

Austin, Helen. See Pook.

Avery, Mary Elizabeth. Assistant in Sewing, 1895—; Instructor, 1900-1905.

Baker, Dinah Skinner. Instructor in Foods and Nutrition, 1946-1947.

Baker, Katherine Haskell Read, Assistant Professor of Child Development and Director of Nursery School, 1941—; Associate Professor, 1944—; Professor, 1947—; Head of Department, 1953-1965; Professor Emeritus of Family Life 1965—.

Band, Bernice. See Dailey.

Beers, Ruby Evangeline. Instructor in Household Administration, 1924-1925.

Bertram, Mary Elizabeth. Graduate Assistant in Household Administration, 1934; Instructor, 1935-1936.

Bibee, Georgia Chapman. See Peavy.

Biles, Jessie. Instructor in Household Art, 1918—; Home Economics Extension Specialist in Clothing and Textiles, 1920—; Instructor in Household Arts 1921-1922.

Blazier, Florence E. Associate Professor of Home Economics Education, 1924—; Professor and Head of Department, 1925-1949.

Blundell, Sue Catharine. Instructor in Clothing and Related Arts, 1926-1927.

Boon, Melva Alice. See Kennen.

Botsford, Mildred Harris. Instructor in Household Administration, 1948-1949.

Bowers, Alice Margaret. Professor of Institution Management and Director of Women's Dormitories, 1925-1926.

Bozorth, Inez Valentia. Secretary, School of Home Economics, 1916-1917; Instructor in Domestic Science, 1917—; in Institutional Management, 1918-1919.

Brandon, Marialta. Instructor in Institution Economics, 1946.

Brandon, Vera Haskell. Instructor in Household Administration, 1928—; Assistant Professor, 1934—; Associate Professor, 1936—; Professor, 1937-1955; Acting Department Head, 1934-1936; 1937-1938; Acting Dean, 1950-1954; Associate Dean, 1954-1955; Professor Emeritus of Home Economics, 1955—.

Brandt, Lula May. Instructor in Household Art, 1919-1924.

Brashear, Vivian. Assistant Professor of Household Administration, 1946-1951.

Brew, Margaret Louise. Instructor in Clothing and Related Arts, 1930-1935.

Brier, Dorris Jacqueline. See Jones.

Brooks, Helen Bryce. Professor and Head of Department of Domestic Art, 1911-1917.

Brucher, Olga. Secretary to Dean, 1924-1925; Instructor in Foods and Nutrition, 1928-1929.

Brumbaugh, Madeline. Instructor in Clothing, Textiles, and Related Arts, 1948-1949.

Brundage, Lois. See Lutz.

Burke, June Clark. Instructor in Household Administration, 1944-1945; Assistant Professor, Home Economics Extension, 1950-1952.

Burns, Amelia Earle. Instructor in Household Science, 1920—; in Foods and Nutrition, 1928-1930.

Buxton, Eileen. See Perdue.

Caldwell, Jean Alice Huffsmith. Instructor in Clothing, Textiles, and Related Arts, 1947-1949.

Calvin, Henrietta Willard. Professor of Domestic Science and Dean of the School of Domestic Science and Art, 1912—; of School of Home Economics, 1914-1915.

Campbell, John Carl. Home Economics Extension Specialist in Housing, 1948-1954.

Carpenter, Phyllis May. Research Assistant in Foods and Nutrition, 1943-1944.

Carter (Lohr), Myrtle Mae. Home Economics Extension Specialist in Home Furnishings, 1946-1947;—in Clothing and Textiles, 1946-1949;—in Home Furnishings, 1949-1957.

Case (Greutzmacher), Lucy Ada. Home Economics Extension Specialist in Nutrition, 1924-1947.

Castleberry, Anna. Instructor in Domestic Art, 1915-1916.

Chamberlain, Mildred. Associate Professor of Clothing and Related Arts, 1930-1935; Acting Head of Department, 1932-1933.

Chappell, Bess. State Supervisor of Home Economics, Teacher Trainer, 1924-1929.

Charley, Helen Geneva. Assistant Professor of Foods and Nutrition, 1944—; Associate Professor, 1951—; Professor, 1962—.

Cheney, Laura Jean. Instructor in Domestic Science, 1915-1920.

Clark, Ava Milam. See Milam.

Clark, Ruth McNary Smith. See Smith.

Cleaveland, Laura Mae. Graduate Assistant in Institution Economics, 1940-1941; Assistant Professor, 1946—; Associate Professor, 1962—.

Clinton (Hall), Frances. Teaching Fellow in Foods and Nutrition, 1929-1930; Extension Agent, 1944—; Assistant State Leader of Home Economics Extension, 1946—; State Leader, 1952-1958; Extension Agent, 1961-1964; County Agent Emeritus, 1964—.

Coleman (Warrell), Commery Wallace. Instructor in Home Economics Education, 1946-1948.

Cooley, Esther Belle. Home Economics Extension Specialist in Clothing and Textiles, 1921-1927.

Cordley, Dorothea McLouth. See Muth.

Cowgill, Helen Julia. Supervisor of Girls' Club Work-Extension, 1914—; Assistant State 4-H Club Leader, 1936-1947.

Cruise, Winnona Ethel. Instructor in Household Science, 1919-1921.

Dahlberg, Hatty Roselle. Instructor in Home Economics Education, 1918—; Assistant Professor, 1919—; Associate Professor, 1921—; Professor, 1924; Head of Department, 1922-1924.

Dailey, Bernice Elizabeth Band, Assistant Professor of Clothing, Textiles, and Related Arts, 1936-1940.

Daniels, Miriam Olive. Instructor in Household Administration, 1949-1951.

Davis, Bertha Stewart. Instructor in Domestic Science, 1915—; Assistant Professor of Home Economics Education, 1917—; Associate Professor, 1920-1922.

Davis, Helen Lee. Associate Professor of Household Arts, 1917—; Professor and Head of Department of Clothing, Textiles, and Related Arts, 1919-1930; Vice Dean of the School of Home Economics, 1924-1930.

Deter, Wanda Annette. Instructor in Clothing, Textiles, and Related Arts, 1947-1948.

Diedesch, Marie. Graduate Assistant in Clothing, Textiles, and Related Arts, 1941; Assistant Professor, 1945—; Associate Professor, 1949—.

Dixon, Beryl. Graduate Assistant, 1935; Instructor in Household Administration, 1935-1936.

Dolman, Alice Marks. Instructor in Domestic Science, 1912—; Assistant Professor, 1915-1919.

Du Bois, May. Assistant Professor of Home Economics Education, 1939—; Associate Professor, 1946—; Professor and Head of Department, 1949-1968; Professor, 1968—.

Edaburn, Clara W. Instructor in Clothing, Textiles, and Related Arts, 1939—; Assistant Professor, 1945—; Associate Professor, 1949—; Professor, 1961—; Acting Chairman of Department, 1965-1967; Professor Emeritus, 1968—.

Edbert, Manette Henderson. Instructor in Clothing, Textiles, and Related Arts, 1948-1949.

Eichwith, Blanche. Instructor and Home Demonstration Agent-at-Large, 1935-1937.

Ewing, Ariel Miriam. Instructor in Domestic Art, 1908-1911.

Failyer, Lois. Instructor in Domestic Science, 1911-1912.

Fenner, Dorothy Harstad. Graduate Assistant in Foods and Nutrition, 1940-1941; Instructor, 1948; 1955-1957; 1959-1961.

Feigenson, Tina. See Adams.

Feike, Zelta Fern. See Rodenwold.

Ferguson, Myrtle. Professor of Household Science and Head of Department, 1921-1922.

Fincke, Margaret Louise. Associate Professor of Foods and Nutrition, 1935—; Professor, 1943—; Head of Department, 1944—; Acting Dean, 1963-1965.

Flora, Elizabeth. Instructor in Institutional Management, 1923-1924.

Forest, Ruth Morris. Critic Teacher, 1931—; Assistant State Supervisor of Home Economics Education, 1938-1944.

Francis, Lillian Wiles. Instructor in Domestic Science, 1915-1918.

Freeman (Polkinghorne), Edith Jeffers. Home Economics Extension Specialist in Family Relations, 1946-1954.

Frank, May Caroline. Instructor in Household Administration, 1926-1927; Assistant Professor, 1929-1930.

Fritchoff, Alma Catherine. Instructor in Household Arts, 1918-1922; in Clothing, Textiles, and Related Arts, 1925—; Assistant Professor, 1926—; Associate Professor and Acting Head of Department, 1928—; Professor and Head of Department 1930-1948; Professor Emeritus of Home Economics, 1948—.

Fulmer, Winnifred K. Gillen, Associate Professor, Home Demonstration Agent, 1938—; Professor, State Extension Agent, 1947—; Head Adviser, School of Home Economics, 1958—.

Gardner, Josephine. Assistant Professor of Foods and Nutrition, 1944-1946.

Garrison, Evra Alta. Instructor in Foods and Nutrition, 1930—; Assistant Professor, 1933-1959; Professor Emeritus, 1959—.

Gatton, Dorothy. Associate Professor of Clothing, Textiles, and Related Arts, 1940—; Professor, 1951-1967; Professor Emeritus, 1958—.

Gaylord, Thelma. Home Demonstration Agent, 1930—; Acting State Leader of Home Economics Extension, 1935-1936.

Geiger, Beatrice Jane. Assistant Professor of Foods and Nutrition, 1926—; Associate Professor, 1929-1931.

Gerber, Alice Anne. Instructor in Household Administration, 1949-1950.

Gillett, Grace Patton. Instructor in Domestic Art, 1915-1917.

Gleiser, Fern Willard. Instructor in Institution Economics and Supervisor of Tearoom, 1925-1928; Professor of Institution Management, 1964.

Grant, Phyllis Emogene. Graduate Assistant in Clothing, Textiles, and Related Arts, 1949; Instructor, 1949—; Assistant Professor, 1952—.

Greer (Bridwell), Juliet. Professor of Domestic Science and Dean of the School of Domestic Science and Art, 1908-1911.

Gregg, Bertha Kohlhagen. See Kohlhagen.

Greutzmacher, Lucy Ada Case. See Case.

Guyer, Muriel Jean. Instructor in Institution Economics, 1945-1946.

Hadjimarkos, Demetrios Markos. Research Associate, Home Economics Dental Research, 1947-1952.

Hadwen, Sibylla. Housekeeper, Women's Dormitory, 1913-1916; Preceptress, Waldo Hall, 1916-1921; Professor and Head of Department of Institutional Management and Director of Dormitories, 1921-1926.

Haight, Katherine Barbara. Preceptress of Cauthorn Hall, 1914—; Instructor in Home Nursing, 1919-1932.

Hall, Frances Clinton. See Clinton.

Hall, Irene Sanborn. Assistant Professor of Foods and Nutrition, 1936-1937.

Halverson, Lucile. Instructor in Foods and Nutrition, 1945-1946.

Hammond, Ruth Gill. Assistant Professor of Household Administration, 1936-1939.

Harley, C. Winifred. Acting Professor of Home Economics, 1937-1938.

Harstad, Dorothy. See Fenner.

Hawthorne, Betty Eileen. Instructor in Foods and Nutrition, 1946—; Assistant Professor, 1949—; Associate Professor, 1955—; Professor, 1962—; Dean of the School of Home Economics, 1965—.

Hayes, Lenore Reynolds. Instructor in Clothing, Textiles, and Related Arts, 1946.

Hazen, Winifred. Assistant Instructor in Institutional Management, 1921; Tearoom Manager, 1922.

Heiner, Mary Koll. Instructor in Household Science, 1917-1919; Acting Associate Professor in Household Administration, 1935.

Hitchcock, Katherine Monell. Instructor in Domestic Art, 1913-1915.

Hodgson, Marion. See Oliver.

Hollandsworth, Helen Lorena. Instructor in Home Economics Education, 1948-1953.

Holman, Miriam Elizabeth Macpherson. Instructor in Foods and Nutrition, 1944—; Assistant Professor, 1946-1950; 1962-1965.

Hoppe, Gertrude Nerissa. Research Assistant in Nutrition, 1942-1944.

Huffsmith, Jean. See Caldwell.

Hull, Dorothy Eidem. Instructor in Foods and Nutrition, 1944.

Hunter, Melissa. Instructor in Institutional Management, 1919—; Professor of Institution Economics and Head of Department and Director of Dormitories, 1926-1944.

Jacobson, Elsie Elvera. Instructor in Clothing and Related Arts, 1929-1930.

Jefferson, Ruth Elizabeth. Instructor in Household Administration Nursery School Program, 1945-1946.

Jenks, Forena. Assistant in Home Management and Home Economics Radio Service, 1930; Home Economics Extension Specialist in Home Management, 1939.

Jensen, Elvira Batilda. Assistant Professor of Clothing, Textiles, and Related Arts, 1945-1946.

Jensen, Frances. Instructor in Foods and Nutrition, 1946.

Jensen, Izola Dorothy. See Parker.

Johnson, Alma Grace. Instructor in Domestic Science, 1915—; Assistant Professor, 1917—; Associate Professor, 1919—; Professor, 1922-1933; Head of Household Administration Department, 1919-1933.

Johnson, Gladys Viola. Instructor in Millinery, 1924—; in Clothing, Textiles, and Related Arts, 1927-1930.

Jonasson, Frances Maurine Wright. State Supervisor and Teacher Trainer in Vocational Home Economics, 1929-1935. Instructor in Household Administration, 1936-1937.

Jones, Alice Harriet. Instructor in Clothing, Textiles, and Related Arts, 1949-1950.

Jones, Dorris Jacqueline Brier. Instructor in Household Administration, 1937—; Home Demonstration Agent, 1940-41.

Joyce, Alice Virginia. Assistant State Leader in Boys' and Girls' Club work, 1918.

Judd, Dorothy. Instructor in Household Administration, 1936-1937.

Kalbus, Minnie. Instructor in Domestic Science, 1916-1918; Home Demonstration Agent, 1918; Assistant State Leader in Home Economics Extension, 1919-1921.

Kay, Helen Boak. Instructor in Household Art, 1924-1925.

Keatley, Dorothy. Assistant in Domestic Art, 1913-1915.

Keiffer, Mary. Instructor in Household Science, 1919-1920.

Kennen, Melva Alice. Instructor in Household Administration, 1947-1949.

Kennedy, Ruth Henrietta. See Tartar.

Kirkendall, Lester Allen. Associate Professor of Family Life, 1949—; Professor, 1955—.

Kleinsorge, Elizabeth Wiley. Associate Professor of Clothing, Textiles, and Related Arts, 1937-1942.

Klippstein, Ruth Nitchals. Nutritional Chemist, Home Economics Research, 1946—; County Extension Agent, 1948-1950; 1956-1957; Extension Specialist in Foods and Nutrition, 1957-1961.

Kohlhagen, (Gregg) Bertha. State Supervisor and Teacher Trainer in Vocational Home Economics, 1935-1963.

Koll, Mary Elizabeth. See Heiner.

Kolshorn, Agnes. Assistant Professor of Foods and Nutrition, 1929—; Associate Professor, 1939—; Professor and Home Economics Extension Specialist in Nutrition, 1948-1958; Professor Emeritus of Nutrition, 1961—.

Landquist, Virginia. Research Assistant in Nutrition, 1942-1943.

Lane, Lassie. Home Demonstration Agent-at-Large, 1919-1920; Home Economics Extension Specialist in Nutrition, 1919-1921.

Lane (McCullough), Lucy Rocena. Home Economics Extension Specialist in Clothing and Textiles, 1938-1953.

Layton, Lida Meredith. Instructor in Domestic Science, 1911-1912.

Ledbetter, Marie. Instructor in Household Administration, 1946—; in Clothing, Textiles, and Related Arts, 1946—; Assistant Professor, 1950—; Associate Professor, 1959—.

Leech, Esther Vestal. Assistant in Domestic Science and Art, 1911-1912; Preceptress of Women's Dormitory, 1913.

Lewis, Sarah Louise. Instructor in Domestic Science, 1912—; Assistant Professor, 1915—; Associate Professor and Head of Department, 1919-1920.

Little, Erma Holliday. Home Economics Extension Specialist in Family Life Relationships, 1946-1947.

Loe, Edna Mae. Instructor in Household Administration, 1944-1945.

Lohr, Myrtle M. See Carter.

Lowe, Jessie Opal. Instructor in Institution Economics, Supervisor of Memorial Union Dining Service, 1928-1929.

Lutz (Brundage), Lois Aileen. Home Demonstration Agent, 1936-1940; Home Economics Extension Specialist in Home Management, 1940-1946.

Lyford, Carrie Alberta. Assistant in Household Economy and Hygiene, 1896-1898.

MacCloskey, Ruth Hudson. Instructor in Clothing, Textiles, and Related Arts, 1942-1945.

Mack, Mabel Clair. Home Demonstration Agent, 1929—; Assistant Professor, 1931—; Acting State Leader of Home Economics Extension, 1934—; Associate Professor, 1935—; Extension Specialist in Home Management, 1946; Assistant State Leader of Home Economics Extension, 1946-1951; Assistant Director of Extension, 1951-1963; Professor Emeritus, 1963—.

Mackey, Andrea Overman. Instructor in Foods and Nutrition, 1938—; Assistant Professor, 1941—; Associate Professor, 1945—; Professor, 1951—.

Maclay, Eleanor Reed. Assistant Professor of Household Science, 1924-1926.

Mallalieu, Jessalee Ahrens. Home Economics Extension Specialist in Recreation, 1948-1964; Associate Professor Emeritus, 1964—.

Manning, Juanita Chaney. Teaching Fellow in Household Administration, 1930-1931; Instructor, 1931-1932.

Maris (Mockmore, Steinmetz), Buena Margason. Instructor in Household Administration, 1937—; Assistant Professor and Home Economics Extension Specialist in Family Life, 1939-1941. Dean of Women, 1941-1948.

Martilla, Martha Kennedy. Instructor in Institution Economics, 1946-1949.

May, Lula Litten. See Brandt.

McCall, Margaret. Assistant in Domestic Science, 1912—; Instructor, 1913-1914.

McClew, Ann. Supervising Teacher (Instructor) in Home Economics Education, 1937-1940.

McComb, Jessie Dunlavey. Assistant State Leader of Home Economics Extension, 1917—; State Leader, 1919-1930.

Macpherson, Miriam E. See Holman.

McCullough, Helen E. Assistant Professor of Home Economics Research, 1939-1943.

McFaul, Helen. Instructor in Household Art, 1918-1924.

McQuesten, Isabella F. Assistant Professor of Home Economics Education, 1948—; Associate Professor, 1949—.

Mengler, Mary Ruth Turnbull. Assistant Professor of Foods and Nutrition, 1948-1950; 1952-1954.

Merklin, Gayle Timmons. Instructor in Foods, 1946-1949.

Milam (Clark), Ava Bertha. Assistant Professor of Domestic Science, 1911—; Professor, 1916—; Dean of the School of Home Economics, 1917—; Dean and Director of Home Economics, Oregon State System of Higher Education, 1932-1950; Professor Emeritus of Home Economics, 1950—.

Miller, Cora Elizabeth Platt. Instructor in Domestic Art, 1915-1920.

Miller, Ruth Catherine. Research Assistant, 1947. Instructor in Household Administration, 1949.

Minden, Mary Beth. Home Economics Extension Specialist in Home Management, 1947-1958.

Mockmore, Buena. See Maris.

Moore, Barbara. Assistant in Domestic Science, 1912—; Instructor, 1913-1919.

Moore, Christie. Instructor in Domestic Science, 1914-1918.

Moore, Martha Kenney. Instructor in Institution Economics, 1946-1948.

Moore (Smith), Willetta. Instructor in Foods and Nutrition, 1925-1932.

Morehouse, Margaret. Instructor in Domestic Art, 1915—; Assistant Professor of Household Administration, 1927—; in Clothing, Textiles, and Related Arts, 1928-1929.

Morgan, Ethel Pope. Instructor in Household Administration, 1925-1926; in Foods and Nutrition, 1945-1959.

Morse, Maud Mueller. See Walker.

Moser, Ruth Annetta. Graduate Assistant in Clothing, Textiles, and Related Arts, 1946—; Instructor, 1947—; Assistant Professor, 1949—; Associate Professor, 1959—.

Mulhern, Helen. Assistant Professor of Institution Economics and Supervisor of Memorial Union Dining Service, 1944—; Acting Head of Department and Assistant Director of Dormitories, 1948—; Assistant Professor of Institution Management and Head of Department, 1955—; Associate Professor, 1957-1962.

Murray, Marian. Instructor in Home Economics Education, 1946-1947.

Muth, Dorothea Cordley. Instructor in Clothing, Textiles, and Related Arts, 1930-1931; 1935-1939.

Nitchals, Ruth. See Klippstein.

Nye, Claribel. Professor and State Leader of Home Economics Extension, 1930-1935.

Oehler, Eleanor May Spike. Critic Teacher in Home Economics Education, 1930—; Teaching Fellow, 1931; Instructor in Household Administration, 1932—; Assistant Professor, 1936—; Associate Professor, 1938—; Director of Home Management Houses, 1938-1946.

Oliver, Marion Hodgson. Instructor in Household Art, 1921-1925; in Clothing, Textiles, and Related Arts, 1930-1931; 1936.

O'Neale, Lila Morris. Assistant Professor of Household Art, 1919-1926.

Overman, Andrea. See Mackey.

Paddock, Elizabeth Gertrude. Assistant Professor of Child Development and Director of Nursery School, 1939-1941.

Palmiter, Jessie. Instructor and Home Demonstration Agent-at-Large, 1936-1938.

Parker, Izola Jensen. Home Economics Extension Specialist in Recreation, and in Community Social Organization, 1936-1943.

Patterson, James Russell. Associate Professor of Clothing and Related Arts, 1929.

Patterson, Joan. Instructor in Clothing, Textiles, and Related Arts, 1936—; Assistant Professor, 1938—; Associate Professor, 1940—; Professor, 1951—; Home Economics Extension Specialist in Home Management, 1936-1940.

Peabody, Kenneth Earl. Instructor in Clothing, Textiles, and Related Arts, 1949-1950.

Peavy, Georgia Chapman Bibee. Instructor in Institution Economics, 1926—; Assistant Professor and Director of MU Dining Service, 1930—; Head of Department and Director of Dormitories, 1944-1948; Instructor in Foods and Nutrition, 1951-1953.

Peer, Helen. See Robinson.

Perdue (Buxton), Eileen Catherine. Acting Specialist in Clothing and Textiles, 1937—; Home Demonstration Agent-at-Large, 1936-1937.

Peterson, Emmajean Stephens. Supervising Teacher, Home Economics Education, 1941-1942; Instructor in Clothing, Textiles, and Related Arts, 1946-1947.

Peterson, Gladys Loraine. Instructor in Millinery, 1924—; in Household Administration, 1926—; in Clothing and Related Arts, 1927-1928.

Phinney, Julianne Wise. Home Demonstration Agent, 1943—; Assistant Professor of Household Administration and Director of Home Management Houses, 1945-1952.

Pohland-Schilling, Olivia. Assistant in Domestic Art, 1914—; Instructor, 1916-1919.

Pook (Cornelius), Helen Austin. Instructor in Home Economics Education, 1944-1945.

Prentiss, Sara Watt. Instructor in Domestic Science, 1917—; Assistant Professor of Household Administration, 1926—; Professor of Child Development and Parent Education, 1930—; Acting Head of Household Administration Department, 1932-1934; Head of Department, 1936-1952; Professor Emeritus of Child Development, 1952—.

Price, Anna Charlotte. Instructor in Costume Design, 1929—; in Clothing and Related Arts, 1930-1932.

Platt, Cora Elizabeth. See Miller.

Raber, Elta Marie. Assistant in Domestic Art, 1912—; Instructor, 1913-1914.

Rea, Jocelyn. See Skinner.

Read, Katherine Haskell. See Baker.

Reynolds, Lucile Winifred. Associate Professor of Household Administration, 1933-1934.

Rhyne, Edith. Associate Professor of Clothing, Textiles, and Related Arts, 1935-1940; Acting Department Head, 1940.

Rich, Joy Hoerner. Instructor in Home Economics, 1946.

Riedesel, Mildred. Instructor in Foods and Nutrition, 1946-1948 (?).

Robbins, Lulie Wiles. Assistant Professor of Domestic Science and Art, Extension Service, 1913-1914.

Roberts, Vivian Mae. Instructor in Foods and Nutrition, 1937—; Assistant Professor, 1941-1943.

Robinson, Annie Lois. Instructor in Domestic Art, 1912—; Assistant Professor, 1914-1915.

Robinson, Helen Peer. Instructor in Domestic Art, 1914-1918; in Clothing, Textiles, and Related Arts, 1930-1931; 1936-1938.

Rodenwold, Zelta Feike. Secretary to Dean of Home Economics, 1919-1921; Home Economics Extension Specialist in Home Management, 1930-1932; Director of Home Economics Radio Programs, 1932-1944.

Roskie, Gertrude. Assistant Professor (Assistant State Supervisor), 1944-45.

Romtvedt, Alvhild. Assistant in Domestic Science and Art, 1910-1911.

Roth, Evelyn Swaim. See Swaim.

Runkle, Markie Weatherford. Instructor in Clothing, Textiles, and Related Arts, 1946-1947.

Sager, Azalea Linfield. Home Economics Extension Specialist in Clothing, 1932—; Professor of Extension Methods and State Leader of Home Economics Extension, 1936-1952; Professor Emeritus, 1954—.

Sanford, Gertrude Skow. Home Demonstration Agent, 1920—; Agent-at-Large, 1934—; Extension Specialist in Community Social Organization, 1935; Extension Specialist in Recreation, 1935-1936.

Sansom, Amelia Grace. Instructor in Household Administration, 1940-1942.

Saylor, Nelma Laura. Graduate Assistant in Institution Economics, 1939-1940; Instructor and Supervisor of Memorial Union Dining Service, 1940-41.

Scales, Murle. Home Economics Extension Specialist in Clothing. 1947—; State Extension Agent, 1957—.

Schneider, Louise Alberta. Instructor in Domestic Art, 1917-1921; Critic Teacher, 1923-1924.

Schreiner, Dorothy Smith. Assistant in Home Economics Research, 1932.

Seeley, June. Instructor in Domestic Art, 1915-1918.

Seleen, Esther Bertha. Instructor in Domestic Art, 1911-1913.

Seymour, Elizabeth. Supervisor of Tearoom, 1922; Instructor in Institution Management, 1924.

Shank, Dorothy. Professor and Head of Department of Household Science, 1922-1923.

Sinnard, Harriet King. Home Economics Extension Specialist in Clothing, 1930-1931; Instructor in Clothing and Related Arts, 1934-1936; Instructor in Family Life and Home Administration, 1963—; Assistant Professor of Home Management, 1965—.

Skinner, Jocelyn Anne Rea. Instructor in Household Administration, 1946-1949.

Skow, Gertrude Lonette. See Sanford.

Smith, Elmer James. Assistant Professor of Household Administration, 1948.

Smith, Laura Belle. Assistant Professor of Clothing, Textiles, and Related Arts, 1946-1954; 1956; 1959-1961; 1966.

Smith, Natalie Ann. Instructor in Household Administration, 1949-1951.

Smith, Margery May. Home Economics Extension Specialist in Nutrition, 1921-1924.

Smith (Clark), Ruth McNary. Assistant in Domestic Science, 1911; Instructor in Domestic Science, 1911-1912; 1913-1915.

Smith, Willetta. See Moore.

Snell, Margaret Comstock. Professor of Household Economy and Hygiene, 1889—; of Household Science and Hygiene, 1900-1908; Head of Department, 1889-1908.

Spike, Eleanor. See Oehler.

Sprague, Hazel. Assistant Preceptress, Waldo Hall, and Instructor in Household Science, 1920-1922.

Staton, Maryanne Kennedy. Instructor in Household Administration, 1949-1951; Assistant Professor of Family Life, 1958—; Associate Professor of Family Life and Assistant Dean, School of Home Economics, 1966—.

Stainken, Catherine Hedwig. Instructor in Foods and Nutrition, 1937-1938.

Stephens, Emmajean. See Peterson.

Stevens, Blanche Whittier. Instructor in Household Art, 1920-1921.

Storvick, Clara A. Associate Professor of Foods and Nutrition, 1945—; Professor, 1948—; Chairman of Home Economics Research, 1955—; Director, Nutrition Research Institute, 1965—.

Stout, Evelyn Emma. Assistant Professor of Clothing, Textiles, and Related Arts, 1948-1949.

Strickland, Gertrude. Instructor in Household Art, 1920—; Assistant Professor of Clothing, Textiles, and Related Arts, 1936—; Associate Professor, 1946—; Professor and Acting Head of Department, 1948—; Head of Department, 1949-1953.

Struve, Louise Christine. Instructor in Clothing, Textiles, and Related Arts, 1927-1929.

Sullivan, June H. Assistant Research Professor, Home Economics Dental Research, 1946-1949.

Sutherland, Mary Elizabeth. Instructor in Dressmaking, 1905-1908.

Swaim (Roth), Harriet Evelyn. Instructor in Home Economics Education, 1941-1943; Assistant State Supervisor, Home Economics Education, 1945-1946.

Tapscott, Alma Frances. Assistant Professor of Clothing, Textiles, and Related Arts, 1946-1948.

Taskerud, Esther Adelia. Assistant State 4-H Club Leader, 1947—; State Extension Agent, 1954—; State Leader of Home Economics Extension, 1958—; Assistant Director of Extension, 1963—.

Tartar, Ruth Kennedy. Assistant in Household Science, 1920—; Instructor, 1921-1924; in Foods and Nutrition, 1927.

Taylor, Lillian Catherine. Instructor in Household Science, 1919—; in Foods and Nutrition, 1928—; Assistant Professor, 1937-1944.

Thomas (Nichols), Helen Ann. Instructor and Home Demonstration Agent-at-Large, 1937—; County Home Demonstration Agent, 1938-1940.

Thomas, Isabelle Rose. Instructor in Foods and Nutrition, 1941-1942.

Thurston, Flora Martha. Acting Professor of Child Development and Parent Education, 1934—; Professor of Family Life, 1935-1936.

Timmons, Gayle Curinne. See Merklin.

Tobin, Helen Hyde. Instructor in Domestic Art, 1908-1911.

Troeger, Elsie Margaret. Instructor in Institution Economics, 1925.

Tuller, Margaret Huston. Home Economics Extension Specialist in Housing, 1947-1954.

Turley, Anna M. State Leader of Home Economics Extension, 1914-1919; Instructor in Household Science, 1920-1921.

Turnbull, Mary Ruth. See Mengler.

Van Deusen, Myrtie Clark. Instructor in Domestic Science, 1909—; Assistant Professor, 1911.

Van Horn, Edna Marjorie. Assistant Professor of Household Administration, 1939-1940; 1942-1943; 1944—; Associate Professor, 1957—; Professor, 1961-1963; Professor Emeritus of Home Administration, 1963—.

Van Kirk, Mary Standerwick. Instructor in Household Art, 1918—; in Household Administration, 1919—; in Clothing, Textiles, and Related Arts, 1928-1931.

Van Liew, Marion Syddum. Instructor in Domestic Science, 1908—; Assistant Professor, 1910-1911.

Van Syckle, Calla. Instructor and Home Agent-at-Large, Home Economics Extension, 1936-1937.

Vasanoja, Hertta. Supervisor of Tearoom, 1923-1924; Instructor in Institution Management, 1925-1926.

Wait, Bernice Cornelia. Instructor in Household Science, 1921-1925.

Waldo, Clara H. Special Lecturer, Short Course in Household Science, 1908.

Walker (Stepleton), Maud Mueller Morse. Fellow in Household Administration, 1932-1933; Home Economics Extension Specialist in Child Development and Parent Education, 1935-1938; Specialist in Group Development and Sociology, 1956-1959.

Walker, Shirley Aileen. Instructor in Clothing, Textiles, and Related Arts, 1949-1951.

Walsh, Helen Elizabeth. Assistant Professor of Household Administration, 1940-1942.

Ware, Margaret Christian. Instructor in Foods and Nutrition, 1945—; Assistant Professor, 1951-1962; Assistant Professor Emeritus, 1966—.

Warrell, Commery Coleman. See Coleman.

Warren, Evelyn Lee. Instructor in Foods and Nutrition, 1949.

Warrington, Earl W., Professor of Household Administration, 1945-1949.

Weiser, Virginia Ruth. Instructor in Foods and Nutrition, 1949—; Home Demonstration Agent, 1951-1954; Extension Specialist in Foods and Nutrition, 1961-1965.

Weld, Emma Skinner. Instructor in Household Administration, 1919—; Assistant Professor, 1925-1926.

Wells, Donald A. Assistant Professor of Household Administration, 1946-1948.

Wells, Vera. Instructor in Clothing, Textiles, and Related Arts, 1948—; Assistant Professor, 1958—.

Whipple (Goode), Gladys. Critic Teacher, 1918—; Instructor in Home Economics Education, 1920—; in Household Art, 1924—; in Household Administration, 1924-1926.

White, Marjorie Tye. Home Demonstration Agent, 1941-1946; 1950-1952; Home Economics Extension Specialist in Clothing and Textiles, 1946.

Wiggenhorn, Miriam Augusta. Assistant Professor of Household Administration, 1946—; Associate Professor, 1949-1958; Associate Professor of Family Life, 1965—.

Wiley, Elizabeth Cecelia. See Kleinsorge.

Williams (McKenzie), Jean Alyce. Home Economics Extension Specialist in Recreation, 1946-1947.

Williams, Jessamine Chapman. Professor of Household Science, 1923—; of Foods and Nutrition, 1927-1947; Head of Department, 1924-1944; Professor Emeritus of Foods and Nutrition, 1944-1963.

Wilson, Lena Eveline. Instructor in Clothing and Related Arts, 1926.

Wilson, Marjorie Ann. Instructor in Clothing, Textiles, and Related Arts, 1946-1947.

Wilson, Maud Mathes. Professor and Head of Home Economics Research, 1925-1950. Professor Emeritus, 1950—.

Wise, Julianne. See Phinney.

Wood, Mabel Altona. Assistant Professor of Foods and Nutrition, 1930-1932. Professor of Home Economics and Head of Department, University of Oregon, 1932-1965.

Woodruff, Sybil. Instructor in Household Science, 1920-1921.

Wright, Frances M. See Jonasson.

Young, Kathryn Wells. Instructor in Institution Economics, 1949-1951.

Zimmer, Helen. Home Management House Adviser and Instructor in Household Administration, 1944-1946.

Index

Abdullah, king of Jordan assassination, 317, 318, 319, 320, 326
Abel, Mary H., 30, 73
Act of International Development, 329
Adak, Alaska, 244
Adams, Mary H., 293
Addams, Jane, 28, 35, 156, 209
Agency for International Development, 329, 345, 346
Agricultural Experiment Station, research bulletins, 175, 177, 178, 181; see also notes in appendix; Jardine, director, 176, 192; Withycombe, director, 62
Agriculture, School of, 2, 47, 128-129, 165, 203, 238
Agriculture, Ministry of, in Syria, 303, 304
Ahern, Ierne, in Tearoom, 104
air travel, 243, 244, 248, 254, 255, 256, 259, 260, 262, 265, 267, 299, 300, 326, 340, 383
Albany, Oregon, *Democrat*, quoted, 42
Aleppo, Syria, 305, 306, 307, 308, 315
Aleutian Islands, Alaska, 212, 243-244
Allahabad, India, 190, 191
Allen, Mrs. John, 61
Allen, L. J., 4-H club leader, 70
Alter, Neale, in Lebanon, 301-302
alumnae, in Orient 243-250, 264; files, 274-285; conferences for, 285-293; newsletter, 271, 274
American Colony, Jerusalem, 194-196, 320
American Dietetics Association, LeVelle Wood, president, 278; requirements met, 241
American Express Company, 213, 214, 215, 220
American Home Economics Association, v, 109, 179; Betty Lamp symbol, 137; executive secretary, 136, 238; international scholarships, 207, 307; meetings, 84-88, 132-136; organization and development, v, 30-31, 131-132, 137, 379;

presidency, 30-31, 85, 88, 131, 132-133, 136, 280; Mrs. Richards, 30-31, 137, 379
Amidon, Edna, 345
amoebic dysentery, 158
Amman, Jordan, 317
Andrews, Benjamin R., Columbia U., 82, 110, 235; manuscript assistance, 170; retirement, 367; secretary AHEA, 31; summer lecturer, 130; summer tour to Orient, 212, 222, 223
anniversaries, 286-289; 289-293
Apperson, J. T., OAC regent, 38
apple varieties, research, 175, 179
archaeology, 319, 335-336
Armstrong, Dr. Helen M., 275-276
Armstrong, Mary Louise, biographical sketch, 283-284
Arnold, Benjamin L., OAC president, 38
Arnold, Dean Sarah Louise, biographical sketch, 87-88; food conservation,88-89, 111; president AHEA, 84-88, 131; quoted, 79, 85-87
Arnold, Sarah Louise (niece), 91, 209, 373
ascorbic acid, research, 100
Ashby, Sir Eric, 199, 200
Asia Foundation, 330
Associated Country Women of the World, 289
Association of Christian Schools and Colleges, Philippines, 259, 268, 269
Association of Land-Grant Colleges, 66, 192
Associated Mission Treasurers, 248
Aston, Kathleen (Casey), biographical sketch, 281-282
Astor House, Tientsin, China, 215-216, 220
Ayer, W. B., food administrator, 112, 201

Baalbek and Biblos, Lebanon, 302
baby care, in home management houses, 122-124; Japan, 187; Jerusalem, 195